DIVINE ENCOUNTERS
explores such questions as . . .

- How did God communicate with Adam and Eve?
- How have archaeological discoveries validated and corroborated biblical records?
- What is revealed in the Dead Sea Scrolls?
- What are the earliest reports of spacecraft?
- What do the visions of the Prophets tell us?
- What have been the missions of divine emissaries through the ages?
- In what way do angels appear to man?
- What powers do angels have to guide and protect us?
- How do dreams foretell the future?
- What is God's divine and universal everlasting plan?

and much, much more

Other Avon Books by
Zecharia Sitchin

THE EARTH CHRONICLES
Book I: The 12th Planet
Book II: The Stairway to Heaven
Book III: The Wars of Gods and Men
Book IV: The Lost Realms
Book V: When Time Began
Genesis Revisited

Avon Books are available at special quantity discounts for bulk purchases for sales promotions, premiums, fund raising or educational use. Special books, or book excerpts, can also be created to fit specific needs.

For details write or telephone the office of the Director of Special Markets, Avon Books, Dept. FP, 1350 Avenue of the Americas, New York, New York 10019, 1-800-238-0658.

DIVINE ENCOUNTERS

A GUIDE TO VISIONS, ANGELS, AND OTHER EMISSARIES

ZECHARIA SITCHIN

AVON BOOKS ◆ NEW YORK

If you purchased this book without a cover, you should be aware that this book is stolen property. It was reported as "unsold and destroyed" to the publisher, and neither the author nor the publisher has received any payment for this "stripped book."

DIVINE ENCOUNTERS is an original publication of Avon Books. This work has never before appeared in book form.

AVON BOOKS
A division of
The Hearst Corporation
1350 Avenue of the Americas
New York, New York 10019

Copyright © 1995 by Zecharia Sitchin
Published by arrangement with the author
Library of Congress Catalog Card Number: 95-94624
ISBN: 0-380-78076-3

All rights reserved, which includes the right to reproduce this book or portions thereof in any form whatsoever except as provided by the U.S. Copyright Law. For information address Avon Books.

First Avon Books Printing: January 1996

AVON TRADEMARK REG. U.S. PAT. OFF. AND IN OTHER COUNTRIES, MARCA REGISTRADA, HECHO EN U.S.A.

Printed in the U.S.A.

RA 10 9 8 7 6 5 4 3 2 1

Dedicated to the memory of my parents,
Isaac and Genia (née Barsky),
my link to my ancestors

CONTENTS

1

THE FIRST ENCOUNTERS

Divine Encounters are the ultimate human experience—the maximal, the utmost possible when alive, as when Moses encountered the Lord upon Mount Sinai; and the final, terminal, and conclusive, as that of Egyptian Pharaohs who at death assumed an eternal Afterlife by joining the gods in their Divine Abode.

The human experience of Divine Encounters as recorded in scriptures and texts from the ancient Near East is a most amazing and fascinating saga. It is a powerful drama that spans Heaven and Earth, involving worship and devotion, eternity and morality on the one hand, and love and sex, jealousy and murder on the other; ascents unto space and journeys to the Netherworld. A stage on which the actors are gods and goddesses, angels and demigods, Earthlings and androids; a drama expressed in prophecies and visions, in dreams and omens and oracles and revelations. It is a story of Man, separated from his Creator, seeking to restore a primeval umbilical cord and, by so doing, reach for the stars.

Divine Encounters are the ultimate human experience perhaps because they were also the very first human experience; for when God created Man, Man met God at the very moment of being created. We read in Genesis, the first book of the Hebrew Bible, how the first human, "The Adam," was brought into being:

> *And God said:*
> *Let us make Man*
> *in our image, after our likeness . . .*

1

> *And God created the Adam in His image,*
> *in the image of* Elohim *created He him.*

We can only surmise that the newborn, at the moment of being brought forth, was hardly aware of the nature and significance of that first Divine Encounter. Nor, it appears, was The Adam fully aware of an ensuing crucial encounter, when the Lord God (in the creation version attributed to Yahweh) decided to create a female mate for The Adam:

> *And Yahweh* Elohim
> *caused a deep sleep to fall upon*
> *the Adam, and he slept.*
> *And he took one of his ribs*
> *and closed up the flesh instead of it.*
> *And Yahweh* Elohim *formed the rib*
> *which He had taken from the Adam*
> *into a woman.*

The first man was thus deeply anesthetized during the proceedings, and therefore oblivious to this crucial Divine Encounter in which the Lord Yahweh displayed his surgical talents. But The Adam was soon informed of what had happened, for the Lord God "brought the woman unto the man" and introduced her to him. The Bible then offers a few words of commentary on why men and women become "one flesh" as they marry and ends the tale with the observation that both the man and his wife "were naked, but were not ashamed." While the situation seemed not to bother the First Matchmaker, why does the Bible imply otherwise? If the other creatures roaming in the Garden of Eden, "the beasts of the field and the fowl of the skies," were unclothed, what on Earth should have caused (but did not) Adam and Eve to be ashamed of being naked? Was it because the ones in whose image the Adam was created were wearing clothing? It is a point to be kept in mind—a clue, an inadvertent clue provided by the Bible, regarding the identity of the *Elohim*.

No one after Adam and Eve could attain the experience of being the first humans on Earth, with the attendant first Divine Encounters. But what has ensued in the Garden of Eden has endured as part of human yearning unto our own days. Even chosen Prophets must have longed to be so privileged, for it was there, in the Garden of Eden, that God spoke directly to the first human beings, instructing them regarding their nourishment: They can eat of all the garden's fruits, except the fruit of the Tree of Knowing.

The chain of events leading to the Expulsion from Paradise raises a lasting question: How did Adam and Eve hear God— how does God communicate with humans at such, or any, Divine Encounters? Can the humans see the divine speaker, or just hear the message? And how is the message conveyed—face-to-face? Telepathically? In a holographic vision? Through the medium of dreams?

We shall examine the ancient evidence for the answers. But as far as the events in the Garden of Eden are concerned, the biblical text suggests a physical divine presence. The place was not a human habitat; rather, it was a divine abode, an orchard deliberately planted "in Eden, in the east," where God "put the Adam whom He had fashioned" to serve as a gardener, "to till it and to keep it."

It is in this garden that Adam and Eve, through the intervention of the Divine Serpent, discover their sexuality after eating of the fruit of the Tree of Knowing that "makes one wise." Having eaten the forbidden fruit, "they knew that they were naked, and they sewed fig leaves together and made themselves aprons."

Now the Lord God—*Yahweh Elohim* in the Hebrew Bible—enters the stage:

> *And they heard the sound of the Lord God*
> *walking in the garden in the cool of the day;*
> *And Adam and his wife hid themselves*
> *from the presence of the Lord God*
> *amongst the trees of the garden.*

God is physically present in the Garden of Eden, and the sound of his strolling about the garden can be heard by the humans. Can they see the deity? The biblical narrative is silent on the issue; it makes clear, however, that God can see them—or, in this instance, was expecting to see them but could not because they were hiding. So God used his voice to reach them: "And the Lord God called unto the Adam, and said unto him: Where art thou?"

A dialogue (or more correctly a trialogue) ensues. The tale raises many issues of great import. It suggests that The Adam could talk from the very beginning; it brings up the question of how—in what tongue—did God and Man converse. For the moment let us just pursue the biblical tale: Adam's explanation, that he hid on hearing God's approach "because I am naked" leads to the questioning of the human pair by the deity. In the full-scale conversation that follows the truth comes out and the sin of eating the forbidden fruit is admitted (though only after Adam and Eve blame the Serpent for the deed). The Lord God then declares the punishment: the woman shall bear children in pain, The Adam shall have to toil for his food and earn his bread by the sweat of his brow.

By this time the encounter is clearly face-to-face, for now the Lord God not only makes skin-coats for Adam and his wife, but also clothes them with the coats. Although the tale undoubtedly is intended to impress upon the reader the significance of being clothed as a "divine" or major dividing element between humans and beasts, the biblical passage cannot be treated as only symbolical. It clearly lets us know that in the beginning, when The Adam was in the Garden of Eden, humans encountered their Creator face-to-face.

Now, unexpectedly, God gets worried. Speaking again to unnamed colleagues, *Yahweh Elohim* expresses his concern that "now that the Adam has become as one of us, to know good and evil, what if he shall put forth his hand and also take of the Tree of Life, and eat, and live forever?"

The shift of focus is so sudden that its significance has been easily lost. Dealing with Man—his creation, procreation, abode, and transgression—the Bible abruptly echoes the concerns of the Lord. In the process, the almost-divine nature of Man is highlighted once more. The decision to create The Adam stems from a suggestion to fashion him "in the image and after the likeness" of the divine creators. The resulting being, the handiwork of the *Elohim,* is brought forth "in the image of Elohim." And now, having eaten the fruit of Knowing, Man has become godlike in one more crucial respect.

Looking at it from the viewpoint of the deity, "the Adam has become as one of us" except for Immortality. And so the other unnamed colleagues of Yahweh concur in the decision to expel Adam and Eve from the Garden of Eden, placing Cherubim with a "revolving flaming sword" to block the humans' way back if they ever tried.

Thus did Man's very Creator decree Man's mortality. But Man, undaunted, has searched for immortality ever since through the medium of Divine Encounters.

Is this yearning for Encounters based on a recollection of real happenings, or an illusionary search based on mere myths? How much of the biblical tales is fact, how much fiction?

The diverse versions relating the creation of the first humans, and the alternating between a plural *Elohim* (deities) and a single Yahweh as the creator(s), have been just one of the indications that the editors or redactors of the Hebrew Bible had in front of them some earlier texts dealing with the subject. Indeed, chapter 5 of Genesis begins by stating that its brief record of the generations that followed Adam is based on "the Book of the Generations of Adam" (starting from "the day Elohim had created Adam in the likeness of Elohim"). Verse 14 in Numbers 21 refers to the *Book of the Wars of Yahweh*. Joshua 10:13 refers the reader for more details of miraculous events to the *Book of Jashar*, which is also listed as a known source text in II Samuel 1:18. These are but passing references to what must have been a much more extensive trove of earlier texts.

The veracity of the Hebrew Bible (Old Testament)—be it its tales of Creation, of the Deluge and Noah's Ark, of the Patriarchs, of the Exodus—has come into doubting criticism in the nineteenth century. Much of that skepticism and disbelief has been muted and countered by archaeological discoveries that increasingly validated the biblical record and data in an ever-receding order—from the near past to the earlier times, carrying the corroboration farther and farther back through historical times to prehistorical ones. From Egypt and Nubia in Africa to the Hittite remains in Anatolia (today's Turkey), from the Mediterranean coast and the islands of Crete and Cyprus in the east to the borders of India in the west, and especially in the lands of the Fertile Crescent that began in Mesopotamia (nowadays Iraq) and curved to embrace Canaan (today's Israel), as one ancient site after another—many known previously only from the Bible—have been uncovered, texts written on clay tablets or papyrus and inscriptions carved on stone walls or monuments have resurrected the kingdoms, the kings, the events, the cities listed in the Bible. Moreover, in many instances, such writings found at sites such as Ras Shamra (the Canaanite Ugarit) or more recently at Ebla have shown familiarity with the same sources as those on which the Bible had relied. However, unencumberd by the monotheistic constraints of the Hebrew Bible, the writings of Israel's neighbors in the ancient Near East spelled out the identities and names of the "us" of the biblical *Elohim*. In doing so, such writings paint a panorama of prehistoric times and raise the curtain on a fascinating record of gods and humans in a series of varied Divine Encounters.

Until the start of purposeful archaeological excavations in Mesopotamia, "The Land Between the Rivers" (the Tigris and Euphrates) some 150 years ago, the Old Testament was the sole source of information on the Assyrian and Babylonian empires, their great cities and haughty kings. As earlier scholars pondered the veracity of the biblical data concerning the existence of such empires three thousand years ago, their credulity was stretched even more by the biblical assertion that Kingship began even earlier, with a "mighty hunter by the grace of Yaweh" called Nimrod, and that there had been royal capitals (and thus an advanced civilization) in the distant past in "the Land of Shine'ar." This assertion was linked to the even more incredible tale of the Tower of Babel (Genesis chapter 11) when Mankind, using clay bricks, embarked on the erection of a "tower whose head can reach the heavens." The place was a plain in the "Land of Shine'ar."

That "mythical" land has been found, its cities unearthed by archaeologists, its language and texts deciphered thanks to the knowledge of Hebrew and thus of its parent tongue, Akkadian, its monuments and sculptures and artworks treasured in major world museums. Nowadays we call the land

Sumer; its people called it *Shumer* ("Land of the Guardians"). It is to ancient Sumer that we have to go to understand the biblical tale of Creation and the ancient Near Eastern record of Divine Encounters; for it is there, in Sumer, that the recording of those events began.

Sumer (the biblical Shine'ar) was the land where the first known and fully documented civilization sprang up after the Deluge, appearing suddenly and all at once some six thousand years ago. It gave Humankind almost every "first" in all that matters as integral components of a high civilization—not just the first brickmaking (as mentioned above) and the first kilns, but also the first high-rise temples and palaces, the first priests and kings; the first wheel, the first kiln, the first medicine and pharmacology; the first musicians and dancers, artisans and craftsmen, merchants and caravaneers, law codes and judges, weights and measures. The first astronomers and observatories were there, and the first mathematicians. And perhaps most important of all: it was there, as early as 3800 B.C., that writing began, making Sumer the land of the first scribes who wrote down on clay tablets in the wedgelike script ("cuneiform") the most astounding tales of gods and humans (as this "Creation of Man" tablet, Fig. 1). Scholars regard these ancient texts as myths. We, however, consider them to be records of events that have essentially happened.

The archaelogists' spades not only verified the existence of Shine'ar/Sumer. The finds also brought to light ancient texts from Mesopotamia that paralleled the biblical tales of Creation and the Deluge. In 1876 George Smith of the British Museum, piecing together broken tablets found in the royal library of Nineveh (the Assyrian capital), published *The Chaldean Genesis* and showed beyond doubt that the biblical tale of Creation was first written down in Mesopotamia millennia of years earlier.

In 1902 L.W. King, also of the British Museum, in his book *The Seven Tablets of Creation*, published a fuller text, in the Old Babylonian language, that required seven clay tablets—so long and detailed it was. Known as the Epic of Creation or as *Enuma elish* by its opening words, its first six tablets describe the creation of the heavens and the Earth and all upon Earth, including Man, paralleling the six "days" of

Figure 1

creation in the Bible. The seventh tablet was devoted to the exaltation of the supreme Babylonian deity Marduk as he surveyed his marvelous handiwork (paralleling the biblical seventh "day" on which God "rested from all His work that He had made"). Scholars now know that these and other "myths" in their Assyrian and Babylonian versions were translations of earlier Sumerian texts (modified to glorify the Assyrian or Babylonian supreme gods). *History,* as the great scholar Samuel N. Kramer has so excellently expounded in his 1959 book of that title, *Begins at Sumer.*

It all began, we learn from the various texts, a very long time ago, with the splashing down in the waters of the Persian Gulf or the Arabian Sea of a group of fifty ANUNNAKI— a term literally meaning "Those Who from Heaven to Earth Came." They waded ashore under the leadership of E.A ("He Whose House Is Water"), a brilliant scientist, and established the first extraterrestrial colony on Earth, calling it E.RI.DU ("House in the Faraway Built"). Other settlements followed in pursuit of the visitors' mission: Obtaining gold by distilling the waters of the Persian Gulf—gold needed urgently back on the home planet of the Anunnaki so that their dwindling atmosphere could be protected by a shield of suspended gold particles. As the expedition expanded and the operations were set in motion, Ea acquired the additional title or epithet EN.KI—"Lord of Earth."

But all did not go well. The home planet (called NIBIRU) was not receiving the required gold. A change of plans was soon decided, calling for the obtainment of the gold the hard way, by mining it in the AB.ZU—southeastern Africa. More Anunnaki arrived on Earth (in the end they numbered 600); another group, the IGI.GI ("Those Who Observe and See") remained skyborne, operating shuttlecraft and spacecraft and space stations (they numbered, Sumerian texts assert, 300 in all). To make sure there were no failures this time, ANU ("The Heavenly One"), ruler of Nibiru, sent to Earth a half brother of Enki/Ea, EN.LIL ("Lord of the Command"). He was a strict disciplinarian and a firm administrator; and while Enki was sent to oversee the mining of gold ores in the Abzu, Enlil took over command of the seven Cities of the Gods in the E.DIN ("Home of the Righteous Ones"), the place where more than 400,000 years later the Sumerian civilization blossomed out. Each such city was assigned specialized functions: a Mission Control Center, a Spaceport, a center for metallurgy; even a medical center under the supervision of NIN.MAH ("Great Lady"), a half sister of both Enki and Enlil.

The evidence, presented and analyzed by us in books I-V of *The Earth Chronicles* series and the companion book *Genesis Revisited,* indicated a vast elliptical orbit for Nibiru that lasts 3,600 Earth-years, a period called SAR in Sumerian. Sumerian records of prehistoric times, called King Lists, measured the passage of time as applied to the Anunnaki in Sars. Scholars who have uncovered and translated these texts find the lengths of the tours of duty of named Anunnaki commanders nothing short of "legendary" or "fantastic," for such individual "reigns" lasted 28,800 or 36,000 or even 43,200 years. But in fact the Sumerian King Lists state that this or that commander was in charge of a certain settlement for 8 or 10 or 12 *Sars.* Converted to Earth-years these numbers become the "fantastic" 28,800 (8 x 3,600) and so on;

but in Anunnaki terms they were just eight or ten of *their* years, a perfectly reasonable (and even short) length of time.

Therein, in the *Sars,* lies the secret to the *apparent* immortality of the ancient "gods." A year, by definition, is the time it takes the planet one lives on to complete one orbit around the Sun. The orbit of Nibiru lasts 3,600 *Earth*-years; but for those who live on Nibiru, that amounts to only one of *their* years. The Sumerian and other Near Eastern texts speak of both the birth and the death of those "gods"; except that, in the eyes of the Earthlings (for that, literally, is what *Adam*—"He of Earth"—meant in Hebrew), the life cycles of the Anunnaki were such that, in human terms, they were immortal for all practical purposes.

The Anunnaki arrived on Earth 120 Sars before the Deluge—432,000 Earth-years before that avalanche of water that was a watershed event in more than physical ways. Man, The Adam, was not yet on Earth when the Anunnaki arrived. For forty Sars the Anunnaki who were sent to the Abzu toiled mining the gold; but then they mutinied. A text in Akkadian (the mother tongue of Babylonian, Assyrian, and Hebrew) called *Atra Hasis* describes the mutiny and the reasons for it in vivid detail. Enlil called for disciplinary measures to force the Anunnaki to continue toiling and to punish the mutiny's instigators. Enki was for leniency. Anu was consulted; he sympathized with the mutineers. How was the impasse to be resolved?

Enki, the scientist, had a solution. *Let us create a Primitive Worker,* he said, that will take over the backbreaking toil. The other leaders of the Anunnaki present wondered: How can it be done, how can an *Adamu* be created? To which Enki gave this answer:

> *The creature whose name you uttered,*
> *it exists!*

He found the "creature"—a hominid, the product of evolution on Earth—in southeast Africa, "above the Abzu." All that we need to do to make it an intelligent worker, Enki added, was to:

Bind upon it the image of the gods.

The assembled gods—the Anunnaki leaders—agreed enthusiastically. On Enki's suggestion they summoned Ninmah, the Chief Medical Officer, to assist in the task. "You are the midwife of the gods," they said to her—"Create Mankind! Create a Mixed One that he may bear the yoke, let him bear the yoke assigned by Enlil, let the Primitive Worker toil for the gods!"

In Chapter 1 of Genesis the discussion that led to this decision is summed up in one verse: "And *Elohim* said: Let us make the Adam in our image, after our likeness." And, with the implied consent of the assembled "us," the task was carried out: "And *Elohim* created the Adam in His image; in the image of *Elohim* created He him."

The term *image*—the element or process by which the existing "creature" could be raised to the level desired by the Anunnaki, akin to them except for Knowing and Longevity—can best be understood by realizing who or what the existing "creature" was. As other texts (e.g. one that scholars title *The Myth of Cattle and Grain*) explain,

> *When Mankind was first created*
> *They knew not the eating of bread,*
> *knew not the wearing of garments.*
> *They ate plants with their mouths,*
> *like sheep;*
> *They drank water from the ditch.*

This is a fitting description of hominids roaming wildly as, and with, other beasts. Sumerian depictions, engraved on stone cylinders (so-called "cylinder seals") show such hominids mingling with animals but standing erect on two feet—an illustration (regrettably ignored by modern scientists) of a Homo erectus (Fig. 2). It was upon that Being, that already existed, that Enki had suggested to "bind upon it the image of the gods," and create through genetic engineering an Earthling, *Homo sapiens*.

A hint of the process involved in the genetic makeover is made in the Yahwist Version (as scholars refer to it) in chap-

Figure 2

ter 2 of Genesis, in which we read that "*Yahweh Elohim* formed The Adam with clay of the earth, and breathed into his nostrils the breath of life; and the Adam became a living being." In *Atra Hasis* and other Mesopotamian texts a much more complex process involving the Being is described. It was a creative process not without frustrating trials and errors until the procedure was perfected and the desired result was attained by Enki and Ninmah (whom some texts, in honor of her memorable role, granted her the epithet NIN.TI—"Lady of Life").

Working in a laboratory called *Bit Shimti*—"House where the wind of life is breathed in"—the "essence" of the blood of a young Anunnaki male was mixed with the egg of a female hominid. The fertilized egg was then inserted into the womb of a female Anunnaki. When, after a tense waiting period, a "Model Man" was born, Ninmah held the newborn baby up and shouted: "I have created! My hands have made it!"

Sumerian artists depicted on a cylinder seal that breathtaking final moment, when Ninmah/Ninti held up the new Being for all to see (Fig. 3). Thus, captured in an engraving on a small stone cylinder, is a pictorial record of the *first Divine Encounter!*

In ancient Egypt, where the gods were called *Neteru* ("Guardians") and identified by the hieroglyphic symbol of a mining axe, the act of creating the first Man out of clay was attributed to the ram-headed god *Khnemu* ("He who

Figure 3

Figure 4

joins''), of whom the texts said that he was ''the maker of men ... the father who was in the beginning.'' Egyptian artists too, as the Sumerians before them, depicted pictorially the moment of the First Encounter (Fig. 4); it showed Khnemu holding up the newly created being, assisted by his son Thoth (the god of science and medicine).

The Adam, as one version in Genesis relates, was indeed created alone. But once this Model Man proved the validity of this process of creating "test-tube babies," a project of mass replication was embarked upon. Preparing more mixtures of TI.IT—"That which is with life," the biblical "clay"—genetically engineered to produce Primitive Workers of both sexes, Ninmah placed seven lumps of the "clay" in a "male mould" and seven in a "female mould." The fertilized eggs were then implanted in the wombs of female Anunnaki "birth goddesses." It was to this process of bringing forth seven male and seven female "Mixed Ones" at each shift that the "Elohist Version" (as scholars call it) in Genesis referred when it stated that when Humankind was created by Elohim, "male and female created He them."

But, like any hybrid (such as a mule, the result of the mating of a horse and a she-ass), the "Mixed Ones" could not procreate. The biblical tale of how the new being acquired "Knowing," the ability to procreate in biblical terminology, covers with an allegorical veneer the second act of genetic engineering. The principal actor in the dramatic development is neither Yahweh-Elohim nor the created Adam and Eve, but the Serpent, the instigator of the crucial biological change.

The Hebrew word for "serpent" in Genesis is *Nahash*. The term, however, had two additional meanings. It could mean "He who knows or solves secrets"; it could also mean "He of the copper." The last two meanings appear to have stemmed from the Sumerian epithel for Enki, BUZUR, which meant both "He who solves secrets" and "He of the metal mines." Indeed, the frequent Sumerian symbol for Enki was that of a serpent. In an earlier work (*Genesis Revisited*) we have suggested that the associated symbol of Entwined Serpents (Fig. 5a), from which the symbol for healing has remained to this day, was inspired—already in ancient Sumer!—by the double helix DNA (Fig. 5b) and thus of genetic engineering. As we shall show later on, Enki's use of genetic engineering in the Garden of Eden also led to the double helix motif in Tree of life depictions. Enki bequeathed this knowledge and its symbol to his son Ningishzidda (Fig. 5c), whom we have identified as the Egyptian god Thoth; the Greeks called him Hermes; his staff bore the emblem of the Entwined Serpents (Fig. 5d).

As we trace these double and triple meanings of Enki's

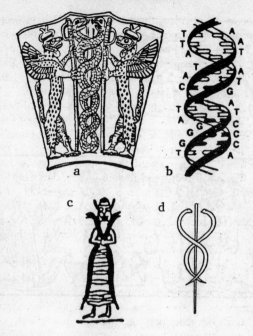

Figures 5a, 5b, 5c, and 5d

epithets (Serpent-copper-healing-genetics), it behooves us to recall the biblical tale of the plague that befell the Israelites during their wanderings in the Sinai wilderness: it stopped after Moses has made a "copper serpent" and held it up to summon divine help.

It is nothing short of mind-boggling to realize that this second Divine Encounter, when Humankind was given the ability to procreate, was also captured for us by ancient "photographers"—artists who carved the scene in reverse on the small stone cylinders, images that were seen in positive after the seal was rolled on wet clay. But such depictions too, in addition to the ones depicting the creation of The Adam, have been found. One shows "Adam" and "Eve" seated, flanking a tree, and the serpent behind Eve (Fig. 6a). Another shows a great god seated atop a thronelike mound from which two

Figures 6a and 6b

serpents emanate—undoubtedly Enki (Fig. 6b). He is flanked
on the right by a male whose sprouting branches are penis-
shaped, and on the left by a female whose branches are va-
gina-shaped and who holds a small fruit tree (presumably
from the Tree of Knowing). Watching the goings-on is a
menacing great god—in all probability an angry Enlil.

All these texts and depictions, augmenting the biblical narrative, have thus combined to paint a detailed picture, a course
of events with identifiable principal participants, in the saga of
Divine Encounters. Nevertheless, scholars by and large persist
in lumping all such evidence as ''mythology.'' To them the tale
of events in the Garden of Eden is just a myth, an imaginary
allegory taking place in a nonexistent place.

But what if such a Paradise, a place with deliberately
planted fruit-bearing trees, had really existed at a time when
everywhere else nature alone was the gardener? What if in

the earliest times there had been a place called "Eden," a real place whose events were real occurrences?

Ask anyone where Adam was created, and the answer will in all probability be: In the Garden of Eden. But it is not there where the story of Humankind begins.

The Mesopotamian tale, first recorded by the Sumerians, places the first phase at a location "above the Abzu"—farther north than where the gold mines were. As several groups of "Mixed Ones" were brought forth and pressed into service for the purpose for which they were created—to take over the toil in the mines—the Anunnaki from the seven settlements in the E.DIN clamored for such helpers too. As those in southeastern Africa resisted, a fight broke out. A text which scholars call *The Myth of the Pickax* describes how, led by Enlil, the Anunnaki from the E.DIN forcefully seized some of "the Created Ones" and brought them over to Eden, to serve the Anunnaki there. The text called *The Myth of Cattle and Grain* explicitly states that "when from the heights of Heaven to Earth Anu had caused the Anunnaki to come," grains that vegetate, lambs and kids were not yet brought forth. Even after the Anunnaki in their "creation chamber" had fashioned food for themselves, they were not satiated. It was only

> *After Anu, Enlil, Enki and Ninmah*
> *had fashioned the black-headed people,*
> *Vegetation that is fruitful they multiplied*
> *in the land ... In the Edin they placed them.*

The Bible, contrary to general assumptions, relates the same tale. As in the *Enuma elish*, the biblical sequence (chapter 2 of Genesis) is, first, the forming of the Heavens and of Earth; next, the creation of The Adam (the Bible does not state where). The Elohim then "planted a garden in Eden, eastward" (of where the Adam was created); and only thereafter did the Elohim "put there" (in the Garden of Eden) "the Adam whom he had fashioned."

> *And Yahweh Elohim took the Adam,*
> *and placed him in the Garden of Eden*
> *to till it and to keep it.*

An interesting light is shed on the "Geography of Creation" (to coin a term) and, consequently on the initial Divine Encounters, by the *Book of Jubilees.* Composed in Jerusalem during the time of the Second Temple, it was known in those centuries as *The Testament of Moses,* because it began by answering the question, How could Humankind know about those early events that even preceded the creation of Humankind? The answer was that it was all revealed to Moses on Mount Sinai, when an Angel of the Divine Presence dictated it to Moses by the Lord's command. The name *Book of Jubilees,* applied to the work by its Greek translators, stems from the chronological structure of the book, which is based on a count of the years by "jubilees" whose years are called "days" and "weeks."

Obviously drawing on sources that were available at the time (in addition to the canonical Genesis), such as the books that the Bible mentions and other texts that Mesopotamian libraries cataloged but which are yet to be found, the *Book of Jubilees,* using the enigmatic count of "days," states that Adam was brought by the angels into the Garden of Eden only "after Adam had completed forty days in the land where he had been created"; and "his wife they brought in on the eightieth day." Adam and Eve, in other words, were brought into being elsewhere.

The *Book of Jubilees,* dealing with the expulsion from Eden later on, provides another morsel of valuable information. It informs us that "Adam and his wife went forth from the Garden of Eden, and they dwelt in the Land of Nativity, the land of their creation." In other words, from the Edin they went back to the Abzu, in southeastern Africa. Only there, in the second Jubilee, did Adam "know" his wife Eve and "in the third week in the second jubilee she gave birth to Cain, and in the fourth she gave birth to Abel, and in the fifth she gave birth to a daughter, Awan." (The Bible states that Adam and Eve had thereafter other sons and daughters; noncanonical books say that they numbered sixty-three in all.)

Such a sequence of events, that places the start of Humankind's proliferation from a single primordial mother not in the Mesopotamian Eden but back in the Abzu, in southeastern Africa, is now fully corroborated by scientific discoveries that have led to the "Out of Africa" theories regarding the origin and spread of Humankind. Not only finds of fossil remains of the earliest hominids, but also genetic evidence concerning the final line of *Homo sapiens,* confirms southeast Africa as the place where Humankind originated. And as to *Homo sapiens,* anthropological and genetic researchers have placed an "Eve"—a single female of whom all of present day humans stem—in the same area at about 250,000 years ago. (This finding, at first based on DNA that is passed only by the mother, has been corroborated in 1994 by genetic research based on Nuclear DNA that is passed from both parents and expanded in 1995 to include an "Adam" circa 270,000 years ago.) It was from there that the various branches of *Homo sapiens* (Neanderthals, Cro-Magnons) later arrived in Asia and Europe.

That the biblical Eden was one and the same place settled by the Anunnaki and the one to which they brought over Primitive Workers from the Abzu, is almost self-evident linguistically. The name *Eden,* hardly anyone now doubts, stemmed from the Sumerian E.DIN via the intermediary of the *Edinnu* in Akkadian (the mother tongue of Assyrian, Babylonian, and Hebrew). Moreover, in describing the profusion of waters in that Paradise (an impressive aspect for readers in a part of the Near East wholly dependent on rains in a short winter season), the Bible offered several geographical indicators that also pointed to Mesopotamia; it stated that the Garden of Eden was located at the head of a body of water that served as the confluence of four rivers:

> *And a river went out of Eden*
> *to water the garden;*
> *And from there it was parted*
> *and became four principal streams.*
> *The name of the first is* Pishon,
> *the one which winds through the land*
> *of Havilah, where the gold is—*
> *the land whose gold is good—*
> *there [too] is the bdellium and onyx stone.*

And the name of the second river is Gihon;
*it is the one that circles
all of the land Kush.
And the name of the third river is* Hiddekel,
*the one that flows east of Assyria.
And the fourth is the* Prath.

Clearly, two of the Rivers of Paradise, the Hiddekel and the Prath, are the two major rivers of Mesopotamia (that gave the land its name, which means "The Land Between the Rivers"), the Tigris and Euphrates as they are called in English. There is complete agreement between all scholars that the biblical names for these two rivers stem from their Sumerian names (via the intermediary Akkadian): *Idilbat* and *Purannu.*

Though the two rivers take separate courses, at some points almost coming together, at others separating substantially, they both originate in the mountains of Anatolia, north of Mesopotamia; and since this is where the headwaters are as riverine science holds, scholars have been searching for the other two rivers at that "headpoint." But no suitable candidates for the Gihon and Pishon as two more rivers flowing from that mountain range and meeting the other qualifications have been found. The search, therefore, spread to more distant lands. Kush has been taken to mean Ethiopia or Nubia in Africa, and the *Gihon* ("The Gusher") to be the Nile River with its several cataracts. A favorable guess for *Pishon* (possibly "The one who had come to rest") has been the Indus River, equating therefore Havilah with the Indian subcontinent, or even with landlocked Luristan. The problem with such suggestions is that neither the Nile nor the Indus confluates with the Tigris and Euphrates of Mesopotamia.

The names Kush and Havilah are found in the Bible more than once, both as geographical terms and as names of nation-states. In the Table of Nations (Genesis chapter 10) Havilah is listed together with Seba, Sabtha, Raamah, Sabtecha, Sheba, and Dedan. They were all nation-lands which various biblical passages linked with the tribes of Ishmael, the son of Abraham by the handmaiden Hagar, and there is no doubt that their domains were in Arabia. These traditions have been corroborated by modern researchers that have identified the tribal locations throughout Arabia. Even the name Hagar was found to be the name of an ancient city in eastern Arabia. An updated study by E.A. Knauf (*Ismael,* 1985) conclusively deciphered the name *Havilah* as the Hebrew for "Sand Land," and identified it as the geographic name for southern Arabia.

The problem with such convincing conclusions has been that no river in Arabia could qualify as the biblical river Pishon, if for no other reason than the simple fact that the whole of Arabia is arid, a huge desert land.

Could the Bible be so wrong? Could the whole tale of the Garden of Eden, and thus of the events and Divine Encounters in it, be just a myth?

Starting with a firm belief in the veracity of the Bible, the following question came to our mind: Why does the biblical narrative go to relatively great lengths to describe the geography and mineralogy of the land (Havilah) where the Pishon was; list the land and describe the circular course of the Gihon River; merely identify the location ("east of Assyria") of the Hiddekel; and just name the fourth river, Prath, without any additional identifying landmarks? Why this descending order of information?

The answer that had occurred to us was that while there was no need whatsoever to tell the reader of Genesis where the Euphrates was, and a mere mention of Assyria was enough to identify the Tigris (Hiddekel) River, it was necessary to explain that the Gihon—evidently, a lesser-known river by then—was the river that encompassed the land of Kush; and that the apparently totally unknown river Pishon was in a land called Havilah, which, devoid of landmarks, was identified by the products that came from it.

These thoughts began to make sense when, in the late 1980s, it was announced that scanning of the Sahara desert (in North Africa, in western Egypt) with soil-penetrating radar from Earth-orbiting satellites and with other instruments aboard the space shuttle *Columbia,* revealed under layers of desert sand dry beds of rivers that once flowed in this region. Subsequent research on the ground established that the area was well watered, with major rivers and many tributaries, since perhaps 200,000 years ago and until about 4,000 years ago, when the climate changed.

The discovery in the Sahara desert made us wonder: Could the same have happened in the Arabian desert? Could it be that when the version in chapter 2 of Genesis was written— obviously at a time when Assyria was already known—the Pishon River had entirely vanished under the sands as the climate changed in past millennia?

Confirmation of the validity of this line of reasoning took place quite dramatically in March 1993. It was an announcement by Farouk El-Baz, director of the Center for Remote Sensing at Boston University, concerning the discovery of a lost river under the sands of the Arabian peninsula—a river that flowed for more than 530 miles from the mountains of western Arabia all the way eastward to the Persian Gulf. There it formed a delta that covered much of today's Kuwait and reached as far as the present-day city of Basra, merging—"confluing"—there with the Tigris and Euphrates rivers. It was a river that was about fifty feet deep throughout its entire length and more than three miles wide at some points.

After the last Ice Age, between 11,000 and 6,000 years ago, the Boston University study concluded, the Arabian climate was wet and rainy enough to support such a river. But some 5,000 years ago the river dried up because of climatic changes that resulted in the aridity and desertlike conditions in the peninsula. In time, wind-driven sand dunes covered the river's channel, obliterating all evidence of the once-mighty river. High-resolution imaging by Landsat satellites, however, revealed that the dune patterns changed as the sand crossed a line that extended for hundreds of miles, a line that ended in mystifying deposits of gravel in Kuwait and near Basra—gravel of rocks that came from the Hijaz Mountains in western Arabia. Ground-level inspections then confirmed the existence of the ancient river (Fig. 7).

Dr. El-Baz has given the lost river the name Kuwait River. *We suggest that it was called Pishon in antiquity,* cutting across the Arabian peninsula that indeed was an ancient source of gold and precious stones.

And what about the river Gihon, "the one that meanders in all of the land of Kush"? *Kush* is listed twice in the Table

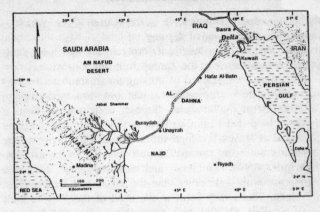

Figure 7

of Nations, first with the Hamitic-African lands of Egypt, Put (Nubia/Sudan) and Canaan; and a second time as one of the Mesopotamian lands where Nimrod was lord, he "whose first kingdoms were Babylon and Erech and Akkad, all in the land of Shine'ar" (Sumer). The Mesopotamian Kush was in all probability east of Sumer, the area of the Zagros Mountains. It was the homeland of the *Kushshu* people, the Akkadian name for the *Kassites,* who in the second millennium B.C. swept down from the Zagros Mountains and occupied Babylon. The ancient name was retained as *Kushan* for the district of Susa (the "Shushan" of the biblical Book of Esther) well into Persian and even Roman times.

There are several noteworthy rivers in that part of the Zagros Mountains, but they have not caught the attention of scholars because none of them share headwaters with the Tigris and Euphrates (which begin hundreds of miles to the northeast). Here, however, another thought came into play: Could the ancients have spoken of rivers that join together not at their headwaters, but at their confluence into the Persian Gulf? If so, the Gihon—the fourth river of Eden—would have been a river that joins the Tigris, the Euphrates, and the newly discovered "Kuwait River" at the head of the Persian Gulf!

If the problem is looked at thus, the obvious candidate for

the *Gihon* easily emerges. It is the Karun River, which is indeed the major river of the ancient land of Kushshu. Some five hundred miles in length, it forms an unusual loop, starting its tortuous flow in the Zardeh-Kuh range in what is now southwestern Iran. Instead of flowing down south to the Persian Gulf, it flows "upward" (as one looks at a modern map) in a northwesterly direction, through deep gorges. Then it makes a loop and begins to flow southward in a zigzagging course as it leaves the high mountains of the Zagros range and starts a descent toward the gulf. Finally, in its last hundred miles or so, it mellows and meanders gently toward a confluence with none other than the Tigris and Euphrates in the marshy delta they form at the head of the Persian Gulf (the so-called Shatt-el-Arab, nowadays contested between Iran and Iraq).

The location, the circular course, the gushing, the confluence with the other three rivers at the head of the Persian Gulf, all suggest to us that *the Karun River could well be the biblical river Gihon* that circled the land of Kush. Such an identification, combined with the space-age discoveries of the major river in Arabia, by so delineating and identifying the location of the Garden of Eden in southern Mesopotamia, confirm the physical existence of such a place and *form a sound foundation of fact, not myth, under the related tales of Divine Encounters.*

Confirmation of southern Mesopotamia, ancient Sumer, as the E.DIN, the original biblical Eden, does more than create a geographic congruency between the Sumerian texts and the biblical narrative. It also identifies the group with whom Humankind had Divine Encounters. The E.DIN was the abode ("E") of the DIN ("The Righteous/Divine Ones"). Their full title was DIN.GIR, meaning "The Righteous Ones of the Rocketships," and was written pictographically as a two-stage rocket whose command module could separate for landing (Fig. 8a). As the script evolved from pictographic to the wedgelike cuneiform, the pictograph was replaced by a star symbol meaning "Heavenly Ones"; later on, in Assyria and Babylon, the symbol was simplified to crossed wedges (Fig.

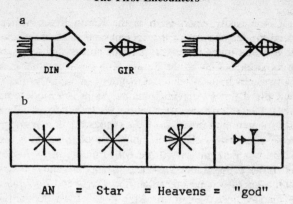

AN = Star = Heavens = "god"

Figures 8a and 8b

8b) and its reading, in the Akkadian language, changed to *Ilu*—"The Lofty Ones."

The Mesopotamian Creation texts provide not just the answer to the puzzle of who were the several deities involved in the creation of The Adam, causing the Bible to employ the plural *Elohim* ("The Divine Ones") in a monotheistic version of the events and to retain the "us" in "Let *us* make Man in *our* image and after *our* likeness"; they also provide the background for this achievement.

The evidence leaves little room for doubting that the *Elohim* of Genesis were the Sumerian DIN.GIR. It was to them that the feat of creating The Adam was attributed, and it was their diverse (and often antagonistic) leaders—Enki, Enlil, Ninmah—who were the "us" whom the first *Homo sapiens* first encountered.

The explusion from the Garden of Eden brought to an end the first chapter in this relationship. Losing Paradise but gaining knowledge and the ability to procreate, Humankind was henceforth destined to be bonded with Earth—

> *In the sweat of thy brow*
> *shalt thou eat bread,*
> *until your return to the earth,*

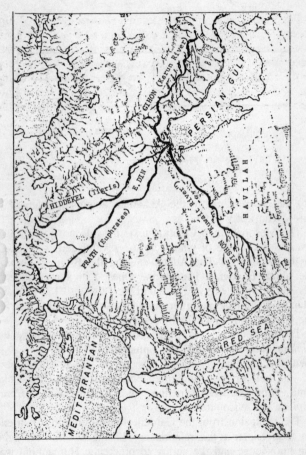

The E.DIN and its four rivers

> *for from it wast thou taken.*
> *For thou art earthdust*
> *and unto earthdust thou shalt return.*

But that is not how Humankind saw its destiny. Being created in the image, after the likeness, and with the genes of the *Dingir/Elohim,* it saw itself part of the heavens—the other planets, the stars, the universe. It strives to join them in their celestial abode, to gain their immortality. To do so, the ancient texts tell us, Man has continued to seek Divine Encounters without weapons-bearing Cherubim blocking the way.

THE FIRST LANGUAGE

Could Adam and Eve speak, and in what language did they converse with God?

Until a few decades ago modern scholars held that human speech began with Cro-Magnon Man some 35,000 years ago and that languages developed locally among diverse clans no more than 8,000 to 12,000 years ago.

This is not the biblical view according to which Adam and Eve conversed in an understandable language, and that prior to the Tower of Babel incident "the whole Earth was of one language and one kind of words."

In the 1960s and 1970s word comparisons led scholars to conclude that all the thousands of different languages—including those of Native Americans—could be grouped into three primary ones. Later fossil discoveries in Israel revealed that 60,000 years ago Neanderthals could already speak as we do. The conclusion that there indeed had been a single Mother Tongue some 100,000 years ago has been confirmed in mid-1994 by updated studies at the University of California at Berkeley.

The advances in genetic research, now applied to speech and language, suggest that these abilities, distinguishing humans from apes, are of a genetic origin. Genetic studies indicate that there indeed had been an "Eve," a sole mother of us all—and that she appeared 200,000–250,000 years ago with "the gift of gab."

Some Fundamentalists would believe that the Mother Tongue was Hebrew, the language of the Holy Bible. Perhaps, but probably not: Hebrew stems from Akkadian (the first "Semitic" language) that was preceded by Sumerian. Was it then Sumerian, the language of the people who had settled in Shine'ar? But that was only after the Deluge, whereas Mesopotamian texts refer to a pre-Diluvial language. Anthropologist Kathleen Gibson of the University of Texas at Houston believes that humans acquired language and mathematics at the same time. Was the First Language that of the Anunnaki themselves, taught to Mankind as all other knowledge?

2

WHEN PARADISE WAS LOST

The Expulsion of Adam and Eve from the Garden of Eden, on the face of it a deliberate and decisive breaking of the links between The Adam and his creators, was not that final after all. Were it to be final, the records of Divine Encounters would have ended right then and there. Instead, the Expulsion was only the start of a new phase in that relationship that can be characterized as hide-and-seek, in which direct encounters become rare and visions or dreams become divine devices.

The beginning of this post-Paradise relationship was far from auspicious; it was, in fact, a most tragic one. Unintentionally it brought about the emergence of new humans, *Homo sapiens sapiens.* And as it turned out, both the tragedy and its unexpected consequence planted the seeds of divine disillusionment with Humankind.

It was not the Expulsion from Paradise, such a cherished topic for preachings on the "Fall of Man," that was at the root of the plan to let the Deluge wipe Humankind off the face of the Earth. Rather, it was the incredible act of fratricide: When all of humanity consisted of four (Adam, Eve, Cain, and Abel), one brother killed the other!

And what was it all about? It was about Divine Encounters . . .

The story as told in the Bible begins almost as an idyll:

> *And the Adam knew Eve his wife*
> *and she conceived and gave birth to Cain;*
> *and she said:*
> *"Alongside Yahweh a man I brought to be."*

> *Again she gave birth, to his brother Abel.*
> *And Abel became a shepherd of flocks*
> *and Cain a tiller of the land.*

Thus, in just two verses, does the Bible introduce the
reader to the entirely new phase of human experience and
sets the stage for the next Divine Encounter. In spite of the
seeming break between God and Man, Yahweh is still watching over Humankind. Somehow—the Bible does not elaborate
how—grains and cattle have been domesticated, with Cain
becoming a farmer and Abel a shepherd. The brothers' first
act is to offer the first fruits and yearlings to Yahweh in
gratitude. The act implies a recognition that it was thanks to
the deity that the two ways of obtaining food became feasible.
The privilege of a Divine Encounter was expected; but—

> *Yahweh paid heed unto Abel and his offering;*
> *unto Cain and his offering He paid no heed.*
> *So Cain was very resentful*
> *and his countenance was sullen.*

Perhaps alarmed by this development, the deity speaks,
directly, to Cain, trying to dissipate his anger and disappointment. But to no avail; when the two brothers were alone in
the field, "Cain came upon his brother Abel and killed him."

Yahweh was soon demanding an accounting from Cain.
"What hast thou done?" the Lord cried out in anger and
despair; "the voice of thy brother's blood cries unto me from
the ground!" Cain is punished to become a wanderer upon the
Earth; but the Earth too is accursed, to cease its fertility. Recognizing the magnitude of his crime, Cain is afraid of being killed
by unnamed avengers. "So Yahweh put a mark on Cain, so
that whoever shall find him should not smite him."

What was this "mark of Cain"? The Bible does not say,
and countless guesses are just that—guesses. Our own guess
(in *The Lost Realms*) was that the mark might have been a
genetic change, such as depriving the line of Cain of facial
hair—a mark that would be immediately obvious to whoever
shall find them. Since this is a mark of recognition of Amer-
indians, we have suggested that since Cain "went away from

the presence of Yahweh and resided in the Land of Nod, east of Eden,'' his wanderings took him and his offspring farther into Asia and the Far East, in time crossing the Pacific to settle in Mesoamerica. When his wanderings ended, Cain had a son whom he named Enoch and built a city "called by the name of his son.'' We have pointed out that Aztec legends called their capital *Tenochtitlán,* ''City of Tenoch,'' in honor of ancestors who came from the Pacific. Since they prefixed many names by the sound ''T,'' the city could have really been named after Enoch.

Whatever the destination of Cain or the nature of the mark were, it is clear that this final act in the Cain-Abel drama required a direct Divine Encounter, a close contact between the deity and Cain so that the ''mark'' could be emplaced.

This, as the unfolding record of the relationship between Man and God will show, was a rare occurrence after the Expulsion from Paradise. According to Genesis it was not until the seventh pre-Diluvial Patriarch (in a line that began with Adam and ended with Noah) that the *Elohim* engaged in a direct Divine Encounter; it had to do with Enoch, who at age 365 (a number of years paralleling the number of days in a year) ''walked with the Elohim'' and then was gone ''for the Elohim had taken him'' to join them in their abode.

But if God so rarely revealed himself, yet Humankind— according to the Bible—continued to ''hear'' him, what were the channels of indirect encounters?

To find answers regarding those early times, we have to fish for information in the extra-biblical books, of which the *Book of Jubilees* is one. Called by scholars Pseudepigrapha of the Old Testament, they include the *Book of Adam and Eve* that survived in several translated versions ranging from Armenian and Slavonic to Syriac, Arabic, and Ethiopic (but not the original Hebrew). According to this source, the slaying of Abel by Cain was foretold to Eve in a dream in which she saw ''the blood of Abel being poured into the mouth of Cain his brother.'' To prevent the dream from coming true, it was decided to ''make for each of them separate dwellings, and they made Cain an husbandman and Abel they made a shepherd.''

But the separation was to no avail. Again Eve had such a dream (this time the text calls it ''a vision''). Awakened by her, Adam suggested that they "go and see what has happened to them." "And they both went, and found Abel murdered by the hand of Cain."

The events, as recorded in the *Book of Adam and Eve,* then describe the birth of *Sheth* (meaning "Replacement" in Hebrew) "in place of Abel." With Abel dead and Cain banished, Seth (as the name is spelled in English translations of the Bible) was now the patriarchal heir and successor to Adam. And so it was that when Adam fell sick and was close to death, he revealed to Seth "what I heard and saw after your mother and I had been driven out of paradise:"

> There came to me Michael the archangel,
> an emissary of God.
> And I saw a chariot like the wind,
> and its wheels were as on fire.
> And I was carried up unto
> the Paradise of the Righteous Ones
> and I saw the Lord sitting;
> But his face was a flaming fire
> that could not be endured.

Though he could not face the awesome sight, he could hear God's voice telling him that because he had transgressed in the Garden of Eden, he was fated to die. Then the archangel Michael took Adam away from the vision of Paradise and brought him back to whence he had come. Concluding the account, Adam admonished Seth to avoid sin and to be righteous and to follow God's commandments and statutes that will be delivered to Seth and his descendants when "the Lord shall appear in a flame of fire."

Since the death of Adam was the first natural passing of a mortal, Eve and Seth knew not what to do. They took the dying Adam and carried him to the "region of Paradise," and there sat at the Gates of Paradise until Adam's soul departed from his body. They sat bewildered, mourning and crying. Then the Sun and Moon and the stars darkened, "the heavens opened," and Eve saw celestial visions. Raising her eyes she saw "coming from the heavens a chariot of light, borne by four bright eagles. And she heard the Lord instruct the angels Michael and Uriel to bring linen cloths and shroud Adam as well as Abel (who has not yet been buried); so were Adam and Abel consecrated for burial. Then the two of them were carried by the angels and buried, "according to the commandment of God, in the place where the Lord obtained the soildust" for the creation of Adam.

There is a wealth of pertinent information in this tale. It establishes prophetic dreams as a channel for divine revelations, a Divine Encounter through telepathic or other subconscious means. It introduces into the realm of Divine Encounters an intermediary: an "angel," a term known from the Hebrew Bible whose literal meaning was "emissary, messenger." And it also brings into play yet another form of Divine Encounter, that of "visions" in which the "Chariot of the Lord" is seen—an "awesome sight" of a "chariot like the wind," whose "wheels were as on fire" when seen by Adam and as a "chariot of light, borne by four bright eagles," when seen by Eve.

Since the *Book of Adam and Eve*, as the other Pseudepigraphic books, was written in the last centuries before the Christian era, one could of course argue that its information regarding dreams and visions could have been based on knowledge or beliefs from a much closer time to the writers than the pre-Diluvial events. In the case of prophetic dreams (of which more later) such a throwback in time would only serve to reinforce the fact that such dreams have indeed been deemed an undisputed channel between the deities and humans throughout recorded history.

In regard to visions of divine chariots, one could also argue that what the author of the *Book of Adam and Eve* had attributed to prehistoric, pre-Diluvial times also reflected much later events, such as Ezekiel's vision of the Divine Chariot (at the end of the seventh century B.C.), as well as familiarity with extensive references to such aerial vehicles in Mesopotamian and Egyptian texts. But in this matter, visions or sightings of what we nowadays call UFOs, there exists actual, physical evidence of such sightings from the days *before* the Deluge—*pictorial evidence* whose authenticity is undeniable.

Let us be clear: We are not referring to Sumerian depictions (starting with the pictograph for GIR) and other depictions from the ancient Near East in the post-Diluvial era. We are talking about actual depictions—drawing, paintings—*from an era preceding the Deluge* (that had occurred, by our calculations, some 13,000 years ago), and preceding it not by a short time but by thousands and tens of thousands of years!

The existence of pictorial depictions from that far back in prehistory is no secret. What is virtually a secret is the fact that besides animals, and some human figures, those drawings and paintings also depicted what we nowadays call UFOs.

We refer to what is known as Cave Art, the many drawings found in caves in Europe where Cro-Magnon Man made his home. Such "decorated caves" as scholars call them have been found especially in the southwest of France and the north of Spain. More than seventy such decorated caves have been found (one, whose entrance is now under the waters of the Mediterranean sea, as recently as 1993); there, Stone Age artists used the cave walls as giant canvases, sometimes talentedly using the natural contours and protrusions of the walls to attain tridimensional effects. Sometimes using sharp stones to engrave the images, sometimes clay to mold and shape, but mostly a limited assortment of pigments—black, red, yellow, and a dull brown—they created astoundingly beautiful works of art. Occasionally depicting humans as hunters, and sometimes their hunting weapons (arrows, lances), the depictions by and large are those of Ice Age animals: bison, reindeer, ibexes, horses, oxen, cows, felines, and here and there also fish and birds (Fig. 9). The drawings, engravings, and paintings are sometimes life-size, always naturalistic. There is no doubt that the anonymous artists painted what they had actually seen. Timewise they span millennia, from about 30,000 to 13,000 years ago.

In many instances the more complex, more vividly colored, more lifelike depictions are in the deeper parts of the caves, which were, of course, also the darkest parts. What means the artists used to light the inner recesses of the caves so that they could paint, no one knows, for no remains of charcoal or torches or the like have been found. Nor, to judge by the absence of remains, were these caves habitats. Many scholars, therefore, tend to view these decorated caves as shrines,

Figure 9

where the art expressed a primitive religion—an appeal to the gods, by painting the animals and hunting scenes, to make forthcoming hunting expeditions successful.

The inclination to view the Cave Art as religious art also stems from the plastic finds. These consist mainly of "Venus" figurines—statuettes of females known as the Willendorf Venus (Fig. 10a) whose date is approximately 23000 B.C. Since the artists could also render the female shape per-

Figures 10a and 10b

Figure 11

fectly naturally, as this find in France from circa 22000 B.C. shows (Fig. 10b), it is believed that the ones with exaggerated reproductive parts were intended to symbolize or seek— "pray for"—fertility; so that while the natural ones represented "Eves," the exaggerated ones ("Venuses") expressed veneration of a goddess.

The discovery of another "Venus" at Laussel in France, dating to the same period, reinforces the deity rather than the human identification, because the female is holding in her right hand the symbol of a crescent (Fig. 11). Although some suggest that she is merely holding a bison's horn, the symbolism of a celestial connection (here with the Moon) is inescapable, no matter of what material the crescent was made.

Many researchers (e.g. Johannes Maringer in *The Gods of Prehistoric Man*) believe that "it appears highly probable that the female figurines were idols of a 'great mother' cult, practiced by non-nomadic Upper Stone Age mammoth hunters." Others, like Marlin Stone (*When God Was A Woman*) considered the phenomenon "dawn of a Stone Age Garden of Eden" and linked this worship of a Mother Goddess to the later goddesses of the Sumerian pantheon. One of the nicknames of Ninmah, who had assisted Enki in the creation of Man, was *Mammi*; there is no doubt that it was the origin of the word for "mother" in almost all the languages. That she was revered already some 30,000 years ago is no wonder— for the Anunnaki had been on Earth for far longer, with Ninmah/Mammi among them.

The question is, though, how did Stone Age Man, more

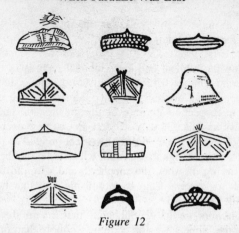

Figure 12

specifically Cro-Magnon Man, know of the existence of these "gods"?

Here, we believe, come into play another type of drawings found in the Stone Age caves. If they are mentioned at all (which is rarely), they are referred to as "markings." But these were not scratches or incoherent lines. These "markings" depict well-defined shapes—shapes of objects that, nowadays, are referred to as UFOs . . .

The best way to make the point is to reproduce these "markings." Fig. 12 reproduces depictions by Stone Age artists—the illustrating reporters of their time—in the Altamira, La Pasiega, and El Castillo caves in Spain, and the Font-de-Gaume and Pair-non-Pair caves in France. These are by no means all of the illustrations of this kind, but the ones that, in our view, are the most obvious Stone Age depictions of celestial chariots. Since all the other depictions in the decorated caves are of animals, etc., actually seen and most accurately rendered by the cave artists, there is no reason to assume that in the case of the "markings" they depicted objects that were abstract imaginings. If the depictions are of flying objects, then the artists must have actually seen them.

Thanks to those artists and their handiwork, we can rest assured that when Adam and Eve—in pre-Diluvial times—

claimed to have seen "celestial chariots," they were recording fact, not fiction.

Reading the biblical and extra-biblical records in the light of Sumerian sources will add greatly to our understanding of those prehistoric events. We have already examined such sources in respect to the tale of the creation of The Adam and of Eve and the Garden of Eden. Let us now examine the Cain-Abel tragedy. Why did the two feel obliged to offer the first fruits or yearlings to Yahweh, why did he pay heed only to the offering of Abel, the shepherd, and why did the Lord then rush to appease Cain by promising him that he, Cain, would rule over Abel?

The answers lie in a realization that, as in the tale of creation, the biblical version compresses more than one Sumerian deity into a single, monotheistic one.

Sumerian texts include two that deal with disputes and conflicts between farming and shepherding. They both hold the key to an understanding of what had happened by going back to a time before the domestication of either grains or cattle, a "time when grains had not yet been brought forth, had not yet vegetated ... when a lamb had not yet been dropped, there was no she-goat." But the "black-headed people" had already been fashioned and placed in the Edin; so the Anunnaki decided to give to NAM.LU.GAL.LU—"civilized Mankind"—the knowledge of and tools for "the tilling of the land" and the "keeping of sheep"; not, however, for the sake of Mankind but "for the sake of the gods," to assure their satiation.

The task of bringing forth the two forms of domestication fell to Enki and Enlil. They went to the DU.KU, the "purification place," the "creation chamber of the gods," and brought forth *Lahar* ("woolly cattle") and *Anshan* ("grains"). "For Lahar they set up a sheepfold ... to Anshan a plough and yoke they presented." Sumerian cylinder seals depicted the presentation of the first-ever plough to Mankind (Fig. 13a)—presumably by Enlil who had created Anshan, the farmer (although a presentation by Enlil's son Ninurta, who was nicknamed "the ploughman," should not be ruled out); and a ploughing scene in which the plough is pulled by a bull (Fig. 13b).

After an initial idyllic period, Lahar and Anshan began to quarrel. A text named by scholars *The Myth of Cattle and Grain* reveals that in spite of the effort to separate the two by "establishing a house," a settled way of life, for Anshan (the farmer) and putting up sheepfolds in the grazing lands for Lahar (the shepherd), and in spite of the abundant crops and bountiful sheepfolds, the two began to quarrel. The quarrel began as the two offered those abundances to the "storehouse of the gods." At first each just extolled his own achievements and belittled those of the other. But the argument became so volatile, that both Enlil and Enki had to intervene. According to the Sumerian text, they declared Anshan—the farmer—the more surpassing.

More explicit in its choice between the two food producers and two ways of life is a text known as *The Dispute Between Emesh an Enten,* in which the two come to Enlil for a decision as to who of them is the more important. Emesh is the one who "made wide stalls and sheepfolds"; Enten, who dug canals to water the lands, asserts that he is the "farmer of the gods." Bringing their offerings to Enlil, each seeks to be granted primacy. Enten boasts how he made "farm touch farm," his irrigation canals "brought water in abundance,"

Figures 13a and 13b

how he "made grain increase in the furrows" and be "heaped high in the granaries." Emesh points out that he "made the ewe give birth to the lamb, the goat to give birth to the kid, cow and calf to multiply, fat and milk to increase," and also how he obtained eggs from nests made for the birds and caught fish from the sea.

But Enlil rejects the pleas of Emesh, even reprimands him: "How could you compare yourself to your brother Enten!" he tells him, for it is Enten "who is in charge of the life-producing waters of all the lands." And water spells life, growth, abundance. Emesh accepts the decision,

> The exalted word of Enlil,
> whose meaning is profound;
> A verdict that is unalterable,
> no one dares transgress it!

And so, "in the dispute between Emesh and Enten, Enten, the faithful farmer of the gods, having proved himself the winner, Emesh his knee bent before Enten, offered him a prayer," and gave him many presents.

It is noteworthy that in the above-quoted lines Enlil calls Emesh a brother of Enten—the same relationship as that between Cain and Abel. This and other similarities between the Sumerian and biblical tales indicate that the former were the inspiration for the latter. The preference of the farmer over the shepherd by Enlil can be traced to the fact that he was the one to introduce farming while Enki accounted for the domestication of livestock. Scholars tend to translate the Sumerian names as "winter" for Enten and "summer" for Emesh. Strictly speaking EN.TEN meant "Lord of Resting," the time after the harvests and thus the winter season, without a clear affinity to a specific deity. E.MESH ("House of Mesh"), on the other hand, is clearly associated with Enki, one of whose epithets was MESH ("Proliferation"); he was thus the god of shepherding.

All in all, there can be little doubt that the Cain-Abel rivalry reflected a rivalry between the two divine brothers. It flared up from time to time, as when Enlil arrived on Earth to take over command from Enki (who was relegated to the

Abzu), and on subsequent occasions. Its roots, however, went back to Nibiru, their home planet. Both were the sons of Anu, Nibiru's ruler. Enki was the firstborn, and thus the natural heir to the throne. But Enlil, though born later, was born by the official spouse of Anu (and presumably a half sister of his)—a fact that made Enlil the legal heir to the throne. Birthright clashed with succession rules; and though Enki accepted the outcome, the rivalry and anger often burst into the open.

A question rarely asked is, where did Cain obtain the very notion of *killing*? In the Garden of Eden Adam and Eve were vegetarians, eating only fruits of the trees. No animal was slaughtered by them. Away from the Garden there were only four humans, none of whom has yet died (and certainly not as a result of foul play). In such circumstances, what made Cain "come upon his brother Abel and kill him"?

The answer, it seems, lies not among men but among the gods. Just as the rivalry between the human brothers reflected a rivalry between the divine brothers, so did the killing of one human by another emulate the killing of one "god" by another. Not of Enki by Enlil or vice versa—their rivalry never reached such vehemence—but still the killing of one leader of the Anunnaki by another.

The tale is well documented in Sumerian literature. Scholars called it *The Myth of Zu*. It relates events that took place after the rearrangement of the command on Earth, with an ample production of gold ores in the Abzu under Enki's direction and their processing, smelting, and refining in the Edin under Enlil's supervision. Six hundred Anunnaki are engaged in all of these operations on Earth; another three hundred (the IGI.GI, "Those Who Observe and See") stay aloft, manning the shuttlecraft and spacecraft that transport the purified gold to Nibiru. Mission Control Center is in Enlil's headquarters in Nippur; it is called DUR.AN.KI, "The Bond Heaven-Earth." There, atop a raised platform, the vital instruments, celestial charts and orbital-data panels ("Tablets of Destinies") are kept in the DIR.GA, a restricted innermost holy-of-holies.

The Igigi, complaining that they get no respite from their orbital duties, send an emissary to Enlil. He is an AN.ZU,

Figure 14

"One Who Knows the Heavens," and is called ZU for short. Admitted into the Dirga, he finds out that the Tablets of Destinies are the key to the whole mission. Soon he begins to think evil thoughts, "to plot aggression:" to steal the Tablets of Destinies and "govern the decrees of the gods."

At first opportunity he carried out his scheme, and "in his Bird" took off to hide in the "Mountain of Skychambers." In the Duranki, everything came to a standstill; the contact with Nibiru was disrupted, all operations were thrown into havoc. As one effort after another to recapture the tablets fails, Ninurta, Enlil's Foremost Son and warrior, undertakes the dangerous mission. Aerial battles with weapons that emit brilliant rays ensue. Finally, Ninurta managed to penetrate Zu's protective force-field shields and shot Zu's "Bird" down. Zu was captured and put on trial before the "seven Anunnaki who judge." He was found guilty and was sentenced to death. His vanquisher, Ninurta, carried out the sentence.

The execution of Zu has been depicted on an archaic sculpted relief found in central Mesopotamia (Fig. 14). It all happened long before Mankind was created; but as these texts show, the tale was recorded and known in ensuing millennia. If that is where Cain obtained the notion of killing, Yahweh's anger was understandable, for Zu was killed after a trial; Abel was just murdered.

Sumerian texts, the origin of and inspiration for the tales of Genesis, not only fill the bare-bones biblical versions with details; they also provide the background for understanding the events. One more aspect of the human experience thus far can be explained by the divine records. The sins of Adam/ Eve and of Cain are punished by nothing more severe than Expulsion. That too appears to be an application of an Anunnaki form of punishment to the created humans. It was once meted out to Enlil himself, who "date-raped" a young Anunnaki nurse (who in the end became his wife).

By combining the biblical and Sumerian data, we are now in a position to put the record of Mankind's beginnings in a time frame supported by modern science.

According to the Sumerian King Lists, 120 *Sars* ("Divine Years" or orbits of Nibiru), equaling 432,000 Earth-years, passed from the arrival of the Anunnaki on Earth until the Deluge. In chapter 6 of Genesis, in the preamble to the tale of Noah and the Deluge, the number "one hundred and twenty years" is also given. It has been generally held that it refers to the limit God had put on the extent of a man's life; but as we have pointed out in *The 12th Planet,* the Patriarchs lived after the Deluge much longer—Shem, the son of Noah, 600 years; his son Arpakhshad 438, his son Shelach 433, and so on through Terah, Abraham's father, who lived to be 205. A careful reading of the biblical Hebrew verse, we have suggested, actually spoke of the *deity's* years completing 120 by then—a count of Divine Years, not those of Earthlings.

Out of those 432,000 Earth-years, the Anunnaki were alone on Earth for forty Sars, when the mutiny occurred. Then, some 288,000 Earth-years before the Deluge, i.e. about 300,000 years ago, they created the Primitive Worker. After an interval whose length is not stated in those sources, they gave the new being the ability to procreate, and returned the First Couple to southeast Africa.

A point that is usually ignored, but which we find highly significant, is that all through the narratives concerning Man's creation, the Garden of Eden episode, and—most intriguing— in the story of the birth of Cain and Abel, the Bible refers to the human as THE Adam, a generic term defining a certain species. Only in chapter 5 of Genesis, that begins with the words "This is the book of the genealogies of Adam," does the Bible drop the "the." It is only then that it starts to deal with a specific forefather of the human generations; but significantly, this listing omits Cain and Abel and proceeds from the person called Adam straight on to his son Seth, the father of Enosh. And it is only for Seth's son Enosh that the Hebrew term meaning "human being" is employed; for that is what *Enosh* meant: "He who is human." To this day the Hebrew word for "Humankind" is *Enoshut*, "that which is like, that which stems from, Enosh."

The link between the biblical narrative and its Sumerian origins emerges most interestingly in this name of the son of Adam, Enosh, whom the Bible considers the real progenitor of Humankind as it came to be in the ancient Near East. A list of months and the gods associated with them (known as IV R 33), which begins with Nisan as the month associated with Anu and Enlil (the first month of the Assyrian-Babylonian year), lists next the month Ayar with the notation *"sha Ea bel tinishti"*—"That of Ea, lord of Mankind." The Akkadian term *tinishti* has the same meaning as the *Enoshut* in Hebrew (which derived from the Akkadian). The Akkadian term, in turn, was paralleled in the Sumerian by the term AZA.LU.LU which can best be translated as "the people who serve"; and once again, this conveys—and explains—the biblical statement that expounds on Enosh, the meaning of his name, and his time.

It is in respect to Enosh that the Bible states (Genesis 4:26) that it was in his time that Humankind "began to call upon the name of Yahweh." It must have been an important development, a new phase in Humankind's history, for the *Book of Jubilees* states in almost identical words that it was Enosh "who began to call on the name of the Lord on Earth." Man has discovered God!

Who was this new human, "Enosh-man," from a scientific point of view? Was he the progenitor of what we call Neanderthal Man, the first true *Homo sapiens?* Or was he already the ancestor of Cro-Magnon Man, the first true *Homo sapiens sapiens* that still walks the Earth as the current human beings? Cro-Magnon Man (so named after the site in France where his skeletal remains were found) appeared *in Europe* some 35,000 years ago, replacing there the Neanderthal Man (so named after the discovery site in Germany) who can be traced there to 100,000 years ago. But, as skeletal remains discovered in recent years in caves in Israel reveal, Neanderthals were migrating through the Near East at least some 115,000 years ago, and Cro-Magnons had dwelt in the area already 92,000 years ago. Where do The Adam and Eve, the first created humans, and Adam and Eve, the progenitors of Seth and Enosh, fit into all that? What light do the Sumerian King Lists and the Bible shed on the issue, and how does it all correlate to modern scientific discoveries?

While fossil remains discovered in Africa, Asia, and Europe suggest that hominids first appeared in southeastern Africa and then branched out to the other continents possibly half a million years ago, the true predecessors of today's humanity made their appearance in southeastern Africa somewhat later. The genetic markers for *Homo sapiens,* first studied through the Mitochondrial DNA that is passed by the female alone, and then through studies of Nuclear DNA that is inherited from both parents (reports at the April 1994 annual meeting of the American Association of Physical Anthropologists) indicate that we all stem from a single "Eve" that had lived in southeast Africa between 200,000 and 250,000 years ago. Studies released in May 1995 of the Y chromosome indicate a single "Adam" ancestor some 270,000 years ago.

The Sumerian data, we have concluded, places the creation of The Adam at about 290,000 years ago—well within the time scales for the two progenitors that modern science now suggests. How long the stay at the Garden of Eden, the attainment of the ability to procreate, the expulsion back to southeast Africa, and the Cain-Abel birth had taken place, the ancient texts do not state. Fifty thousand years? One hundred thousand years? Whatever the exact time lapse, it seems evident that the "Eve" who was back in southeast Africa, bearing offspring to The Adam, fits well chronologically with the current scientific data.

With those early humans gone from the stage, the time came for the specific Adam and his line to appear. According to the Bible the pre-Diluvial patriarchs, who enjoyed life spans ranging in most cases almost 1,000 years, account for

1,656 years from Adam (the specific individual) to the Deluge:

Age of Adam when he begot Seth	130 years
Age of Seth when he begot Enosh	105 years
Age of Enosh when he begot Kenan	90 years
Age of Kenan when he begot Mahalalel	70 years
Age of Mahalalel when he begot Jared	65 years
Age of Jared when he begot Enoch	162 years
Age of Enoch when he begot Metushelah	65 years
Age of Metushelah when he begot Lamech	187 years
Age of Lamech when he begot Noah	182 years
Age of Noah when the Deluge occurred	600 years
Total time from birth of Adam to Deluge	1,656 years

There has been no shortage of attempts to reconcile these 1,656 years with the Sumerian 432,000, especially so since the Bible lists ten pre-Diluvial patriarchs from Adam to Noah, and the Sumerian King Lists also name ten pre-Diluvial rulers the last of whom, Ziusudra, was also the hero of the Deluge. More than a century ago, for example, Julius Oppert (in a study titled *Die Daten der Genesis*) showed that the two numbers share a factor of 72 (432,000 : 72 = 6,000 and 1656 : 72 = 23) and then engaged in mathematical acrobatics to arrive at a common source for the two. About a century later the "mythologist" Joseph Campbell (*The Masks of God*) noted with fascination that 72 represented the number of years Earth, in its orbit around the Sun, retards by 1° (the phenomenon called Precession) and thus saw a connection to the zodiacal houses of 2,160 years each (72 x 30° = 2,160). These and other ingenious solutions fail to recognize the error in comparing 432,000 with 1,656 because of treatment of all the ancient texts as just "myth." If the ancient records would be treated as reliable data, it should be noted that the Primitive Worker (still only THE Adam) was brought forth not 120 Sars before the Deluge but only 80 Sars before the watery ordeal, i.e. only 288,000 Earth-years before the Deluge. Moreover, as we have shown earlier in this chapter, THE Adam and the person Adam were not one and the same. First there was the interlude in the Garden of Eden, then the

Expulsion. How long that interlude lasted, the Bible does not say.

Since, as we have shown, the biblical narrative is based on Sumerian sources, the simplest solution to the problem is also the most plausible. In the Sumerian sexagesimal ("base 60") mathematical system, the cuneiform sign for "1" could mean one or could mean sixty, depending on the position of the sign, just as "1" could mean one or ten or one hundred depending on the digit's position in the decimal system (except that we make distinction easy by the use of "0" to indicate position, writing 1, 10, 100 etc.). Could it not then be that the redactors of the Hebrew Bible, seeing in the Sumerian sources the sign "1", took it to mean One rather than Sixty?

Based on such an assumption, the numbers 1,656 (the birth of Adam), 1,526 (the birth of Seth) and 1,421 (the birth of Enosh) are converted to 99,360, 91,560 and 85,260 respectively. To determine how long ago that was, we have to add the 13,000 years since the Deluge; the numbers then become

> Adam born 112,360 years ago
> Seth born 104,560 years ago
> Enosh born 98,260 years ago

The solution offered here by us leads to astounding results. It places the Adam-Seth-Enosh line right in the time slot when Neanderthals and then Cro-Magnons passed through the Lands of the Bible as they spread toward Asia and Europe. It means that the individual (not the generic) *Adam* **was the biblical Man whom we term Neanderthal, and that** *Enosh,* **whose name meant "Human," was the biblical term for what we call Cro-Magnon—the first** *Homo sapiens sapiens, indeed the forefather of Enoshut,* **today's humanity.**

It was then, the Bible asserts, that humanity "began to call upon the name of Yahweh." Man was ready for renewed Divine Encounters; and some that then occurred were truly astounding.

THE FIRST AMERICANS

The long-held notion that America was settled by hunters who had crossed over a frozen Bering Strait during the last Ice Age had seemed implausible to us all along, for it required familiarity with an ice-free, warmer hunting continent thousands of miles away by people who, by definition, had not known of "America." If they did know of such a land, others must have preceded them!

This notion, according to which the First Americans came down the Pacific coast and established their first settlement at a North American site called Clovis is now completely discredited, primarily owing to the discovery of much earlier settlements in the eastern parts of North America, and even more so of settlements dating back 20,000, 25,000 and even 30,000 years in South America, both near the Pacific and the Atlantic coasts.

This is way before such candidates as Africans or Phoenicians (who had certainly been to Mesoamerica) or Vikings (who had probably reached North America); indeed, it is way *before the Deluge*, and thus in the time frame of the pre-Diluvial descendants of Adam.

According to local lore, the arrivals were by sea. The latest estimate, of some 30,000 years ago from Asia via the Pacific Ocean, requires seafaring knowledge at such an early date. This is no longer deemed outlandish by scientists, since it has been established by now that the first settlers in Australia arrived there—*by boat*—some 37,000 years ago. Australia and the Pacific Islands are now considered logical stepping-stones en route from Asia to the Americas.

Rock art by Australian Aborigines includes depictions of boats. So do the rock paintings of Cro-Magnon Man in Europe—as we show in the next chapter.

3

THE THREE
WHO TO HEAVEN ASCENDED

Divine Encounters, as even Humankind's earliest experiences have shown, can take many forms. Whether in the form of direct contact, through emissaries, by only hearing the god's voice, in dreams or visions, there is one aspect common to all the experiences thus far described: they all take place on Earth.

Yet there was one more form of Divine Encounter, the utmost, and thus reserved for only a handful of chosen mortals: To be taken aloft to join the gods in Heaven.

In much later times, Egyptian Pharaohs were subjected to elaborate mortuary rituals so that they might enjoy an Afterlife journey to the Divine Abode. But in the days before the Deluge, selected individuals ascended to Heaven and lived to tell about it. One ascent is recorded in Genesis; two are related in Sumerian texts.

All three require accepting as truthful the Sumerian assertion that there had been a developed civilization *before* the Deluge, one that was wiped out and buried under millions of tons of mud by the avalanche of water that engulfed Mesopotamia. This Sumerian assertion was not doubted by later generations. An Assyrian king (Ashurbanipal) boasted that he could "understand the enigmatic words in the stone carvings from the days before the Flood," and Assyrian and Babylonian texts often spoke of other knowledge and knowing individuals, of events and urban settlements, long ago before the Deluge. The Bible, too, describes an advanced civilization

Figure 15

with cities, crafts, and arts in respect to the line of Cain. Though no such details are provided in respect to the line of Seth, the very tale of Noah and the construction of the ark implies a state of affairs where people could already build seagoing vessels.

That such a civilization expressed itself in urban centers in Mesopotamia (the core of such advances) but in only magnificent artistry among the European branch of Cro-Magnons is quite possible. As a matter of fact, some of the images painted or drawn by the cave artists depict inexplicable structures or objects (Fig. 15). They become meaningful if one accepts the possibility that Cro-Magnons had seen (or perhaps even traveled by) masted seagoing vessels—a possibility that could explain how Man crossed the two oceans 20,000 or even 30,000 years ago to reach America from the Old World. (Native American legends of prehistoric arrivals by sea across the Pacific include the tale of Naymlap, the leader of a small armada of balsamwood boats, who carried in his lead boat a green stone through which he could hear the divine instructions for navigation and the point of landfall).

Indeed, the Sumerian tales of the two chosen individuals who ascended to Heaven pertain to the origins of human civilization and explain how it came about (*before* the Deluge). The first one is the tale recounted in what scholars call *The Legend of Adapa*. An intriguing aspect of the tale is that, prior to the heavenly ascent, Adapa was involved in an involuntary sea crossing to an unknown land because his boat was blown off course—an episode that is perhaps reflected in the recollections of early Americans and in the Cro-Magnon cave depictions.

Adapa, according to the ancient text, was a protégé of Enki. Allowed to live in Enki's city Eridu (the very first settlement of the Anunnaki on Earth), "daily he attended the sanctuary of Eridu." Choosing him to become "as a model of men," Enki (in this text called by his initial epithet-name, E.A) "gave him wisdom, but did not give him eternal life." It is not just the similarity between the names Adapa and Adam, but also this statement, that led various scholars to see in the ancient tale of Adapa the forerunner (or inspiration for) the tale of Adam and Eve in the Garden of Eden, who were allowed to eat of the Tree of Knowing but not of the Tree of Life. The text then describes Adapa as a busybody, in charge of the services for which the Primitive Workers were brought over to the Edin: he supervises the bakers, assures water supplies, oversees the fishing for Eridu, and as an "ointment priest, clean of hands," tends to the offerings and prescribed rites.

One day "at the holy quay, the Quay of the New Moon" (the Moon was then the celestial body associated with Ea/Enki) "he boarded the sailboat," perhaps intending to just sail to catch fish. But then calamity struck:

> *Then a wind blew thither,*
> *and without a rudder his boat drifted.*
> *With the oar he steered his boat;*
> *[he drifted] into the broad sea.*

The following lines in the clay tablet were damaged, so that we are missing some details of what happened once Adapa had found himself adrift in the "broad sea" (the Persian Gulf). As the lines become legible again we read that a major storm, the South Wind, began to blow. It apparently unexpectedly changed direction, and instead of blowing from the sea toward land it blew toward the open ocean. For seven days the storm blew, carrying Adapa to an unknown distant region. There, stranded, "at the place which is the home of the fishes, he took up a residence." We are not told how long he was stranded at that southern location, nor how he was finally rescued.

In his heavenly abode, according to the tale, Anu wondered

why the South Wind "has not blown toward the land for
seven days." His vizier Ilabrat answered him that it was
because "Adapa, offspring of Ea, had broken the wing of
the South Wind." Perplexed, Anu ("rising from his throne")
said, "Let them fetch him hither!"

"At that, Ea, he who knows what pertains to Heaven,"
took charge of the preparations for the celestial journey.
"He made Adapa wear his hair unkempt, and clothed him
in mourning garb." He then gave Adapa the following
advice:

> You are about to go before Anu, the king;
> The road to heaven you will be taking.
> When you approach the gate of Anu
> the gods Dumuzi and Gizzida
> at the gate of Anu will be standing.
> When they see you, they will ask you:
> "Man, on account of whom do you look thus,
> for whom so you wear mourning garb?"

To this question, Ea instructed Adapa, you must give the
following answer: "Two gods have vanished from our land,
that is why I am thus." When they question you who the
two gods were, Ea continued, you must say, "Dumuzi and
Gizzida they are." And, since the two gods whose names
you tell as being the vanished gods for whom you mourn
will be the very same two who guard the gate of Anu, Ea
explained, "They will glance at each other, and laugh a lot,
and will speak to Anu a good word about you."

This strategy, Ea explained, will get Adapa past the gate
and "cause Anu to show you his benign face." But once
inside, Ea warned, Adapa's true test will come:

> As you stand before Anu,
> they will offer you bread;
> it is Death, do not eat!
> They will offer you water;
> it is Death, do not drink!
> They will offer you a garment;
> put it on.

> *They will offer you oil;*
> *anoint yourself with it!*

"You must not neglect these instructions," Ea cautioned Adapa; "to that which I have spoken, hold fast!"

Soon thereafter the emissary of Anu arrived. Anu, he said, gave the following instructions: "Adapa, he who broke the South Wind's wing—bring him to me!" And so speaking,

> *He made Adapa take the way to heaven,*
> *and to heaven he ascended.*

"When he came to Heaven," the text continued, "and approached the gate of Anu," Dumuzi and Gizzida were standing there, as Ea had predicted. They questioned Adapa also as predicted, and Adapa answered as instructed, and the two gods brought him "before the presence of Anu." Seeing him approach, Anu shouted, "Come closer, Adapa; Why did you break the South Wind's wing?" In reply, Adapa related the story of his sea voyage, making sure that Anu realized it was all in the service of Ea. Hearing that, Anu's anger to Adapa subsided, but grew instead at Ea. "It was he who did it!"

A nagging aspect of the tale thus far is the lack of clarity regarding the true circumstances of the sea voyage. Was the arrival in a distant land the result of an accidental blowing off course, or somehow deliberate? The damaged lines that deal with that portion of the events make a determination impossible; but a feeling that the whole excuse of a "broken wing" of the South Wind was a cover for some deliberate plan by Ea comes to us as we read and reread the ancient text. Evidently Anu had such suspicions right then and there, for having heard Adapa's tale he was puzzled, and asked:

> *Why did Ea to an unworthy human*
> *disclose the ways of heaven*
> *and the plans of Earth—*
> *rendering him distinguished,*
> *making a* Shem *for him?*

And, continuing such rhetorical questions, Anu asked: "As for us, what shall we do about him?"

Since Adapa was not to blame for the whole incident, Anu wished to reward him. He ordered that bread, "the Bread of Life," be offered to Adapa; but Adapa, having been told by Ea that it will be the Bread of Death, refused to eat of it. They brought to him water, "the Water of Life"; but Adapa, forewarned by Ea that it would be the Water of Death, refused to drink. But when they brought a garment he put it on, and when they brought oil he anointed himself.

Adapa's peculiar behavior amazed Anu. "Anu looked at him, and laughed at him." "Come now, Adapa," Anu said, "why did you not eat, why did you not drink?" To which Adapa responded, "Ea, my master, commanded me, 'you shall not eat, you shall not drink.'"

"When Anu heard this, wrath filled his heart." He dispatched an emissary, "one who knows the thoughts of the great Anunnaki," to discuss the matter with the lord Ea. The emissary, the partly damaged tablet relates, repeated the events in Heaven word for word. The tablet then becomes too damaged and illegible, so that we do not know Ea's explanation for his odd instructions (that were, obviously, intended to sustain his decision to give Adapa knowledge but not immortality).

No matter how the discussion ended, Anu decided to send Adapa back to Earth; and since Adapa did use the oil to anoint himself, Anu decreed that back in Eridu Adapa's destiny will be to start a line of priests who will be adept at curing diseases. On the way back

> Adapa, from the horizon of heaven
> to the zenith of heaven cast a glance;
> and he saw its awesomeness.

The interesting question, what was the mode of transportation by which Adapa had made the round-trip, seeing in the process the awesome expanse of the heavens, is answered by the ancient text only indirectly, when Anu wonders out loud why did Ea "make a *Shem*" for Adapa. This Akkadian word is usually translated "name." But as we have elaborated in

Figures 16a, 16b, and 16c

The 12th Planet, the term (MU in Sumerian) obtained this meaning from the shape of the stones erected to "commemorate the name" of a king—a shape that emulated the pointed skychambers of the Anunnaki. What Anu wondered, then, was, Why did Ea provide a *skyrocket* for Adapa?

Mesopotamian depictions show "Eaglemen"—Anunnaki astronauts in their dress uniforms—flanking and saluting a rocketlike *Shem* (Fig. 16a). Another depiction shows two such "Eaglemen" guarding the gateway of Anu (illustrating perhaps the gods Dumuzi and Gizzida of the Adapa tale). The gate's lintel (Fig. 16b) is decorated with the emblem of the Winged Disc, the celestial symbol of Nibiru, which establishes where the gateway was. The celestial symbol of Enlil (the seven dots that stood for Earth as the seventh planet, counting from outside inward) and the celestial symbol of Enki, the Moon's crescent, together with the depiction of the whole solar system (a central deity surrounded by a family of eleven planets) complete the heavenly background. We also find the winged "Eaglemen, whose depictions undoubtedly inspired later notions of winged angels, flanking a Tree of Life; significantly, it often evoked the double helix of DNA (Fig. 16c), a reminder of the Garden of Eden tale.

Mesopotamian kings, boasting of their great knowledge, claimed that they were "scions of the wise Adapa." Such claims reflected the tradition that Adapa was granted not just priestly status, but was also taught scientific knowledge that in antiquity was associated with the priesthood, passed from one generation of priests to another in the sacred precincts. Tablets that cataloged literary works kept on shelves in the library of Ashurbanipal in Nineveh mention, in their undamaged portions, at least two "books" relating to Adapa's knowledge. One, whose title is damaged at its start, was on a shelf next to a text of "Writings from Before the Flood," and its second line reads ". . . which Adapa wrote at his dictation." The suggestion that Adapa had written down knowledge dictated to him by a deity is enhanced by the title of another work attributed to Adapa by Sumerian sources. It was titled *U.SAR Dingir ANUM Dingir ENLILA*—"Writings Regarding Time, [from] Divine Anu and Divine Enlil"—and confirms the traditions that Adapa was tutored not only by Ea/Enki but also by Anu and Enlil, and that his knowledge ranged from that of curing diseases to astronomy, timekeeping, and the calendar.

One other book (i.e. a set of tablets) by Adapa that was listed on the shelves of the library of Nineveh was titled "Celestialship which to the Sage of Anu, Adapa [was given]." The *Legend of Adapa* texts repeatedly refer to the fact that Adapa was shown "the ways of heaven," enabling him to travel from Earth to the heavenly abode of Anu. The implication that Adapa was shown a celestial route map ought to be taken as based on fact, for—incredibly—at least one such route map has been found. It is depicted on a clay disc, undoubtedly a copy of an earlier artifact, that was also discovered in the ruins of the royal library of Nineveh and that is now kept in the British Museum in London. Divided into eight segments, it depicted (as evident from the undamaged portions, Fig. 17a) precise geometric shapes (some, such as an ellipse, unknown from other ancient artifacts), arrows,

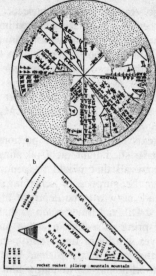

Figures 17a and 17b

and accompanying notations in Akkadian that referred to various planets, stars, and constellations. Of particular interest is an almost-intact segment (Fig. 17b) whose notations (translated here into English) of space flight instructions identify it as the Route of Enlil from a mountainous planet (Nibiru) to Earth. Beyond Earth's skies (the "Way of Enlil") lie four celestial bodies (which other texts identify as Sun, Moon, Mercury, and Venus). In between, the flight passes by seven planets.

The count of seven planets is signficant. We consider Earth to be the third planet, counting from the Sun outward: Mercury, Venus, Earth. But for someone arriving from the outer limits of the solar system, the count would be Pluto as the first, Neptune as the second, Uranus as the third, Saturn and Jupiter as the fourth and fifth, Mars as the sixth, and Earth would be the seventh. In fact, Earth was so depicted (by the symbol of seven dots) on cylinder seals and monuments, oftentimes with Mars (the sixth) as a six-pointed "star" and Venus (the eighth) as an eight-pointed one.

Significant, too, though in other respects, is the fact that the route passes between the planets named in Sumerian DIL-GAN (Jupiter) and APIN (Mars). Mesopotamian astronomical texts referred to Mars as the planet "where the right course is set," where a turn is made as the drawing on the segment indicates. In *Genesis Revisited* we have presented considerable ancient and modern evidence in support of a conclusion that an ancient space base had existed on Mars.

The missing texts or the damaged portions of the Adapa Legend might have shed light on a puzzling aspect of the tale: If Ea foresaw all that would happen at the heavenly abode, what was the purpose of scheming to send Adapa aloft if, in the end, he was to be deprived of Eternal Life?

Tales from post-Diluvial times (such as that of Gilgamesh) indicate that offspring of a human and a god (or goddess) deemed themselves worthy of Immortality, and went to great lengths to join the gods to attain that. Was Adapa such a "demigod," and did he nag Ea to endow him with Immortality? The reference to Adapa as "offspring of Ea" is translated by some literally as "son of Ea," born to Enki by a human female. This would explain Ea's scheme to pretend that Adapa's wish is being granted, while in fact he maneuvered for the opposite result.

Adapa, without doubt, also bore the title "Son of Eridu" (Enki's center). It was an honorific title that signified intelligence and education by schooling in Eridu's renowned academies. In Sumerian times the "Sages of Eridu" were a class unto themselves, ancient savants of blessed memory. Their names and specialties were listed and recorded with great respect and reverence in countless texts.

According to those sources, the Sages of Eridu were seven in number. In her study of Assyrian sources, Rykle Borger ("Die Beschwerungsserie Bit Meshri und die Himmelfahrt Henochs" in the *Journal of Near Eastern Studies*) was intrigued by the fact that in respect to the seventh one, the text stated (in addition to the name and main call on fame, as for all those listed) that it was he "who to heaven ascended." The Assyrian text calls him Utu-Abzu; Professor Borger concluded that he was the Assyrian "Enoch," because according

to the biblical record, it was the seventh pre-Diluvial Patriarch, whom the Bible calls Enoch, who was taken by God
to the heavenly abode.

While the biblical narrative lists for the pre-Diluvial Patriarchs who had preceded Enoch and for those who followed
him their names, age when their firstborn son was begotten,
and the age at which they died, it states in respect to Enoch,
the seventh Patriarch, thus (we quote from the common English translation):

> *And Enoch lived sixty and five years*
> *and begot Methuselah.*
> *And Enoch walked with God*
> *after he had begotten Methuselah*
> *three hundred years,*
> *and begot sons and daughters.*
> *And all the days of Enoch*
> *were three hundred sixty five years,*
> *for Enoch walked with God and was gone,*
> *for God had taken him.*

Even this short biblical report has more to it than meets
the eye in translation because in the original Hebrew it is
stated that "Enoch walked with *the Elohim*," and was taken
aloft "*by Elohim*." The Hebrew term, as we have shown,
stood for DIN.GIR in the Sumerian sources of Genesis. Thus
it was the Anunnaki with whom Enoch "walked" and by
whom he was taken aloft. This gloss, as well as scientific
data that could come only from the Sumerian sexagesimal
system of mathematics and the Sumerian calendar that had
originated in Nippur, are clues to the ancient sources of compositions thanks to which we know much more about Enoch
than the laconic biblical sentence.

The first of these compositions is the *Book of Jubilees* that
we have already mentioned. Filling in the details lacking in
the biblical account of the ten pre-Diluvial Patriarchs, it asserts that Enoch's "walking with the Elohim" was his
"being with the angels of God six jubilees of years, and they
showed him everything which is on Earth and in the
heavens:"

*He was the first among men that are born on Earth
who learnt writing and knowledge and wisdom,
and who wrote down the signs of heaven according to
the order of their months in a book . . .
And he was the first to write a testimony,
and he attested to the sons of Adam by the
generations on Earth, and recounted the weeks of
the jubilees and made known the days of the years;
And set in order the months and recounted the
Sabbaths of the years as the angels made known to him.
And also what he saw in a vision of his sleep, what
was and what will be as it will happen to the children
of men throughout their generations.*

According to this version of Enoch's Divine Encounters,
"he was taken from amongst the children of men" by the
angels, who "conducted him into the Garden of Eden in
majesty and honor." There, according to the *Book of Jubilees,*
Enoch spent his time by "writing down the condemnations
and judgments of the world," on account of which "God
brought the waters of the Flood upon all the land of Eden."

Even greater detail is provided by the Pseudepigraphic
Book of Enoch, in which the tale of Enoch is not part of the
patriarchial tale but the principal subject of a major work.
Composed in the centuries immediately preceding the Christian era, and based on ancient Mesopotamian sources as well
as the biblical ones, it embellishes the old material with an
angelology common in the author's time.

The Hebrew original of the *Book of Enoch* is lost, but had
surely existed because fragments thereof, mixed in with an
Aramaic dialect (Aramaic having become by then the language of common daily usage), have been found among the
Dead Sea scrolls. Widely quoted and translated into Greek
and Latin, it was considered as holy scripture by nearly all
the writers of the New Testament. With all that, the composition has survived mainly owing to much later translations into
Ethiopic (known as "1 Enoch") and Slavonic ("2 Enoch,"
sometimes called *The Book of the Secrets of Enoch*).

The *Book of Enoch* describes in detail not one but two
celestial journeys: the first one to learn the heavenly secrets,

return, and impart the acquired knowledge to his sons. The second journey was one way only: Enoch did not return from it, and thus the biblical statement that Enoch was gone, for the *Elohim* had taken him. In the *Book of Enoch* it is a cadre of angels that perform the divinely ordained tasks.

The Bible states that Enoch "walked with the Elohim" well before he was taken aloft; the *Book of Enoch* enlarges on that pre-ascent period. It describes Enoch as a scribe with prophetic powers. "Before these things Enoch was hidden, and no one of the Children of Adam knew where he was hidden, and where he abode . . . his days were with the Holy Ones." His Divine Encounters began with dreams and visions. "I saw in my sleep what I will now say with my tongue of flesh," he said of the start of his involvement with the Divine Ones. It was more than a dream, it was a vision:

> *And the vision was shown to me thus:*
> *In the vision, clouds invited me*
> *and a mist summoned me;*
> *the course of the stars and lightnings*
> *sped and hastened me;*
> *the winds in the vision caused me to fly*
> *and lifted me upwards,*
> *and bore me unto heaven.*

Arriving in Heaven, he reached a wall "which is built of crystals and surrounded by tongues of fire." He braved the fire and came upon a house built of crystals whose ceiling emulated the starry sky and showed the paths of the stars. In his vision he then saw a second house, larger and more magnificent than the first. Braving the fires that enflamed it, he saw inside a throne of crystal resting upon streams of fire; "its appearance was crystal and the wheels thereof as a shining sun." Seated on the throne was the Great Glory, but not even the angels could approach and behold His face because of the brilliance and magnificence of His glory. Enoch prostrated himself, hiding his face and trembling. But then "the Lord called me with His own mouth, and said, 'Come hither, Enoch, and hear my words.'" Then an angel brought him closer, and he heard the Lord tell him that because he was a scribe and righteous, he will become an interceder for men and will be taught heavenly secrets.

It was after that dream-vision that Enoch's journeys actually took place. They started one night, ninety days before his 365th birthday. As Enoch told it later to his sons,

I was alone in the house. I was in great trouble,
weeping with my eyes, and was resting, and fell
asleep in my couch.
And there appeared to me two men, exceedingly big,
such as I have never seen on Earth. Their faces
shone like the Sun, their eyes were like a burning
light, and fire was coming out of their mouths.
Their clothing, purple in appearance, was different
from each other; and their arms were like golden wings.
They stood at the head of my couch,
and called upon me by my name.

Thus awakened from his sleep, Enoch continued, "I saw clearly those two men standing in front of me." Unlike the first dream-vision, this was more than just a dreamlike vision; this time it was for real!

"I stood up beside my couch, and bowed down to them," Enoch went on, "and was seized with fear, and I covered my face from terror." Then the two emissaries spoke up, saying, "Have courage, Enoch, do not fear, for the Eternal Lord hath sent us to thee. Behold, today thou shalt go up with us to the heavens."

They instructed Enoch to prepare himself for the celestial journey by telling his sons and servants all that they should do in the house while he was gone, and that no one should seek him, "until the Lord return thee to them." Summoning his two oldest sons, Metushelah and Regim, Enoch told them, "I know not whither I go nor what will befall me." Therefore, he instructed them to be righteous and just and keep the faith of one Almighty God. He was still speaking to his sons when "the two angels took him on their wings and bore him up unto the First Heaven." It was a cloudy place, and he saw there "a very great sea, greater than the earthly sea." In that first stop Enoch was shown the secrets of meteorology, after which he was "carried up" to the Second Heaven, where he saw prisoners tormented, their sin having been "not obeying the Lord's commands." In the Third Heaven, whence the two angels then took him, he saw Paradise with the Tree of Life. The Fourth Heaven was the place of the longest stop, where Enoch was shown the secrets of the Sun and Moon, of stars and zodiacal constellations, and of the calendar. The Fifth Heaven was the "end of Heaven and Earth" and the banishment place of "the angels who have connected themselves with women." It was a "chaotic and horrible place," from which "seven stars of heaven" could be seen "bound together." It was there that the first part of the celestial journey was completed.

On the second leg of the journey Enoch encountered the various classes of angels in an ascending order: Cherubim and Seraphim and great Archangels, seven ranks of angels in all. Passing through the Sixth Heaven and the Seventh Heaven, Enoch reached the Eighth Heaven; there the stars that make up the constellations could already be seen; and as Enoch ascended yet higher, he could see from the Ninth Heaven "the heavenly homes of the twelve signs of the zodiac." Finally he reached the Tenth Heaven, where he was "brought before the Lord's face," a sight too awesome, Enoch later said, to be described.

Terrified, Enoch "fell prone and bowed down to the Lord." And then he heard the Lord say, "arise Enoch, have no fear, arise and stand before my face and gain eternity." And the Lord commanded the archangel Michael to change Enoch's earthly garments, clothe him in divine garments, and anoint him. Then the Lord told the archangel Pravuel to "bring out the books from the holy storehouse, and a reed for quickwriting, and give it to Enoch so that he would write down all that the archangel will read to him, all the commandments and teachings." For thirty days and thirty nights Pravuel was dictating and Enoch was writing down all the secrets of "the works of heaven, earth and sea, and all the elements, their passages and goings, and the thunderings of the thunder; and the Sun and Moon, the goings and changes of the stars, the seasons, years, days and hours" and "all human things, the tongue of every human song . . . and all things fitting to learn.'' The writings filled up 360 books.

Then the Lord himself, letting Enoch sit on His left beside the archangel Gabriel, told Enoch how Heaven and Earth and all upon it were created. Then the Lord told Enoch that he would be returned to Earth so that he could relate all that he had learned to his sons, and give them the handwritten books, to pass the books from generation to generation. But his stay on Earth would be for a term of thirty days only, ''and after thirty days I shall send my angel for thee; and he will take thee from Earth and from thy sons, to me.''

And so it was, at the end of the celestial stay, that the two angels returned Enoch to his home, bringing him back to his couch at night. Summoning his sons and all in his household, Enoch related to them his experiences and described to them the contents of the books: the measurements and descriptions of the stars, the length of the Sun's circle, the changes of the seasons due to the solstices and equinoxes, and other secrets regarding the calendar. Then he instructed his sons to be patient and gentle, to give alms to the poor, to be righteous and faithful, and to keep all of the Lord's commandments.

Enoch kept talking and instructing until the last moment, by which time word of his celestial visit and teachings had spread in town and a crowd of two thousand people had assembled to hear him. So the Lord sent a darkness upon the Earth, and the darkness engulfed the crowd and all who were near Enoch. In the darkness, the angels swiftly lifted Enoch and carried him off ''to the highest heaven.''

> *And all the people saw,*
> *but could not understand,*
> *how Enoch had been taken.*
> *And they went back to their homes,*
> *those who had seen such a thing,*
> *and glorified God.*
> *And Metushelah and his brethren,*
> *all the sons of Enoch, made haste*
> *and erected an altar at the place*
> *whence and where Enoch*
> *had been taken up to heaven.*

The second and final ascent of Enoch to Heaven, the scribe of the *Book of Enoch* stated at the book's conclusion, took place exactly on the day and hour he was born, at age 365.

Was this tale of Enoch's heavenly ascent(s) the equivalent of, or inspired by, the Sumerian tale of Adapa?

Certain details that are included in both tales point in that direction. Two angels, paralleling the gods Dumuzi and Gizzida in the Adapa legend, bring the Earthling "before the face of the Lord." The visitor's garments are changed from earthly ones to divine ones. He is anointed. And finally, he is given great knowledge that he writes down in "books." In both instances, the visitor writes what is being dictated to him. These details appear within a framework that without doubt establishes the Sumerian origins of the Enoch "legend."

We have already pointed out that by ascribing Enoch's Divine Encounters to "the *Elohim*," the biblical narrative divulged its Sumerian source. The Sumerian sexagesimal system reveals itself by some key numbers in the Enoch tale, such as in the sixty days of the first heavenly sojourn and the 360 "books" (tablets) dictated to Enoch. Most intriguing, however, is the assertion that the Divine Abode, site of the supreme Divine Encounter, was the *Tenth* Heaven. This goes against all the notions of seven divine heavens, with the seventh most supreme, a notion based on the assumption that the ancient peoples knew only of seven celestial bodies (Sun, Moon, Mercury, Venus, Mars, Jupiter, Saturn) that could be observed in the skies surrounding the Earth. The Sumerians, so much earlier than the Greeks or Romans, knew, however, of the complete makeup of the Solar System, a family they said of twelve members: Sun and Moon; Mercury, Venus, EARTH, Mars, Jupiter, Saturn, Uranus, Neptune, Pluto (we are using the modern names); and a *tenth* planet, Nibiru, the planet that was the abode of Anu, the "king" or "lord" of all the Anunnaki "gods."

(It is noteworthy that in Jewish medieval mysticism known as the *Kaballah*, the abode of God the Almighty is in the tenth *Sefira*, a "brilliance" or heavenly place, a Tenth Heaven. The *Sefirot* (plural) were usually depicted as concen-

Figure 18

tric circles, often superimposed on the image of *Kadmon* ("The Ancient One") (Fig. 18) the center of which is called *Yesod* ("Foundation"), the tenth *Ketter* ("Crown" of God the Most High). Beyond it stretches the *Ein Soff*—infinity, infinite space.)

These are all definite links to the Sumerian sources. But whether it was the tale of Adapa that is reflected in the Enoch record is uncertain, for one can find more similarities between Enoch and a second pre-Diluvial Sumerian individual, EN.-ME.DUR.ANNA ("Master of the Divine Tables of the Heavenly Bond"), also known as EN.ME.DUR.AN.KI ("Master of the Divine Tablets of the Bond Heaven-Earth").

Like the biblical reign-list of ten pre-Diluvian Patriarchs, so does the earlier Sumerian King List name ten pre-Diluvial rulers. In the biblical list, Enoch was the seventh. In the Sumerian list, Enmeduranki was the seventh. And, as in the case of Enoch, Enmeduranki was taken by two divine chaperons heavenward, to be taught a variety of sciences. Whereas in the case of Adapa the possibility (mentioned above) that he was a seventh (sage) is not absolute (some Mesopotamian sources list him as the first of Eridu's seven sages), the seventh position of Enmeduranki is certain; hence the scholarly opinion that it was he who was the Sumerian equivalent of the biblical Enoch. He came from Sippar, where in pre-Diluvial times the Spaceport of the Anunnaki was located, with Utu ("Shamash" in later times), a grandson of Enlil, as its commander.

The Sumerian King Lists record a "reign" of 21,600 years (six *Sars*) for Enmeduranki in Sippar—a detail of much significance. First, it reveals that at a certain point in time the Anunnaki deemed selected humans qualified to act as the EN—"Chief"—of one of the pre-Diluvial settlements (in this case, Sippar)—an aspect of the phenomenon of demigods. Secondly, in line with our suggestion for reconciling the Sumerian and biblical pre-Diluvial patriarchal life spans, it ought to be noted that 21,600 reduced by a factor of 60 results in 360. Although the Bible assigns to Enoch an earthly presence of 365 years, the Book of Enoch gives 360 as the number of books written by Enoch in which he recorded the knowledge given him. These details not only highlight the similarities between Enoch and Enmeduranki, but also support our solution for the Sumerian/biblical treatment of pre-Diluvial time spans.

The text detailing the ascent and training of Enmeduranki was pieced together from fragments of tablets, mostly from the royal library in Nineveh, then collated and published in an edited version by W.G. Lambert ("Enmeduranki and Related Material" in the *Journal of Cuneiform Studies*). The basic source is the record of pre-Diluvial events inscribed on clay tablets by a Babylonian king in support of his claim to the throne because he was a "distant scion of kingship, seed preserved from before the Flood, offspring of Enmeduranki who ruled in Sippar." Having thus asserted his impressive ancestral link to a pre-Diluvial ruler, the Babylonian king went on to tell the story of Enmeduranki:

> *Enmeduranki was a prince in Sippar,*
> *beloved of Anu, Enlil and Ea.*
> *Shamash in the Bright Temple*
> *appointed him as priest.*
> *Shamash and Adad [took him]*
> *to the assembly [of the gods].*

Shamash, as mentioned, was a grandson of Enlil and commander of the Spaceport in Sippar in pre-Diluvial times and of the one of the Sinai peninsula thereafter. Sippar, rebuilt after the Deluge but no longer a Spaceport, was nevertheless revered as the link with the celestial justice of the DIN.GIR ("The Righteous/Just Ones of the Rocketships") and was the location of Sumer's supreme court. Adad (Ishkur in Sumerian) was the youngest son of Enlil, and was granted Asia Minor as his domain. The texts described him as close to his niece Ishtar and his nephew Shamash. It was the two, Adad and Shamash, who chaperoned Enmeduranki to the place where the gods were assembled, presumably for evaluation and approval. Then,

> Shamash and Adad [clothed? purified?] him,
> Shamash and Adad set him on
> a large throne of gold.
> They showed him how to observe
> oil on water—
> a secret of Anu, Enlil and Ea.
> They gave him a Divine Tablet,
> The Kibdu, a secret of Heaven and Earth.
> They put in his hand a cedar instrument,
> a favorite of the great gods . . .
> They taught him how to make
> calculations with numbers.

Having been taught the "secrets of Heaven and Earth," specifically including medicine and mathematics, Enmeduranki was returned to Sippar with instructions to reveal to the populace his Divine Encounter and to make the knowledge available to Humankind by passing the secrets from one priestly generation to another, father to son:

> The learned savant,
> who guards the secrets of the great gods,
> will bind his favored son with an oath
> before Shamash and Adad.
> By the Divine Tablets, with a stylus,
> he will instruct him
> in the secrets of the gods.

The tablet with this text, now kept in the British Museum in London, has a postscript:

Thus was the line of priests created,
those who are allowed
to approach Shamash and Adad.

According to this rendition of the heavenly ascent of Enmeduranki, his abode was in Sippar (the post-Diluvial "cult
center" of Shamash), and it is there that he used the Divine
Tablets to teach secret knowledge to his successor priests.
This detail forges a link with the events of the Deluge, because according to Mesopotamian sources as also reported by
Berossus (a Babylonian priest who in the second century B.C.
compiled a "world history" in Greek), the tablets containing
the knowledge revealed to Mankind by the Anunnaki before
the Deluge were buried for safekeeping in Sippar.

In fact, the two tales—of the Sumerian Enmeduranki and
of the biblical Enoch—contain even stronger links than that
one to the Deluge. For, as we shall examine the story-behind-
the-story, we shall come upon a sequence of events whose
principal motivation was Divine Sex and whose culmination
was a deliberate plan to eradicate Mankind. .

BEFORE COPERNICUS AND NASA

Until the publication by Nicolaus Copernicus of his astronomical work *De revolutionibus orbium coelestium* in 1543 (and for many years thereafter), the established wisdom was that the Sun, Moon and other known planets orbit the Earth. The Catholic Church, which condemned Copernicus for that heresy, officially acknowledged its mistake only 450 years later, in 1993.

The first new celestial objects discovered after the invention of telescopes were the four large moons of Jupiter—by Galileo, in 1610.

Uranus, the planet beyond Saturn, which cannot be seen with the naked eye from Earth, was discovered with the aid of improved telescopes in 1781. Neptune was discovered beyond Uranus in 1846. And Pluto, the outermost known planet, was found only in 1930.

Yet the Sumerians, millennia ago, had already depicted (see Fig. 13 and the detail, "A", opposite) a complete Solar System, with the Sun—not Earth—in the center; a Solar System that includes Uranus, Neptune, and Pluto, and one more large planet ("Nibiru") as it passes between Jupiter and Mars.

It was only in the 1970s that NASA satellites gave us close-up views of our neighboring planets, and only in 1986 and 1989 that Voyager-2 flew by Uranus and Neptune. Yet Sumerian texts (quoted by us in *The 12th Planet*) had already described those outer planets exactly as NASA found them to be.

The first ring surrounding Saturn was not discovered until 1659 (by Christian Huygens). Yet the imprint of an Assyrian cylinder seal on a clay envelope encasing a tablet, that shows in the celestial background the Sun, the Moon (its crescent), and Venus (eight-pointed "star"), also depicts a small planet—Mars—separated from a larger one (Jupiter) (by a straw representing the Asteroid Belt?) followed by *a large ringed planet—Saturn*! ("B" opposite).

4

THE NEFILIM:
SEX AND DEMIGODS

The biblical record of human prehistory moves at a fast clip through the generations following Enoch—his son Metus-helah, who begot Lamech, who begot Noah ("Respite"), get-ting us to the main event—the Deluge. The Deluge was indeed a story of major proportions as newscasters would say nowadays, a global event, a watershed both figuratively and literally in human and divine affairs. But hidden behind the tale of the Deluge is an episode of Divine Encounters of a totally new kind—an episode without which the Deluge tale itself would lose its biblical rationale.

The biblical tale of the Deluge, the great Flood, begins in chapter 6 of Genesis with eight enigmatic verses. Their pre-sumed purpose was to explain to future generation how was it—how could it have happened?—that the very Creator of Humankind turned against it, vowing to wipe Man off the face of the Earth. The fifth verse is supposed to offer both explanation and justification: "And Yahweh saw that the wickedness of Man was great on the Earth, and that every imagination of his heart's thoughts was evil." Therefore (verse six) "Yahweh repented that He had made Man upon the Earth, and it grieved Him at His heart."

But this explanation by the Bible, pointing the accusing finger at humanity, only increases the puzzle of the chapter's first four verses, whose subject is not at all humanity but the deities themselves, and whose focus is the intermarriage between "the sons of God" and "the daughters of the Adam."

And if one wonders, What has all that got to do with the excuse for the Deluge as a punishment of Mankind, the answer can be given in one word: SEX ... Not human sex, but Divine Sex. Divine Encounters for the purpose of sexual intercourse.

The opening verses of the Deluge tale in the Bible, echoing ancient sins and calamitous purgatory, have been a preacher's delight: That was a time that set an example, the time when "there were giants upon the Earth, in those days and also after that, when the sons of God came in unto the daughters of men and they bare children to them."

The above quote follows the common English translation. But that is not what the Bible says. It speaks not of "giants" but of the *Nefilim,* literally meaning "Those who had descended," "sons of the *Elohim*" (not "sons of God") who had come down to Earth from the heavens. And the four initial incomprehensible verses, a remnant (as all scholars agree) of some longer original source, become comprehensible once it is realized that the subject of these verses is not Mankind, but the gods themselves. Properly translated, this is how the Bible describes the circumstances that preceded and led to the Deluge:

> *And it came to pass,*
> *When the Earthlings began to increase in*
> *number upon the face of the Earth,*
> *and daughters were born unto them,*
> *that the sons of the Elohim*
> *saw the daughters of the Earthlings,*
> *that they were compatible.*
> *And they took unto themselves*
> *wives of whichever they chose.*
>
> *The Nefilim were upon the Earth*
> *in those days, and thereafter too,*
> *when the sons of the Elohim*
> *cohabited with the daughters of the Adam*
> *and they bore children to them.*

The biblical term *Nefilim*, the sons of the *Elohim* who were then upon the Earth, parallels the Sumerian *Anunnaki* ("Those Who from Heaven to Earth Came"); the Bible itself (Numbers 13:33) explains that by pointing out that the Nefilim were "sons of *Anak*" (Hebrew rendering of Anunnaki). The time preceding the Deluge was thus a time when the young Anunnaki males began to have sex with young human females; and being compatible, had children by them—offspring part mortal and part "divine": demigods.

That such demigods were present on Earth is amply attested in Near Eastern texts, be it in regard to individuals (such as the Sumerian Gilgamesh) or long dynasties (such as the reported dynasty of thirty demigods in Egypt that preceded the Pharaohs); both instances, however, pertain to postDiluvial times. But in the biblical preamble to the Deluge tale we have an assertion that the "taking of wives" from among the human females by the "sons of the *Elohim*"— sons of the DIN.GIR—had already begun well before the Deluge.

The Sumerian sources that deal with pre-Diluvial times and the origins of Humankind and civilization include the tale of Adapa, and we have already touched upon the question whether having been called "offspring of Ea" simply meant that he was a human descended of The Adam whom Ea had helped create, or more literally (as many scholars hold) an actual son born to Ea by intercourse with a human female, which would make Adapa a demigod. If that would have required Ea/Enki to have sex with a female other than his official spouse, the goddess Ninki, no eyebrows should be raised: several Sumerian texts detail the sexual prowess of Enki. In one instance he was after Inanna/Ishtar, the granddaughter of his half brother Enlil. Among other escapades was his determination to attain a son by his half sister Ninmah; but when only a daughter was born, he continued the sexual relationship with the next and next and next generations of goddesses.

Was Enmeduranki, by all accounts, the seventh and not the last (tenth) ruler of a City of the Gods well before the Deluge, such a demigod? The point is not clarified by the Sumerian texts, but we suspect that he was (in which case his father was Utu/Shamash). Otherwise, why would a City of the Gods (in this case, Sippar) be put under his charge, in a succession in which all the previous six listed rulers were Anunnaki leaders? And how could he reign in Sippar 21,600 years were he not a genetic beneficiary of the relative "Immortality" of the Anunnaki?

Although the Bible itself does not say when the intermarriage began, except to state that it "came to pass when the Earthlings began to increase in number" and to spread upon the Earth, the Pseudepigraphic books reveal that the sexual involvement of young gods with human females became a major issue in the time of Enoch—well before the Deluge (since Enoch was the seventh Patriarch of the ten pre-Diluvial ones). According to the *Book of Jubilees* one of the matters regarding which Enoch had "testified" concerned "angels of the Lord who had descended to Earth and who had sinned with the daughters of men, those who had begun to unite themselves, and thus be defiled, with the daughters of men." According to this source, this was a major sin committed by the "angels of the Lord," a "fornication" "wherein, against the law of their ordinance, they went whoring after the daughters of men, and took themselves wives of all which they chose, thus causing the beginning of uncleanliness."

The *Book of Enoch* throws more light on what had happened:

> And it came to pass when the children of men
> had multiplied, that in those days were born
> unto them beautiful and comely daughters.
> And the angels, the Children of Heaven,
> saw and lusted after them,
> and said to one another:
> "Come, let us choose wives from among the
> children of men, and beget us children."

According to this source, this was not a development resulting from individual acts, from a young Anunnaki here and another one there getting overcome by lust. There is a hint that the sexual urge was augmented by a desire to have offspring; and that the choosing of human wives was a deliberate decision by a group of Anunnaki acting in concert. Indeed, as we peruse the text further, we read that after the idea had germinated,

> *Semjaza, who was their leader, said unto them:*
> *"I fear ye will not agree to do this deed, and I*
> *alone shall have to pay the penalty for a great sin."*
> *And they all answered and said:*
> *"Let us all swear an oath, and all*
> *bind ourselves by mutual imprecations, not to*
> *abandon this plan but to do this thing."*

So they all gathered together and bound themselves by an oath "to do this thing" although it was a violation of "the law of their ordinance." The scheming angels, we learn as we read on, descended upon Mount Hermon ("Mount of Oath"), at the southern edge of the mountains of Lebanon. "Their number was two hundred, those who in the days of Jared came down upon the summit of Mount Hermon." The two hundred divided themselves into subgroups of ten; the *Book of Enoch* provides the names of the group leaders, "the chiefs of Ten." The whole affair was thus a well-organized effort by sex-deprived and childless "sons of the *Elohim*" to remedy the situation.

It is obvious that in the Pseudepigraphic books the sexual involvement of divine beings with the human females was no more than lust, fornication, defilement—a sin of the "fallen angels." The prevalent notion is that that is the viewpoint of the Bible itself; but in fact this is not so. The ones to be blamed and, therefore, to be wiped out are the Children of Adam, not the sons of the *Elohim*. The latter are, in fact, fondly remembered: verse 4 recalls them as "the mighty ones of *Olam,* the people of the *Shem*"—the people of the rocketships.

An insight into the motivation, calculations, and sentiments that brought about the intermarriage and how it was to be judged, might be gleaned from a somewhat similar occurrence related in the Bible (Judges chapter 21). On account of the sexual abuse of a traveler's woman by men from the tribe of Benjamin, the other Israelite tribes made war on the Benjaminites. Decimated and with few childbearing females remaining, the tribe faced extinction. The option of marrying females from other tribes was also blocked, for all the other tribes took an oath not to give their daughters to the Benjaminites. So the Benjaminite men, on the occasion of a national festival, hid themselves along a road leading to the town of Shiloh; and when the daughters of Shiloh came out dancing down the road, they "caught every man his wife" and carried them off to the Benjaminite domain. Surprisingly, they were not punished for these abductions; for in truth, the whole incident was a scheme concocted by the elders of Israel, a way to help the tribe of Benjamin survive in spite of the boycott oath.

Was such a "do what you have to do while I look away" ploy behind the oath-taking ceremony atop Mount Hermon? Was it at least one principal leader, an elder of the Anunnaki (Enki?) who looked away, while another (perhaps Enlil?) was so upset?

A little-known Sumerian text may have a bearing on the question. Regarded as a "mythical tablet" by E. Chiera (in *Sumerian Religious Texts*), it tells the story of a young god named Martu who complained about his spouseless life; and we learn from it that intermarriage with human females was both common and not a sin—providing it was done by permission and not without the young woman's consent:

> In my city I have friends,
> they have taken wives.
> I have companions,
> they have taken wives.
> In my city, unlike my friends,
> I have not taken a wife;
> I have no wife, I have no children.

The city about which Martu was speaking was called Ninab, a "city in the settled great land." The time, the Sumerian text explains, was in the distant past when "the city of Ninab existed, Shed-tab did not exist; the holy tiara existed, the holy crown did not exist." In other words, priesthood existed,

Figure 19

but not Kingship as yet. But it was a time when "cohabitation there was . . . bringing forth of children there was."

The city's High Priest, the text informs us, was an accomplished musician; he had a wife and a daughter. As the people gathered for a festival, offering the gods the roasted meat of the sacrifices, Martu saw the priest's daughter and desired her.

Evidently, taking her as a wife required special permission, for it was an act—to use the words of the *Book of Jubilees*—"against the law of their ordinances." The above-quoted complaint by Martu was addressed to his mother, an unnamed goddess. She wanted to know whether the maiden whom he desired "appreciated his gaze." When it was so determined, the gods gave Martu the needed permission. The rest of the text describes how the other young gods prepared a marriage feast, and how the residents of Nin-ab were summoned by the beat of a copper drum to witness the ceremony.

If we read the available texts as versions of the same prehistoric record, we can envision the predicament of the young Anunnaki males and the unwelcome solution. There were six hundred Anunnaki who had come to Earth and another three hundred who operated the shuttlecraft, spacecraft, and other facilities such as a space station. Females were few among them. There was Ninmah, the daughter of Anu and a half sister of both Enki and Enlil (all three from different mothers) who was the Chief Medical Officer, and with her there came a group of female Anunnaki nurses (a depiction on a Sumerian cylinder seal portrays the group—Fig. 19). One of them eventually became Enlil's official consort (and was given the title-name NIN.LIL, "Lady of the Command"), but only after

the incident of the date-rape for which Enlil was banished—
an incident that also highlights the shortage of females among
the first Anunnaki groups.

An insight into the sexual habits on Nibiru itself can be
gleaned from the records, in various God Lists that the Sumerians and subsequent nations had kept, concerning Anu himself. He had fourteen sons and daughters from his official
spouse Antu; but in addition he had six concubines, whose
(presumably numerous) offspring by Anu were not listed.
Enlil, on Nibiru, fathered a son by his half sister Ninmah
(also known as Ninti in the Creation of Man tales and as
Ninharsag later on); his name was Ninurta. But, though a
grandson of Anu, his spouse Bau (also given the epithet
GULA, "The Great One") was one of the daughers of Anu,
which amonts to Ninurta marrying one of his aunts. On Earth
Enlil, once having espoused Ninlil, was strictly monogamous.
They had a total of six children, four daughters and two sons;
the youngest, Ishkur in Sumerian and Adad in Akkadian, was
also called in some God Lists Martu—indicating that Shala,
his official consort, might well have been an Earthling, the
daughter of the High Priest, as the tale of Martu's marriage
reported.

Enki's spouse was called NIN.KI ("Lady of Earth") and
was also known as DAM.KI.NA ("Spouse who to Earth
came"). Back on Nibiru she bore him a son, Marduk; mother
and son joined Enki on Earth on subsequent trips. But while
he was on Earth without her, Enki did not deprive himself
. . . A text called by scholars "Enki and Ninharsag: A Paradise Myth" describes how Enki stalked his half sister and,
seeking a son by her, "poured the semen into her womb."
But she bore him only daughters, whom Enki also found
worthy of conjugation. Finally Ninharsag put a curse on Enki
that paralyzed him, and forced him to concur in a quick
assignment of husbands to the young female goddesses. This
did not stop Enki, on another occasion, from forcefully "carrying off as a prize" a granddaughter of Enlil, Ereshkigal,
by boat to his domain in southern Africa.

All these instances serve to illustrate the dire shortage of
females among the Anunnaki who had come to Earth. After
the Deluge, as the Sumerian God Lists attest, with second

and third generations of Anunnaki around, a better male-female balance was attained. But the shortage of females was obviously acute in the long pre-Diluvian times.

There was absolutely no intention on the part of the Anunnaki leadership, when the decision to create Primitive Workers was taken, to also create sexmates for the Anunnaki males. But, in the words of the Bible, "when the Earthlings began to increase in number upon the face of the Earth, and daughters were born unto them," the young Anunnaki discovered that the series of genetic manipulations have made these females compatible, and that cohabiting with them would result in children.

The planetary intermarriage required strict permission. With the behavioral code of the Anunnaki viewing rape as a serious offense (even Enlil, the supreme commander, was sentenced to exile when he date-raped the young nurse; he was forgiven after he married her), the new form of Divine Encounters was strictly regulated and required permission which, we learn from the Sumerian text, was given only if the human female "appreciated the gaze" of the young god.

So two hundred of the young ones took matters into their own hands, swore an oath to do it all together and face the results as a group, and swooped down among the Daughters of Men to pick out wives. The outcome—totally unanticipated when The Adam was created—was a new breed of people: Demigods.

Enki, who himself may have fathered demigods, viewed the development more leniently than Enlil; so, evidently, did Enki's cocreator of The Adam, Ninmah, for it was in her city, the medical center called Shuruppak, that the Sumerian hero of the Deluge resided. The fact that he was listed in the Sumerian King Lists as the tenth pre-Diluvial ruler indicates that it was to demigods that key roles as intermediaries between the gods and the people were assigned: kings and priests. The practice resumed after the Deluge; kings especially boasted that they were "seed" of this or that god (and some made the claim even if they were not, just to legitimize their assumption of the throne).

The new kind of Divine Encounters, resulting in a new (though limited) breed of humans, created problems not only for the leadership of the Anunnaki, but also for Mankind. The Bible recognizes the sexual intercourse between Anunnaki and humans as the most significant aspect of the events preceding and leading to the Deluge, doing so by the enigmatic prefacing of the tale of the flood with the verses that record the intermarriage phenomenon. The development is presented as a problem for Yahweh, a cause for grief and being sorry for creating the Earthlings. But as the more detailed pseudepigraphical sources relate, the new kind of Divine Encounters created problems also for the sex partners and their families.

The first reported instance concerns the very hero of the Deluge and his family—Noah and his parents. The report also raises the question whether the hero of the Deluge (called Ziusudra in the Sumerian texts and Utnapishtim in the Akkadian version) was in fact a demigod.

Scholars have long believed that among the sources for the *Book of Enoch* there was a lost text that had been called the *Book of Noah*. Its existence was guessed from various early writings; but what had only been surmised became a certain and verified fact when fragments of such a *Book of Noah* were found among the Dead Sea scrolls in caves in the Qumran area, not far from Jericho.

According to the relevant sections of the book, when Bath-Enosh, the wife of Lamech, gave birth to Noah, the baby boy was so unusual that he aroused tormenting suspicions in the mind of Lamech:

His body was white as snow and red as the blooming
of a rose, and the hair of his head and his locks
were white as wool, and his eyes were fair.
And when he opened his eyes, he lighted up the whole
house like the sun, and the whole house was very bright.
And thereupon he arose in the hands of the midwife,
opened his mouth, and conversed with the Lord of
Righteousness.

Shocked, Lamech ran to his father Metushelah and said:

I have begotten a strange son, diverse from and
unlike Man, and resembling the sons of the God

*of Heaven; and his nature is different, and he
is not like us . . .
And it seems to me that he is not sprung from me
but from the angels.*

In other words, Lamech suspected that his wife's preg-
nancy was induced not by him but by one of the "sons of
the God of Heaven," one of the "Watchers"!

The distraught Lamech came to his father Metushelah not
only to share the problem with him but also to request specific assistance. We learn at this point that Enoch, who was
taken by the *Elohim* to be with them, was still alive and well,
residing in a "dwelling place among the angels"—not in the
distant heavens, but "at the ends of the Earth." So Lamech
asked his father to reach there his father Enoch, and ask him
to investigate whether any of the Watchers had mated with
Lamech's wife. Reaching the place but prohibited from entering it, Metushelah called out for Enoch, and after a while
Enoch, hearing the call, responded. Thereupon Metushelah
related the unusual birth to Enoch, and Lamech's doubts
about the true identity of Noah's father. Confirming that intermarriage resulting in demigod children had indeed begun in
the time of Jared, Enoch nevertheless assured his son that
Noah is a son of Lamech and that his unusual countenance
and brilliant mind are omens that "there shall come a Deluge
and great destruction for one year," but Noah and his family
are destined to be saved. All that, Enoch said, he knows
because "the Lord has showed me and informed me, and I
have read it in the heavenly tablets."

According to the Hebrew-Aramaic fragment of the *Book
of Noah* that was discovered among the Dead Sea scrolls, the
first reaction by Lamech on seeing his highly unusual son
was to question his wife Bath-Enosh ("Daughter/offspring of
Enosh"). As translated by T.H. Gaster (*The Dead Sea Scriptures*) and H. Dupont-Sommer (*The Essene Writings from
Qumran*) column II of the scroll fragment begins with Lamech confessing that, as soon as he saw the baby Noah,

*I thought in my heart that the conception was
from one of the* Watchers, *one of the Holy Ones . . .*

*And my heart was changed within me because of the
child.*
*Then I, Lamech, hastened and went to Bath-Enosh,
my wife, and I said to her: I want you to take an oath
by the Most High, the Lord Supreme, the King of all
the worlds, the ruler of the Sons of Heaven,
that you will tell me the truth whether . . .*

But if one examines the original Hebrew-Aramaic text of
the scroll, one finds that where the modern translators use
the term *Watchers*—as translators have done—the original
text (Fig. 20) actually says *Nefilim* (author's italics).

(The mistranslation of the word as "Watchers" before the
Hebrew-Aramaic text was discovered resulted from reliance
on the Greek versions, which were the product of Greek-
Egyptian translators in Alexandria who took the term to mean
the same as the Egyptian one for "god," *NeTeR,* literally
meaning "Guardian." The term is not without a link to ancient Sumer, or more correctly Shumer, which meant Land
of the Guardians).

Lamech, then, suspected that the child was not his. Asking
his wife to tell him the truth under oath, she responded by
imploring that he "remember my delicate feelings" although
"the occasion is indeed alarming." Hearing this ambiguous,
even evasive answer, Lamech grew even more "excited and
perturbed at heart." Again he implored his wife for the truth
"and not with lies." So, she said, "ignoring my delicate
feelings, I swear to you by the Holy and Great One, the Lord
of Heaven and Earth, that this seed came from you, this
conception was by you, and this fruit was planted by you

Column II

¹ הא באדין חשבת בלבי די מן עירין הריאנתא ומן קדישין הריוזא ולנפילין

² ולבי עלי משתני על עולימא דנא
³ באדין אנה למך אתבהלת ועלת על בתאנוש אנותתי ואמרת

⁴]אנא ועד בעליא במרה רבותא במלך כול עולמים

Figure 20

and not by some stranger or by any of the Watchers, the heavenly beings.''

As we know from the rest of the story, Lamech remained doubting in spite of these reassurances. Perhaps he wondered what Bath-Enosh was talking about when she said that ''her delicate feelings'' should be taken into consideration. Was she covering up the truth after all? As we have already described, Lamech then rushed to his father Metushelah and sought through him Enoch's help in getting to the bottom of the puzzle.

The pseudepigraphical sources conclude the tale with the reassurances about Noah's parentage and the explanation that his unusual features and intelligence were just signs of his forthcoming role as the savior of the human seed. As for us, we must remain wondering, since according to the Sumerian sources of the tale the hero of the Deluge was, in all probability, a demigod.

The sex-oriented Divine Encounters began, according to the sources quoted above, at the time of Jared, the father of Enoch. Indeed, his very name is explained in those sources as stemming from the root *Yrd* which in Hebrew means ''to descend,'' recalling the descent of the plotting sons of the gods upon Mount Hermon. Using the chronological formula that we had earlier adopted, we could calculate when it had happened.

According to the biblical record, Jared was born 1,196 years before the Deluge; his son Enoch 1,034 years before the Deluge; then Metushelah 969 years before the Deluge, Lamech his son 782 years before the Deluge; and finally Noah, the son of Lamech, 600 years before the Great Flood. Multiplying these numbers by 60 and adding 13,000 years, we arrive at the following timetable:

Jared born	84,760 years ago
Enoch born	75,040 years ago
Metushelah born	71,140 years ago
Lamech born	59,920 years ago
Noah born	49,000 years ago

Bearing in mind that these pre-Diluvial patriarchs lived on for many years after giving birth to their successors, these are "fantastic ages" (as scholars say) when expressed in Earth-years—but just a few Nibiru-years when measured in Sars. Indeed, one of the tablets with the Sumerian King Lists data (known as W-B 62, now kept in the Ashmolean Museum in Oxford, England), accords to the hero of the Deluge ("Ziusudra" in Sumerian) a reign of ten Sars or 36,000 Earth-years until the Deluge's occurrence; this is exactly the 600 years the Bible assigns to Noah's age by the time of the Deluge, multiplied by sixty (600 x 60 = 36,000)—corroborating not only the symmetry between the two, but also our suggestion for correlating the biblical and Sumerian pre-Diluvial patriarchal/ruler ages.

Developing a plausible chronology from these combined sources, we thus learn that the new form of Divine Encounter began some 80,000 years ago, in the time of Jared. They continued in the time of Enoch, and caused a family crisis when Noah was born, some 49,000 years ago.

What was the truth about Noah's parentage? Was he a demigod as Lamech had suspected, or his own seed as the offended Bath-Enosh had reassured him? The Bible says of Noah (to follow the common translation) that he was "a just man, perfect in his generations; and Noah walked with God." A more literal translation would be "a righteous man, of perfect genealogy, who walked with the *Elohim*." The last qualification is identical to that employed by the Bible to describe Enoch's divine contacts; and one must wonder whether there is more than meets the eye in the innocuous biblical statement.

Be it as it may, it is certain that the by breaking their own taboos the young Anunnaki/Nefilim launched a chain of events which was full of ironies. They took the daughters of Man as wives because they were genetically compatible; but it was as a consequence of having been so reengineered and perfected, that Mankind was doomed to be terminated . . . It was not the human females who lusted after the young Anunnaki, but the other way around; ironically, it was Mankind that had to bear the brunt of punishment, for "Yahweh had repented that He had made The Adam upon the Earth," and resolved "to wipe The Adam, whom I had created, off the face of the Earth."

But what was supposed to have been the Last Encounter, the Sumerian sources reveal, was undone by a brotherly dispute. In the Bible, the god vowing to wipe Mankind off the face of the Earth is the very same one who then connives with Noah to nullify the decision. In the Mesopotamian original version, the events again unfold against the background of the Enlil-Enki rivalry. The divine "Cain" and "Abel" continued to be at loggerheads—except that the intended victim was not one of them but the Being they had created.

But if a new kind of Divine Encounter—the sexual one—had led to the near-demise of Mankind, it was yet another kind of Divine Encounter—a whispered one—that led to its salvation.

5

THE DELUGE

The story of the Deluge, the Great Flood, is part of human lore and communal memory virtually in all parts of the world. Its main elements are the same everywhere, no matter the version or the epithet-names by which the tale's principals are called: Angry gods decide to wipe Mankind off the face of the Earth by means of a global flood, but one couple is spared and saves the human line.

Except for an account of the Deluge written in Greek by the Chaldean priest Berossus in the third century B.C., known to scholars from fragmentary mentions in the writings of Greek historians, the only record of that momentous event was in the Hebrew Bible. But in 1872 the British Society of Biblical Archaeology was told in a lecture by George Smith that among the tablets of the *Epic of Gilgamesh* discovered by Henry Layard in the royal library of Nineveh, the ancient Assyrian capital, some (Fig. 21) contained a Deluge tale similar to that in the Bible. By 1910 parts of other recensions (as scholars call versions in other ancient Near Eastern languages) have been found. They helped reconstruct another major Mesopotamian text, the *Epic of Atra-hasis,* that told the story of Mankind from its creation until its near-annihilation by the Deluge. Linguistic and other clues in these texts indicated an earlier Sumerian source, and parts of that were found and began to be published after 1914. Although the full Sumerian text is yet to be discovered, the existence of such a prototype on which all the others, including the biblical version, are based, is now beyond doubt.

The Bible introduces Noah, the hero of the Deluge tale

who was singled out to be saved with his family, as "a righteous man, of perfect genealogy; with the *Elohim* did Noah walk." The Mesopotamian texts paint a more comprehensive picture of the man, suggesting that he was the offspring of a demigod and possibly (as Lamech had suspected) a demigod himself. It fills out the details of what "walking with the *Elohim*" had really entailed. Among the many details that the Mesopotamian texts provide, the role played by dreams as an important form of Divine Encounter becomes evident. There is also a precedent for a deity's refusal to show his face to a beseeching mortal—God is heard but is not seen. And there is a vivid, first person report of a Divine Encounter unique in all the annals of the ancient Near East— the blessing of humans by the deity by the physical touching of the forehead.

In the biblical version it is the same deity who resolves to wipe Mankind off the face of the Earth and, contradictorily, acts to prevent the demise of Mankind by devising a way to save the hero of the tale and his family. In the Sumerian original text and its subsequent Mesopotamian recensions, more than one deity is involved; and as in other instances, Enlil and Enki emerge as the chief protagonists: the stricter Enlil, upset by the intermarriages with the daughters of Man, calling for putting an end to Mankind; but the lenient Enki,

Figure 21

deeming Mankind as his "Created Ones," schemes to save it through a chosen family.

The Deluge, furthermore, was not a universal calamity brought about by an angry god, but a natural calamity seized by an upset Enlil to attain the desired goal. It was preceded by a long period of a worsening climate, increasing cold, reduced precipitation, and failing crops—conditions that we have identified in *The 12th Planet* as the last Ice Age that began circa 75,000 years ago and ended abruptly some 13,000 years ago. We have suggested that the accumulating mass of ice atop Antarctica, causing by its sheer weight some of the bottom layers to melt, was nearing a point where the whole mass could slip off the continent; this would have caused an immense tidal wave that, surging from the south, could engulf the land masses to the north. With their IGI.GI ("Those Who Observe and See") orbiting the Earth and with a scientific station at the tip of Africa, the Anunnaki were well aware of the danger. And as the next orbital proximity of Nibiru to Earth was due, they well realized that the heightened gravitational pull on this passage could well trigger the calamity.

Throughout the mounting human suffering as the Ice Age became more severe, Enlil forbade the other gods from helping Mankind; it is evident from the details in the *Epic of Atra-hasis* that his intention was to have Mankind perish by starvation. But Mankind somehow survived, for in the absence of rains crops still grew by dint of a morning mist and a nighttime dew. In time, however, "the fertile fields became white, vegetation did not sprout." "People walked hunched in the streets, their faces looked green." The starvation led to fraternal strife, even cannibalism. But Enki, defying Enlil's command, found ways of helping Mankind sustain itself, mainly by ingenious catches of fishes. He was especially helpful to his faithful follower Atra-hasis ("He who is most wise"), a demigod charged with acting as the go-between to the Anunnaki and their human servants in the settlement of Shuruppak—a city under the patronage of Ninmah/Ninharsag.

As the various texts reveal, Atra-hasis, seeking Enki's guidance and assistance, moved his bed into the temple so as to receive the divine instructions by means of dreams. Keeping constant vigil in the temple, "every day he wept;

bringing oblations in the morning'' and at night ''giving attention to dreams.''

In spite of all the suffering, Mankind was still around. The people's outcry—''bellowing'' in Enlil's words—only increased his annoyance. Previously he explained the need to annihilate Mankind because ''its conjugations deprive me of sleep.'' Now, he said, ''the noise of Mankind has become too annoying; their uproar deprives me of sleep.'' And so he made the other leaders swear that what is about to happen— the avalanche of water—would be kept a secret from the Earthlings, so that they would perish:

> *Enlil opened his mouth to speak*
> *and addressed the assembly of all the gods:*
> *''Come, all of us, and take an oath*
> *regarding the killing Flood!''*

That the Anunnaki themselves were preparing to abandon Earth in their shuttlecraft was another part of the secret that the gods swore to keep from Mankind. But as all the others took the oath, Enki resisted. ''Why will you bind me with an oath?'' he asked, ''Am I to raise my hand against my own humans?'' A bitter argument ensued, but in the end Enki too was made to swear not to reveal ''the secret.''

It was after that fatal oath-taking ceremony that Atra-hasis, staying day and night at the temple, received the following message in a dream:

> *The gods commanded total destruction.*
> *Enlil imposed an evil deed on the humans.*

It was a message, an oracle, that Atra-hasis could not understand. ''Atra-hasis opened his mouth and addressed his god: 'Teach me the meaning of the dream, so that I may understand its meaning.' ''

But how could Enki be more explicit without breaking his oath? As Enki contemplated the problem, the answer came to him. He did swear not to reveal ''the secret'' *to Mankind;* but could he not tell the secret *to a wall?* And so, one day, Atra-hasis heard his god's voice without seeing him. This was no communication by means of a dream, at night. It was daytime; and yet, the encounter was totally different.

The experience was traumatic. We read in the Assyrian recension that the baffled Atra-hasis "bowed down and prostrated himself, then stood up, opened his mouth, and said,"

> Enki, lord-god—
> I heard your entry,
> I noticed steps like your footsteps!

For seven years, Atra-hasis said, "I have seen your face." Now, all of a sudden, he could not see his lord-god. Appealing to the unseen god, "Atra-hasis made his voice heard and spoke to his lord," asking for the meaning, the portent of his dream, that he may know what to do.

Thereupon Enki "opened his mouth to speak, and addressed the reed wall." Still not seeing his god, Atra-hasis heard the deity's voice coming from behind the reed wall in the temple; his lord-god was giving instructions to the wall:

> Wall, listen to me!
> Reed wall, observe my words!
> Discard your house, build a boat!
> Spurn property, save life!

Instructions for the construction of the boat then followed. It had to be roofed over so that the Sun should not be seen from inside it, pitched all over with tar "above and below." Then Enki "opened the water clock and filled it; He announced to him the coming of a killing flood on the seventh night." A depiction on a Sumerian cylinder seal appears to have illustrated the scene, showing the reed wall (in the shape of a water clock?) held by a priest, Enki as a serpent-god, and the hero of the Deluge getting instructions (Fig. 22).

The construction of the boat, obviously, could not have been hidden from the other people; so how could it be done without alerting them, too, to the coming catastrophe? For that, Atra-hasis was instructed (from behind the reed wall) to explain to the others that he was building the boat in order to leave the city. He was to tell them that, as a worshiper of Enki, he could no longer stay in a place controlled by Enlil:

> *My god does not agree with your god.*
> *Enki and Enlil are angry with one another.*
> *Since I reverence Enki,*
> *I cannot remain in the land of Enlil.*
> *I have been expelled from my house.*

The conflict between Enki and Enlil, that earlier had to be surmised from their actions, has thus broken into the open—sufficiently to serve as a believable reason for the banishment of Atra-hasis. The city where the events were taking place was Shuruppak, a settlement under the lordship of Ninmah/Ninharsag. There, for the first time, a demigod was elevated to the status of ''king.'' According to the Sumerian text, his name was Ubar-Tutu; his son and successor was the hero of the Deluge. (The Sumerians called him Ziusudra; in the *Epic of Gilgamesh* he was called Utnapishtim; in Old Babylonian his epithet-name was Atra-hasis; and the Bible called him Noah). As one of the settlements of the Anunnaki in the Edin, it was in the domain of Enlil; to Enki the Abzu, in southern Africa, was allotted. It was that land of Enki beyond the seas, Atra-hasis was to say, that he expected to reach with his boat.

Eager to get rid of the banished man, the elders of the city made the whole town help build the boat. ''The carpenter

Figure 22

brought his axe, the workers brought the tar stones, the young
ones carried the pitch, the binders provided the rest.'' When
the boat was finished, according to the Atra-hasis text, the
townspeople helped him load it with food and water (kept in
watertight compartments), as well as ''with clean animals . . .
fat animals . . . wild creatures . . . cattle . . . winged birds of
the sky.'' The list is akin to the one in Genesis, according
to which the Lord's instructions to Noah were to bring into
the ark two of each species, male and female, ''of every
living thing of flesh . . . of the fowls after their kind and of
the cattle after their kind.''

The embarkation of pairs of animals has been a favorite
subject of countless artists, be it master painters or illustrators
of children's books. It has also been one of the eyebrow
raisers of the tale, deemed a virtual impossibility and thus
more of an allegorical way to explain how animal life continued even after the Deluge. Indirectly, such doubt regarding
an important detail is bound to cast incredulity on the factu-
ality of the whole Deluge story.

It is therefore noteworthy that the Deluge recension in the
Epic of Gilgamesh offers a totally different detail regarding
the preservation of animal life: It was not the living animals
that were taken aboard—it was their *seed* that was preserved!

The text (tablet XI, lines 21–28) quotes Enki speaking thus
to the wall:

> *Reed hut, reed hut! Wall, wall!*
> *Reed hut, hearken! Wall, reflect!*
> *Man of Shuruppak, son of Ubar-Tutu:*
> *Abandon your house, build a ship!*
> *Give up possessions, seek thou life!*
> *Forswear goods, the life keep!*
> *Aboard the ship take thou*
> *the seed of all living things.*

We learn from line 83 in the tablet that Utnapishtim (as
''Noah'' was called in this Old Babylonian recension) had
indeed brought on board ''whatever I had of the *seed of
living beings.*'' Clearly, this is a reference not to plant seeds,
but to that of animals.

The term for "seed" in the Old Babylonian and Assyrian recensions is the Akkadian word *zeru* (*Zera* in Hebrew) which stands for that from which living things sprout and grow. That these recensions stem from Sumerian originals has been clearly established; indeed, in some of the Akkadian versions the technical term for "seed" has been retained by its original Sumerian NUMUN, which was used to signify that by which a man had offspring.

Taking on board "the seed of living beings" rather than the animals themselves not only reduced the space requirements to manageable proportions. It also implies the application of sophisticated biotechnology to preserve varied species—a technique being developed nowadays by learning the genetic secrets of DNA. This was feasible since Enki was involved; for he was the master of genetic engineering, symbolized in this capacity by the Entwined Serpents that emulated the double-helixed DNA (see Fig. 5).

The assigning by the Sumerian/Mesopotamian texts of the role of Mankind's savior to Enki makes much sense. He was the creator of The Adam and of *Homo sapiens,* and thus he understandably called the doomed Earthlings "my humans." As chief scientist of the Anunnaki he could select, obtain, and provide "the seed of all living things" for preservation, and possessed the knowledge of resurrecting those animals from their "seed" DNA. He was also best suited for the role of the designer of Noah's ark—a vessel of a special design that could survive the avalanche of water. All the versions agree that it was built according to exact specifications provided by the deity.

Built so that two-thirds of its great size would be below the waterline, it was given considerable stability. Its wooden structure was made waterproof with bitumen tar both inside and outside, so that when the tidal wave engulfed it even the upper decks would hold off the waters. The flat top had only one small jutting cubicle, whose hatch was also closed and sealed with bitumen when the time came to face the Deluge. Of the many suggestions for the shape of Noah's Ark, the one by Paul Haupt ("The Ship of the Babylonian Noah" in

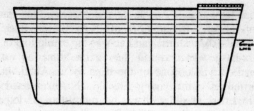

Figure 23

Beiträge zur Assyriologie—Fig. 23) appears to us the most plausible. It also bears a striking resemblance to a modern submarine, with a conning tower whose hatch is closed tight when diving.

No wonder, perhaps, that this specially designed vessel was described in the Babylonian and Assyrian recensions as a *tzulili*—a term which even nowadays (in modern Hebrew, *Tzolelet*) denotes a submersible boat, a *submarine*. The Sumerian term for Ziusudra's boat was MA.GUR.GUR, meaning "a boat that can turn and tumble."

According to the biblical version it was built of gopher wood and reeds, with only one hatch, and was covered with tar-pitch "within and without." The Hebrew term in Genesis for the complete boat was *Teba,* which denotes something closed on all sides, a "box" rather than the commonly translated "ark." Stemming from the Akkadian *Tebitu,* it is considered by some scholars to signify a "goods vessel," a cargo ship. But the term, with a hard "T," means "to sink." The boat was thus a "sinkable" boat, hermetically sealed, so that even if submerged under the tidal wave of the Deluge, it could survive the watery ordeal and resurface.

That it was Enki who had designed the boat also makes sense. It will be recalled that his epithet-name before he was given the title EN.KI ("Lord of Earth") was E.A—"He Whose Home/Abode is Water." Indeed, as texts dealing with the earliest times state, Ea liked to sail the Edin's waters, alone or with mariners whose sea songs he liked. Sumerian depictions (Fig. 24a,b) showed him with streams of water— the prototype of Aquarius (which, as a constellation, was the zodiacal House honoring him). In setting up the gold-mining operations in southeast Africa, he also organized the transportation of the ores to the Edin in cargo vessels; they were nicknamed "Abzu ships" and it was in emulation of them that Atra-hasis was to build the Tzulili. And, as we have mentioned, it was on one of the trips by an Abzu-boat that Ea "carried off" the young Ereshkigal. A seasoned sailor and an expert shipbuilder, it was he, more than any other one of the Anunnaki, who could devise and design the ingenious boat that could withstand the Deluge.

Noah's Ark and its construction are key components of the Deluge tale, for without such a boat Mankind would have perished as Enlil had wished. The tale of the boat has a bearing on another aspect of the pre-Diluvial era; for it restates familiarity with and use of boats in those early times—aspects already mentioned in the Adapa tale. All this corroborates the existence of pre-Diluvial shipping, and thus the incredible Cro-Magnon depictions of boats in their Cave Art—see Fig. 15.

When the construction of the boat was completed and its outfitting and loading done as Enki had directed, Atra-hasis

Figures 24a and 24b

brought his family into the boat. According to Berossus, those coming on board included also some close friends of Ziusudra/Noah. In the Akkadian version, Utnapishtim "made all the craftsmen go on board" to be saved by the boat they helped build. In another detail from the Mesopotamian texts we also learn that the group also included an expert navigator, Puzur-Amurri by name, whom Enki provided and who was instructed where to veer the boat once the tidal wave subsided.

Even though the loading and boarding were completed, Atra-hasis/Utnapishtim himself could not sit still inside and he was entering and leaving the boat constantly, nervously waiting for the signal that Enki had told him to watch for:

> *When Shamash,*
> *ordering a trembling at dusk,*
> *will shower a rain of eruptions—*
> *board thou the ship,*
> *batten up the entrance!*

The signal was to be the launching of spacecraft at Sippar, the site of the Spaceport of the Anunnaki some one hundred miles north of Shuruppak. For it was the plan of the Anunnaki to gather in Sippar and from there ascend into Earth orbit. Atra-hasis/Utnapishtim was told to watch the skies for such a "shower of eruptions," the thunder and flames of the launched spacecraft that made the ground tremble. "Shamash"—then the "Eagleman" in charge of the Spaceport—"had set a stated time," Enki told his faithful Earthling. And when the signs to watch for had appeared, Utnapishtim "boarded the ship, battened up the hatch, and handed over the structure together with its contents to Puzur-Amurri the boatman." The boatman's instructions were to navigate the ship to Mount Nitzir ("Mount of Salvation")—the twin-peaked Mount Ararat.

A few important facts emerge from these details. They indicate that the master of the Salvation Plan was aware not only of the very existence of the Mount so far away from southern Mesopotamia, but also that these twin peaks would be the first to emerge from the tidal wave, being the highest

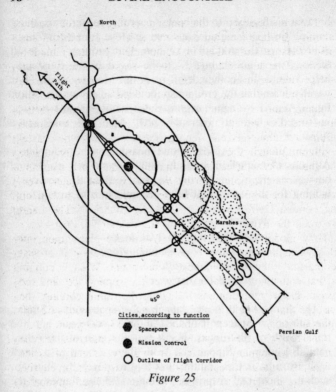

Figure 25

peaks in the whole of western Asia (17,000 and 12,900 feet high). This would have been a well-known fact to any one of the Anunnaki leaders, for when they established their pre-Diluvial Spaceport in Sippar, they anchored the Landing corridor on the twin peaks of Ararat (Fig. 25).

The master of the Salvation Plan, furthermore, was also aware of the general direction in which the avalanche of water will carry the boat; for unless the tidal wave were to come from the south and carry the boat northward, no navigator could redirect the boat (with no oars and no sails) to the desired destination.

These elements of the Geography of the Deluge (to coin an expression) have a bearing on the cause of and nature of the Deluge. Contrary to the popular notion that the watery calamity resulted from an excessive rainfall, the biblical and earlier Mesopotamian texts make clear that—though rains followed as the temperatures dropped—the catastrophe began with a rush of *wind from the south* followed by a *watery wave from the south*. The source of the waters were the "fountains of the Great Deep"—a term that referred to the great and deep oceanic waters beyond Africa. The avalanche of water "submerged the dams of the dry land"—the coastal continental barriers. As the ice over Antarctica slipped into the Indian Ocean it caused an immense tidal wave. Gushing forth across the ocean northward, the wall of water overwhelmed the continental coastline of Arabia and rushed up the Persian Gulf. Then it reached the funnel of The Land Between the Rivers, engulfing all the lands (Fig. 26.)

How global was the Deluge? Was every place upon our globe actually inundated? The human recollection is almost global and suggests an almost-global event. What is certain is that with the eventual melting of the slipped ice, and the rise in global temperatures following the initial cooling, the Ice Age that had held Earth in its grip for the previous 62,000 years abruptly ended. It happened about 13,000 years ago.

One result of the catastrophe was that Antarctica, for the first time in so many thousands of years, was freed of its ice cover. Its true continental features—coasts, bays, even rivers—were available to be seen, *if* there had been anyone at the time to see them. Amazingly (but not to our surprise), such a "someone" was there!

We know that because of the existence of maps showing an ice-free Antarctica.

For the record let it be recalled that in modern times the very existence of a continent at the south pole was not known until A.D. 1820, when British and Russian sailors discovered it. It was then, as it is now, covered by a massive layer of ice; we know the continent's true shape (under the ice cap) by means of radar and other sophisticated instruments used by many teams during the 1958 International Geophysical Year. Yet Antarctica appears on *mapas mundi* (World Maps) from the fifteenth and even fourteenth centuries A.D.—hundreds of years before the discovery of Antarctica—and the continent, to add puzzle to puzzle, is shown ice-free! Of several such maps, ably described and discussed in *Maps of the Ancient Sea Kings / Evidence of Advanced Civilization in the Ice Age* by Charles H. Hapgood, the one that illustrates the enigma very clearly is the 1531 Map of the World by Orontius Finaeus (Fig. 27), whose depiction of Antarctica is compared to the ice-free continent as determined by the 1958 IGY (Fig. 28).

An even earlier map, from 1513, by the Turkish admiral Piri Re'is, shows the continent connected by an archipelago to the tip of South America (without showing the whole of Antarctica). On the other hand, the map shows correctly Central and South America with the Andean mountains, the Ama-

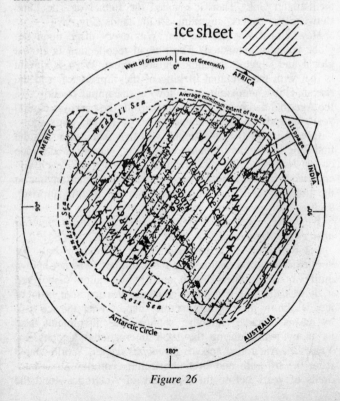

Figure 26

zon River, and so on. How could that be known even before the Spaniards had reached Mexico (in 1519) or South America (in 1531)?

In all these instances, the mapmakers of the Age of Discovery stated that their sources were ancient maps from Phoenicia and ''Chaldea,'' the Greek name for Mesopotamia. But as others who have studied these maps had concluded, no mortal seamen, even given some advanced instruments, could have mapped these continents and their inner features in those early days, and certainly not of an ice-free Antarctica. Only

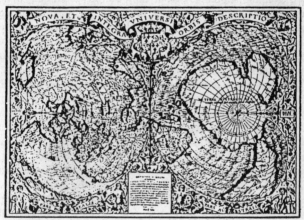

Figure 27

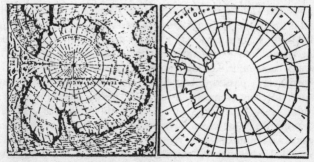

Figure 28

someone viewing and mapping it from the air could have done it. And the only ones around at the time were the Anunnaki.

Indeed, the slippage of Antarctica's ice cover and its effects on the Earth are mentioned in a major text known as the *Erra Epos*. It deals with the events, millennia later, when a deadly dispute arose between the Anunnaki concerning the supremacy on Earth. As the zodiacal age of the Bull (Taurus) was giving way to that of the Ram (Aries), Marduk, the Firstborn son of Enki, asserted that his time had come to take over the supremacy from Enlil and his legal heir. When instruments located at sacred precincts in Sumer indicated that the new age of the Ram had not yet arrived, Marduk complained that they reflected changes that had occurred because "the *Erakallum* quaked and its covering was diminished, and the measures could no longer be taken." *Erakallum* is a term whose precise meaning escapes the scholars; it used to be translated "Lower World" but is now left in scholarly studies untranslated. In *When Time Began* we have suggested that the term denotes the land at the bottom of the world—Antarctica, and that the "covering" that had diminished was the ice cover that had slipped circa 13,000 years ago but grew back to some extent by 4,000 years ago. (Charles Hapgood surmised that the ice-free Antarctica as depicted in the Orontius Finaeus map showed the continent as it was seen circa 4000 B.C., i.e. 6,000 years ago; other studies saw 9,000 years ago as the right time).

As the Deluge overwhelmed the lands and destroyed all upon them, the Anunnaki themselves were airborne, orbiting the Earth in their spacecraft. From the skies they could see the havoc and destruction. Divided into several spacecraft, some "cowered like dogs, crouched against the outer wall." As the days passed "their lips were feverish of thirst, they were suffering cramp from hunger." In the spacecraft where Ishtar was, "she cried out like a woman in travail," lamenting that "the olden days are alas turned to clay." In her spacecraft Ninmah, who shared in the creation of Mankind, bewailed what she was seeing. "My creatures have become like flies, filling the rivers like dragonflies, their fatherhood taken away by the rolling sea." Enlil and Ninurta, accompanied no doubt by the others from Mission Control Center in Nippur, were in another spacecraft. So were Enki, Marduk, and the others of Enki's clan. Their destination, too, was the peaks of Ararat that—as they all well knew—would emerge from under the waters before all else. But all, except Enki, were not aware that a family of humans, saved from the calamity, was also headed that way . . .

The unexpected encounter was full of surprising aspects; their bearing on the human search for Immortality lingered for ten thousand years, and beyond. They also left a permanent human yearning to see the Face of God.

According to the biblical tale, after the ark had come to rest on the peaks of Ararat and the waters receded from the drenched earth, "Noah and his sons and his wife and the wives of his sons who were with him," plus the animals that were in the ark, left the boat. "And Noah built an altar unto Yahweh, and he took of every clean cattle and of every clean fowl, and offered burnt offerings on the altar. And Yahweh smelled the pleasant savor, and said in his heart: 'I will no longer accurse the Earth because of Man.'" And *Elohim* blessed Noah and his sons, and said to them: "Be fruitful and multiply and fill the Earth."

The rapprochement between the angry god and the remnant of Humankind is again described in greater detail and some variation in the Mesopotamian sources. The sequence of events is retained—the cessation of the tidal wave, the falling level of water, the sending out of birds to scout the terrain, the arrival at Ararat, the stepping out of the ark, the building of an altar, and the offering of burnt sacrifices; followed by the recanting triggered by the sweet savory smell of the roasted meat, and the blessing of Noah and his sons.

As Utnapishtim recalled it when he told "the secret of the gods" to Gilgamesh, after he had come out of the boat, he "offered a sacrifice and poured out a libation on the mountaintop, set up seven and seven cult vessels, heaped upon their pot-stands cane, cedarwood and myrtle." The gods, emerging from their spacecraft as they too landed on the mountain, "smelled the sweet savor, crowded like flies about the sacrificer."

Soon Ninmah arrived and realized what had happened. Swearing by the "great jewels which Anu had fashioned for her," she announced that she will never forget the ordeal and what had happened. Go ahead, partake of the offering, she told the rank and file Anunnaki; "but let not Enlil come to the offering; for he, unreasoning, by the deluge my humans consigned to destruction."

But not letting Enlil savor and taste the burnt offering was the least of the problems:

> When at length Enlil arrived
> and saw the ship, Enlil was wroth.
> He was filled with wroth against the Igigi gods.
> "Has some living soul escaped?
> No man was to survive the destruction!"

His foremost son, Ninurta, suspected someone other than the Igigi gods in their orbiters, and said to Enlil:

> Who, other than Ea, can devise plans?
> It is Ea who knows every matter!

Joining the gathering, Ea/Enki admitted what he had done. But, he made sure to point out, he did not violate his oath to secrecy: I did not disclose the secret of the gods, he said. All he did was to "let Atra-hasis see a dream," and this clever human "perceived the secret of the gods" by himself ... Since that is how things had turned out, Enki told Enlil, would it not be wiser to repent? Was not the whole plan to destroy Mankind by the Deluge a big mistake? "Thou wisest of the gods, thou hero, how couldst thou, unreasoning," bring such a calamity about?

Whether it was this sermon, or a realization that he ought to make the best of the situation, the text does not make clear. Whatever the motives, Enlil did have a change of heart. This is how Utnapishtim/Atra-hasis described what ensued:

> Thereupon Enlil went aboard the ship.
> Holding me by the hand, he took me aboard.
> He took my wife aboard and made her kneel

by my side.
Standing between us, he touched our foreheads
to bless us.

The Bible simply states that after Yahweh had repented, "*Elohim* blessed Noah and his sons." From the Mesopotamian sources we learn what the blessing had entailed. It was an unheard-of ceremony, a unique Divine Encounter in which the deity had physically taken the chosen humans by the hand and, standing between them, physically touched their foreheads to convey a divine attribute. There, on Mount Ararat, in full view of the other Anunnaki, Enlil bestowed Immortality upon Utnapishtim and his wife, proclaiming thus:

Hitherto Utnapishtim has been just a human;
henceforth Utnapishtim and his wife
shall be like gods unto us.
Utnapishtim shall reside far away,
at the mouth of the waters.

And "thus they took me and made me reside in the Far Away, at the mouth of the waters," Utnapishtim told Gilgamesh.

The amazing part of this tale is that Utnapishtim was relating it to Gilgamesh some *ten thousand years after the Deluge!*

As a son of a demigod and, in all probability, a demigod himself, Utnapishtim could well have lived another 10,000 years after having lived in Shuruppak (before the Deluge) for 36,000 years. This was not impossible; even the Bible allotted to Noah another 350 years after the Deluge on top of the previous 601. The really extraordinary aspect is that the *wife* of Utnapishtim was also able to live that long as a result of the blessing and the sacred place of residence to which the couple were transported.

Indeed, it was such famed longevity of the Blessed Couple that had led Gilgamesh—a king of the city of Erech, circa 2900 B.C.—to search for the hero of the Deluge. But that is a tale that merits close scrutiny by itself, for it is filled with

Figure 29

a variety of Divine Encounters that enthrall from beginning to end.

As a final act of the Deluge drama, according to the Bible, *Elohim* assured the saved humans that such a calamity shall never occur again; and as a sign, "I placed my bow in the cloud as a token of the covenant between me and the Earth." Though this particular detail does not show up in the extant Mesopotamian versions, the deity who had covenanted with the people was indeed sometimes shown, as in this Mesopotamian depiction, as a bow-holding god in the clouds (Fig. 29).

NEVER AGAIN?

Scientific and public concern about the warming of the Earth as a result of fuel consumption and the diminishing ozone layer over Antarctica has led in recent years to extensive studies of past climates. Accumulated ice over Greenland and Antarctica was drilled to the core, ice sheets were studied with imaging radar; sedimentary rocks, natural fissures, ocean muds, ancient corals, sites of penguin nesting, evidence of ancient shorelines— these and many others have been probed for evidence. They all indicate that the last Ice Age ended abruptly about 13,000 years ago, coinciding with a major global flooding.

The feared catastrophic results from Earth's warming focus presently on the possible melting of Antarctica's ice. The smaller accumulation is in the west, where the ice cap partly rises over water. A warming of only 2° can cause the melting of this ice cap to raise the level of all the world's oceans by 20 feet. More calamitous would be the slippage of the eastern ice cap (see Fig. 26) as a result of a water-mud "lubricant" forming at its bottom from sheer pressure or volcanic activity; that would raise all sea levels by 200 feet (*Scientific American*, March 1993).

If instead of melting gradually the Antarctic ice cap would slip into the surrounding oceans all at once, the tidal wave would be immense, for it would pour all this water in one spill. This, we have suggested, is what had happened when the gravitational pull of the passing Nibiru gave the ice cap its final nudge.

Evidence for "the Earth's greatest flood at the end of the last ice age" has been reported in *Science* (15 January 1993). It was a "cataclysmic flood" whose waters, rushing at the rate of 650 million cubic feet per second (sic!) broke through the ice dams northwest of the Caspian Sea and streamed through the barrier of the Altay Mountains in a 1,500-foot-high wave. Coming from the south (as Sumerian and biblical texts attest) and rushing through the funnel of the Persian Gulf, the initial wave could indeed have overwhelmed all the area's mountains.

6

THE GATES OF HEAVEN

The Sumerians bequeathed to humanity a long list of "firsts" without which ensuing and modern civilizations would have been impossible. To those that were already mentioned, another "first" that has endured almost without a break has been Kingship. As all others, this "first" too was granted to the Sumerians by the Anunnaki. In the words of the Sumerian King Lists, "after the Flood had swept over the Earth, when Kingship was lowered from Heaven, Kingship was in Kish." It was, perhaps, because of this—because "Kingship was lowered from Heaven"—that kings have deemed it a right to be taken aloft, to ascend unto the Gates of Heaven. Therein lie records of attained, attempted, or simulated Divine Encounters filled with soaring aspirations and dramatic failures. In most, dreams play a key role.

The Mesopotamian texts relate that, faced with the reality of a devastated planet, Enlil accepted the fact of Mankind's survival and bestowed his blessings upon the remnants. Realizing that henceforth the Anunnaki themselves could not continue their stay and functioning on Earth without human help, Enlil joined Enki in providing Mankind with the advancements that we call the progress from Paleolithic (Old Stone Age) to Mesolithic and Neolithic (Middle and New Stone Ages) to the sudden Sumerian civilization—in each instance at 3,600-year intervals—that marked the introduction of animal and plant domestications and the switchover from stone to clay and pottery to copper tools and utensils, then to a full-fledged civilization.

As the Mexopotamian texts make clear, the institution of

108

Kingship as an aspect of such high-level civilizations with their hierarchies was created by the Anunnaki to form a partition between themselves and the surging masses of humanity. Before the Deluge Enlil complained that "the noise of Mankind has become too intense" for him, that "by their uproar I am deprived of sleep." Now the gods retreated to sacred precincts, the step-pyramids (ziggurats) at whose center were called the "E" (literally: House, abode) of the god; and a chosen individual who was permitted to approach close enough to hear the deity's words, then conveyed the divine message to the people. Lest Enlil become unhappy again with humanity, the choice of a king was his prerogative; and in Sumerian what we call "Kingship" was called "Enlilship."

We read in the texts that the decision to create Kingship came only after great turmoil and warfare among the Anunnaki themselves—conflicts that we have termed Pyramid Wars in our book *The Wars of Gods and Men*. These bitter conflicts were halted by a peace treaty that divided the ancient settled world into four regions. Three were allocated to Mankind, recognizable as the locations of the three great ancient civilizations of the Tigris-Euphrates (Mesopotamia), the Nile River (Egypt, Nubia) and the Indus Valley. The Fourth Region, a neutral zone, was TILMUN ("Land of the Missiles")—the Sinai peninsula—where the post-Diluvial Spaceport was located. And so it was that

> *The great Anunnaki who decree the fates*
> *sat exchanging their counsels regarding the Earth.*
> *The four regions they created,*
> *establishing their boundaries.*

At that time, as the lands were being divided among the Enlilites and the Enki'ites,

> *A king was not yet established*
> *over all the teeming peoples;*
> *At that time the headband and crown*
> *remained unworn;*
> *The scepter inlaid with lapis lazuli*
> *was not yet brandished;*

The throne-dais had not yet been built.
Scepter and crown, royal headband and staff
still lay in heaven before Anu.

When finally, after the decisions regarding the four regions and the granting of civilizations and Kingship to Mankind were reached, "the scepter of Kingship was brought down from Heaven," Enlil assigned to the goddess Ishtar (his granddaughter) the task of finding a suitable candidate for the first throne in the City of Men—Kish, in Sumer.

The Bible recalls Enlil's change of heart and blessing of the remnants by stating that "*Elohim* blessed Noah and his sons and said unto them: Be fruitful and multiply and replenish the Earth." The Bible then, in what is called the Table of Nations (Genesis chapter 10), proceeds to list the tribal nations that have descended of the three sons of Noah—Shem, Ham, and Japhet—the three major groupings that we still recognize as the Semitic peoples of the Near East, the Hamitic peoples of Africa, and the Indo-Europeans of Anatolia and the Caucasus who had spread to Europe and India. Plunked into the list of sons and sons of sons and grandsons is an unexpected statement regarding the origins of Kingship and the name of the first king—*Nimrod*:

And Kush begot Nimrod,
he who was the first Mighty Man
upon the Earth.
He was a mighty hunter before Yahweh,
wherefore the saying, "A Mighty Hunter
like Nimrod before Yahweh."
And the beginning of his kingdom:
Babel and Erech and Akkad,
all in the Land of Shine'ar.
Out of that land there emanated Ashur,
where Nineveh was built,
a city of wide streets;
and Khalah, and Ressen—the great
city which is between Nineveh and Khalah.

This is an accurate, though concise, history of Kingship

and kingdoms in Mesopotamia. It compresses the data in the Sumerian King Lists wherein Kingship, having begun in Kish (that the Bible calls Kush), indeed shifted to Uruk (*Erech* in the Bible) and after some meandering to Akkad, and in time to Babylon (*Babel*) and Assyria (*Ashur*). They all emanated from Sumer, the biblical *Shine'ar*. The Sumerian "first" in Kingship is further evidenced by the biblical use of the term "Mighty Man" to describe the first king, for this is a literal rendering of the Sumerian word for king, LU.GAL—"Great/ Mighty Man."

There have been many attempts to identify "Nimrod." Since according to Sumerian "myths" it was Ninurta, the Foremost Son of Enlil, who was given the task of instituting "Enlilship" in Kish, *Nimrod* might have been the Hebrew name for Ninurta. If it is a man's name, no one knows what it was in Sumerian because the clay tablet is damaged there. According to the Sumerian King Lists, the Kish dynasty consisted of twenty-three kings who ruled for "24,510 years 3 months and 3½ days," with individual reigns of 1,200, 900, 960, 1,500, 1,560 years and the like. Assuming the mispositioning of "1" as "60" in transcribing over the millennia, one arrives at the more plausible 20, 15, and so on individual reigns and a total of just over four hundred years—a period that is supported by archaeological discoveries at Kish.

The list of names and lengths of reign is deviated from only once, in respect to the thirteenth king. Of him the King Lists state:

> *Etana, a shepherd,*
> *he who ascended to heaven,*
> *who consolidated all countries,*
> *became king and ruled for 1,560 years.*

This historical notation is not an idle one; for there does exist a long epic tale, the *Epic of Etana,* that describes his Divine Encounters in his efforts to reach the Gates of Heaven. Although no complete text has been found, scholars have been able to piece together the story line from fragments of Old Babylonian, Middle Assyrian, and Neo-Assyrian recensions; but there is no doubt that the original version was

Figure 30

Sumerian, for a sage in the service of the Sumerian king Shulgi (twenty-first century B.C.) is mentioned in one of the recensions as the editor of an earlier version.

The reconstruction of the tale from the various fragments has not been easy because the text seems to weave together two separate stories. One has to do with Etana, clearly a beloved king known for a major benevolent achievement (the "consolidation of all countries"), who was deprived of a son and natural successor because of his wife's malady; and the only remedy was the Plant of Birth, which could be obtained only in the Heavens. The story thus leads to Etana's dramatic attempts to reach the Gates of Heaven, borne aloft on the wings of an eagle (a part of the tale that was depicted on cylinder seals from the twenty-fourth century B.C.—Fig. 30). The other story line deals with the Eagle, its friendship at first and then quarrel with a Serpent, resulting in the Eagle's imprisonment in a pit from which it is saved by Etana in a mutually beneficial deal: Etana rescues the Eagle and repairs its wings in exchange for the Eagle's acting as a spaceship that takes Etana to distant heavens.

Several Sumerian texts convey historical data in the form of an allegorical disputation (some of which we had already mentioned), and scholars are uncertain where in the Eagle-Serpent segment allegory ends and a historical record begins. The fact that in both segments it is Utu/Shamash, the commander of the Spaceport, who is the deity that controls the fate of the Eagle and who arranges for Etana to meet the Eagle, suggests a factual space-related event. Moreover, in what scholars call The Historical Introduction to the interwoven episodes, the narrative sets the stage for the related events as a time of conflict and clashes in which the IGI.GI ("Those Who Observe and See")—the corps of astronauts who remained in Earth orbit and manned the shuttlecraft (as distinct from the Anunnaki who had come down to Earth)—"barred the gates" and "patrolled the city" against opponents whose identity is lost in the damaged tablets. All of this spells actuality, a record of facts.

The unusual presence of the Igigi in a city on land, the fact that Utu/Shamash was commander of the Spaceport (by then in the Fourth Region), and the designation of the pilot-cum-spacecraft of Etana as an Eagle, suggest that the conflict echoed in the Etana tale had to do with space flight. Could it be an attempt to create an alternative space center, one not controlled by Utu/Shamash? Could the Eagleman who was involved in the failed attempt, or the intended spacecraft, be banished to languish in a pit—an underground silo? A depiction of a rocketship in an underground silo (showing the command module above ground) has been found in the tomb of Hui, an Egyptian governor of the Sinai in Pharaonic times (Fig. 31), indicating that an "Eagle" in a "pit" was recognized in antiquity as a rocketship in its silo.

Figure 31

If we accept the biblical data as an abbreviated version, yet one that is chronologically and otherwise correct, of the Sumerian sources, we learn that in the aftermath of the Deluge, as Mankind proliferated and the Tigris-Euphrates plain was drying up sufficiently for resettlement, people "journeyed from the east, and they found a plain in the land of Shine'ar and they settled there. And they said to one another: Let us make bricks, and burn them in a kiln. And thus the brick served them for stone, and bitumen served them as mortar."

This is quite an accurate if concise description of the beginning of Sumerian civilization and some of its "firsts"—the brick, the kiln, and the first City of Men; for what ensued was the building of a city and of a "Tower whose head can reach unto heaven."

Nowadays we call such a structure a *launch tower,* and its "head" that can reach the heavens is called a *rocketship* . . .

We have arrived, in the biblical narrative and chronologically, at the incident of the Tower of Babel—the unauthorized construction of a space facility. So "Yahweh came down to see the city and the tower that the Children of Adam were building."

Not liking at all what he was seeing, Yahweh expressed his concerns to unnamed colleagues. "Come, let us descend and confound there their tongue, so that they may not understand one another's speech," he said. And so it was. "And Yahweh scattered them from there upon all over the Earth, and they ceased building the city."

The Bible identifies the place where the attempt to scale the heavens had taken place as Babylon, explaining its Hebrew name *Babel* as derived from the root "to confuse." In fact the original Mesopotamian name, *Bab-ili,* meant "Gateway of the Gods," a place intended by Marduk, the Firstborn son of Enki, to serve as an alternative launch site, free of Enlilite control. Coming in the wake of what we had termed the Pyramid Wars, the incident was timed by us to circa 3450 B.C.—several centuries after the beginning of Kingship in Kish and thus in about the same time frame as that of the Etana events.

Such correspondences between the Sumerian and biblical chronologies shed light on the identity of the divine beings who, like Yahweh in the biblical version, had come down to see what was happening in Babylon, and to whom Yahweh had expressed his concerns. They were the Igigi, who came down to Earth, occupied the city, barred its seven gates against the opposing forces, and patrolled the place until order was restored under a new chosen king capable of "consolidating the lands." That new ruler was Etana. His name can best be translated as "Strongman," and must have been a favorite name for boys in the ancient Near East for it is encountered several times as a personal name in the Hebrew Bible (as *Ethan*). Not unlike executive searches in our times, he too was selected after "Ishtar was looking for a shepherd and searching high and low for a king." After Ishtar had come up with Etana as a candidate for the throne, Enlil looked him over and approved: "A king is hereby affirmed for the land," he announced; and "in Kish a throne-dais for Etana he established." With this done, "the Igigi turned away from the city" and presumably returned to their space stations.

And Etana, having "consolidated the land," turned his mind to the need for a male heir.

The tragedy of a childless spouse, unable to bear a successor for her husband, is a theme encountered in the Bible beginning with the Patriarchal tales. Sarah, the wife of Abraham, was unable to bear children until a Divine Encounter at age ninety; in the meantime, her handmaiden Hagar bore Abraham a son (Ishmael) and the stage was set for a succession conflict between the Firstborn and the younger Legal Heir (Isaac). Isaac in turn had to "entreat Yahweh in behalf of his wife, because she was barren." She was able to conceive only after Yahweh had "let himself be entreated."

Throughout the biblical narratives the belief persists that it is from the Lord that the ability to conceive is granted, and in turn withheld. When Abimelech the king of Gerar took Sarah away from Abraham, "Yahweh closed up every womb in the house of Abimelech" and the affliction was removed only after an appeal by Abraham. Hannah, the wife of Elkanah, was deprived of children because "the Lord had shut her womb." She gave birth to Samuel only after she vowed to give the boy, if she bears a son, "unto the Lord all the days of his life and there shall come no razor upon his head."

In the case of Etana's wife the problem was not an inability to conceive, but rather repeated miscarriages. She was afflicted with a LA.BU disease which prevented her bringing to full term the children that she did conceive. In his desperation, Etana envisioned dire forebodings. In a dream "he saw the city of Kish sobbing; in the city, the people were mourning; there was a song of lamentation." Was it for him, because "Etana cannot have an heir," or for his wife—an omen of death?

Thereafter, "his wife said to Etana: the god showed me a dream. Like Etana my husband, I have had a dream." In the dream she saw a man. He held a plant in his hand; it was a *shammu sha aladi,* a Plant of Birth. He kept pouring cold water on it so that it might "become established in his house." He brought the plant to his city and into his house. From the plant there blossomed a flower; then the plant withered away.

Etana was certain that the dream was a divine omen. "Who would not reverence such a dream!" he said. "The command of the gods has gone forth!" he exclaimed; the remedy to the malady "has come upon us."

Where was this plant, Etana asked his wife. But, she said, in her dream "I could not see where it was growing." Convinced however that the dream was an omen that must come true, Etana went in search of it. He crossed rivers and mountain streams, he rode to and fro. But he could not find the plant. Frustrated, Etana sought divine guidance. "Every day Etana prayed repeatedly to Shamash." Coupling appeals with remonstration, "O Shamash, you have enjoyed the best cuts of my sheep," he said. "The soil has absorbed the blood of my lambs. I have honored the gods!" "The interpreters of dreams," he continued, "have made full use of my incense." Now it was up to the deities themselves, those "who have made full use of my slaughtered lambs," to interpret the dream for him.

If there is such a Plant of Birth, he said in his prayers,

"Let the word go forth from your mouth, O Lord, and give me the Plant of Birth! Show me the Plant of Birth! Remove my shame and provide me with a son!"

The texts do not state where Etana had thus appealed to Utu/Shamash, the commander of the Spaceport. But apparently it was not a face-to-face encounter, for we read next that "Shamash made his voice heard and spoke to Etana." And this was what the divine voice said:

> Go along the road, cross the mountain.
> Find a pit and look carefully at what
> is inside it.
> An Eagle is abandoned down there.
> He will obtain for you the Plant of Birth.

Following the god's instructions Etana found the pit and the Eagle inside it. Demanding to know why Etana had come hither, the Eagle was told of Etana's problem, and told Etana his sad story. Soon a deal was struck: Etana would help raise the Eagle out of the pit and help him fly again; in exchange the Eagle would find for Etana the Plant of Birth. With the aid of a six-runged ladder Etana brought the Eagle up; with copper he repaired his wings. Fit to fly, the Eagle began to search for the magical plant in the mountains. "But the Plant of Birth was not found there."

As despair and disappointment engulfed Etana, he had another dream. What he told about it to the Eagle is partly illegible because of damage to the tablet; but the legible portions refer to the emblems of lordship and authority, coming from "the bright heights of heaven, lay across my path." "My friend, your dream is favorable!" The Eagle said to Etana. Etana then had one more dream in which he saw reeds from all parts of the land assemble into heaps in his house; an evil serpent tried to stop them, but the reeds, "like subject slaves, bowed down before me." Again the Eagle "persuaded Etana to accept the dream" as a favorable omen.

Nothing however happened until the Eagle, too, had a dream. "My friend," he said to Etana, "that same god to me too showed a dream":

We were going through the entrance
of the gates of Anu, Enlil and Ea;
we bowed down together, you and I.
We were going through the entrance
of the gates of Sin, Shamash, Adad and Ishtar;
We bowed down together, you and I.

If we take a look at the route map in Fig. 17, it will at once be realized that the Eagle was describing a reverse journey—from the center of the Solar System where the Sun (Shamash), the Moon (Sin), Mercury (Adad), and Venus (Ishtar) are clustered, toward the outer planets and the outermost one, Anu's domain of Nibiru!

The dream, the Eagle reported, had a second part:

I saw a house with a window without a seal.
I pushed it open and went inside.
Sitting in there was a young woman amidst a brilliance,
adorned with a crown, fair of countenance.
A throne was set for her;
around it the ground was made firm.
At the base of the throne lions were crouching.
As I went forward, the lions gave obeisance.
Then I woke up with a start.

The dream was thus filled with good omens: the "window" was unsealed, the young woman on the throne (the king's wife) was amidst a brilliance; the lions were obliging. This dream, the Eagle said, made it clear what had to be done: "Our objective-target has been made manifest; come, I will bear you to the heaven of Anu!"

What follows in the ancient text is a description of *space flight*, as realistic as any reported by modern astronauts.

Soaring skyward with Etana holding on, the Eagle said to Etana after they had ascended one *beru* (a Sumerian measure of distance and of the celestial arc):

See, my friend, how the land appears!
Peer at the sea at the sides of the Mountain House:

The land has indeed become a mere hill,
the wide sea is just a tub!

Higher and higher the Eagle carried Etana heavenward; smaller and smaller the Earth appeared. After they had ascended another *beru,* the Eagle said to Etana:

> *My friend,*
> *Cast a glance at how the Earth appears!*
> *The land has turned into a furrow . . .*
> *The wide sea is just like a bread-basket . . .*

After they had journeyed another *beru,* the land was seen no larger than a gardener's ditch. And after that, as they continued to ascend, the Earth was totally out of sight. Recording the experience, Etana said thus:

> *As I glanced around,*
> *the land had disappeared;*
> *and upon the wide sea*
> *mine eyes could not feast.*

They were so far out in space that Earth had disappeared from view!

Seized with fright, Etana called out to the Eagle to turn back. It was a dangerous descent, for the Eagle "plunged down" to Earth. A tablet's fragment identified by scholars as "the Eagle's prayer to Ishtar as he and Etana fall from Heaven" (viz. J.V. Kinnier Wilson, *The Legend of Etana: A New Edition*) suggests that the Eagle had called out to Ishtar—whose mastery of the Earth's skies was well attested in both texts and drawings, such as in Fig. 32—to come to their rescue. They were falling toward a body of water that, "though it would have saved them at the top, would have killed them in its depths." With Ishtar's intervention, the Eagle and his passenger landed in a forest.

In the second region of civilization, that of the Nile River, Kingship began circa 3100 B.C.—human Kingship, that is, for

Figure 32

Egyptian traditions held that long before that Egypt was ruled by gods and demigods.

According to the Egyptian priest Manetho, who had written down the history of Egypt when Alexander's Greeks arrived, in times immemorial "Gods of Heaven" came to Earth from the Celestial Disc (Fig. 33). After a great flood had inundated Egypt, "a very great god who had come to Earth in the earliest times" raised the land from under the waters by ingenious damming, dyking, and land reclamation works. His name was *Ptah,* "The Developer," and he was a great scientist who had earlier had a hand in the creation of Man. He was often depicted with a staff that was graduated, very much like surveyors' rods nowadays (Fig. 34a). In time Ptah handed the rule over Egypt to his Firstborn son *Ra* ("The Bright One"—Fig. 34b), who for all time remained head of the pantheon of Egyptian gods.

The Egyptian term for "gods" was NTR—"Guardian, Watcher" and the belief was that they had come to Egypt from *Ta-Ur,* the "foreign/Far Land." In our previous writings we have identified that land as Sumer (more correctly *Shumer,* "Land of the Guardians"), Egypt's gods as the Anunnaki, Ptah as Ea/Enki (whose Sumerian nickname,

Figure 33

NUDIMMUD, meant "The Artful Creator") and Ra as his Firstborn son Marduk.

Ra was followed on the divine throne of Egypt by four brother-sister couples: first his own children *Shu* ("Dryness") and *Tefnut* ("Moisture"), and then by their children *Geb* ("Who Piles Up the Earth") and *Nut* ("The Stretched-out Firmament of the Sky"). Geb and Nut then had four children: *Asar* ("The All-Seeing") whom the Greeks called Osiris, who married his sister *Ast,* whom we know as Isis; and *Seth* ("The Southerner") who married his sister Nebt-hat, alias Nephtys. To keep the peace, Egypt was divided between Osiris (who was given Lower Egypt in the north) and Seth (who was assigned Upper Egypt in the south). But Seth deemed himself entitled to all of Egypt, and never accepted the division. Using subterfuge, he managed to seize Osiris, cut up his body into fourteen pieces, and dispersed the pieces all over Egypt. But Isis managed to retrieve the pieces (all except for the phallus) and put together the mutilated body, thereby resurrecting the dead Osiris to life in the Other World. Of him the sacred writings said:

> He entered the secret gates,
> the glory of the Lord of Eternity,
> in step with him who shines in the horizon,
> on the path of Ra.

Figures 34a and 34b

And thus was born the belief that the king of Egypt, the Pharaoh, if "put together" (mummified) like Osiris after death, could journey to join the gods in their abode, enter the secret Gates of Heaven, encounter there the great god Ra, and, if allowed to enter, enjoy an eternal Afterlife.

The journey to this ultimate Divine Encounter was a simulated one; but to simulate one has to emulate a real, actual precedent—a journey that the gods themselves, and specifically so the resurrected Osiris, had actually taken from the shores of the Nile to *Neter-Khert*, "The Gods' Mountainland," where an Ascender would take them aloft in the *Duat*, a magical "Abode for rising to the stars."

Much of what we know of those simulated journeys comes from the *Pyramid Texts*, texts whose origin is lost in the mists of time that are known from their repeated quoting inside Pharaonic pyramids (especially those of Unas, Teti, Pepi I, Merenra, and Pepi II who had reigned between 2350 and 2180 B.C.). Exiting his burial tomb (which was never inside a pyramid) through a false door, the king expected to be met by a divine herald who would "take hold of the king by the arm and take him to heaven." As the Pharaoh thus began his Journey to the Afterlife, the priests broke out in a chant: "The king is on his way to Heaven! The king is on his way to Heaven!"

The journey—so realistic and geographically precise that one forgets it was supposed to be simulated—began, as stated, by passing through the false door that faced east; the destination of the Pharaoh was thus eastward, away from Egypt and toward the Sinai peninsula. The first obstacle was a Lake of Reeds; the term is almost identical to that of the biblical Sea of Reeds that the Israelites managed to cross when its waters miraculously parted, and undoubtedly refers in both instances to the chain of lakes that still run almost the whole length of the border between Egypt and the Sinai, from north to south.

In the case of the Pharaoh, it was a Divine Ferryman who, after some tough questioning regarding the Pharaoh's qualifications, decided to let the king cross. The Divine Ferryman brought the magical boat over from the lake's far side, but it was the Pharaoh who had to recite magical formulas to make the boat sail back. Once the formulas were recited, the ferryboat began to move by itself and the steering oar directed itself. In every respect, the boat was self-propelled!

Beyond the lake there stretched a desert, and beyond it the Pharaoh could see in the distance the Mountains of the East. But no sooner had the Pharaoh alighted from the boat, than he was stopped by four Divine Guards, who were conspicuous by their black hair that was arranged in curls on their foreheads, at their temples, and at the back of their heads, with braids in the center of their heads. They, too, questioned the Pharaoh, but finally let him pass.

A text (known only from its quotes) titled *The Book of Two Ways* described the alternatives that now faced the Pharaoh, for he could see two passes that led through the mountain range beyond which the Duat was. Such two passes, nowadays called the Giddi and Mitla passes, offered since time immemorial unto the most recent wars the only viable way into the center of the peninsula, be it for armies or nomads or pilgrims. Pronouncing the required Utterances, the Pharaoh is shown the correct pass. Ahead lies an arid and barren land, and Divine Guards pop up unexpectedly. "Where goest thou?" they demand to know of the mortal who appears in the gods' region. The Divine Herald, alternately seen and unseen, speaks up: "The king goes to Heaven, to possess life and joy," he says. As the guards hesitate, the king himself pleads with them: "Open the frontier ... incline its barrier ... let me pass as the gods pass through!" In the end the Divine Guards let the king through, and he has finally reached the Duat.

The Duat was conceived as an enclosed Circle of the Gods, at the headpoint of which the sky (represented by the goddess Nut) opened so that the Imperishable Star (represented by the Celestial Disc) could be reached (Fig. 35); geographically it was an oval valley, enclosed by mountains, through which shallow streams flowed. The streams were so shallow, or sometimes even so dry, that the Barge of Ra had to be towed or, otherwise, moved by its own power as a sled.

The Duat was divided into twelve divisions, which the king had to tackle in twelve hours of the day above ground and in twelve hours of the night below ground, in the *Amen-ta,* the "Hidden Place." It was there that Osiris himself had ascended to an Eternal Life, and the king offered there a prayer to Osiris—a prayer that is quoted in the Egyptian *Book of the Dead* in the chapter titled "Chapter of Making His Name":

> *May be given to me my Name*
> *in the Great House of Two.*
> *May in the House of Fire*
> *a Name to me be granted.*
> *In the night of computing the years*
> *and of telling the months,*
> *May I become a Divine Being,*
> *may I sit on the east side of Heaven.*

As we have already suggested, the "Name"—*Shem* in Hebrew, MU in Sumerian—that ancient kings prayed for was a rocketship that could take them heavenward, and by making them immortal become "that by which they are remembered."

The king can actually see the Ascender for which he prays. But it is in the House of Fire that can be reached only through the subterranean passages. The way down leads through spiraling corridors, hidden chambers, and doors that open and close mysteriously. In each of the twelve parts companies of

Figure 35

Figure 36

gods can be seen; their dress differs; some are headless, some look ferocious, some are with hidden faces; some are menacing, others welcome the Pharaoh. The king is constantly put to the test. By the seventh division, however, the underworld or infernal aspects begin to diminish and celestial aspects, emblems and Birdmen gods (with falcon heads) start to appear. In the ninth hour-zone the king sees the twelve "Divine Rowers of the Boat of Ra," the "Celestial Boat of Millions of Years" (Fig. 36).

In the tenth hour-zone the king, passing through a gate, enters a place astir with activity, whose gods are charged with providing the Flame and Fire for the Celestial Boat of Ra. In the eleventh hour-zone the king encounters more gods with star emblems; their task is to provide "power for emerging from the Duat, to make the Object of Ra advance to the Hidden House in the Upper Heavens." Here is where the gods equip the king for the celestial journey, shedding his earthly clothes and putting on a Falcon-god's garb.

In the final twelfth hour-zone, the king is led through a tunnel to a cavern where the Divine Ladder stands. The cavern is inside the Mountain of the Ascent of Ra. The Divine Ladder is bound together by copper cables and is, or leads to, the Divine Ascender. It is the Ladder of the Gods, used previously by Ra and Seth and Osiris; and the king (as inscribed in the tomb of Pepi) has prayed that the Ladder "may be given to Pepi, so that Pepi may ascend to heaven on it." Some illustrations in the *Book of the Dead* show at this point

Figure 37

the king, receiving the blessings of or being bid good-bye by the goddesses Isis and Nephtys, being led to a winged *Ded* (the symbol of Everlastingness, Fig. 37).

Equipped as a god, the king is now assisted by two goddesses "who seize the cables" to enter the "Eye" of the celestial boat, the command module of the Ascender. He takes his seat between two gods; the seat is called "Truth which makes alive." The king attaches himself to a protruding contraption, and all is ready for takeoff: "Pepi is arrayed in the apparel of Horus" (the commander of the Falcon-gods) "and in the dress of Thoth" (the Divine Recordskeeper); "the Opener of the Ways has opened the way for him; the gods of An" (Heliopolis) "let him ascend the Stairway, set him before the Firmament of Heaven; Nut" (the sky goddess) "extends her hand to him."

The king now offers a prayer to the Double Gates—the "Door of Earth" and the "Door to Heaven"—that they may open. The hour is now daybreak; and suddenly "the aperture of the celestial window" opens up, and "the steps of light are revealed!"

Inside the Ascender's "Eye" "the command of the gods is heard." Outside, the "radiance that lifts" is strengthened so that "the king may be lifted up to heaven." A "might that no one can withstand" can be felt inside the "Eye," the command chamber. There are sound and fury, roaring and quaking: "The Heaven speaks, the Earth quakes, the Earth trembles . . . The ground is come apart . . . The king ascends to Heaven!" "The Roaring Tempest drives him . . . The guardians of Heaven's parts open the *Gate of Heaven* for him!''

The inscriptions within the tomb of Pepi explain to those who were left behind, the king's subjects, what had happened:

> *He flies who flies:*
> *This is the king Pepi who flies away*
> *from you, ye mortals.*
> *He is not of Earth; he is of the Heaven.*
> *This king Pepi flies as a cloud to the sky.*

Having risen in the Ascender toward the east, the king is now orbiting the Earth:

> *He encompasses the sky like Ra,*
> *He traverses the sky like Thoth ...*
> *He travels over the regions of Horus,*
> *He travels over the regions of Seth ...*
> *He has completely encircled the heavens twice.*

The repeated circling of the Earth provides the Ascender with momentum to leave the Earth for the Double Gates of Heaven. Down below, the priests' incantations tell the king: "The Double Gates of Heaven are opened for thee!" and assure him that the Goddess of Heaven will protect and guide him in this celestial journey: "She will lay hold of your arm, she will show you the way to the horizon, to the place where Ra is." The destination is the "Imperishable Star" whose symbol is the Winged Disc.

The sacred utterances assure the faithful that when the departed king shall reach his destination, "when the king shall stand there, on the star which is on the underside of heaven, he shall be judged as a god."

The incantation utterances envision that when the king shall approach the Double Gates of Heaven, he will be met by "the four gods who stand on the *Dam*-scepters of Heaven." He will call out to them to announce the king's arrival to Ra; and without doubt, Ra himself will step forward to greet the king and lead him past the Gates of Heaven and into the Celestial Palace:

Figure 38

> *Thou findest Ra standing there.*
> *He greets thee, lays hold on thy arm.*
> *He leads thee into the celestial Double Palace.*
> *He places thee upon the throne of Osiris.*

After a series of Divine Encounters with major and minor deities, the Pharaoh now experiences the utmost Divine Encounter, with the Great God RA himself. He is offered the throne of Osiris, making him eligible for Eternity. The celestial journey is complete, but not the mission. For though the king has become eligible for Eternity, he now must find and attain it—one final detail in the translation to an everlasting Afterlife: the king now must find and partake of the "Nourishment of Everlasting," an elixir which keeps rejuvenating the gods in their celestial abode.

The priestly incantations now address this last hurdle. They appeal to the gods to "take this king with you, that he may eat of that which you eat, that he may drink of that which you drink, that he may live on that which you live. Give sustenance to the king from your eternal sustenance."

Some of the ancient texts describe where the king now goes as the Field of Life; others refer to it as the Great Lake of the Gods. What he has to obtain is both a beverage that is the Water of Life and a food that is the Fruit of the Tree of Life. Illustrations in the *Book of the Dead* show the king (sometimes accompanied by his queen, Fig. 38) within the

Great Lake of the Gods, drinking the Waters of Life—waters out of which the Tree of Life (a date-palm tree) grows. In the *Pyramid Texts* it is the Great Green Divine Falcon who leads the king to the Field of Life, to find the Tree of Life that grows there. There the goddess who is the Lady of Life meets the king. She holds four jars with whose contents she "refreshes the heart of the Great God on the day when he awakens." She offers the divine elixir to the king, "therewith giving him Life."

Watching the proceedings, Ra is happy. Behold, he calls out to the king—

> *All satisfying Life is given to thee!*
> *Eternity is thine ...*
> *Thou perishest not,*
> *Thou passest not away,*
> *for ever and ever.*

With this last Divine Encounter on the Imperishable Star, the "king's lifetime is eternity, its limit is everlastingness."

THE CONFUSION OF LANGUAGES

According to Genesis (chapter 11) Mankind had "one language and one kind of words" before Sumer was settled. But as a result of the Tower of Babel incident, Yahweh, who had come down to see what was going on, said to (unnamed) colleagues: "Behold, they are one people and they all have one tongue . . . Let us descend and confound there their tongue so that they may not understand each other's speech." It happened, by our calculations, circa 3450 B.C.

This tradition reflects Sumerian assertions that "once upon a time," in an idyllic past when "man had no rivals" and all the lands "rested in security," "the people in unison to Enlil in one tongue gave speech."

Those idyllic times are recalled in a Sumerian text known as *Enmerkar and the Lord of Aratta* that deals with a power struggle and a test of wills between Enmerkar, a ruler of Uruk (the biblical Erech), and the king of Aratta (in the Indus Valley) circa 2850 B.C. The dispute concerned the extent of the powers of Ishtar, Enlil's granddaughter, who could not make up her mind whether to reside in faraway Aratta or stay in the then-unimportant Erech.

Viewing the expansion of Enlilite control unfavorably, Enki sought to inflame the War of Words between the two rulers by confusing their language. So "Enki, the lord of Eridu, endowed with knowledge, *changed the speech in their mouths*" to create contentions between "prince and prince, king and king."

According to J. van Dijk ("La confusion des langues" in *Orientalia* vol. 39), the last verse in this passage should be translated "the language of Mankind, once upon a time one, *for the second time* was confused" (italics by the author).

Whether the verse means that it was Enki who for the second time confused the languages, or simply that it was he who was responsible for the second confusion but not necessarily for the first one, is not clear from the text.

7

IN SEARCH OF IMMORTALITY

Circa 2900 B.C. Gilgamesh, a Sumerian king, refused to die.

Five hundred years before him Etana, king of Kish, sought to achieve Immortality by preserving his seed—his DNA—by having a son. (According to the Sumerian King Lists he was followed on the throne by "Balih, the son of Etana"; but whether this was a child by his official spouse or by a concubine, the records do not say).

Five hundred years after Gilgamesh, Egyptian Pharaohs sought to achieve Immortality by joining the gods in an Afterlife. But to embark on the journey that would translate them to an Everlastingness, they had first to die.

Gilgamesh sought to achieve Immortality by refusing to die ... The result was an adventure-filled search for Immortality whose tale became one of the most famous epics of the ancient world, known to us primarily from an Akkadian recension written on twelve clay tablets. In the course of this search Gilgamesh—and with him the readers of the *Epic of Gilgamesh*—meet a robotic man, an artificial guardian, the Bull of Heaven, gods and goddesses, and the still-living hero of the Deluge. With Gilgamesh we arrive at the Landing Place and witness the launch of a rocketship, and go to the Spaceport in the forbidden region. With him we climb the Cedar Mountains, go under in a sinking boat, traverse a desert where lions roam, cross the Sea of Death, reach the Gates of Heaven. All along Divine Encounters dominate the saga, omens and dreams determine its course, visions fill its dramatic stages. Indeed, as the *Epic*'s opening lines state,

Figure 39

> *He saw everything to the ends of Earth,*
> *All things experienced, gained complete wisdom.*
> *Secret things he saw, the mysteries he laid bare.*
> *He brought back a tale of times before the Flood.*

According to the Sumerian King Lists, after the reign of twenty-three kings in Kish, "Kingship was removed to the Eanna." The E.ANNA was the House (temple-ziggurat) of Anu in the sacred precinct of Uruk (the biblical Erech). There a semidivine dynasty began with Meskiaggasher, "the son of the god Utu," who was the high priest of the Eanna temple and became king as well. He was followed on the royal throne by his son Enmerkar ("He who built Uruk," the great city beside the sacred precinct) and his grandson Lugalbanda—both rulers of whom heroic tales were written down. After a brief interregnum by the divine Dumuzi (whose life, loves, and death are a tale by themselves), Gilgamesh (Fig. 39) ascended the throne. His name was sometimes written with the "Dingir" prefix, to indicate his divinity: for his mother was a full-fledged goddess, the goddess Ninsun; and that, as the great and long *Epic of Gilgamesh* explained, made him "two-thirds divine." (His father, Lugalbanda, was apparently only the High Priest when Gilgamesh was born.)

At the beginning of his reign Gilgamesh was a benevolent king, enlarging and reinforcing his city and caring for its citizens. But as the years passed (he ruled, according to the

King Lists, 126 years which, reduced by a factor of six, would have really been only twenty-one), his aging began to bother him and he was seized with the issues of Life and Death. Appealing to his godfather Utu/Shamash, he said:

> *In my city man dies; oppressed is my heart.*
> *Man perishes; heavy is my heart . . .*
> *Man, the tallest, cannot stretch to heaven;*
> *Man, the widest, cannot cover the earth.*

"I peered over the wall, saw the dead bodies," Gilgamesh said to Shamash, referring perhaps to a cemetery. "Will I too 'peer over the wall,' will I too be fated thus?" But his godfather's answer was not reassuring. "When the gods created Mankind," Shamash responded, "death for Mankind they allotted; life they retained in their own keeping." Therefore, Shamash advised, live day by day, enjoy life while you can—"Let full be thy belly, make thou merry day and night! On each day make thou a feast of rejoicing, day and night dance thou and play!"

Though the god's admonition concluded with the advice that Gilgamesh let his spouse "delight in thy bosom," Gilgamesh read into the words of Shamash a different meaning. "Make merry day and night," he was told in reply to his concerns about aging and looming death; and he took it as a hint that "joyful sex" would keep him young. He thus made it a habit of roaming the streets of Uruk by night, and when he came upon a just-married couple, he demanded the right to have the first sex with the bride.

As the people's outcry reached the gods, "the gods hearkened to the plaint" and decided to create an artificial man who would be a match for Gilgamesh, wrestling him to exhaustion and distracting him from his sexual escapades. Given the task, Ninmah, using the "essence" of several gods and guided by Enki, created in the steppe a "savage man" with copper sinews. He was called ENKI.DU—"Enki's Creature"—and given by Enki "wisdom and broad understanding" in addition to immense strength. A cylinder seal, now in the British Museum, depicts Enkidu and his creators, as

Figure 40

well as Gilgamesh and his mother, the goddess Ninsun (Fig. 40).

Many verses in the epic tale are devoted to the process by which this artificial creature was humanized, by having unceasing sex with a harlot. When that was achieved, Enkidu was instructed by the gods what his task was: to wrestle, subdue, calm, and then befriend Gilgamesh. So that Gilgamesh should not be overcome by surprise, the gods informed Enkidu, Gilgamesh would be forewarned by means of dreams. That *dreams would be used by the gods in such a premeditated manner* is made unmistakenly clear by the text (Tablet I, column v, lines 23–24):

> *Before thou comest down from the hills,*
> *Gilgamesh will see thee in dreams in Uruk.*

No sooner was this planned than Gilgamesh did have a dream. He went to his mother, "beloved and wise Ninsun who is versed in all knowledge," and told her of his dream:

> *My mother, I saw a dream last night.*
> *There appeared stars in the heavens.*
> *Something from the heavens kept coming at me.*
> *I tried to lift it; it was too heavy for me.*
> *I tried to turn it over, but could not budge it.*
> *The people of Uruk were standing about it,*
> *the nobles thronged around it,*

my companions were kissing its feet.
I was drawn to it as to a woman;
I placed it at your feet; you made it vie with me.

"That which was coming toward you from the heavens," Ninsun told Gilgamesh, is a rival: "A stout comrade who rescues a friend is come to thee." He will wrestle you with his might, but he will never forsake you.

Gilgamesh then had a second omen-dream. "On the ramparts of Uruk there lay an axe." The populace was gathered around it. After some difficulty Gilgamesh managed to bring the axe to his mother, and she made him vie with it. Again Ninsun interpreted the dream: "The copper axe that you saw is a man," one equal to you in strength. "A strong partner will come to you, one who can save the life of a comrade." He was created on the steppe, and he will soon arrive in Uruk.

Accepting the omens, Gilgamesh said: "Let it fall then, according to the will of Enlil."

And then, one night, as Gilgamesh went out to have his sexual joys, Enkidu barred his way and would not allow Gilgamesh to enter the house where newlyweds were about to go to bed. A struggle ensued; "they grappled each other, holding fast like bulls." Walls shook, doorposts shattered as the two wrestled. At last, "Gilgamesh bent the knee." He lost the match to a stranger, and "bitterly he was weeping." Enkidu stood perplexed. Then "the wise mother of Gilgamesh spoke" to both of them: it was all meant to be, and from now on the two were to be comrades, with Enkidu acting as the protector of Gilgamesh. Foreseeing future dangers—for well she knew that there was more to the dreamomen than she had told Gilgamesh—she beseeched Enkidu always to go ahead of Gilgamesh and be a shield unto him.

As the two settled into a friendship, Gilgamesh began to tell his comrade of his troubled heart. Recalling his first omen-dream, the "something from the heaven" was now described by him as "the handiwork of Anu," an object that became embedded in the ground as it fell from the skies. When he was finally able to dislodge it, it was because the strongmen of Uruk "grabbed its lower part" as he, Gilgamesh, "pulled it up by the forepart." The dreamlike recollection became a vividly remembered vision as Gilgamesh described his efforts to open up the object's top:

> *I pressed strongly its upper part;*
> *I could neither remove its covering*
> *nor raise its Ascender.*

Retelling his dream-vision, unsure no more ¡of whether it was a recollection of an obscured reality or a nighttime fantasy, Gilgamesh was now describing an *Ascender* that had crashed to Earth, the "handiwork of Anu," a mechanical contraption with an upper part that served as a covering. Determined to see what was inside, Gilgamesh continued,

> *With a destroying fire*
> *its top I then broke off*
> *and moved into its depth.*

Once inside the Ascender, "its movable That-which-pulls-forward"—its engine—"I lifted, and brought it to my mother." Now, he wondered out loud, was it not a sign that Anu himself was summoning him to the Divine Abode? It was undoubtedly an omen, an invitation. But how could he answer the call? "Who, my friend, can scale heaven?" Gilgamesh asked Enkidu, and gave his own answer: "Only the gods, by going to the underground place of Shamash"—the Spaceport in the forbidden region.

But here Enkidu had a surprising bit of information. There is a Landing Place in the Cedar Mountain, he said. He discovered it while he was roaming the land, and he can show Gilgamesh where it is! There is, though, a problem: The place is guarded by a guardian artfully created by Enlil, a "siege engine" whose "mouth is fire, whose breath is death, whose roaring is a flood-storm." The monster's name is Huwawa, "as a terror to mortals Enlil has appointed him." And no one can even come near him, for "at sixty leagues he can hear the wild cows of the forest."

The danger only encouraged Gilgamesh to try and reach the Landing Place. If he succeeds, he will attain immortality;

and if he fails, his heroism will be forever remembered: "Should I fall," he told Enkidu, " 'Gilgamesh against fierce Huwawa had fallen' they will say long after my offspring will be born."

Determined to go, Gilgamesh prayed to Shamash, his godfather and commander of the Eaglemen, for help and protection. "Let me go, O Shamash!" he intoned, "my hands are raised in prayer . . . to the Landing Place give command . . . establish over me your protection!" Receiving no favorable response, Gilgamesh revealed his plan to his mother, seeking her intercession with Shamash. "A far journey I have boldly undertaken," he said, "to the place of Huwawa; an uncertain battle I am about to face; unknown pathways I am about to tread. O my mother, pray thou to Shamash on my behalf!"

Heeding her son's entreating, Ninsun donned the garb of a priestess, "a smoke-offering set up, and to Shamash raised her hands." "Why, having given me Gilgamesh for a son, with a restless heart didst thou endow him? And now thou didst affect him to go on a far journey, to the place of Huwawa, to face an uncertain battle." Give him your protection, she asked Shamash, "Until he reaches the Cedar Forest, until he has slain the fierce Huwawa, until the day that he goes and returns." Turning to Enkidu, Ninsun announced that she had adopted him as a son, "though not from the same womb as Gilgamesh" he was, thus "putting an obligation on Enkidu's shoulders." Let Enkidu go in front, she told the comrades, "for he who goes in front saves his comrade."

And so, with newly made weapons, the comrades were off on their perilous journey to the Landing Place in the Cedar Mountains.

The fourth tablet of the *Epic of Gilgamesh* begins with the journey to the Cedar Mountains. Moving as fast as they could, the comrades "at twenty leagues ate their ration, at thirty leagues they stopped for the night," covering thus fifty leagues during a day. "The distance took them from the new moon to the full moon then three days more"—a total of seventeen days. "Then they came to *Lebanon*," in whose mountains the unique cedars of biblical fame have been growing.

When the two arrived at the green mountain, the comrades were awestruck. "Their words were silenced . . . they stood still and gazed at the forest. They looked at the height of the cedars; they looked at the entrance to the forest: where Huwawa was wont to move was a path: straight were the tracks, a fiery channel. They beheld the Cedar Mountain, abode of the gods, the crossroads of Ishtar." They had indeed arrived at their destination, and the sight was awesome.

Gilgamesh made an offering to Shamash and asked for an omen. Facing the mountain, he called out: "Bring me a dream, a favorable dream!"

For the first time we learn here that *a ritual had been practiced for bringing about such requested omen-dreams.* The six verses describing the rite are partly damaged, but the undamaged portions give an idea of what had taken place:

> *Enkidu arranged it for him, for Gilgamesh.*
> *With dust . . . . . . he fixed . . . . . .*
> *He made him lie down inside the circle and*
> *. . . . . . . like wild barley . . . .*
> *. . . . . . . blood . . . .*
> *Gilgamesh sat with his chin on his knees.*

The ritual, it appears, called for the making of a circle with dust, the use of wild barley and blood in some magical way, and the sitting of the subject inside the circle with knees pulled up and the chin touching the knees. The rite worked, for next we read that "sleep, which spills out over people, overcame Gilgamesh; in the middle of the watch sleep departed from him; a dream he tells to Enkidu." In the dream, "which was extremely upsetting," Gilgamesh saw the two of them at the foot of the high mountain; suddenly the mountain toppled, and the two of them "were like flies" (meaning unclear). Reassuring Gilgamesh that the dream was favorable and that its meaning will become clear at dawn, Enkidu urged Gilgamesh to go back to sleep.

This time Gilgamesh awoke with a start. "Did you arouse me?" he asked Enkidu, "Did you touch me, did you call my name?" No, said Enkidu. Then perhaps it was a god who had passed by, Gilgamesh said, for in his second dream he again saw a mountain topple; "it laid me low, trapped my feet." There was an overpowering glare and a man appeared; "the fairest in the land was he. From under the toppled ground he pulled me out; he gave me water to drink, my heart quieted; on the ground he set my feet."

Again Enkidu reassured Gilgamesh. The "mountain" that toppled was the slain Huwawa, he explained. "Your dream is favorable!" he said to Gilgamesh, urging him to go back to sleep.

As they both fell asleep, the tranquility of the night was shattered by a thunderous noise and a blinding light, and Gilgamesh was not sure whether he was dreaming or seeing a true vision. This is how the text quotes Gilgamesh:

> *The vision that I saw was wholly awesome!*
> *The heavens shrieked, the earth boomed!*
> *Though daylight was dawning, darkness came.*
> *Lightning flashed, a flame shot up.*
> *The clouds swelled, it rained death!*
> *Then the glow vanished; the fire went out.*
> *And all that had fallen was turned to ashes.*

Did Gilgamesh realize, right then and there, that he had witnessed the launching of a *Shem,* a skyrocket—the shaking of the ground as the engines ignited and roared, the clouds of smoke and "raining death," darkening the dawn sky; the brilliance of the engine's flames seen through the thick cloud, as the skyrocket rose up; and then the vanishing glow, and the burnt ashes falling back to Earth as the only final evidence of the rocket's launch. Did Gilgamesh realize that he had indeed arrived at the "Landing Place," where he could find the *Shem* that would make him immortal? Apparently he did, for in spite of cautionary words by Enkidu, he was certain that it was all a good omen, a signal from Shamash that he ought to press on.

But before the Cedar Forest could be penetrated and the Landing Place be reached, the terrifying guardian, Huwawa, had to be overcome. Enkidu knew where a gate was, and in the morning the comrades made their way toward it, careful to avoid "weapon-trees that kill." Reaching the gate, Enkidu tried to open it. An unseen force threw him back, and for twelve days he lay paralyzed. The narrative reveals that Enkidu rubbed himself with plants, creating a "double mantle of radiance" that made "paralysis leave the arms, impotence leave the loins."

While Enkidu was lying immobilized, Gilgamesh made a discovery: he found a tunnel that led into the forest. Its entrance was overgrown with trees and bushes and it was blocked by rocks and soil. "While Gilgamesh cut down the trees, Enkidu dug up" the rocks and soil. After a while they found themselves inside the forest, and saw ahead a path—the path "where Huwawa made tracks as he went to and fro."

For a while the comrades stood awestruck. Motionless "they beheld the Cedar Mountain, the dwelling place of the gods, shrine-place of Inanna." They "gazed and gazed at the height of the cedars, gazed and gazed at the pathway into the forest. The path was well trodden, the road was excellent. The cedars held up their luxuriance all upon the mountain, their shade was pleasant; it filled one with happiness."

Just as the two were feeling so good, terror struck: "Huwawa made his voice heard." Somehow alerted to the presence of the two inside the forest, Huwawa's voice boomed death and doom for the intruders. In a scene that brings to mind the much later encounter between the boy David and the giant Goliath, when the latter felt insulted by the uneven match and threatened to "give thy flesh unto the fowls of the air and to the beasts of the field," so did Huwawa belittle and threaten the twosome: "You are so very small that I regard you as a turtle and a tortoise," his voice announced; "were I to swallow you, I would not satisfy my stomach . . . So I shall bite your windpipe and neck, Gilgamesh, and leave your body for the birds of the forest and for the roaring beasts."

Seized with fear, the comrades now saw the monster appear. He was "mighty, his teeth as the teeth of a dragon, his face the face of a lion, his coming like the onrushing floodwaters." From his forehead there emanated a "radiant beam; it devoured trees and bushes." From this weapon's "killing force, none could escape." A Sumerian cylinder seal

Figure 41

which depicts a mechanical monster (Fig. 41) might have had Huwawa in mind. It shows the monster, the heroic king, Enkidu (on the right) and a god (on the left), the latter representing Shamash who, according to the epic tale, came at this crucial moment to the rescue. "Down from the skies divine Shamash spoke to them," revealing a weakness in Huwawa's armor and devising a strategy for the comrades' attack. Huwawa, the deity explained, usually protects himself with "seven cloaks," but now "only one he had donned, six are still off." They could therefore slay Huwawa with the weapons they had, if only they could approach him closely enough; and to make that possible, Shamash said, he would create a whirlwind that "would beat against the eyes of Huwawa" and neutralize his death-beam.

Soon the ground began to shake; "white clouds grew black." "Shamash summoned up great tempests against Huwawa" from all directions, creating a massive whirlwind. "Huwawa's face grew dark; he could not charge forward, nor could he move backward." The two then attacked the incapacitated monster. "Enkidu struck the guardian, Huwawa, to the ground. For two leagues the cedars resounded" with the monster's fall. Wounded but not dead, Huwawa spoke up, wondering why he had not slain Enkidu as soon as he had discovered his entering the forest. Turning to Gilgamesh, Huwawa offered him all the wood he wished from the luxuriant cedars—undoubtedly a most precious prize. But Enkidu urged Gilgamesh not to listen to the enticements. "Finish him off, slay him!" he shouted to Gilgamesh. "Do it before the leader Enlil hears it in Nippur!" And seeing Gilgamesh hesitate, "Enkidu Huwawa put to death."

Figure 42

"Lest the gods be filled with fury at them," and as a way to "set up an eternal memorial," the comrades cut down one of the cedar trees, made poles of it, and formed of them a raft with a cabin on it. In the cabin they put the head of Huwawa, and pushed the raft down a stream. "Let the Euphrates carry it to Nippur," they said.

And thus rid of the monstrous guardian of the path to the Landing Place, the two stopped to rest at the stream. Gilgamesh "washed his filthy hair, he cleaned his gear, shook his locks over his back, threw away his dirty clothes, put on fresh ones. He clothed himself in robes and tied on a sash." There was no need to rush; the way to the "secret abode of the Anunnaki" was no longer blocked.

He totally forgot that the place was also "the crossroads of Ishtar."

Using the Landing Place for her sky-roaming, Ishtar was watching Gilgamesh from her skychamber (Fig. 42). Whether or not she had witnessed the battle with Huwawa is not reported. But she was certainly watching Gilgamesh take off his clothes, bathe and groom himself, clothe himself in fine robes. And "glorious Ishtar raised an eye at the beauty of Gilgamesh." Wasting no time, she directly addressed Gilgamesh: "Come, Gilgamesh, be thou my lover! Grant me the fruit of thy love!"

If he were to become her lover, Ishtar promised, kings, princes, and nobles would bow to him; he shall be given a chariot adorned with lapis and gold; his flocks would double and quadruple; the produce of field and mountain shall be his fill ... But, to her surprise, Gilgamesh turned down her invitation. Listing only the few worldly possessions that he could offer her, he foresaw her quick tiring of him and his lovemaking. Sooner or later, he said, she would get rid of him as of "a shoe that pinches the foot of its owner."

I will obtain for you eternal life, Ishtar announced. But that, too, could not convince Gilgamesh. Listing all her known lovers, whom she used and discarded, "which of your lovers lasted forever?" Gilgamesh asked, "which of your masterful paramours went to heaven?" And, he concluded, "if you will love me, you shall treat me just like them."

"When Ishtar heard this, Ishtar was enraged, and to the skies flew off.'" In her fury at being rejected, she appealed to Anu to punish Gilgamesh, who "had disgraced me." She asked Anu for the Bull of Heaven so that it might smite Gilgamesh. At first Anu refused, but in the end he yielded to the pleas and threats of Ishtar, and "put the reins of the Bull of Heaven in her hands."

(GUD.ANNA, the Sumerian term employed in the ancient texts, is commonly translated "Bull of Heaven," but it could also be understood to more literally mean the "Bull of Anu." The term was also the Sumerian name for the celestial constellation of the Bull (Taurus), which was associated with Enlil. The "Bull of Heaven" that was kept in the Cedar Forest guarded by Enlil's monster could have been a specially selected bull, or the "prototype" bull seeded from Nibiru to create bulls on Earth. Its counterpart in Egypt was the sacred Apis Bull.)

Attacked by the Bull of Heaven, the comrades forgot all about the Landing Place and the search for Immortality, and fled for their lives. Aided by Shamash, the "distance of a month and fifteen days in three days they traversed." Arriving in Uruk, Gilgamesh sought protection behind its ramparts while Enkidu waited outside, to face the attacker. Hundreds of the city's warriors came out too; but the snorts of the Bull of Heaven opened up pits in the earth into which the warriors

Figure 43

fell. Seeing an opportunity when the sky monster turned, Enkidu leapt on its back and seized it by the horns. With all its might, and whipping its tail, the Bull of Heaven fought Enkidu off. Desperate, Enkidu called out to Gilgamesh: "Plunge your sword in, between the base of the horns and the neck tendons!"

It was a call that has echoed in bullfighting arenas to this very day . . .

In this first-ever recorded bullfight, "Enkidu seized the Bull of Heaven by its thick tail and spun it around. Then Gilgamesh, like a butcher, between neck and horns thrust his sword." The heavenly creature was defeated, and Gilgamesh ordered celebrations in Uruk. But "Ishtar, in her abode, set up a wailing; she arranged a weeping over the Bull of Heaven."

Among the numerous cylinder seals that have been unearthed throughout the Near East that depict scenes from the *Epic of Gilgamesh,* one (found in a Hittite trading outpost on the border with Assyria, Fig. 43) shows Ishtar addressing Gilgamesh with the seminaked Enkidu watching; in the space between the goddess and Gilgamesh the severed head of Huwawa, as well as that of the Bull of Heaven, are shown.

And so it was that while Gilgamesh was celebrating in Uruk, the gods held a council. Anu said: "Because they have slain the Bull of Heaven and Huwawa, the two of them must

die.'' Enlil said: "Enkidu shall die, let Gilgamesh not die.''
But Shamash, accepting part of the blame, said: "Why should
innocent Enkidu die?''

While the gods discussed his fate, Enkidu was struck with
a coma. Hallucinating, he envisioned being sentenced to
death. But the final decision was to commute his death sentence to hard labor in the "Land of Mines," a place where
copper and turquoise were obtained by backbreaking toil in
dark tunnels.

Here the saga, already filled with more dramatic and unexpected twists and turns than the best of thrillers, took yet
another unforeseen turn. The "Land of Mines" was located
in the Fourth Region, the Sinai peninsula; and it dawned on
Gilgamesh that here was a second chance for him to join the
gods and attain immortality, for the "Land of Living"—the
Spaceport where the *Shem* rocketships were based, commanded by Shamash—was also there, in the Fourth Region.

So, if Shamash could arrange for him to accompany Enkidu, he (Gilgamesh) would reach the Land of Living! Seeing
this unique opportunity, Gilgamesh appealed to Shamash:

> *O Shamash,*
> *The Land I wish to enter;*
> *be thou my ally!*
> *The Land which with the cool cedars is aligned,*
> *I wish to enter; be thou my ally!*
> *In the places where the* Shems *have been raised,*
> *Let me set up my* Shem!

When Shamash responded by describing to Gilgamesh the
hazards and difficulties of the land route, Gilgamesh had a
bright idea: He and Enkidu would sail there by boat! A
Magan boat—a "ship of Egypt"—was outfitted. And, accompanied by fifty heroes as sailors and protectors, the two
comrades sailed away. The route, by all indications, was
down the Persian Gulf, around the Arabian peninsula, and up
the Red Sea until the Sinai coast was to be reached. But the
planned voyage was not to be.

When Enlil demanded that "Enkidu shall die," and the
death sentence was commuted to hard labor in the Land of

Figures 44a and 44b

Mines, it was decreed by the gods that two emissaries, "clothed like birds, with wings for garments," shall take Enkidu by the hand and carry him thereto (Fig. 44a). The sea voyage contradicted that, and the wrath of Enlil was yet to come. Now, as the ship sailed close to the Arabian coast and the sun was setting, those on board could see someone— "if a man he be, or a god he be"—standing on a mound "like a bull," equipped with a ray-emitting device (Fig. 44b). As if by an unseen hand, the "three ply cloth" that was the ship's sail suddenly tore apart. Next, the ship itself was thrust on its side and capsized. It sank fast, like a stone in water, and all aboard with it, except Gilgamesh and Enkidu. As Gilgamesh swam out of the ship and up, dragging Enkidu along, he could see the others seated where they were, "as though living creatures." In the sudden death, they just froze in whatever position they were.

The two sole survivors reached the shore and spent the night on an unknown coast discussing what to do. Gilgamesh was undeterred in his desire to reach the Land of Living; Enkidu advised that they seek the way back to Uruk. But the die was already cast for Enkidu; his limbs became numb, his insides were disintegrating. Gilgamesh exhorted his comrade to hold on to life, but to no avail.

For six days and seven nights Gilgamesh mourned Enkidu; then he walked away, roaming the wilderness aimlessly, wondering not when but how he too shall die: "When I die, shall I not be like Enkidu?"

Little did he know that after all the previous adventures, after the diverse Divine Encounters, after the dreams and visions, the real and the imagined, the fights and the flights, and now all alone—that only now his most memorable saga was about to begin.

How long Gilgamesh roamed aimlessly in the wilderness, the ancient epic does not tell. He trod unbeaten paths encountering no man, hunting for food. "What mountains he had climbed, what streams he had crossed, no man can know," the ancient scribes noted. Finally he took hold of himself. "Must I lay my head inside the earth and sleep through all the years?" he asked himself, and join his comrade in death, or would the gods "let mine eyes behold the sun?" Again he was filled with determination to avoid a mortal's fate by reaching the Land of Living.

Guided by the rising and setting sun—the celestial counterpart of Shamash—Gilgamesh trekked in a purposeful manner. As day followed day, the terrain began to change: the flat desert wilderness, home of lizards and scorpions, was ending and he could see mountains in the distance. The wildlife was also changing. "When at night he arrived at the mountain pass, Gilgamesh saw lions and grew afraid."

> *He lifted his head to Sin and prayed:*
> *"To the place where the gods rejuvenate*
> *my steps are directed . . .*
> *Preserve thou me!"*

The change from Shamash to Sin (the father of Shamash) as the protecting deity to whom the prayer is addressed is made in the text without pause or comment; and we are left to presume that somehow Gilgamesh had realized that he had reached a region dedicated to Sin.

Gilgamesh "went to sleep and awoke from a dream," in which he saw himself "rejoice with life." He took it as a favorable omen from Sin, that he would manage to cross the mountain pass despite the lions roaming there. Gathering his weapons, "Gilgamesh like an arrow descended among the lions," striking the beasts with all his strength: "He smote them, he hacked away at them." But by midday his weapons shattered and Gilgamesh threw them away. Two lions were

Figures 45a, 45b, 45c, and 45d

still left facing him; and Gilgamesh now had to fight them with his bare hands.

The fight with the lions, in which Gilgamesh was the victor, was commemorated by artists throughout the ancient Near East, and not only in Mesopotamia (Fig. 45a). It was depicted by the Hittites (Fig. 45b) to the north, the Cassites in Luristan to the east (Fig. 45c), even in ancient Egypt (Fig. 45d). In later times such a feat—vanquishing lions with bare hands—was attributed in the Bible only to Samson, he of the god-given superhuman power (Judges 14:5–6).

Clad in the skin of one of the lions, Gilgamesh traversed the mountain pass. In the distance he saw a body of water, like a vast lake. In the plain beyond the inland sea he could see a city "closed-up about," a city surrounded by a fortified wall. It was, the epic text explains, a city where "the temple to Sin was dedicated." Outside the city, "down by the low-lying sea," Gilgamesh could see an inn. As he approached the inn, he could see inside "Siduri, the ale-woman." There were vat stands, fermentation vats, inside; and the ale-woman, Siduri, was holding a jug of ale and a bowl of yellow porridge. Gilgamesh paced around, seeking a way to enter; but Siduri, seeing an unkempt man wearing a lion's skin, "his belly shrunk, his face like that of a wayfarer from afar," was frightened and bolted the door. With great difficulty Gilgamesh managed to convince her of his true identity.

Fed and rested, Gilgamesh told Siduri all about his adventures, from the first journey to the Cedar Forest, the slaying of Huwawa and of the Bull of Heaven, the second voyage and the death of Enkidu, followed by his wanderings and the slaying of the lions. His destination, he explained, was the Land of Living; Immortality could be attained there, for Utnapishtim of Deluge fame was still living there. What is the way to the Land of Living? Gilgamesh asked Siduri. Must he go the long and hazardous way around the sea, or could he sail across it? "Now, ale-woman, which is the way to Utnapishtim? Give me the directions!"

Crossing the sea, the ale-woman answered, was not possible, for its waters are "the Waters of Death:"

> *Never, Gilgamesh, has there been a crossing;*
> *From days of long ago,*
> *no one arrived from across the sea.*
> *Valiant Shamash did cross the sea,*
> *but other than Shamash, who can cross it?*

As Gilgamesh fell silent, Siduri revealed to him that there could be a way, after all, to cross the Waters of Death: Utnapishtim has a boatman; his name is Urshanabi. Urshanabi can cross the Waters of Death because "with him are the Stone Things." He comes across to pick up *Urnu* (meaning unclear) in the woods. Go and wait for him, Siduri said to Gilgamesh, "let him see your face." If it suits him, he will take you across. So advised, Gilgamesh went to the shore to await the boatman Urshanabi.

When Urshanabi saw him, he wondered who Gilgamesh was, and Gilgamesh told him the long story. Convinced of the true identity of Gilgamesh and his legitimate wish to reach the Land of Living, Urshanabi took Gilgamesh aboard. But no sooner than this was done, Urshanabi accused Gilgamesh of smashing the "Stone Things" required for the crossing. Reprimanding Gilgamesh, Urshanabi told him to go back to the forest, cut to shape 120 poles; and use up the poles in groups of twelve as they sailed across. After three days, they reached the other side.

Where shall I go now? Gilgamesh asked Urshanabi. Urshanabi told him to go straight ahead until he reached "a regular

way" that leads toward "the Great Sea." He was to follow
that road until he reached two stone columns that serve as
markers. Turning there, he would come to a town named (in
the Hittite recension of the epic) Itla, sacred to the god Ullu-
Yah. That god's permission was needed in order to cross
into the Forbidden Region where Mount Mashu was; that,
Urshanabi said, is your destination.

Itla proved a mixed blessing for Gilgamesh. Arriving there
he ate and drank, washed and changed to proper attire. On
the advice of Shamash, he offered sacrifices to Ullu-Yah
(meaning, perhaps, "He of the Peaks"). But the Great God,
learning of the king's wish for a *Shem,* vetoed the idea. Seeking the intercession of Shamash, Gilgamesh then pleaded with
the gods for an alternative: "Let me take the road to
Utnapishtim, the son of Ubar-Tutu!" And that, after some
deliberation, was permitted.

After a journey of six days, Gilgamesh could see the sacred
mountain of which Urshanabi the boatman had spoken:

> *The name of the mountain is* Mashu.
> *At the mountain of Mashu he arrived,*
> *where daily the* Shems *he watched*
> *as they depart and come in.*
> *On high, to the Celestial Band it is connected;*
> *below, to the Lower World it is bound.*

There was a way to go inside the mountain, but the entrance was guarded by awesome "Rocket-men:"

> *Rocket-men guard its gate.*
> *Their terror is awesome, their glance is death.*
> *Their dreaded spotlight sweeps the mountains.*
> *They watch over Shamash as he ascends and descends.*

Caught in the sweep of the deadly spotlight, Gilgamesh
shielded his face; unharmed, he paced toward the Rocket-men
(a scene depicted on a cylinder seal might have illustrated this
episode—Fig. 46). They were astounded to see that the death
rays did not affect Gilgamesh, and realized that "he who
comes, the flesh of the gods is his body." Allowed to ap-

proach, they questioned Gilgamesh; and he told them who he was and that he was indeed two-thirds divine. "On account of Utnapishtim, my forefather, have I come," he told the guards, "he who the congregation of the gods has joined; about Death and Life I wish to ask him."

"No mortal has passed through the mountain's inaccessible tract!" the guards told Gilgamesh. However, recognizing that he was not a mere mortal, they let him through. "The gate of the Mount is open to thee!" they announced.

The "inaccessible tract" was a subterranean "path of Shamash." The passage through it lasted twelve double-hours. "The darkness was dense, there was no light." Gilgamesh could not see "ahead or behind." In the eighth double-hour something made him scream with fear. In the ninth double-hour "he felt a north wind fanning his face"—he was nearing an opening to the sky. In the eleventh double-hour he could see dawn breaking. Finally, in the twelfth double-hour, "it had grown bright; he came out in front of the sun."

Out of the subterranean passage through the sacred mountain, in sunlight, Gilgamesh came upon an incredible sight. He saw "an enclosure of the gods" wherein there was a garden; but the "garden" was made up entirely of artificially carved precious stones: "All kinds of thorny Prickly Bushes

Figure 46

were visible, blooming with gemstones; Carnelian bore fruit hanging in clusters, its vines too beautiful to behold. The foliage was of lapis lazuli; and grapes, too lush to look at, of . . . stones were made." The partly damaged verses go on to list other kinds of fruit-bearing trees and the variety of precious stones—white and red and green—of which they were made. Pure water ran through the garden, and in its midst he saw "like a Tree of Life and a Tree of . . . that of *An-gug* stones were made."

Enthralled and amazed, Gilgamesh walked about the garden. Clearly, he found himself in a simulated Garden of Eden!

Unbeknown to him, he was being watched by Utnapishtim. "Utnapishtim was looking from a distance, pondered and spoke to himself, took counsel with himself:" who is this man and how did he show up here? he wondered; "he who comes here is not one of my men"—no one who has been with him on the ark . . .

As he approached Gilgamesh, Gilgamesh was astounded: the hero of the Deluge from thousands of years ago was not at all older than he, Gilgamesh, was! "He said to him, to Utnapishtim, the Far-Distant: As I look upon thee, Utnapishtim, thou art no different at all; even as I art thou!"

But who are you, why and how did you get here? Utnapishtim wanted to know. And, as he had done with Si-duri and the boatman, Gilgamesh related the whole story of his Kingship, ancestry, comradeship with Enkidu, and the adventures in search of Immortality, including the latest ones. "So I thought of going to see Utnapishtim, the Far-Distant, of whom people speak," Gilgamesh concluded. Now, he told Utnapishtim, tell me the secret of your Immortality! Tell me "how you came to join the congregation of the gods, and attained eternal life?"

> *Utnapishtim spoke to him, to Gilgamesh:*
> *I will reveal to thee, Gilgamesh,*
> *a hidden matter, a secret of the gods*
> *I will tell thee.*

And then followed the story of the Deluge reported in the first person by Utnapishtim, in all its details from beginning to end, until Enlil, on the Mount of Salvation where the ark came to rest, "holding me by the hand, took me aboard the ship; he took my wife aboard and made her kneel by my side. Standing between us, he touched our foreheads to bless us. Hitherto Utnapishtim has been mortal (Enlil said), henceforth Utnapishtim and his wife shall be as we gods are; Utnapishtim shall reside far away, at the mouth of the rivers. Thus they took me and made me reside far away, at the mouth of the rivers."

That, Unapishtim concluded, is the whole truth about his escaping a mortal's fate. "But now, who will for thy sake call the gods to Assembly, that the Life which thou seekest thou mayest find?"

Realizing that only a decree of the gods meeting in Assembly could give him Immortality, and not his own searches, Gilgamesh passed out; for a week he lay unconscious. When he came to, Utnapishtim called upon Urshanabi the boatman to take Gilgamesh back, "that he may return safe on the way by which he came." But as Gilgamesh was ready to depart, Utnapishtim, pitying him, decided to disclose to him yet another secret: *Everlasting life is attained not by being immortal—it is attained by staying forever young!*

> *Utnapishtim said to him, to Gilgamesh:*
> *Thou hast come hither, toiling and straining.*
> *What shall I give thee to take back to your land?*
> *Let me disclose, Gilgamesh,*
> *a closely-guarded hidden matter—*
> *a secret of the gods I will tell thee:*
> *A plant there is,*
> *like a prickly berrybush is its root.*
> *Its thorns are like a brier-vine's;*
> *thine hands the thorns will prick.*
> *[But] if with thine own hands the plant*
> *you could obtain,*
> *Rejuvenation you will find.*

The plant grew underwater, perhaps in the well or spring in the splendid garden. Some kind of a pipe led to the source or depths of these Waters of Life. No sooner did Gilgamesh hear the secret, than he "opened the water-pipe, tied heavy

stones to his feet; they dragged him down to the abyss."
And there he saw the plant.

> *He took the plant himself*
> *though it pricked his hands.*
> *He cut the heavy stones from his feet;*
> *the second one cast him back*
> *to where he had come from.*

Urshanabi, who had been summoned by Utnapishtim, was
waiting for him. Triumphant and exhilarated, Gilgamesh
showed him the Plant of Rejuvenation. Overcome with excite-
ment, he said to the boatman:

> *Urshanabi,*
> *This plant of all plants is unique:*
> *By it a man can regain the breath of life!*
> *I will take it to ramparted Uruk,*
> *there the plant to cut and eat.*
> *Let its name be called*
> *"Man becomes young in old age."*
> *Of this plant I shall eat*
> *and to my youthful state shall I return.*

With these high hopes for rejuvenation the two started on
the way back. "At thirty leagues they stopped for the night.
Gilgamesh saw a well whose water was cool. He went down
into it to bathe in the water. A snake smelt the fragrance of
the plant; it came up silently and carried off the plant. As it
took it away, the snake shed its scaly skin." It was indeed
a rejuvenating plant; but it was the snake, not Gilgamesh,
who ended up rejuvenated . . .

> *Thereupon Gilgamesh sits down and weeps,*
> *his tears running down his face.*
> *He took the hand of Urshanabi the boatman.*
> *"For whom" (he asked) "have my hands toiled?*
> *For whom is spent the blood of my heart?*
> *For myself I have not obtained a boon;*
> *For a snake the boon I affected."*

Brooding over his misfortune, Gilgamesh recalled an incident during his dive for the plant "which must have been an omen." "While I was opening the pipe, arranging the gear," he told Urshanabi, "I found a door seal; it must have been placed as an omen for me—a sign to withdraw, to give up." Now Gilgamesh realized that he was not fated to obtain the Plant of Rejuvenation; and having plucked it out of its waters, he was fated to lose it.

When he finally returned to ramparted Uruk, Gilgamesh sat down and had the scribes write down his odyssey. "Let me make known to the country him who the Tunnel had seen; of him who knows the waters let me the full story tell." And it was with those introductory words that the *Epic of Gilgamesh* was recorded, to be read, translated, rewritten, illustrated, and read again for generations thereafter—for all to know that Man, even if two-thirds divine, cannot change his fate.

The *Epic of Gilgamesh* is replete with geographical markers that enhance its authenticity and identify the targets of that ancient search for Immortality.

The first destination was the Landing Place in the Cedar Forest, in the Cedar Mountains. There was only one such place in the whole of the ancient Near East, renowned for its unique cedars: Lebanon (whose national emblem, to this very day, is the cedar tree). Lebanon is specifically mentioned by name as the land the two comrades reached after the journey of seventeen days from Uruk. In another verse, describing how the earth shook as the skyrocket was launched, the facing peaks "Sirara and Lebanon" are described as "splitting apart." In the Bible (Psalms 27) the majestic Voice of the Lord is described as "breaking the cedars of Lebanon" and making "Lebanon and Sirion skip like a calf." There is no doubt that *Sirion* is Hebrew for *Sirara* in the Mesopotamian text.

There is also no doubt that a Landing Place had existed there, for the simple reason that that vast platform is still there to this very day. Located at a place nowadays called Baalbek, the immense stone platform, some *five million* square feet in area, rests upon massive stone blocks that

Figure 47

Figure 48

weigh hundreds of tons; three stone blocks, weighing more
than one thousand tons each and known as the Trilithons
(Fig. 47), were quarried in a valley miles away, where one
of the colossal stones still sticks out of the ground, its quar-
rying not having been completed (Fig. 48). There is no modern equipment that can lift such weight; yet in bygone days

Figure 49

"someone"—local lore says "the giants"—quarried, lifted, and emplaced these stone blocks with great precision.

Greeks and Romans followed Canaanites and others before them in deeming the platform a sacred site, on which to build and rebuild temples to the great gods. We have no picture of what had stood there in the days of Gilgamesh; but we do know what had been there afterward, in Phoenician times. We know, because the platform, with an enclosure, held a skyrocket poised upon a crossbeamed pedestal—as depicted on a coin from Byblos (Fig. 49).

The most telling geographical detail in the second journey of Gilgamesh is the body of water he had reached after crossing the wilderness. It is described as a "low-lying sea," a sea that looked like "a vast lake." It was called the sea of the "Waters of Death." These are all identifying features of the landlocked sea that is still called the Dead Sea, which is indeed the lowest-lying sea in the world.

In the distance Gilgamesh could see a city that was "closed-up about," a city surrounded by a wall, whose temple was dedicated to Sin. Such a city—one of the oldest in the world—is still there; it is known as Jericho, which in Hebrew (*Yeriho*) means "City of the Moon God," who indeed was Sin; the city was famous for its walls, whose miraculous toppling is recounted in the Bible. (One must also wonder to what extent the biblical tale of the spies of Joshua who hid in the inn of Rahab in Jericho, reflects the brief stay of Gilgamesh at Siduri's inn).

Having crossed the Sea of Death, Gilgamesh followed a way that led "toward the Great Sea." This term too is found in the Bible (e.g. Numbers 34, Joshua 1) and undisputably referred to the Mediterranean Sea. Gilgamesh, however, stopped short of going all the way and instead stopped at the town called Itla in the Hittite recension. Based on archaeological discoveries and the biblical narrative of the Exodus, Itla was the same place that the bible called Kadesh-Barnea; it was an ancient caravan town situated at the border of the restricted Fourth Region in the Sinai peninsula.

One can only speculate whether the mountain to which Gilgamesh was directed, Mount Mashu, bore a name that is almost identical to the Hebrew name of Moses, *Moshe*. The subterranean journey of Gilgamesh inside this sacred mountain, lasting twelve double-hours, is clearly paralleled by the description in the Egyptian *Book of the Dead* of the Pharaoh's subterranean journey through twelve hour-zones. The Pharaohs, like Gilgamesh, asked for a *Shem*—a rocketship—with which to ascend heavenward and join the gods in an eternal abode. Like Gilgamesh before them, the Pharaohs had to cross a body of water and be assisted by a Divine Boatman. There is no doubt that both the Sumerian king's and Egyptian Pharaoh's destination was one and the same, except that they went there from opposite starting points. The destination was the Spaceport in the Sinai peninsula, where the *Shems,* in their underground silos (see Fig. 31) were.

As in pre-Diluvial times (Fig. 25), the post-Diluvial Spaceport (Fig. 50) was also anchored on the peaks of Ararat. But with the plain of Mesopotamia totally covered by muddy waters, the Spaceport was shifted to the firm ground of the Sinai peninsula. Mission Control Center shifted from Nippur to where Jerusalem (JM) is now located. The new landing corridor, anchored at its end on two artificial mountains that are still standing as the two great pyramids of Giza (GZ) and the high peaks in southern Sinai (KT and US), incorporated the immense pre-Diluvial platform of Baalbek in the Cedar Mountains (BK).

It was to the platform at Baalbek and toward the Spaceport (SP) that Gilgamesh had journeyed.

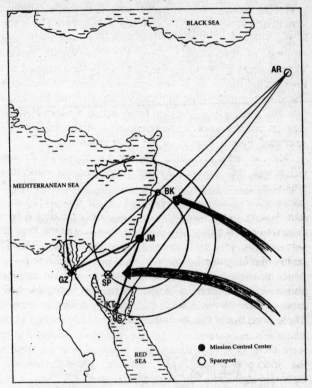

Figure 50

GILGAMESH IN AMERICA

Familiarity with the epic tale of Gilgamesh in South America is one facet of the evidence for prehistoric contacts between the Old and New Worlds.

The hallmark of such familiarity was the depiction of Gilgamesh fighting the lions. Amazingly, such depictions—in a continent that has no lions—have been found in the lands of the Andes.

One concentration of such depictions on stone tablets ("A" and "B" below) has been found in the Chavin de Huantar/Aija area in northern Peru, a major gold-producing area in prehistoric times, where other evidence (statuettes, carvings, petroglyphs) indicates the presence of Old World peoples from 2500 B.C. on; they are similar to the Hittite depictions (Fig. 45b).

Another area where such depictions proliferated was near the southern shores of Lake Titicaca (now in Bolivia), where a great metalworking metropolis—Tiahuanacu—had once flourished. Begun by some accounts well before 4000 B.C. as a gold-processing center, and becoming after 2500 B.C. the world's foremost source of tin, Tiahuanacu was the place where bronze appeared in South America. Among the artifacts discovered there were depictions, in bronze, of Gilgamesh wrestling with lionlike animals ("C" below)—artwork undoubtedly inspired by the Cassite bronzemakers of Luristan (Fig. 45c).

8

ENCOUNTERS IN THE GIGUNU

More than 2,500 years after the epic search for Immortality by Gilgamesh, another legendary king—Alexander of Macedonia—emulated the Sumerian king and Egyptian Pharaohs in the very same arena. In his case, too, the claim to Immortality was based on being partly divine. The evidence suggests that Alexander, through his teacher Aristotle, was aware of the earlier searches; but what he probably did not know was that the root of his specific claim to divine parentage lay in Uruk's GIPAR (''Nighttime House'') and its inner sanctum, the GIGUNU.

Soon after Alexander was crowned king of Macedonia in lieu of the assassinated Philip II, he went to Delphi in Greece to consult its famed Oracle. Only twenty years old at the time, he was shocked to hear the first of several prophecies predicting for him fame, but a very short life. The prophecies served to increase his belief in rumors that had been circulating in the Macedonian court, according to which Philip II was not really his father; but that he was really the son of an Egyptian Pharaoh by name of Nectanebus who had visited the Macedonian court and secretly seduced Olympias, Alexander's mother. And Nectanebus—a master magician and diviner—so the whispering went, was in fact the Egyptian god Amon, who disguised himself as a man in order to sire the future conqueror of the world.

No sooner did Alexander reach Egypt (in 332 B.C.) than, after paying homage to Egyptian gods and priests, he set his course to the oasis of Siwah in the western desert, the seat of a renowned Oracle of Amon. There (so the historians who had accompanied him reported) the great god himself confirmed Alexander's divine parentage. Thus affirmed as truly the son of a god, the Egyptian priests proclaimed him a Divine Pharaoh. But instead of waiting to die and attain immortality in the Afterlife, Alexander set out to find the famed Waters of Life right away. His searches took him to subterranean places filled with magic and angels in the Sinai peninsula, then (on orders of a Winged Man) to Babylon. In the end, as the Delphic Oracle prophesied, he died famous but young.

In his search for immortality Alexander, leaving his troops behind, went toward the Land of Darkness, to find there a mountain called Mushas. At the edge of the desert he left his few trusted companions and proceeded alone. He saw and followed "a straight path that had no wall, and it had no high or low place in it." He walked therein twelve days and twelve nights, at which point "he perceived the radiance of an angel." As he drew nearer the radiance became "a flaming fire," and Alexander realized that he was at the "mountain from which the whole world is surrounded."

Speaking to Alexander from the flaming fire, the angel questioned him, "Who art thou, and for what reason art thou here, O mortal?" and wondered how Alexander had managed "to penetrate into this darkness, which no other mortal hath been able to do." Alexander explained that God himself had guided him and gave him strength to arrive at this place, "which is Paradise." But the angel told him that the Water of Life was somewhere else; "and whosoever drinketh therefrom, if it be but a single drop, shall never die."

To find the "Well of the Water of Life" Alexander needed a savant who knew such secrets, and after much searching such a man was found. Magical and miraculous adventures took place on their way. To be certain that the well is the right one, the two had with them a dead dried fish. One night, reaching a subterranean fountain, and while Alexander was sleeping, the guide tested the water and the fish came alive. Then he himself immersed in the waters, becoming thereby *El Khidr*—"The Evergreen"—the One Who Is Forever Young of Arab legends. In the morning Alexander rushed to the indicated place. It was "inlaid with sapphires and emeralds and jacinths." But there two birds with human features blocked his way. "The land on which you stay belongs to God alone," they announced. Realizing that he could not change his fate, Alexander gave up the search and instead started to build cities bearing his name, thereby to be forever remembered.

The numerous details of the Alexander search that are virtually identical to those of Gilgamesh—the location, the name of the mountain, the twelve periods of the subterranean journey, the winged Birdmen, the questioning by the guards, the immersion in the well of the Waters of Life—indicate a familiarity with the *Epic of Gilgamesh;* not only with the literary work (which continued to survive to our times), but also with the *raison d'être* for the search—the partial divinity, the divine parentage, of Gilgamesh.

Indeed, even the claims by Egyptian Pharaohs that they were fathered by gods or, in the very least, nourished with mother's milk by a goddess, can be traced to the time and place of Gilgamesh; for it was in Uruk that the custom and tradition began with the dynasty to which Gilgamesh belonged.

The Kingship began in Uruk, it will be recalled, when the future city consisted almost entirely only of the sacred precinct. There, according to the Sumerian King Lists, "Mes-kiag-gasher, the son of the god Utu, became high priest as well as king." Then, after reigns by Enmerkar and Lugal-banda and an intermediate reign by the divine Dumuzi, Gilgamesh ascended the throne; and he, as stated, was the son of the goddess Ninsun.

These are astounding revelations, especially in light of the episode of the taking of human wives by the *Nefilim* that caused Enlil to seek the annihilation of Mankind. It took Mankind, the Anunnaki, and the Earth itself millennia to recover from the trauma of the Deluge. It took millennia for the Anunnaki to gradually, and step by careful step, grant Mankind knowledge, technology, domestication, and, finally, full-fledged civilizations. It took the better part of a millennium to develop, in Kish, the institution of Kingship. And then, so unexpectedly, *boom!* Kingship is transferred to Uruk, and the first dynasty is begun by a son of a god (Utu/Shamash) and a human female . . .

While the sexual shenanigans of other deities (some already mentioned, more to come) have been recorded in the

Figure 51

Figure 52

ancient texts, Utu/Shamash does not appear to be one of them. His official spouse and consort was the goddess Aia (Fig. 51) and the texts do not ascribe any infidelities to him. Yet here we encounter a son of his by a human female, a son whose name, functions, and locale are clearly stated. What was going on? Have the taboos been removed, or just ignored by the new generation?

Even more peculiar was the case of Ninsun, the mother of Gilgamesh (Fig. 52). Her own genealogy and the record of her offspring are illustrative of the mixing of generations that was taking place among the Anunnaki—perhaps as a result of the fact that some retained the longevities acquired on Nibiru (and counted in *Sars*), others (the first generation on Earth) partly affected by Earth's shorter cycles, and yet others (third and fourth generations) more Earthlike than Nibiruan.

Figure 53

Anu, who besides his official spouse Antu had numerous concubines and (at least in one instance) ventured even farther afield, had as a result a great number of official and unofficial offspring; we have met so far Enki, Enlil, and Ninmah, all three half brothers and half sister of each other (i.e. born of different mothers). It turns out that Anu had yet another, younger daughter, named Bau, who became the wife of Ninurta, Enlil's son by his half sister Ninmah. As far as one can judge from the texts, Ninurta and Bau (Fig. 53) led an immaculate marriage, unmarred by any infidelities. It was a marriage blessed by two sons and seven daughters, of whom Ninsun (''Lady Wild Cow'') was the best-known one. This genealogy made her at one and the same time a granddaughter of Anu as well as a granddaughter of Anu's son Enlil. (Enlil, it ought to be mentioned here, begot Ninurta on Nibiru; after Enlil had espoused Ninlil on Earth, he was scrupulously monogamous).

No less confusing was the makeup of Ninsun's offspring. On the one hand she was the mother of Gilgamesh. The Sumerian King Lists state that his father was the High Priest of the sacred precinct of Uruk; the *Epic of Gilgamesh* and other narrative texts concerning him assert that his father was Lugalbanda, the third ruler of Uruk. Since the first such ruler, Meskiaggasher, was both High Priest and king, the assumption is that Lugalbanda, too, held both posts. The upshot is that Ninsun, whether officially espoused to the mortal Lugalbanda or not, had sexual relations with him and bore him a son.

But on the other hand Ninsun was also having sex with gods, or at least one god. According to the Sumerian King Lists the young god Dumuzi reigned briefly in Uruk, between Lugalbanda and Gilgamesh. The Lists recognize the full divinity of Dumuzi, for he was a son of Enki. What the Lists do not mention, but what is attested by considerable literary texts dealing with the life, loves, and death of Dumuzi, is that his mother was the goddess Ninsun—the very same goddess who was the mother of Gilgamesh.

Ninsun thus had sexual liaisons with both gods (Enki) and men (Lugalbanda). In this new phase of Divine Encounters, she was emulating not only Utu/Shamash (whose spouse was the goddess Aia, yet had a son by a mortal female), but also Inanna/Ishtar, the twin sister of Utu/Shamash. The fact that all these encounters in one way or another involved Uruk was no accident; for it was in Uruk that the GIGUNU—the "Chamber of Nighttime Pleasures"—was first established in the Gipar.

Unlike Utu/Shamash and Ninsun, Inanna/Ishtar is not mentioned in the Sumerian King Lists in connection with Uruk; but in the *Epic of Gilgamesh* she joins the two as a featured divine actor in the saga. In a way she belonged in the tale perhaps more than they, for she was the patron-goddess of Uruk and it was due to her that what was only a sacred precinct became a major great city. How she achieved that was described in a text known as "Enki and Inanna" that we shall soon examine; but first one should explain how Inanna became associated with Uruk—indeed, how she came to be called "Inanna" to begin with.

When Kingship was transferred from Kish to Uruk at the beginning of the third millennium B.C., Uruk consisted only of a sacred precinct, the *Kullab*. That sacred precinct had existed by then for almost a thousand years, for it was originally built mainly to accommodate Anu and Antu on their state visit to Earth. Clay tablets found in the ruins of Uruk, copies of earlier texts recording the pomp and circumstance of the event, retained enough detail to follow the carefully prescribed rites and ceremonies as well as the nature of the sacred compound and its various buildings. Besides temples and shrines, each with specified functions, the compound also included special sleeping quarters for the divine visitors. The two of them, however, do not seem to have shared the same bedroom.

Once the banquet and other ceremonies were completed and the meal of the night was served, the two divine visitors were led through the main courtyard to two separate courts. Antu was escorted to the "House of the Golden Bed," and "the Divine Daughters of Anu and the Divine Daughters of Uruk" kept watch outside till daybreak. Anu was escorted by male gods to his own quarters, a house known as the *Gipar;* we know from a number of Sumerian and Akkadian texts that it was a "taboo" place, a harem if you will (for that, "taboo," is the meaning of the Arabic word "harim")—the place where the *Entu,* a chosen virgin, was awaiting the god.

In later times the Entu was a daughter of the king, and her role as a Hierodule, a "sacred maiden," was deemed a great honor. In the case of Anu and his visit to the Kullab, however, it was not a mortal female who was chosen to await him in the Gipar; it was his great-granddaughter Irninni. They spent the night in the closed-off chamber inside the Gipar, the Gigunu ("Chamber of Nighttime Pleasures"). And after that Irninni was renamed *IN.ANNA*—"Anu's Beloved."

While we may view the encounter as an abhorrent case of incest, it was not so deemed at the time. Sumerian hymns extolled the fact that Inanna was Anu's beloved, his beautiful Hierodule. A *Hymn to Ishtar* written on a tablet from Uruk (tablet AO.4479 in the Louvre Museum) described Ishtar "clothed with love, feathered with seduction, a goddess of joy," "with Anu together occupying the closed-off Gigunu, the Chamber of Joy, as the other gods stand in front." Indeed, another text (AO.6458) reveals that the very idea of selecting Irninni for the honor of sleeping with Anu was not at all Anu's idea—but that of Ishtar herself. It was through the other gods that she was introduced to Anu, and it was they who persuaded Anu to agree . . .

Since Anu (and Antu) were only visiting, they had no permanent need for the E.ANNA temple; and so it was that as a reward, Anu granted use of the temple to Inanna:

*After the Lord had assigned
a great destiny to the daughter of Sin,
the temple Eanna he bestowed on her
as a gift of betrothal.*

With this gift of the Eanna temple came the Gipar house, "a place of fragrant woods," and its inner Chamber of Nighttime Pleasures, the Gigunu; and in time Inanna put the place to good use.

But a sacred precinct was not a city, and the Sumerian King Lists record that it was only the son of the first priestking, Enmerkar, "who built Uruk." It was then that Inanna decided that if Uruk was her cult center, it ought to be a full-fledged center of urban civilization. To achieve that she needed the ME's.

The ME's were portable objects which held all the knowledge and other aspects of a high civilization. In the current state of modern technology, one can envision them as some kind of computer disks or memory chips which, in spite of their minute size, hold vast amounts of information. In a few decades, with more advanced technology, one might compare them to some other marvelous store of information (yet to be invented). When Nippur was to become (after the Deluge) a City of Men, Enlil complained to Anu that Enki was keeping all the ME's to himself, using them solely to enhance Eridu and Enki's hideaway in the Abzu; and Enki was forced to share those essential ME's with Enlil. Now that Inanna wished to make Uruk a great urban center, she set out to Enki's abode to pry some essential ME's out of her greatuncle.

A text known as "Inanna and Enki" and subtitled by modern scholars "The Transfer of the Arts of Civilization from Eridu to Erech" describes how Inanna journeyed in her "Boat of Heaven" to the Abzu in southeastern Africa, where Enki had secreted away the ME's. Realizing that Inanna was coming to call on him unchaperoned—"the maiden, all alone, has directed her step to the Abzu"—Enki ordered his chamberlain to prepare a banquet meal, with plenty of wine made of sweet dates. After Inanna and Enki had feasted and Enki's heart became happy with drink, Inanna brought up the subject of the ME's.

Gracious with drink, Enki presented to her some ME's that would make Uruk a seat of Kingship: the ME for "Lordship," the ME for "the exalted and enduring tiara," the ME for "the throne of Kingship;" and "bright Inanna took them"—but asked for more. As Inanna worked her charms on her aging host, Enki made to her a second presentation; this time he gave her the ME's needed for "the exalted scepter and staff, the exalted shrine, and righteous Rulership." And "bright Inanna took them too." As the feasting and drinking went on, Enki parted with another seven ME's that provided for the functions and attributes of a Divine Lady— the status of a Great Goddess: a temple and its rituals, priests and attendants; justice and courts; music and arts; masonry and woodworking; metalworking, leatherwork and weaving; scribeship and mathematics; and last but not least, weapons and the art of warfare.

Holding in her hands all these essentials for a high civilization, Inanna slipped away and took off in her Boat of Heaven back to Uruk. When Enki sobered up and realized what he had done, Enki ordered his chamberlain to pursue Inanna in her "Great Heavenly Skychamber" and retrieve the ME's. He caught up with her in Eridu, back in Sumer. But Inanna handed the ME's to her pilot, who flew off to Uruk while Inanna kept arguing with the chamberlain in Eridu. The people of Uruk forever recalled how their city became a seat of Kingship and civilization in a hymn titled *Lady of the ME's;* it was read responsively by the congregation on festive occasions:

> *Lady of the ME's,*
> *Queen brightly resplendent.*
> *Righteous, clothed in radiance,*
> *Beloved of Heaven and Earth.*
> *Hierodule of Anu,*
> *Wearing great adorations.*
> *For the exalted tiara appropriate,*
> *For the high-priesthood suitable.*
> *The seven ME's she attained,*

> *In her hand she is holding.*
> *Lady of the great ME's,*
> *Of them she is a guardian.*

Whether Enki actually managed to seduce Inanna is not clear (an assumption that he did could help resolve the enigma of who the mother of Enki's son Ningishzidda was). It does seem certain that as a result of her experiences with Anu and Enki, Inanna's femininity was aroused. As Anu's Beloved, she was made the patron-goddess of the city of Aratta in the Third Region (the Indus Valley civilization). One purpose of seeking the ME-tablets for Uruk was to make Uruk a major center so that Inanna could reign where it really mattered, not in faraway Aratta. Several texts have been found dealing with the contest of wills between the new king of Uruk, Enmerkar ("He who built Uruk") and the king of Aratta; the prize was not simply where Inanna would spend her time—but also where she would engage in lovemaking with the king.

In one passage in the text called *Enmerkar and the Lord of Aratta* the latter, sure of being the favorite of Inanna, taunted Enmerkar thus:

> *He will live with Inanna*
> *[separated] by a wall;*
> *I will live with Inanna*
> *in the lapis-lazuli house in Aratta.*
> *He will gaze upon Inanna only in a dream;*
> *I will lie with her sweetly on an ornate bed.*

It appears that these liaisons were frowned upon by Inanna's parents and, even more so, by her brother Utu/Shamash. When he reprimanded her, Inanna retorted by asking who will then take care of her sexual needs—

> *As for my vulva—*
> *Who will plough the hillock for me?*
> *My vulva, a watered ground,*
> *who will place the ox there?*

To which Utu had an answer: "O lordly maiden, "he said, "Dumuzi, of lordly seed, he will plow it for you."

DUMUZI ("Son who is Life"), a shepherd-god whose domain was in the African lands of Enki's clan, was—as we have noted above—the son of Ninsun, and thus partly an Enlilite. If there had been a hidden agenda to the proposed union, Utu did not belabor it; instead he extolled the merits of having a shepherd as a husband: "His cream is good, his milk is bright." But Inanna was thinking of a farmer-god as a husband: "I, the maiden, a farmer will marry," she announced; "the farmer grows many plants, the farmer grows much grain."

In the end, genealogy and the peace dividend prevailed, and Inanna and Dumuzi were engaged.

The poetic texts dealing with the courtship, love, and marriage of Inanna and Dumuzi—texts of which quite a collection has been unearthed—read as the best love songs of all time, explicit yet tender. When, after the parental approval was given on both sides, the marriage was proclaimed, Inanna awaited the consummation of the marriage in the Gipar in Uruk. In anticipation of the moment, Inanna, "dancing and singing, sent a message to her father" about the Gipar:

> In my house, my Gipar-house,
> my fruitful bed will be set up.
> With plants the color of lapis-lazuli
> it shall be covered.
> I will bring there my sweetheart;
> He will put his hand by my hand,
> he will put his heart by my heart.
> In my house, in my Gipar-house,
> let him "make it long" for me.

The great love between scions of the warring clans—a granddaughter of Enlil, a son of Enki—meant, no doubt, to enhance the peace between the two camps—did not last long. Marduk, the Firstborn of Enki and the claimant to supremacy over all the regions, opposed the union from the very beginning. When Dumuzi went back to his pastoral domain in Africa, promising Ishtar to make her Queen of Egypt, Inanna

was elated but Marduk was enraged. Using an indiscretion
by Dumuzi as a pretext, Marduk sent "sheriffs" to arrest
Dumuzi and bring him to trial. But Dumuzi, having seen
death in an omen-dream, tried to escape and hide. In the
ensuing pursuit, Dumuzi was accidentally killed.

When the news reached Inanna, she raised a great wailing.
So great was the shock and grief also among the people, to
whom this Romeo-and-Juliet love affair came to symbolize
Love and its joys, that the anniversary of Dumuzi's death
became a day of mourning for a long time thereafter. Almost
two thousand years after the event the Prophet Ezekiel was
abhorred to see the women of Israel sitting and "weeping
for Tammuz" (the Hebrew rendering of Dumuzi).

It took Inanna a long time to get over her grief; and in
her search for consolation, she turned to the Gipar and its
Gigunu chamber as the place where she could forget her lost
love. There she perfected the rites of sex to a new form of
Divine Encounter. It came to be known as the rite of the
Sacred Marriage.

When Ishtar invited Gilgamesh "come, be my lover," he
refused by listing her many previous lovers whom she used
and discarded. It began, Gilgamesh pointed out, after the
death of Dumuzi/Tammuz, "the lover of your youth." For
him, Gilgamesh continued, "thou hast ordained a wailing
year after year." And it was, the text implies, on those anniversaries that Ishtar invited man after man to spend the night
with her. "Come, let us enjoy your vigor! Put your hand and
touch my vulva!" she would tell them. But, Gilgamesh asked,
"which lover did you love forever? Which of your paramours
pleased you all the time?" Then he mentioned some of those
discarded lovers and their fates: One, a shepherd, had his
"wing" broken after he had spent the night with her. Another, strong as a lion, was buried in a pit. A third one was
smitten and turned into a wolf; yet another, "your father's
gardener," was hit and turned into a frog. "And how about
me?" Gilgamesh asked at the end, "you will love me and
then treat me just like them." It was no wonder that with
such a reputation, Ishtar was as often as not depicted by

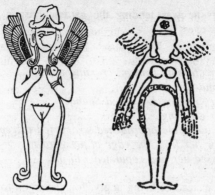

Figure 54

ancient artists as a naked beauty, taunting and inviting men to see her (Fig. 54).

Between those bittersweet anniversaries, Ishtar spent her time roaming Earth's skies in her Skychamber (see Fig. 42) and thus as often as not depictions showed her as a winged goddess. She was, as mentioned, the city goddess of Aratta in the Indus Valley, and paid there periodic flying visits.

It was on one of her flights to the distant domain that Inanna/Ishtar had a sexual encounter in reverse: *she was raped by a mortal;* and, in such a reversal of roles, the man who did it lived to tell about it.

He is known from historical records as Sargon of Aggade, the founder of a new dynasty that was installed in a new capital (usually called Akkad). In his autobiography, a text in the Akkadian language known by scholars as *The Legend of Sargon,* the king describes the circumstances of his birth in terms that remind us of the story of Moses: "My mother was a high priestess; I knew not my father. My mother, the high priestess who conceived me, in secret she bore me. She set me in a basket of reeds, its lid sealed with bitumen. She cast me into the river; it did not sink [with] me. The river bore me up, it carried me to Akki the irrigator. Akki the irrigator lifted me up when he drew water. Akki the irrigator as a son made me and reared me. Akki, the irrigator, appointed me as his gardener."

Then, as he was tending the garden, Sargon could not believe his eyes:

> *One day the queen,*
> *After crossing heaven, crossing earth,*
> *Inanna—*
> *After crossing Elam and Shubur,*
> *After crossing ...*
> *The hierodule approached weary, fell asleep.*
> *I saw her from the edge of my garden;*
> *I kissed her and copulated with her.*

Inanna, instead of being angry, found Sargon to be a man to her liking. Sumer, its civilization a millennium and a half old by then, needed a strong hand at the helm of its Kingship—a Kingship that, after the glorious one in Uruk, kept changing capitals; the changes led to conflicts among the cities and eventually between their patron-gods. Seeing in Sargon a man of action and resolve, Inanna recommended him as the next king over all of "Sumer and Akkad." He also became her constant lover. As Sargon stated in another text known as the *Sargon Chronicle,* "When I was a gardener, Ishtar granted me her love, and for four and fifty years I exercised Kingship."

It was in the reign of the successors of Sargon as kings of Sumer and Akkad that Inanna/Ishtar incorporated the conjugations with the king into the ceremonies of the New Year Festival, formalizing them into the rite of the Sacred Marriage.

In earlier times it was the gods who gathered to relive and retell, on the occasion of the New Year, the epic of Creation and the odyssey of the Anunnaki in coming to and staying on Earth; the festival was called A.KI.TI—"On Earth build Life." After Kingship was introduced, and after Inanna began to invite the king to her Gigunu, a reenactment of the death of her sex partner—and then his replacement by the king—was incorporated into the festival's proceedings. The essence of the procedure was to find a way to have the king spend the night with the goddess without ending up dead ... On the outcome depended not only the king's personal fate, but also the fate of the land and its people—prosperity and abundance or the lack of them in the coming year.

For the first four days of the festival, the gods alone participated in the reenacts. On the fifth day the king came on the scene, leading the elders and other dignitaries in a procession through a special Way of Ishtar (in Babylon the processional way assumed monumental proportions and architectural grandeur that inspire awe to this day; it has been reconstructed in the Vorderasiatisches Museum in Berlin). Arriving at the main temple, the king was met by the High Priest, who took away the king's insignia and placed them before the deity in the Holy of Holies. Then, returning to the dethroned king, the High Priest struck him in the face and made him kneel down for a ceremony of Atonement in which the king had to recite a list of sins and seek divine forgiveness. Priests then led the king out of town to a pit of symbolic death; the king stayed there imprisoned while above the gods debated his Destiny. On the ninth day he reemerged, was given back his insignia and royal robes, and led back the procession to the city. There, at evetime, washed and scented, he was led to the Gipar in the sacred precinct.

At the entrance to the Gigunu he was met by Inanna's personal attendant, who made the following appeal to the goddess in behalf of the king:

> *The sun has gone to sleep,*
> *the day has passed.*
> *As in bed you gaze upon him,*
> *as you caress him—*
> *give Life unto the king . . .*
> *May the king whom you have called to heart*
> *enjoy long days at your holy lap . . .*
> *Give him a reign favorable and glorious,*
> *Grant his throne an enduring foundation . . .*
> *May the farmer make the fields productive,*
> *May the shepherd multiply the sheepfolds . . .*
> *In the palace let there be long life.*

The king was then left alone with the goddess in the Gigunu for the conjugal encounter. It lasted the whole night. In the morning the king emerged, for all to see that he had survived the night. The Sacred Marriage had taken place; the king could reign on for another year; the land and people were granted prosperity.

"The Sacred Marriage Rite was celebrated joyously and rapturously all over the ancient Near East for some two thousand years," the great Sumerologist Samuel N. Kramer wrote in *The Sacred Marriage Rite.* Indeed, long after the days of Dumuzi and Gilgamesh, Sumerian kings described poetically the ecstasy of such memorable nights with Ishtar. The biblical Song of Songs described the pleasures of love in the *Ta'annugim* and several of the Prophets foresaw the demise of the "House of *Annugim*" (House of Pleasures) of the "Daughter of Babylon" (Ishtar); and it is apparent to us that the Hebrew term stemmed from the Sumerian *Gigunu,* indicating familiarity with the Chamber of Pleasures and the rite of the Sacred Marriage well into the middle of the first millennium B.C.

In the olden days the Gipar was the separate structure to which the god and his official spouse retired for the night. The gods who stayed monogamous—Enlil, Ninurta—have kept it that way. Ishtar, in her city Uruk, met her betrothed Dumuzi there but turned the inner chamber, the Gigunu, to a place of one-night stands. The changes introduced by Ishtar—the use of the Gipar for a new form of Divine Encounter—gave ideas to some of the *male deities* of that time.

Some of the best-preserved records in this regard concern Nannar/Sin (the father of Inanna/Ishtar) and the Gipar in his sacred precinct in Ur. The role played by the male king in Ishtar's rites was played by an *Entu,* a "God's Lady," (NIN.-DINGIR in Sumerian). Excavations there unearthed the quarters of the Entu in the southeastern part of the sacred precinct, not too far from the ziggurat of Sin and clearly away from the temple-abode of his spouse Ningal. Near the Gigunu of the Entu the archaeologists found a cemetery where generations of Entus were buried. The cemetery, and the uncovered structures, confirmed that the practice of having a "God's Lady" besides the official spouse extended from the early Dynastic Period well into Neo-Babylonian times—a span of time exceeding two millennia.

Herodotus, the fifth century B.C. Greek historian and traveler, described in his writings (*History,* Book I, 178–182) the sacred precinct of Babylon and the temple-ziggurat of Marduk (whom he called ''Jupiter Bellus'')—quite accurately, as modern archaeology has shown. According to his testimony,

> On the topmost tower there is a spacious temple, and inside the temple stands a couch of unusual size, richly adorned, with a golden table by its side. There is no statue of any kind set up in the place, nor is the chamber occupied of nights by any one but a single native woman, who, as the Chaldeans, the priests of this god affirm, is chosen for himself by the deity out of all the women of the land.

> They also declare—but I for my part do not credit it— that the god comes down in person into this chamber, and sleeps upon the couch. This is like the story told by the Egyptians of what takes place in their city of Thebes, where a woman always passes the night in the temple of the Theban Jupiter. In each case the woman is said to be debarred all intercourse with men. It is also like the custom of Patara, in Lycia, where the priestess who delivers the oracles, during the time that she is so employed ... is shut up in the temple every night.

Although the statements by Herodotus give the impression that any maiden in the lands could have qualified for this widespread practice, it was not really so.

One of the inscriptions found in the ruins of the Gipar at Ur was by an Entu named Enannedu, who has been identified as the daughter of Kudur-Mabuk, a king of the Sumerian city Larsa circa 1900 B.C. ''I am magnificently suited to be a Gipar-woman, the house which in a pure place for the Entu is built,'' she wrote. Interestingly, votive objects found in the Ningal temple bore inscriptions identifying them as gifts from Enannedu, suggesting to some scholars (e.g. Penelope Weadock, *The Giparu at Ur*) that while serving as the human consort of the god Nannar, the Entu also had to be on good

terms with the official spouse, "providing for the comfort
and adornment of the goddess Ningal."

Other instances where kings sought the Entu office for
their daughters abound. The reason that emerges from the
inscriptions is that by having such intimate access to the god,
the Entu could plead the case and cause of the king for "long
days of life and good health"—the very requests made by
the male king on the occasion of the Sacred Marriage with
Ishtar. With such a direct access to the city god through the
"God's Lady," no wonder that successive kings all over the
ancient Near East built and rebuilt the Gipars in their cities,
making sure that their daughters, and no one else, would be
the Entu. This high and unique office was totally different
from that of a variety of priestesses who served in the temples
as "holy prostitutes," referred to by the general term *Qad-
ishtu*—an occupation frequently mentioned derogatively in
the Bible (and specifically prohibited for the Daughters of
Israel: Deuteronomy 23:18). The *Entu* was different from the
concubines that gods (and kings, or Patriarchs) had, in that
the Entu did not and apparently could not (through unknown
procedures) bear children, while the concubines could and
did.

These rules and customs meant that kings seeking or claiming divine parentage had to find other ways than descent from
an Entu (who could not bear children) or a concubine (whose
offspring lost out to those of the official spouse). It is thus
no wonder that during the last glorious era of Sumer, the
time of the Third Dynasty of Ur, some of its kings, emulating
Gilgamesh, claimed that they were mothered by the goddess
Ninsun. The Assyrian king Sennacherib, unable to make such
a claim, asserted instead in one of his inscriptions that "the
Mistress of the gods, the goddess of procreation, looked upon
me with favor (while I was still) in the womb of the mother
who bore me and watched over my conception; Ea provided
a spacious womb, and granted me keen understanding, the
equal of the master Adapa." In other instances Mesopotamian
kings asserted that this or that goddess raised them or breast-
fed them.

In Egypt, too, claims of divine births were made (and de-

Figure 55

picted on temple walls—Fig. 55) by various kings and
queens, especially during the eighteenth dynasty (1567–1320
B.C.). The mother of the first Pharaoh of this dynasty was
given the title (probably posthumously) ''Spouse of the god
Amon-Ra,'' and the title passed from mother to daughter
in succession. When the Pharaoh Thothmes I (also spelled
Thothmose, Thutmosis) died, he left behind a daughter (Hatshepsut) mothered by his legitimate wife and a son born by a
concubine. In order to legitimize his reign after their father
died, the son (known as Thothmes II) married his half sister
Hatshepsut; but when he died after a short reign, the only
son he had was a young boy mothered by a harem girl;
Hatshepsut herself bore one or two daughters, but had no
son. (In our opinion Hatshepsut, when still a princess bearing
the title The Pharaoh's Daughter, was the biblical Pharaoh's
Daughter who raised the Hebrew boy, calling him ''Mose''
after the divine prefix of her dynasty, eventually adopting
him as her son; but that is another subject).

At first Hatshepsut held the reins as a coregent with her
half brother (who some twenty-two years later became the
Pharaoh Thothmes/Tuthmose III). But then she decided that
the Kingship was rightfully only hers, and had herself
crowned as a Pharaoh (accordingly, her depictions on temple
walls showed her with an attached false beard . . .).

To legitimize her coronation and ascension to the throne
of Osiris, Hatshepsut had the following statement put into
the Egyptian royal records regarding her mother's conception
of her:

Figure 56

*The god Amon took the form of his majesty the
king, of this [queen's] husband the king. Then he
went to her immediately; then he had intercourse
with her.*
*These are the words which the god Amon, Lord of the
Thrones of the Two Lands, spoke thereafter in her
presence:*
*"Hatshepsut-by-Amon-created shall be the name of this
my daughter whom I have planted in thy body ... She
is to exercise the beneficent kingship in this entire
land."*

One of ancient Egypt's most imposing royal temples is that
of queen Hatshepsut in Deir-el-Bahari, a section of Thebes on
the western side of the Nile (Fig. 56). A series of ramps and
terraces took yesteryear's worshiper (and today's visitor) up
to the level of magnificent colonnades where (on the left) the
queen's expedition to Punt was depicted in reliefs and murals,
and (on the right) her divine birth. In this section the painted
reliefs show the god Amun being led by the god Thoth to
queen Ahmose, the mother of Hatshepsut. The accompanying
inscription can well be considered one of the most poetic and
tender records of a sexual Divine Encounter, as the god—

disguised as the queen's husband—entered the inner sanctum
of the queen's nighttime chamber:

Then came the glorious god, Amun himself,
Lord of the thrones of the Two Lands,
When he had taken the form of her husband.

They found her sleeping in the beautiful sanctuary;
She awoke at the perfume of the god,
merrily laughed in the face of his majesty.

Enflamed with love, he hastened toward her;
She could behold him, in the shape of a god,
When he had come nearer to her.

She exulted at the sight of his beauty;
His love entered into all her limbs.
The place was filled with the god's sweet perfume.

The majestic god did to her all that he wished.
She gladdened him with all of herself;
She kissed him.

To further strengthen her claim to divinely ordained Kingship, Hatshepsut asserted that she was nursed by the goddess
Hathor, mistress of the southern Sinai where the turquoise
mines were and whose Egyptian name, *Hat-Hor* ("House/
Abode of Horus"), signified her role in raising and protecting
the young god after his father Osiris was slain by Seth. Hathor, whose nickname was The Cow, was depicted with cow's
horns or alternatively as a cow; and the decorations in Hatshepsut's temple showed the queen being nursed by the god-
dess-cow, suckling on her udder (Fig. 57).

In the absence of a claim to semidivinity, the son and
successor of Thothmes III, called Amenophis II, also asserted
that he was suckled by Hathor, and ordered that he so be
depicted on temple walls (Fig. 58). But a later successor,
Ramses II (1304–1237 B.C.) asserted again that his was a
divine birth by recording the following secret revelation by
the god Ptah to the Pharaoh:

I am thy father . . .
I assumed my form as a ram, Lord of Mendes,
and begot thee inside thy august mother.

And a thousand years later, as we have mentioned, Alexander the Great heard the rumors of his semidivine ancestry, conceived when his mother had a Divine Encounter in her bedchamber with the god Amon.

Figure 57

Figure 58

WHEN GODS GREW OLD

The Immortality of the gods that Earthlings sought to attain was, in reality, only an apparent longevity due to the different life cycles on the two planets. By the time Nibiru completed one orbit around the Sun, someone born there was just one year old. An Earthling born at the same moment would have been, however, 3,600 years old by the end of one Nibiruan year, for Earth would have orbited the Sun 3,600 times by then.

How did coming and staying on Earth affect the Anunnaki? Did they succumb to Earth's shorter orbital time, and thus to Earth's shorter life cycles?

A case in point is what had happened to Ninmah. When she arrived on Earth as the Chief Medical Officer, she was young and attractive (see Fig. 19); so attractive that when Enki—no novice in sex matters—saw her in the marshlands, "his phallus watered the dykes." She was depicted still youthful and with long hair when (as Ninti, "Lady Life") she helped create The Adam (Fig. 3). When Earth was divided, she was assigned the neutral region in the Sinai peninsula (and was called Ninharsag, "Lady of the Mountainpeaks"). But when Inanna rose to prominence and was made patron-goddess of the Indus Civilization, she also took the place of Ninmah in the pantheon of twelve. By then the younger Anunnaki, who referred to Ninmah as *Mammi*, "Old Mother," called her "The Cow" behind her back. Sumerian artists depicted her as an aging goddess, with cow's horns ("A" p. 184).

The Egyptians called the Mistress of the Sinai Hathor, and always depicted her with cow's horns ("B" p. 184).

As the younger gods broke taboos and reshaped Divine Encounters, the Olden Gods appear more aloof, less involved, stepping into the breach only when events were getting out of hand. The gods, indeed, did grow old.

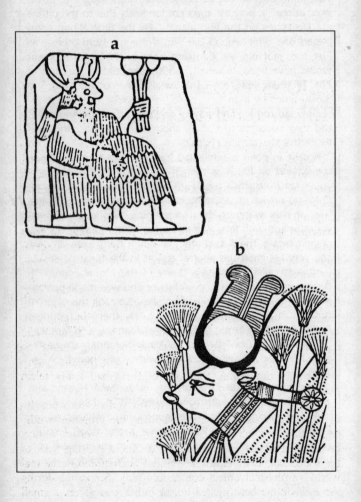

9

VISIONS FROM
THE TWILIGHT ZONE

Rod Serling's popular television series "The Twilight Zone" held viewers spellbound for many years (and still does so in reruns) by putting the episodes' heroes in obviously dangerous circumstances—a fatal accident, a terminal illness, a trapping in a time warp—from which they miraculously emerged unharmed because of some incredible twist of fate. In most instances, the miracle was the handiwork of a person, seemingly ordinary, who proved to have extraordinary powers—an "angel," if you wish.

But the fascination for the viewer was the Twilight Zone; for when all was said and done, the episode's hero—and with him or her the viewer—was uncertain of what had happened. Was the danger only imagined? Was it all just a dream—and thus the "miracle" that resolved the inevitable ending no miracle at all; the "angel" no angel at all; the time warp not another dimension, for none of them had really taken place . . .

In some episodes, however, the hero's and viewer's puzzlement was given a final twist that made the program worthy of its name. At the very end, as hero and viewer are almost certain that it was all imagined, a dream, a passing trick of the subconscious mind, a tale that has no foothold in the real world—a physical object comes into play. Sometime during the episode the hero picked up, or rather was given, a small object that he absentmindedly put in his/her pocket, or a ring put on the finger, or a talisman worn as a necklace. As all other aspects of the imagined and unreal episode, the object too had to be imagined and nonreal. But as the viewer and the hero are certain that all had faded into its nonreality, the hero finds the object in his pocket or on his finger—a reality left over from the unreality. And thus, Rod Serling has shown us, between reality and nonreality, between the rational and the irrational, we were passing through a Twilight Zone.

Four thousand years earlier, a Sumerian king found himself in such a Twilight Zone, and recorded his experience on two clay cylinders (that are now on display in the Louvre Museum in Paris).

The king's name was Gudea and he reigned in the Sumerian city Lagash circa 2100 B.C. Lagash was the "cult center" of Ninurta, the Foremost Son of Enlil, and he dwelt with his spouse Bau in the city's sacred precinct called the Girsu—hence his local epithet NIN.GIRSU, "Lord of the Girsu." At about that time, owing to an intensification of the struggle for supremacy on Earth that pitted primarily Enki's Firstborn Marduk against Enlil's clan, Ninurta/Ningirsu obtained the permission of his father Enlil to build a new temple in the Girsu—a temple so magnificent that it would express the rights of Ninurta to the supremacy. As it turned out, Ninurta's plan was to build in Mesopotamia a most unusual temple, one that would emulate the Great Pyramid of Giza on the one hand and that, upon its vast platform, would hold stone circles that could serve as sophisticated astronomical observatories. The need to find a reliable and faithful worshiper to carry out the grandiose plans and to follow intelligently the designs of the Divine Architects served as the background for the ensuing events recorded by Gudea.

The series of events began with a dream that Gudea had one night; it was a vision of Divine Encounters. And it was so vivid that it transported the king into a Twilight Zone; for when Gudea awoke, *an object that he had seen only in his dream was now physically on his lap.* Somehow, the boundary between unreality and reality had been crossed.

Utterly perplexed by the occurrence, Gudea asked for and received permission to seek the advice of the oracle goddess Nanshe in her "House of Fate-Solving" in another city. Reaching the place by boat and offering prayers and sacrifices

Figure 59a and Figure 59b

so that she would solve the riddle of his nighttime vision,
Gudea proceeded to tell her what had happened (we read
from column IV in Cylinder "A," verses 14–20, as transcribed by Ira M. Price, *The Great Cylinder Inscriptions A
and B of Gudea,* Fig. 59a):

> *In the dream [I saw]*
> *a man who was bright, shining like Heaven*
> *—great in Heaven, great on Earth—*
> *who by his headdress was a* Dingir *(god).*
> *At his side was the divine Storm Bird;*
> *Like a devouring storm under his feet*
> *two lions crouched, on the right and on the left.*
> *He commanded me to build his temple.*

A celestial omen then followed whose meaning, Gudea

told the dream-solving goddess, he did not understand: the Sun upon *Kishar* (the planet Jupiter) was suddenly seen on the horizon. A female then appeared and gave Gudea celestial instructions (column IV, verses 23–26):

> *A woman—*
> *who was she? Who was she not?*
> *the image of a temple-structure*
> *she carried on her head—*
> *in her hand she held a holy stylus;*
> *The tablet of the favorable star of heaven*
> *she bore.*

As the "woman" was consulting the star tablet, a third divine being appeared (we follow column V, verses 2–10, Fig. 59b); he was a male:

> *A second man appeared, he had the*
> *look of a hero, endowed with strength.*
> *A tablet of lapis lazuli in his hand he held.*
> *The plan of a temple he drew on it.*
> *He placed before me a holy carrying basket;*
> *Upon it he placed a pure brickmaking mold;*
> *the destined brick was inside it.*
> *A large vessel stood before me;*
> *on it was engraved the* Tibu *bird which shines*
> *brilliantly day and night.*
> *A freight-ass crouched to my right.*

The text suggests that all these objects somehow materialized during the dream, but regarding one of them there is absolutely no doubt that it was made to cross from the dream dimension to the dimension of physical reality; for when Gudea awoke, he found the lapis lazuli stone tablet on his lap, with the plan of the temple etched upon it. He commemorated the miracle in one of his statues (Fig. 60a). The statue shows both the tablet and the Divine Stylus with which the plan was etched. Modern studies suggest that, ingeniously, the markings on the margin (Fig. 60b) are diminishing scales

Figures 60a and 60b

for constructing all of the seven stages of the temple with one single design.

The other objects, that may have also materialized, are known through various archaeological finds. Other Sumerian kings have depicted themselves with the "holy carrying basket" that the king carried to begin the sacred construction (Fig. 61a); brick molds, and bricks embossed with a "destiny" statement, have been found (Fig. 61b); and a silver

Figures 61a, 61b, and 61c

vase that bears the image of the *Tibu* bird of Ninurta has been found in the ruins of the Girsu of Lagash (Fig. 61c).

Repeating the details of the dream-vision one by one in the manner reported by Gudea, the oracle goddess proceeded to tell the king what it meant. The first god to appear, she said, was Ninurta/Ningirsu, announcing to Gudea that he was chosen to build the new temple: "For thee to build his temple he commanded." Its name was to be E.NINNU—"House of Fifty"—to signify that Ninurta has the claim to Enlil's rank of fifty and thus the only one below Anu, whose rank was sixty.

The sighting of the heliacal rising of Jupiter "is the god Ningishzidda," meant to show the king the exact point in the skies to which the temple's observatories should be oriented, indicating precisely where the Sun will rise on the day of the New Year. The female who appeared in the vision, carrying on her head the image of a temple-structure, was the goddess Nisaba; with her stylus that she grasped in one hand and the celestial map that she held in the other hand, "to build the temple in accordance with the Holy Planet she instructed thee." And the second male, Nanshe explained, was the god Nindub; "to thee the plan of the temple he gave."

She also explained to Gudea the meaning of the other objects that he had seen. The carrying basket signified Gudea's role in the construction; the mold and "destiny brick" indicated the size and shape of the bricks to be used, molded of clay; the *Tibu* bird that "brilliantly shines day and night" meant that, throughout the construction, "no good sleep shall come to thee." If that did not mar Gudea's joy at being selected for the sacred task, the interpretation of the freight-Ass symbolism should have: it meant that, like a beast of burden, Gudea shall toil in the temple's building . . .

Back in Lagash Gudea contemplated the words of the oracle goddess and studied the divine tablet that had materialized on his lap. The more he thought about the varied instructions, the more he was baffled, especially so regarding the astronomical orientation and timing. He sought to understand the secrets of temple construction by going into the existing temple "day by day, and again at sleeping time." Still perplexed, he went into the temple's Holy of Holies and appealed to

"Ningirsu, son of Enlil," for additional guidance: "My heart remains unknowing, the meaning is far from me as the middle of the ocean; as the midst of heaven from me it is distant." "Lord Ningirsu," Gudea cried out in the darkness, "the temple I will build for thee, but my omen is not yet clear to me!"

He asked for a second omen, and received it. In what scholars call Gudea's second dream, the position of the king and the encountered deity seem to be crucial. The text (column IX, verses 5–6) states that "for the second time, by the prostrate one, by the prostrate one, the god took his stand." The Sumerian term used, NAD.A, conveys more than the "lying flat, lying stretched out" that the English term "prostrate" conveys. It implies an element of not-seeing by lying facedown. Gudea, in other words, had to lie down in a manner assuring that he would not see the deity. The god, on his part, had to position himself at the head of Gudea. If Gudea was asleep, or in a trance, did the god actually speak to him—or was the position near the king's head intended to facilitate some other, metaphysical method of communication? The text does not make this point clear; it does relate that Gudea was given promises of constant divine help, especially by the god Ningishzidda. The help of this deity, whom we have identified as the Egyptian deity Thoth, seemed especially important to Ninurta/Ningirsu, as was the expected homage that *Magan* (Egypt) and *Meluhha* (Nubia) would pay to Ninurta once his new temple would proclaim his rank of Fifty, "the fifty names of Lordship that by Anu were ordained." This, he explained to Gudea, was why the temple was to be called E.NINNU—"House of Fifty." He promised Gudea that the new temple will not only glorify the deity; it will also bring fame and prosperity to all of Sumer and to Lagash in particular.

The deity then explained to Gudea various details of the temple's architecture, including the design of the special enclosures for the Divine Black Bird and the Supreme Weapon; the *Gigunu* for the divine couple; an oracle chamber, and a place for the assembly of the gods. Details of utensils and furnishings were also given. Then the god assured Gudea that "for the building of my temple I will give thee a sign; my commands will teach thee the sign by the heavenly planet."

The construction, he told Gudea, should begin on the "day of the new moon." The particular new moon day will become known to the king by a divine omen—a signal from the skies. The day will start with winds and great rains; by nightfall, the god's hand shall appear in the skies; it will hold a flame "that shall make the night as light as day:"

> At night a light shall shine;
> it will cause the fields to be
> brightly lit, as by the sun.

Hearing all that "Gudea understood the favorable plan, a plan that was the clear message of his vision-dream." "Now he was greatly wise and understood great things." After presenting offerings and prayers "to the Anunnaki of Lagash, the faithful shepherd, Gudea, engaged in the work with joy." Losing no time, he proceeded to "purify the city," then "levied taxes upon the land." The taxes were payable in kind—oxen, wild asses, wood and timbers, copper. He amassed building materials from near and far and organized a labor force. As Nanshe had foreseen, he toiled like a Freight-Ass and "good sleep did not come to him."

With everything ready, it was time to start making the bricks. They had to be made from clay according to the mold and sample that appeared to Gudea in his first vision-dream. We read in column XIX, verse 19, that Gudea "brought the brick, placed it in the temple." It follows from this statement that Gudea had the brick (and by inference the required mold) in his physical possession; *the brick and mold were thus two more objects (in addition to the lapis lazuli tablet) that crossed the boundary in a Twilight Zone.*

Now Gudea contemplated "the sketched ground plan of the temple." But "unlike the goddess Nisaba who always understands the meaning of dimensions," Gudea was stymied. Again he needed additional divine guidance; and again he resorted to the method that had worked before—but only after obtaining, through divination, a "go-ahead." The method he used for divination involved the "passing of quiet waters over seeds" and determining the course of action by the appearance of the wet seeds. "Gudea examined the omens, and his omens were favorable."

> *So Gudea laid down his head,*
> *prostrated himself.*
> *The command-vision emerged:*
> *"The building of thy Lord's House,*
> *the Eninnu, thou shall complete—*
> *from its foundation below to*
> *its top that rises skyward."*

Though scholars consider this episode "Gudea's third dream," the text's terminology is significantly different. Even on the previous occasions the term translated "dream," MA-MUZU, is more akin to the Hebrew/Semitic *Mahazeh* which better translates as "a vision." Here, on the third time, the term employed is DUG MUNATAE—a "command-vision that emerges." On this time around, in this "command-vision" by request, Gudea was shown how to start the building of his Lord's temple. In front of his very eyes the process of the completion of the Eninnu, "from its foundation below to its top that rises skyward," was taking shape. The *vision of a simulated demonstration of the whole process,* from the bottom up, "engaged his attention." What was to be done finally became clear; and "with joy he took up the task."

How the work then proceeded, how Gudea was helped by a team of Divine Architects and gods and goddesses of astronomy to orient the temple and erect its observatories, how and when calendrical requirements were met, and the ceremonies that inaugurated the new temple, are all told in the balance of Cylinder "A" and in Cylinder "B" of the Sumerian king. We have dealt with this part of the records in *When Time Began.*

A tablet that appears in a dream and then materializes with powerful effects in the subsequent awakened condition plays a key role in the tale of a Babylonian "Job," a righteous sufferer. The text, titled *Ludlul Bel Nemeqi* ("I will praise the Lord of Wisdom") after its opening line, tells the story of Shubshi, a righteous man, who laments his misfortune, having been forsaken by his god, "cut off" by his protective goddess, abandoned by his friends. He loses his house, his possessions, and—worst of all—his health. He wonders Why?, hires diviners and "interpreters of dreams" to find out the reasons for his sufferings, calls upon exorcists to "appease the divine wrath." But nothing seems to work or help. "I am perplexed at these things," he writes. Debilitated, coughing, limp, with terrible headaches, he is ready to die; but as he reaches the depths of misery and desperation, salvation comes in a series of dreams.

In the first dream he sees "a remarkable young man of outstanding physique, splendid in body, clothed in new garments." As he awakens, he catches a glimpse of this apparition, actually sees the young man "clothed in splendor, robed in awesomeness." The action or speech that take place in the course of this dream come true are lost by damage to the tablet.

In the second dream a "remarkable Washed One" appeared, "holding in his hand a piece of purifying tamarisk wood." The apparition recited "life-restoring incantations" and poured "purifying waters" over the diseased sufferer.

The third dream was even more remarkable, for it contained a dream within a dream. "A remarkable young woman of shining countenance," a goddess by all counts, appeared. She spoke to the Babylonian "Job" of deliverance. "Fear not," she said, "I will . . . in a dream deliver you from your wretched state." And so, in his dream, the sufferer dreamed that he was *seeing in a dream* "a bearded young man wearing a head-covering, an exorcist":

> *He was carrying a tablet.*
> *"Marduk has sent me," [he said].*
> *"To Shubshi, the Righteous Dweller,*
> *from Marduk's pure hands*
> *I have brought thee wellbeing."*

When he awakens, Shubshi finds the tablet that appeared to him in the dream within a dream actually in his possession. The boundary that is the Twilight Zone has been crossed, the metaphysical has become physical. There is cuneiform writing on the tablet, and Shubshi can read it: "in the waking hours, he sees the message." He regains enough strength to "show the favorable sign to my people."

Miraculously, the "illness was quickly over." His fever was broken. The headache was "carried away," the Evil Demon was banished to its domain; the chills were "flowed away to the sea," the "clouded eyes" cleared up, the "obstructions to the hearing" were removed, the toothache was gone—the list of afflictions that disappeared when the mysterious-miraculous tablet appeared goes on and on, leading to the punch line: "Who but Marduk could have restored the dying to life?"

The tale ends with a description of the libations, sacrifices, and offerings by the hero of the tale in honor of Marduk and his spouse Sarpanit as the erstwhile sufferer proceeds to the great ziggurat-temple via the sacred precinct's twelve gates.

The ancient records include additional instances that belong in the Twilight Zone, where objects—or actions—that are part of the dream-vision dimension appear in the ensuing awakened reality. Though they lack the clear-cut pictorial evidence available in the case of the tablet with the temple's plan, the other reports suggest that the phenomenon, though rare, was not unique to Gudea. Even there, though Gudea himself does not hold them up for posterity to see, we know from the text that at least two additional objects—the mold and the Brick of Destiny—also materialized into the rational dimension.

Physical objects and actions that transcend the boundary are also encountered in the dreams of Gilgamesh. The "handiwork of Anu" that descended from the skies is reported in Tablet I as seen in a dream; but when the episode is repeated in Tablet II of the *Epic of Gilgamesh,* the dream becomes a vision of real happenings. Gilgamesh struggles to extract the artifact's inner whirring part, and when he finally succeeds he takes the mysterious object to his mother and puts it at her feet.

Later on, as Gilgamesh and Enkidu encamp at the foothills of the Cedar Mountain, Gilgamesh falls asleep, has three dreams, and each time a dreamed-of action—a call, a touch— is transformed into real action that awakens him. The call, the touch are so real that he suspects Enkidu of doing that; but after Enkidu firmly denies calling or touching Gilgamesh, the king realizes that it was the god in his dream that had touched him so realistically that his flesh became numb. And finally there was the dream-vision of the launched rocket-etship—a "dream" in which Gilgamesh sees an object the likes of which he had never seen before, a launching the likes of which no one in Uruk had seen (for it was neither a Spaceport nor a Landing Place). He did not end up holding the object in his hand once the vision had dissipated; but we could still see it depicted in the Byblos coin (Fig. 49).

The dream-visions of Daniel, a Jewish captive in the court of Nebuchadnezzar (king of Babylon in the sixth century B.C.), contain even more direct parallels to the physical aspects of the Twilight Zone encounters of Gilgamesh and Gudea. Describing one of his Divine Encounters at the banks of the Tigris River (the Book of Daniel, chapter 10), he wrote:

> *I lifted up mine eyes, and behold,*
> *I saw a sole man clothed in linen*
> *whose loins were girded with Ophir gold.*
> *His body gleamed like topaz,*
> *his face shone like lightning,*
> *his eyes flamed like torches,*
> *his arms and feet were the color of bronze,*
> *and his voice was a booming one.*

"I alone could see the apparition," Daniel wrote; but though the other people who were with him could not see it, they felt an awesome presence and ran away to hide. He, too, felt suddenly immobilized, able to only hear the divine voice; but

> *As soon as I heard the voice of his words*
> *I fell asleep face down,*
> *my face touching the ground.*

This position was akin to that described by Gudea; ensuing is the similarity to the awakenings that puzzled Gilgamesh,

Figure 62

when in his dreams he experienced an actual, physical touch and voice of ''a god.'' Continuing his narrative, Daniel wrote that as he fell asleep facedown,

> *Suddenly a hand touched me*
> *and pulled me up, to be*
> *upon my knees and the palms of my hands.*

The divine person then revealed to Daniel that he was to be shown the future. Overwhelmed, with his face still down, Daniel was speechless. But then the person—''of the appearance of the sons of Man''—touched the lips of Daniel, and Daniel was able to speak. When he apologized for his weakness, the divine person touched him again, and Daniel ''regained his strength.'' All that had taken place while Daniel was seized by a trancelike sleep.

More memorable than the dream-visions of Daniel is the Twilight Zone incident of the *Handwriting-on-the-Wall*. It took place in the reign of Nebuchadnezzar's successor as regent in Babylon, Bel-shar-utzur (''Lord, the Prince preserve'') whom the bible calls Belshazzar, circa 540 B.C. As related in chapter 5 of the Book of Daniel, Belshazzar made a great banquet for a thousand of his nobles and was feasting and drinking wine—a scene known from several Babylonian and Assyrian depictions of royal banquets (Fig. 62). Drunk with too much wine, he gave orders to fetch the gold and silver vessels that Nebuchadnezzar had seized from the Temple in Jerusalem, so that ''he and his nobles, his concubines and his courtesans might drink from them. So the vessels of

gold and silver from the sanctuary in the House of God in
Jerusalem were brought in; and the king and his nobles, his
concubines and courtesans, drank from them; they drank wine
and praised the gods of gold and silver, of bronze and iron
and of wood and stone." As the pagan merriment and defilement of the sacred objects from Yahweh's temple
continued,

> *Suddenly,*
> *There appeared the fingers of a*
> *human hand,*
> *and it wrote upon the plaster of*
> *the palace wall,*
> *opposite the candelabra;*
> *And the king could see the wrist of*
> *the hand as it wrote.*

The sight of a human hand—disembodied, floating by itself
unconnected to an arm and a body—was disconcerting; the
suddenness of the appearance only added to the sense of
foreboding. "The king's mind was filled with terror, his
countenance turned pale, every limb of his became limp, his
knees knocked together." He must have realized that the
desecration of the vessels from the Temple of Yahweh had
triggered an ominous Divine Encounter with some unknown
dire consequences.

He shouted for the seers and diviners of Babylon to be
rushed in. Addressing the "wise men of Babylon" he announced that whoever could read the writing and interpret
the meaning of the apparition shall be rewarded and elevated
to the third highest rank in the kingdom. But none could
interpret the vision nor understand the written message. And
"Belshazzar sat pale and utterly scared and his nobles all
perplexed."

Upon this scene of fear and desperation in walked the
queen; and when she heard what had happened, she pointed
out that the wise man Daniel had been known for his ability
to understand and interpret dreams and divine messages. So
Daniel was called in and was told of the promised rewards.
Refusing the rewards, he nevertheless agreed to interpret the

vision. By then the writing hand must have vanished, but the writing on the wall remained. Confirming that the bad omen was the result of the desecration of the Temple's vessels that were consecrated to the God Most High, the Lord of Heaven, Daniel explained the writing and its meaning:

> *This is why by Him the hand was sent,*
> *and why this writing was inscribed.*
> *These are the words of the writing:*
> Mene, mene, tekel u Pharsin.

> *And here is the words' interpretation:*
> Mene: *God hath numbered the days of thy kingdom,*
> *and it is finished.*
> Tekel: *Thou are weighed in the balance,*
> *and found wanting.*
> U Pharsin: *Thy kingdom shall be divided,*
> *to the Medes and Persians it shall be given.*

Belshazzar kept his promise, and ordered that Daniel be robed in purple and honored with a chain of gold around his neck, and proclaimed third in rank in the kingdom. But "that very night, Belshazzar king of the Chaldeans was slain, and Darius of the Medes took the kingdom" (Daniel 5:30–31). The message from the Twilight Zone was promptly fulfilled.

Gudea's Twilight Zone dream-visions, in which he was given divine instructions and plans for the construction of the Eninnu temple in Lagash, preceded by more than a millennium similar divine communications regarding Yahweh's temple in Jerusalem.

Following the detailed instructions given by Yahweh to Moses on Mount Sinai, the Children of Israel built for the Lord a portable *Mishkan*—literally, "Residence"—in the Sinai wilderness; its most important component was the *Ohel Moed* ("Tent of Appointment") in whose holiest part the Ark of the Covenant that contained the Tablets of the Law and that was protected by the Cherubim was kept. After the arrival in Canaan, the Ark of the Covenant was temporarily located at the principal places of worship, awaiting its final and permanent installation in the "House of Yahweh" in Jerusalem. Circa 1000 B.C. David succeeded King Saul as King of Israel. After making Jerusalem his capital, it was the hope and ambition of King David to build there the sacred Temple in whose Holy of Holies the Ark of the Covenant could finally come to rest at a spot held sacred from time immemorial. But divine communications—principally through dreams—had willed otherwise.

As the biblical record tells it, David shared his intention to build the temple with the Prophet Nathan, who gave it his blessing. But "it came to pass that very night, that the word of Yahweh came to Nathan, instructing him to tell King David that because he had been involved in wars and the shedding of blood, it would be his son, rather than David himself, who would build the temple."

How the Prophet Nathan had received the divine communication "that very night" is explained at the end of the tale (II Samuel 7:17): "And Nathan related to David all these words, the whole of this *vision*." It was thus not just a dream, but an epiphany; not a *Chalom* ("dream") but a *Hizzayon* ("envisioning"), in which not only were the words heard but the speaker was also "envisioned," as had been explained by Yahweh to the brother and sister of Moses in the Sinai encampment.

So King David went "and sat before Yahweh," in front of the Ark of the Covenant. He accepted the Lord's decision, but wished to make sure of both its parts—that he would not build the Temple, and that his son will. Thus sitting before the Ark of the Covenant by means of which Moses had communicated with the Lord, David repeated the Prophet's words. The Bible does not report the Lord's answer; but in that "sitting before Yahweh" may lie a key to understanding a puzzle—the mystery of the origin of the Temple's plans. For we read in I Chronicles chapter 28 that as David neared the end of his days he called together the leaders and elders of Israel and told them of Yahweh's decision regarding the building of the Temple. Announcing that his successor would be Solomon, "David gave Solomon his son the *Tavnit*" of the Temple with all its parts and chambers, "the *Tavnit* of all that he had by the Spirit."

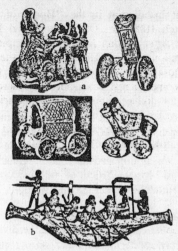

Figures 63a and 63b

The Hebrew word *Tavnit* is commonly translated "pattern," and this term suggests that it could be a design, an architectural plan. But the biblical term implies more accurately a "constructed model" rather than a *Tokhnit* ("plan" in Hebrew). It was a physical model that apparently was small enough to be handed over by David to Solomon—something that nowadays would be spoken of as a "scale model."

As archaeological finds in Mesopotamia and Egypt attest, scale models were not unknown in the ancient Near East; we can illustrate the fact by showing some of the objects discovered in Mesopotamia (Fig. 63a), as well as some of the numerous Egyptian ones (Fig. 63b). In some Sumerian cylinder seal depictions a temple-tower (Fig. 64a) is shown no taller than the human and divine personages in the scene, as is the case of a priestess shown decorating a model of a temple (Fig. 64b). It has been assumed that the structures were drawn not to true scale simply to make them fit the space on the seal; but the discovery of *actual* clay scale models of temples and shrines (Fig. 64c)—paralleling the biblical references to the *Tavnit,* suggests that perhaps in Mesopotamia, too, kings were shown actual models of the temples and shrines they were instructed to build.

The term *Tavnit* appears earlier in the Bible, in connection with the building of the portable Residence for Yahweh during the Exodus. It was when Moses went up Mount Sinai to meet the Lord, staying there forty days and forty nights, that "Yahweh spoke unto Moses" regarding the *Mishkan* (a term usually translated Tabernacle but that literally means a "Residence"). After listing a variety of materials needed for the construction—to be obtained from the Israelites as voluntary contributions, not as imposed taxation as Gudea had done—Yahweh showed Moses a *Tavnit* of the Residence and a *Tavnit* of the instruments thereof, saying (Exodus 25:8–9):

> *And they shall make me a sanctuary,*
> *and I will reside in the midst of them.*
> *In accordance with all that I show thee—*
> *the* Tavnit *of the* Mishkan *and*
> *the* Tavnit *of all the instruments thereof—*
> *so shall ye make it.*

Detailed architectural measurements and instructions for

Figures 64a, 64b, and 64c

Figure 65

the making of the Ark of the Covenant with its two Cherubim, and the Curtain, and the ritual Table and its utensils, and the Candelabra then followed; and the instructions were only interrupted for the admonition, "and see and make them in accordance with their *Tavnit* that you are being shown on the Mount," after which the explicit architectural directives continued (taking up two additional chapters in the Book of Exodus). Clearly then, Moses was *shown* models—presumably scale models—of everything that had to be made. The biblical accounts of the architectural instructions for the Residence in the Sinai and the Temple in Jerusalem, and for the various utensils, ritual instruments, and accessories, are so detailed that modern scholars and artists had no problem in depicting them (Fig. 65).

The account in I Chronicles chapter 28, reporting the materials and instructions handed over by King David to Solomon for the construction of the Temple, uses the term *Tavnit* four times, leaving no doubt regarding the existence of such a model. After the fourth and last mention, David told Solomon that the *Tavnit* with all its details were literally given him by Yahweh, *accompanied by written instructions:*

All this,
in writing by his hand,
did Yahweh made me understand
all of the workings of the Tavnit.

All that, according to the bible, was given to David "by the Spirit" as he "sat before Yahweh" in front of the Ark of the Covenant (in its temporary location). How the "Spirit" imparted to David the instructions, including the writings by the hand of Yahweh and the extraordinarily detailed *Tavnit*, remains a mystery—a Divine Encounter that befits the Twilight Zone.

The Temple that Solomon eventually built was destroyed by the Babylonian king Nebuchadnezzar (in 587 B.C.), who took most of the Judean leaders and nobles into exile in Babylon. Among them was Ezekiel; and when the Lord deemed that the time for the rebuilding of the Temple was nigh, the Divine Spirit—the "Spirit of *Elohim*"—was upon Ezekiel and he began to prophesy. His experiences truly belong in the Twilight Zone.

And it came to pass in the thirtieth year,
in the fourth month, on the fifth day thereof,
as I was among the captives by the river Chebar,
that the heavens were opened
and I saw Divine Visions.

Thus begins the biblical Book of Ezekiel. Its forty-eight chapters are replete with visions and Divine Encounters; *the opening vision, that of a Divine Chariot, is one of the most remarkable records of a UFO witnessed in antiquity.*

The detailed technical description of the Chariot and the manner in which it could move in any direction as well as up and down, has intrigued generations of biblical scholars from early on all the way to modern times, and became part of the mystery lore of the Jewish Kaballah, whose study was limited only to Knowing Initiates. (In recent years the technical interpretation by Joseph Blumrich, an ex-NASA engineer, in *The Spaceships of Ezekiel* (Fig. 66a) has received favorable attention. An early Chinese depiction of a Flying Chariot

(Fig. 66b), attests to the widespread awareness of the phenomenon in antiquity in all parts of the world).

Inside the Chariot Ezekiel could vaguely see, seated upon what appeared to be a throne, "the likeness of a man" within a brilliance or a fiery halo; and as Ezekiel fell upon his face, he heard a voice speaking. Then he saw "a hand stretched out" toward him, and the hand held a written scroll. "And it was unrolled before me, and, behold, it was covered with writing front and back."

The vision of just a hand representing the deity recalls the Writing on the Wall seen by Belshazzar; and in the Gudea inscriptions it was stated that he was told that, to signal the propitious day for the temple, a god's hand holding a torch shall appear in the sky. In this regard an eleventh century bronze plaque in the Hildsheim (Germany) cathedral, showing Cain and Abel making their offerings to God, in which the Lord is represented only by a divine hand appearing from the clouds (Fig. 67) is truly inspired.

The word "dream" does not appear in the book of Ezekiel

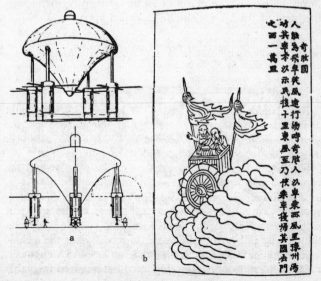

Figures 66a and 66b

even once; instead the Prophet uses the term "vision." "The heavens opened and I saw Divine Visions," Ezekiel states in the very first paragraph of his book. The term used in the Hebrew is actually "*Elohim* visions," visions relating to the DIN.GIR of Sumerian texts. The term retains some ambiguity as to the nature of the "vision"—the actual seeing of a scene, or an induced mental image that is created, somehow, in the mind's eye only. What is certain is that from time to time reality intrudes into these visions—an actual voice, an actual object, a visible hand. In that, the visions of Ezekiel belong in the Twilight Zone.

Among the several Divine Encounters that move Ezekiel along his prophetic path, more than one are instances where the unreal includes a reality that in turn fades into unreality. One has elements of Gudea's initial dream-vision in which divine beings show him a plan of a temple and hold architectural tools that end up materially in the king's possession.

"It was in the sixth year, in the sixth month, in the fifth day thereof," Ezekiel relates in chapter 8. "As I was sitting in my home, and the elders of Judah were sitting before me, the hand of the Lord Yahweh happened upon me,"

And I looked up, and beheld an apparition,
the likeness of a man.

Figure 67

From his waist down the appearance was of fire,
and from the waist up the appearance was of a
brightness, like the sheen of electrum.

The wording here reveals the Prophet's own uncertainty regarding the nature of the vision—a reality or a nonreality. He calls what he sees an "apparition," the being that he sees is only a *likeness* of a man. Is whoever had appeared *clad* in fire and brilliance, or is he *made* of fire and brilliance, a make-believe image? Whatever it was, it was able to perform physically:

And he put forth the shape of a hand,
and seized me by a lock on my head.
And the spirit carried me
between the earth and the heaven,
and brought me to Jerusalem—
in Elohim *visions—*
to the door of the inner gate that faces north.

The narrative then described what Ezekiel had seen in Jerusalem (including the women mourning Dumuzi). And when the prophetic instructions were completed, and the Divine Chariot "lifted off from the city and rested upon the mount that is to the east of the city,"

The spirit carried me and brought me
to Chaldea, to the place of exile.
[It was] in a Vision of the Spirit of Elohim.
And then the vision that I had seen
was lifted off me.

The biblical text stresses more than once that the airborne journey was in a Divine Vision, a "Vision of the Spirit of *Elohim.*" Yet there clearly is a description of a physical visit to Jerusalem, discussions with its residents, and even the "putting of a mark on the foreheads" of the righteous ones who were to be spared the predicted carnage and final destruction of the city. (Chapter 33 records the arrival of a refugee from Jerusalem in the twelfth year of the first exile,

Figure 68

informing the exiles in Babylon that the prophecy regarding Jerusalem had come to pass).

Fourteen years later, in the twenty-fifth year of the first exile, on New Year's Day, "the hand of Yahweh came upon" Ezekiel once more, and the hand took him to Jerusalem. "In *Elohim* Visions he brought me to the Land of Israel, and placed me on a very high mountain, by which was the model of a city, to the south."

> *And as he brought me there, behold—*
> *There was a man whose appearance was that*
> *of copper*
> *He held a cord of flax in his hand,*
> *and a measuring rod;*
> *and he stood at the gate.*

(A measuring cord and rod have been depicted in Sumerian times as sacred objects granted by a Divine Architect to a king chosen to build a temple—Fig. 68.)

The Divine Measurer instructed Ezekiel to pay attention to everything he would hear and see, and especially so to note all the measurements, so that he could report it all accurately back to the exiles. No sooner were these instructions given, than the image in front of Ezekiel changed. Suddenly the scene of a distant man changed to that of a wall surrounding a large house—as though, in terms from our time, a camera

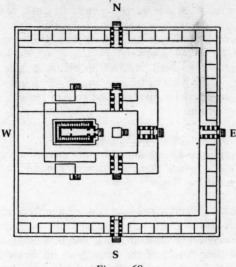

Figure 69

was refocused to a telescopic lens. From a close-up, Ezekiel could see "the man with the measure" starting to take the measurements of the house.

From the scene outside the house, at the surrounding wall, Ezekiel could now see the measurer as he kept going and measuring; and as this went on, the scene—as though a television camera was following the man—kept changing; and instead of the outside scenes Ezekiel could see images of the inner parts of the house—courtyards, chambers, chapels. From an examination of the general architecture the images now switched to the perception of details of construction and decorative fine points. It became evident to Ezekiel that he was being shown the *future, rebuilt Temple,* with its Holy of Holies and sacred utensils, and the locations for the priests, and the place of the Cherubim.

The description, which takes up three long chapters in the Book of Ezekiel, is so detailed and the measurements and architectural data so precise, that modern draftsmen were able to draw the Temple's plans with little difficulty (Fig. 69).

As one envisioned scene followed the other, in a simulation

that beats the most advanced "Virtual Reality" techniques that are still being developed at the end of the twentieth century A.D., Ezekiel was then—more than 2,500 years ago— *taken into the vision.* As though physically, he was led to the east-facing gate to the Temple compound; and there he saw "the glory of the God of Israel" coming through the eastern entrance, in a "vision like the vision seen before" on two previous occasions.

> *And the spirit lifted me up*
> *and brought me into the inner court;*
> *and I beheld that the Glory of Yahweh*
> *filled the Temple.*

And now he heard a voice addressing him from inside the Temple. It was not the "man" whom he had seen before with the measuring cord and rod, for that man was now standing beside him. And the voice from inside the Temple announced that that would be where the Divine Throne will be placed, and where the Lord's feet shall touch the ground. Finally, Ezekiel was instructed to inform the House of Israel of all that he had heard and seen, and give them the plan's measurements, so that the New Temple could be properly built.

The Book of Ezekiel then ends with long instructions for the sacred services in the future Temple. It mentions that Ezekiel "was brought back" to see the Glory of Yahweh through the north gate. Presumably, it was therefrom that Ezekiel was returned from his Divine Vision; but the Book of Ezekiel leaves this unstated.

Ancient Holograms, Virtual Reality?

When Gudea kept being baffled by the architectural instructions for the temple he was to build, he was shown a "command-vision that *emerges*" in which he could dream-see the temple taking shape from the initial groundstone to its completion stage by stage—a feat more than 4,000 years ago which can now be attained by computer simulations.

Ezekiel was not only miraculously transported (twice) from Mesopotamia to the Land of Israel. The second time he was shown, in what nowadays we would call a "Virtual Reality" technology, scene by scene, details of *something that did not yet exist*—the *future* Temple; the House of Yahweh that was to be built according to the architectural details revealed to Ezekiel in this Twilight Zone vision. How was it done?

Ezekiel called the vision, at the very beginning, a *Tavnit*—the term that was used earlier in the Bible in connection with the Residence and the Temple. But if they might have been only scale models, the one envisioned by Ezekiel had to be a full-sized "construction model," for the Divine Measurer was taking actual measurements with a rod that was six cubits long, measuring a length of sixty cubits here, a height of twenty-five cubits there. Was what Ezekiel was being shown based on a "Virtual Reality" or holographic technology? Was he shown "computer" simulations, or seeing an actual temple somewhere else through holography?

Visitors to science museums are often fascinated by the holographic displays in which two beams project images that when combined seem to enable one to see an actual, three-dimensional image floating in the air. Techniques developed at the end of 1993 (*Physical Review Letters,* December 1993) can make long-distance holograms appear with the aid of only one laser beam focused on a crystal. Were these kinds of techniques, undoubtedly far more advanced, used to enable Ezekiel to see, visit, and even enter the "constructed model" that was actually somewhere else—perhaps all the way in South America?

10

ROYAL DREAMS, FATEFUL ORACLES

"To sleep, perchance to dream," says Hamlet in Shakespeare's *Hamlet, Prince of Denmark*—a tragedy in which an apparition of the murdered king is seen by Hamlet in a vision, and celestial omens come to play. In the ancient Near East dreams were not considered a matter of chance; they were all, to varying degrees, Divine Encounters: in the least, omens that portend things to come; throughout, channels for conveying divine will or instructions; and in the utmost, carefully staged and premeditated epiphanies.

According to the ancient scriptures, dreams have accompanied Earthlings from the very beginning of Humankind, starting from the First Mother, Eve, who had an omen-dream about the slaying of Abel. After the Deluge, when Kingship was instituted to create both a barrier and a link between the Anunnaki and the mass of people, it was the kings whose dreams accompanied the course of human affairs. And then, when human leaders strayed, the Divine Word was conveyed through the dreams and visions of Prophets. Within that long record of dreams and visions, some, as we have seen, stand out by crossing into the Twilight Zone, where the unreal becomes real, a metaphysical object assumes a physical existence, an unspoken word becomes a voice actually heard.

The Bible is replete with records of dreams as a major form of Divine Encounter, as channels for conveying the deity's decision or advice, benevolent promise or strict verdict. Indeed, in Numbers 12:6, Yahweh is quoted as explicitly stating (to the brother and sister of Moses) that "if there be a prophet among you"—a person chosen to convey God's word—"I the Lord will make myself known to him in a vision and will speak unto him in a dream." The significance of the statement is enhanced by the precision of the wording: In a vision Yahweh makes himself *known*, recognizable, visible; in a dream he makes himself *heard*, granting oracles.

Informative in this regard is the tale in I Samuel chapter 28. Saul, the Israelite king, faced a crucial battle with the Philistines. The Prophet Samuel, who on Yahweh's command had anointed Saul king and had provided him with the Lord's word, has died. The apprehensive Saul is trying to obtain divine guidance on his own; but although he had "inquired of Yahweh" "both by dreams and by omens and by prophets," Yahweh did not respond. In this instance, dreams are listed as the first or foremost method of divine communication; omens—celestial signs or unusual terrestrial occurrences—and oracles, divine words through prophets, follow.

The manner in which Samuel himself had been chosen to become a Prophet of Yahweh also hinges on the use of dream for divine communication. It was a sequence of three "theophany dreams" in which scholars, such as Robert K. Gnuse (*The Dream Theophany of Samuel*), find remarkable parallels to the three dreams-cum-awakenings of Gilgamesh.

We have already mentioned how Samuel's mother, unable to bear children, promised to dedicate the child to Yahweh if she be blessed with a son. Keeping her vow, the mother brought the boy to Shiloh, where the Ark of the Covenant was kept in a temporary shrine under the supervision of Eli the Priest. But since Eli's sons were lewd and promiscuous, Yahweh decided to choose the pious Samuel as successor to Eli. It was a time, we read in I Samuel 3:1, when "the word of Yahweh was seldom heard and a vision was not frequent."

*And it came to pass on that day
that Eli was lying in his usual place,
and his eyes began to wax dim
and he could not see.
The lamp of Elohim did not yet go out;
and Samuel was lying in the sanctuary*

Figure 70

> *of Yahweh, where the Ark of* Elohim *was.*
> *And Yahweh called out to Samuel;*
> *and Samuel answered* "Here I am,"
> *and ran to Eli, saying:*
> "Here I am, for thou hast called me."

But Eli said no, he had not called Samuel, and told the boy to go back to sleep. Once again Yahweh called Samuel, and once again Samuel went to Eli only to be told that the priest did not call him. But when that happened the third time, "Eli understood that it was Yahweh calling the boy." So he instructed him to answer, if it ever happens again, "Speak O Yahweh, for thy servant listens." And thereafter "Yahweh came, and stood upright, and called 'Samuel, Samuel' from time to time; and each time Samuel answered 'speak, for thy servant listens'." An artist in thirteenth century A.D. France did his best to depict the first dream theophany and the final Divine Encounter of Samuel with Yahweh in a medieval illustrated Bible (Fig. 70).

It will be recalled that the Divine Spirit that provided King David with the *Tavnit* and written instructions for the Jerusalem Temple came upon him as he sat himself before the Ark of the Covenant. The call upon Samuel also occurred as "he was lying in the sanctuary of Yahweh, where the Ark of

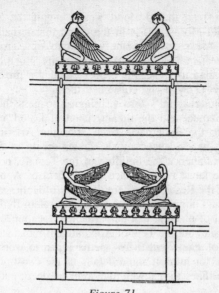

Figure 71

Elohim was.'' The Ark, made of acacia wood and inlaid with gold inside and out, was intended to safekeep the two Tablets of the Law. But its main purpose, as stated in the Book of Exodus, was to serve as a *Dvir*—literally, a ''Speaker.'' The Ark was to be topped by the two Cherubim made of solid gold, with their wings touching (the two possibilities of this detail are illustrated in Fig. 71). ''It is there that I shall keep appointments with you,'' Yahweh told Moses, ''and I will speak to you from above the cover, from between the two Cherubim which shall be upon the Ark'' (Exodus 25:22). The innermost part of the sanctuary, the Holy of Holies, was separated from the forepart by a veil that could not be parted except by Moses and then by his brother Aaron, who was appointed by Yahweh to serve as High Priest, and the three sons of Aaron, who were anointed as priests. And they were to enter the sacred place only after performing certain rites and wearing special clothing. Furthermore, when these consecrated priests would enter the Holy of Holies, they had to burn incense (whose composition was also strictly prescribed by the Lord) so that a cloud would engulf the Ark; for, Yahweh told Moses, "it is in the cloud that I shall appear, above the Ark's cover." But when two of Aaron's sons "brought near before the Lord a strange fire," one that (presumably) failed to create the proper cloud, "a fire went out from before Yahweh and consumed them."

Such "supernatural" forces, bringing to pass the dream-oracle of Samuel and the dream-vision of David, continued to permeate the Tabernacle even after the Ark itself was moved out, as evidenced by the dream-oracle of Solomon. Ready to commence the building of the Temple, he went to Gibeon, the latest resting place of the Tent of Appointment (the part of the Residence where the Holy of Holies was). The Ark itself had already been moved to Jerusalem by David, in anticipation of placing it in its permanent location within the future Temple; but the Tent of Appointment remained in Gibeon, and Solomon went there—perhaps just to worship, perhaps to see for himself some details of the construction. He offered sacrifices to Yahweh and went to sleep; and then—

> *And it was in Gibeon*
> *that Yahweh appeared unto Solomon*
> *in a nighttime dream.*
> *And Elohim said:*
> *"Ask what I shall give thee."*

The epiphany developed into a two-way conversation in which Solomon asked to be granted "an understanding heart to judge my people, that I may discern between good and bad." Yahweh liked the answer, for Solomon had asked neither for riches nor for long life, nor for the death of his enemies. Therefore, said Yahweh, he would grant him extraordinary Wisdom and Understanding, as well as riches and long life.

> *And Solomon awoke,*
> *and lo—it was a dream!*

Although the relevant section in the Bible begins with the statement that it was a dream epiphany, the vision and dialogue seemed so real to Solomon that when the conversation came to an end, Solomon was astounded that it was only a dream; and he did realize that what had taken place represented a reality, with lasting effects: thereafter he was indeed endowed with extraordinary Wisdom and Understanding. In a verse that indicates familiarity with the Mesopotamian and Egyptian civilizations at that time, the Bible added that "the wisdom of Solomon was greater than the wisdom of all the Sons of the East and of all of the wisdom of Egypt."

Whereas in the Sinai it was Yahweh who selected and instructed two artisans to carry out the intricate and artful architectural details, "filling up with the Spirit of *Elohim,* with wisdom and understanding and knowledge" Bezalel of the tribe of Judah and "putting wide wisdom in the heart" of Aholiab of the tribe of Dan, Solomon relied on the artisans of the Phoenician king of Tyre for the required experts. And when the Temple was completed, Solomon prayed to the Lord Yahweh that He accept the House as an eternal abode and as a place from which the prayers of Israel would be heard. It was then that Solomon had his second dream epiphany: "Yahweh appeared unto Solomon for the second time, in the manner seen to him in Gibeon."

Although the Temple in Jerusalem was literally called a "house" for the Lord, echoing the Sumerian term "E" for the temple-house, it is evident from the prayer of Solomon that he did not share the Mesopotamian view of temples as actual divine dwelling places, but rather as a sacred place for divine communication, a place where Man and God can hear each other, a permanent substitute for the desert Tent of Appointment for the Divine Presence.

No sooner had the priests brought the Ark of the Covenant into its place in the Holy of Holies, "the *Dvir* section of the Temple" and put it "under the wings of the Cherubim," than they had to leave hurriedly "on account of the cloud of Yahweh's Glory that filled the House." It was then that Solomon began his prayer, addressing "Yahweh, who would dwell in the dark cloud." "The heavens are thy dwelling place," Solomon said; "would *Elohim* then come to dwell on Earth? If the heaven and the highest heaven cannot contain thee, would this House that I have built?" Realizing that,

Solomon asked only for the Lord to hear the prayers that emanate from the temple; "hear in your dwelling place, in the heavens, the prayers and supplications, and judge the people accordingly."

It was then "that Yahweh appeared unto Solomon for a second time, in the manner that he was seen to him in Gibeon. And Yahweh said to him: I have heard thy prayer and thy supplications that thou hast made before me, and have sanctified this House that thou hast built, to place my *Shem* in it forever, so that my eyes and my heart shall be there in perpetuity."

The term *Shem* is traditionally translated "name," that by which someone is known or remembered. But as we have shown in *The 12th Planet,* quoting biblical, Mesopotamian, and Egyptian sources, the term paralleled the Sumerian MU that, though in time it came to mean "that by which one is remembered," originally referred to the Skychambers or flying machines of the Mesopotamian gods. Thus, when the people of Babylon (*Bab-Ili,* "Gateway of the Gods") set out to build the tower so as to make a *Shem* for themselves, they were building a launch tower not for a "name" but for skyborne vehicles.

In Mesopotamia, it was upon the temple platforms that special enclosures—some depicted as designed to withstand heavy impacts—were built specifically to serve the coming and going of these skychambers. Gudea had to provide in the sacred precinct such a special enclosure for the Divine Black Bird of Ninurta, and when the construction was done expressed the hope that the new temple's "MU shall hug the lands from horizon to horizon." A hymn to Adad/Ishkur extolled his "ray-emitting MU that can attain the heaven's zenith," and a hymn to Inanna/Ishtar described how, after putting on the pilot's garb (see Fig. 33), "over all the peopled lands she flies in her MU." In all these instances the usual translation is "name" for MU, reading for Adad a "name" that hugs the lands and attains the highest heavens, for Inanna/Ishtar that "over all the peopled lands she flies in her name." In fact, however, the reference was to the gods' flying machines and their landing pads within the sacred precincts. One depiction of such aerial vehicles, discovered by archaeol-

Figure 72

ogists excavating in behalf of the Vatican at Tell Ghassul across the Jordan River from Jericho, bring to mind the Chariot that Ezekiel described (Fig. 72).

In his instructions for building the original ziggurat-temple in Babylon, the E.SAG.IL ("House of the Great God"), Marduk specified the requirements for the skychamber:

> *Construct the Gateway of the Gods . . .*
> *Let its brickwork be fashioned.*
> *Its* Shem *shall be in the designated place.*

In time, because of the deterioration that afflicted all these stage-towers that were built of clay bricks as well as as a result of deliberate destruction by enemy attackers, temples required restoring and rebuilding. One instance concerning the Esagil, reported in the annals of the Assyrian king Esarhaddon (680–669 B.C.) contains several other key elements of the royal dreams recorded in the Bible in regard to the Temple in Jerusalem. These recurring elements include the Wisdom granted to Solomon, the architectural instructions, and the need for artisans to be divinely inspired or trained so as to understand these instructions.

Esarhaddon, here seen on his stela on which the twelve members of the Solar System are depicted by their symbols (Fig. 73), reversed previous Assyrian policy of confrontation and war with Babylon and saw no harm in revering Marduk (the national god of Babylon) in addition to worshiping Ashur (Assyria's national god). "Both Ashur and Marduk gave me wisdom," Esarhaddon wrote, granting him "the exalted understanding of Enki" for the task of "civilizing"—conquering and subjugating—other nations. He was also instructed by oracles and omens to start a program of temple restorations, beginning with Marduk's temple in Babylon. But the king knew not how.

It was then that Shamash and Adad appeared to Esarhaddon in a dream in which they showed the king the temple's architectural plans and construction details. In answer to his bafflement, they told him to gather all the needed masons, carpenters, and other artisans and lead them to the "House of Wisdom" in Ashur (the Assyrian capital city). They also told him to consult a seer regarding the right month and day in which to start the building work. Acting on what "Shamash and Adad had shown me in the dream," Esarhaddon wrote, he assembled the workforce and marched at their head to the "Place of Knowing." Consulting a seer, on the auspicious day the king carried on his head the foundation stone and laid it in the precise olden spot. With a mold made of ivory he fashioned the first brick. As the rebuilt temple was completed, he installed in it ornate doors of cypress wood

Figure 73

overlaid with gold, silver, and bronze; he fashioned golden vessels for the sacred rites. And when all was done, the priests were summoned, sacrifices were offered, and the prescribed temple service was renewed.

The language employed in the Bible to describe the unexpected realization by Solomon, suddenly awakened, that the experienced sight and sound were just a dream, duplicated an earlier instance of such a sudden realization—that of a Pharaoh:

> *And Pharaoh awoke,*
> *and lo—it was a dream!*

It was the dream series, described in chapter 41 of Genesis, that began with the Pharaoh's dream of seven cows—some translations prefer the more archaic-sounding "kine"—"of good appearance and fat-fleshed," that came up out of the Nile River to pasture. They were followed by seven "ill-favored and lean of flesh" cows; and the latter ate up the former. In a following dream the Pharaoh saw seven ears of corn, "rank and good," grow on one stalk, followed by seven thin and wind-withered ears of corn; and the latter swallowed the former. "And the Pharaoh awakened, and lo—it was a dream." The envisioned double scene was so real that the awakened Pharaoh was astonished to realize that it was just a dream. Troubled by the reality of the dream, he summoned the sages and magicians of Egypt to tell him the meaning of the dream; but none could offer an interpretation.

Thus began the rise to prominence in Egypt of the Hebrew youth Joseph, who, wrongfully imprisoned, interpreted correctly the dreams that two of the Pharaoh's ministers, also in prison, had. Now one of them, the Chief Wine Steward who was reinstated to his position, told that to the Pharaoh and suggested that Joseph be summoned to help solve the Pharaoh's two dreams. And Joseph said to the Pharaoh: The two dreams are but one single dream; "that which the *Elohim* will be doing to the Pharaoh has been told." It was, in other words, an *omen-dream,* a divine revelation of what will happen in the future by God's design. It is a foretelling of seven

a mn m ht
n t
Amen.em.het

Figure 74

years of plenty that will be overwhelmed by the subsequent seven years of shortages and hunger, he said: "That which *Elohim* will be doing did He reveal to Pharaoh." And the dream was repeated twice, he added, because "the thing is firmly resolved by the *Elohim,* who will hasten it to come to pass."

Now then, realizing that Joseph was possessed of the "Spirit of *Elohim,*" the Pharaoh appointed him Overseer over all the Land of Egypt to help avert the hunger. And Joseph found ways to double and treble the crops during the seven plentiful years, and stored the food. And when the famine came, "affecting all the lands," there was food in Egypt.

Although the Bible does not identify the Pharaoh of Joseph's time by name, other biblical data and chronologies have enabled us to identify him as Amenemhet III of the Twelfth Dynasty, who reigned over Egypt from 1850 to 1800 B.C. His granite statue (Fig. 74) is on display in the Cairo Museum.

The biblical tale of this Pharaoh's dream of the seven cows undoubtedly echoes Egyptian beliefs that seven cows, called

Figure 75

the Seven Hathors (after the goddess Hathor, who, as we have mentioned, was depicted as a cow) could foretell the future—forerunners of the Sibylline oracle goddesses of the Greeks. Nor is the very notion of seven lean years a biblical invention, for such cycles in the level of the waters of the Nile—the only source of water in rainless Egypt—continue to our own times. In fact, there exists an earlier *Egyptian* record of such a cycle of seven years of plenty followed by seven lean years. It is a hieroglyphic text (transcribed by E.A.W. Budge in *Legends of the Gods*—Fig. 75); it relates that the Pharaoh Zoser (Circa 2650 B.C.) received a royal dispatch from the governor of Upper Egypt, in the south, of a grave famine, because "the Nile had not come in for the space of seven years."

So the king "extended his heart back to the beginnings," and asked the Chamberlain of the gods, the Ibis-headed god Thoth, "What is the birthplace of the Nile? Is there a god there, and who is that god?" And Thoth answered that there

Figure 76

indeed was a god there who regulates the waters of the Nile from two caverns (Fig. 76) and that he was his father Khnum (alias Ptah, alias Enki), the god who had fashioned Mankind (see Fig. 4).

How exactly Zoser managed to speak to Thoth and receive his answer is not made clear in the hieroglyphic text. The text does tell us that once Zoser had been told that the god in whose hands the fate of the Nile and Egypt's sustenance was Khnum, residing far away on the island of Elephantine in Upper Egypt, the king knew what to do: he went to sleep . . . Expecting an epiphany, he had one:

> *And as I slept,*
> *with life and satisfaction,*
> *I discovered the god*
> *standing over against me!*

In his sleep—dreaming, envisioning—Zoser says, ''I propitiated him with praise; I prayed to him in his presence,'' asking for the restoration of the Nile's waters and the land's fertility. And the god

Revealed himself to me.
Concerning me, with friendly face,
these words he declared:
"I am Khnum, thy fashioner."

The god announced that he would heed the king's prayers if the king would undertake to "rebuild temples, to restore what is ruined, and to hew out new shrines" for the deity. For that, the god said, he will be giving the king new stones as well as "hard stones which have existed from the beginning of time."

Then the god promised that in exchange he would open the sluices in two caverns that are beneath his rock chamber and that as a result the waters of the Nile will begin to flow again. Within a year, he said, the river's banks will be green again, plants will grow, starvation will disappear. And when the god finished speaking, and his image vanished, Zoser "awoke refreshed, my heart relieved of weariness," and decreed permanent rites of offerings to Khnum in eternal gratitude.

The god Ptah and a vision of him is the central theme of two other Egyptian dream epiphanies; one of them brings to mind the biblical tales of the woman who cannot bear a male heir.

The first, describing how a Divine Encounter turned the tide of warfare, is contained in a long inscription by the Pharaoh Merenptah (circa 1230 B.C.) on the fourth pylon in the great temple in Karnak. Though the son of the warring Pharaoh Ramses II, Merenptah found it beyond his capabilities to protect Egypt from a rising tide of invaders, both by land (Libyans from the west) and by sea ("pirates" from across the Mediterranean). The warfare reached its culmination when Libyan forces reinforced by the "pirates" were poised to seize Memphis, the olden capital of Egypt. Merenptah, desponded, was ill prepared to face the attackers. Then, in the night before the decisive battle, he had a dream. In the dream the god Ptah appeared; promising the king victory, the god said: "Take this now!" and with those words handed to Merenptah a sword, saying further: "and banish from yourself your troubled heart."

The hieroglyphic text is partly damaged at this point, making it unclear what happened next; but the inference is that as Merenptah awoke, he found the divine sword physically in his hand. Reassured by the god's words and the divine sword, Merenptah led his troops to battle; it resulted in a complete victory for the Egyptians.

In the other instance wherein Ptah appears, it was in a dream by a princess (Taimhotep) who was the wife of the High Priest. She bore three daughters but no male heir, wherefor she "prayed to the majesty of this august god, great of wonders and able to give a son to one who has none." One night, as the High Priest was asleep, Ptah "came to him in a revelation" and said to the High Priest that in exchange for carrying out certain construction works, "I shall make you in return for it a male child."

> On this the high priest awoke
> and kissed the ground of this august god.
> He commissioned the prophets, the chiefs
> of mysteries, the priests, and the
> sculptors of the House of Gold,
> to carry out at once the beneficent work.

The construction work was carried out in accordance with the wishes of Ptah; and after that, the princess states in the inscription, she became pregnant and did bear a male child.

Though not in its details but in its essential theme, the Egyptian tale (from Ptolmeic times) bears a resemblance to the much earlier biblical record of the appearance of the Lord, accompanied by two other divine beings, to Abraham and predicting that his aging and childless wife Sarah will bear a male heir.

Among other instances of royal oracle dreams found in Egyptian records, the most famous is that by the prince who later ascended the throne to be crowned as Thothmes IV. His dream is well-known because he describes it on a stela that he had erected between the paws of the great Sphinx in Giza—where it still stands for all to see.

As recorded on the stela (Fig. 77), the prince "used to occupy himself with sport on the desert highland of Memphis.'' One day he lay to rest near the necropolis of Gizah, next to ''the divine way of the gods to the horizon ... the holy place of primeval times.'' That, the inscription says, was where ''the very great statue of the Sphinx rests, great of fame, majestic of awe.'' It was noontime, the sun was strong; so the prince chose to lie down in the shadow of the Sphinx, and he fell asleep.

As he was sleeping, he heard the Sphinx speak ''with his own mouth, saying:''

> *Look at me, my son, Thothmose ...*
> *Behold, my state is that of one in need,*
> *my whole body is going to pieces.*
> *The sands of the desert above which I had stood*
> *have encroached upon me ...*

What the Sphinx was saying to the sleeping prince was a request that the desert sands that had engulfed the Sphinx and covered most of it—a situation not unlike that found by Napoleon's men in the nineteenth century (Fig. 78)—be removed so that the Sphinx could be seen in its full majesty.

Figure 77

In exchange, the Sphinx—representing the god Harmakhis—promised him that he would be the successor on Egypt's throne. "When the Sphinx finished these words," the inscription continues, "the king's son awoke." Though it was a dream, its contents and meaning were crystal clear to the prince. "He understood the speech of this god." At first opportunity he carried out the divine request, to clear the Sphinx of the sands that buried it almost completely; and indeed, in 1421 B.C., the prince ascended Egypt's throne to become Thothmes IV.

Such a divine nomination to Kingship was not unique in Egyptian annals. In fact, it has been recorded in connection with a predecessor, Thothmes III. The tale of miraculous happenings and a vision of the "Glory of the Lord" has been inscribed by this king on the temple walls in Karnak. In this case the god did not speak out; rather, he indicated his choice of a future monarch through the "working of miracles."

As Thothmes himself related it, when he was still a youth training as a priest, he was standing in the colonnaded part of the temple. Suddenly, the god Amon-Ra appeared in his glory from the horizon. "He made heaven and Earth festive with his beauty; then he began to perform a great marvel: he

Figure 78

directed his rays into the eyes of Horus-of-the-Horizon'' (the
Sphinx). The king offered the arriving god incense, sacrifices,
and oblations, and led the god into the temple in a procession.
As the god walked by the young prince, Thothmes reported,

> He really recognized me and he halted.
> I touched the ground; I bowed myself down
> in his presence.
> He stood me up, set me before the king.

Then, as an indication that this prince was the divinely
chosen one for the succession, the god "worked a marvel"
over the prince. What ensued, Thothmes III wrote, as incredible as it sounds, as mysterious these things are, really
happened:

> He opened for me the doors of Heaven;
> He spread open for me the portals of its horizon.
> I flew up to the sky as a Divine Falcon,
> able to see his mysterious form
> which is in Heaven,
> that I might adore his majesty.
> [And] I saw the being-form of the
> Horizon God in his mysterious
> Ways of Heaven.

On this heavenly flight, Thothmes III wrote in his annals,
he "was made full with the Understanding of the gods." The
experience, and its claims, surely bring to mind the heavenly
ascents of Enmeduranki and Enoch, and the "Glory of Yahweh" seen by the Prophet Ezekiel.

The conviction that dreams were divine oracles, foretelling
things to come, was a firmly held belief throughout the ancient Near East. Ethiopian kings also believed in the power
of dreams as guidelines for actions to be taken (or avoided)
and of events about to happen.

One instance, recorded on a stela by the Ethiopian king
Tanutamun, relates that in the first year of his reign "his
majesty saw a dream in the night." In the dream the king

saw "two serpents, one on his right, one on his left." The vision was so real that when the king awoke, he was astonished not to find the serpents actually beside him. He called the priests and seers to interpret the dream, and they said that the two serpents represented two goddesses, representing Upper and Lower Egypt. The dream, they said, meant that he could conquer the whole of Egypt "in its length and in its breadth; there is no other to share it with you." So the king "went forth, and a hundred thousand followed him," and he conquered Egypt. So, he wrote on the stela commemorating the dream and its aftermath, "true indeed was the dream."

A divine oracle given by the god Amon, though in broad daylight rather than in a dream, is reported in an inscription on a stela found in Upper Egypt near the Nubian border. It relates that when an Ethiopian king was leading his army into Egypt, he suddenly died. His commanders were "like a herd without a herdsman." They knew that the next king had to be chosen from among the king's brothers, but which one? So they went to the Temple of Amon to obtain an oracle. After the "prophets and major priests" performed the required rites, the commanders presented one of the king's brothers to the god, but there was silence. They then presented the second brother, born to the king's sister. This time the god spoke up, saying: "He is your king ... He is your ruler." So the commanders crowned this brother, who assumed the Kingship after the deity assured him of divine support.

This tale of the selection of a successor to the Ethiopian king includes a detail that usually goes unnoticed—the fact that the divinely chosen successor was the son born to the king by his sister. We find a parallel in the biblical tale of Abraham and his beautiful wife Sarah, whom Abimelech, the Philistine king of Gerar, fancied. Once before, when they visited the Pharaoh's court in Egypt, when the Pharaoh wished to take Sarah away from Abraham, Abraham asked her to say that she was his sister (not his wife) so that his life would be spared. Wisened by the experience, Abraham again asked Sarah to say that she was only a sister of Abraham. But when Abimelech proceeded with his plan, the Lord intervened:

And Elohim *came to Abimelech*
in a nighttime dream, saying to him:
"Indeed thou shalt die on account of the
woman whom thou hast taken, for she is
a man's wife."

"And Abimelech did not come near her," explaining to
the Lord that he was innocent, for Abraham "did say to me,
'She is my sister' and she too hath said, 'He is my brother'."
So "*Elohim* said to him, in the dream," that if so he would
not be punished as long as he returned Sarah to Abraham
untouched. Afterward, when Abimelech demanded an explanation from Abraham, Abraham explained that fearing for his
life he did tell the truth but not the whole truth: "Indeed she
is my sister, the daughter of my father but not the daughter
of my mother, so she could become my wife." By being his
half sister Sarah assured that her son (Isaac), even if not the
Firstborn, would be the successor. These rules of succession,
emulating the customs of the Anunnaki themselves, prevailed
throughout the ancient Near East (and were even copied by
the Incas in Peru).

The Philistines called their principal deity *Dagon,* a name
or epithet that can be translated as "He of the Fishes"—the
god of Pisces, an attribute of Ea/Enki. This identification,
however, is not so clear-cut and certain, because when this
deity appears elsewhere in the ancient Near East, his name
is spelled *Dagan,* which could mean "He of the Grains"—
a god of farming. Whatever his true identity, this god featured
in several omen-dreams reported in the state archives of the
kingdom of Mari, a city-state that flourished at the beginning
of the second millennium B.C. until its destruction by the
Babylonian king Hammurabi in 1759 B.C.

One report from Mari pertains to a dream whose contents
were deemed so significant that it was at once brought by
messenger to the attention of Zimri-Lim, the last king of
Mari. In the dream the man saw himself journeying with
others. Arriving at a place called Terqa, he entered the temple
to Dagan and prostrated himself. At that moment the god
"opened his mouth" and asked the traveler whether a truce
had been declared between the forces of Zimri-Lim and those

of the Yaminites. When the traveler answered in the negative, the god complained why he had not been kept abreast of developments and instructed the dreamer to take a message to the king, demanding that he send messengers to update the god on the situation. "This is what this man saw in his dream," the urgent report to the king stated, adding that "this man is trustworthy."

Another dream concerning Dagan and the wars in which Zimri-Lim was engaged was reported by a temple priestess. In the dream, she stated, "I entered the temple of the goddess Belet-ekallim ("Mistress of Temples") but she was not in residence nor did I see the statues presented to her. As I saw this I began to weep." Then I heard "an eery voice crying, saying over and over again: 'Come back, O Dagan, come back, O Dagan!' This it was crying over and over." Then the voice became more ecstatic, filling the temple of the goddess with the voice, saying: "O Zimri-Lim, do not go on an expedition, stay in Mari, and then I alone will take responsibility."

The goddess who spoke out in this dream, offering to do the fighting for the beleaguered king, is named in the report *Annunitum,* a Semitic rendering of Inanna, i.e. Ishtar. Her reported willingness to so act for Zimri-Lim makes historical sense, for she was the one who anointed Zimri-Lim to be king of Mari—a divine act that was commemorated in the magnificent murals found in the palace of Mari (Fig. 79) when it was unearthed by French archaeologists.

The priestess who had reported the dream as related, Addu-duri by name, was an oracle priestess. In her report she pointed out that while her oracles were based in the past on "signs," this was the first time she had had an oracle dream. Her name is mentioned in another dream report, but this time of a dream by a male priest in which he saw the Goddess of Oracles speak to him about the king's "negligence in guarding himself." (In other instances oracle priestesses reported to the king divine messages obtained while they were in a self-induced trance, rather than sleeping and dreaming).

Mari was situated on the Euphrates River where Syria and Iraq meet today, and served as the way station from Mesopotamia to the Mediterranean coastlands (and thence to Egypt) on a route that crossed the Syrian desert to the Cedar Mountains of Lebanon. (A longer route but through the Fertile Crescent led via Harran on the Upper Euphrates). No wonder, then, that the Canaanites of the coastal lands, as their neighbors the Philistines, believed in (and reported) dreams as a form of Divine Encounter. Though their writings (of which we know primarily from finds in Ras Shamra, the ancient Ugarit, on the Mediterranean coast in Syria) dealt mostly with legends or ''myths'' of the god Ba'al, his companion the goddess Anat, and their father the aging god El, they do mention oracle dreams by patriarchal heroes. Thus, in the *Tale of Aqhat,* a patriarch by name of Danel who is without a male heir is told by El in a dream-omen that he would have a son within a year—just as Abraham was told by Yahweh regarding the birth of Isaac. (When the boy, Aqhat, grows up, Anat lusts for him and, as she had done with Gilgamesh, promises him longevity if he would become her lover. When he refuses, she causes him to be slain).

Dreams as a venerated form of divine communication were also recorded in the lands on the Upper Euphrates and all the way into Asia Minor. With the coastal lands that are nowadays Israel, Lebanon, and Syria serving both as a land bridge as well as a battlefield between contending Egyptian Pharaohs and Mesopotamian kings—each claiming to act on

Figure 79

orders of their gods—no wonder that in that meeting and melting zone the omen-dreams also reflected the clash of cultures and mixing of omens.

Egyptian records of royal omen-dreams include a text known to scholars as the *Legend of the Possessed Princess*—one of the oldest records, *inter alia,* of exorcism. Written on a stela that is now in the Louvre Museum in Paris, it tells how the Prince of Bekhten (the land Bactria on the Upper Euphrates), who had married an Egyptian princess, sought the help of the Pharaoh Ramses II to cure the princess of the ''spirits that possessed her.'' The Pharaoh sent over one of his magicians, but to no avail. So the Prince of Bekhten asked that an Egyptian *god* ''be brought to contend with this spirit.''

Receiving the petition in his capital Thebes during a religious festival, the Pharaoh went to the temple of the god Khensu, described as a son of Ra and usually depicted with a falcon's head on which the Moon rests in its crescent. There the king related to the god, ''the great god who expels disease-demons,'' what the problem was, and requested divine help. As he spoke, ''there was much nodding of the head of Khensu,'' indicating a favorable hearing. So the king put together a great caravan that went to Bekhten accompanying the god (or his ''prophet, the carrier of the plans,'' or the god's statue—as some scholars suggest). And using the divine magical powers, the ''evil spirit'' was exorcised.

Witnessing the magical powers of Khensu, the Prince of Bekhten ''then schemed in his heart, saying: 'I will cause this god to stay here in Bekhten.' '' But having caused a delay in the god's return to Egypt, while ''the Prince of Bekhten was sleeping in his bed,'' he had a dream. In the dream he saw ''this god coming to him outside the shrine. He was a falcon of gold, and he flew to the sky and off to Egypt.'' The prince ''awoke with panic,'' and realized that the dream was a divine omen, instructing him to let the god return to Egypt. So the prince ''let this god proceed to Egypt, after he had given him much tribute of every good thing.''

Farther north of Bactria, in the Land of the Hittites in Asia Minor, the conviction that royal dreams were divine revelations was also firmly held. One of the longest extant texts that reflect that conviction is called by scholars *The Plague Prayers of Mursilis,* a Hittite king who reigned from 1334 to 1306 B.C. As confirmed by historical records, a plague had afflicted the land decimating the population; and Mursilis could not figure out what had angered the gods. He himself had been pious and deeply religious, "celebrated all the festivals, never preferred one temple for another." So what was wrong? In desperation, he included the following words in his prayer:

> *Hearken to me, ye gods, my lords!*
> *Drive ye forth the plague from the Hittite land!*
> *Let the reason for which the people are dying*
> *be established—either by an omen,*
> *or let me see it in a dream,*
> *or let a prophet declare it.*

It should be noted that the three methods of obtaining divine guidance—an oracle dream, an omen, or a communication through a prophet—are exactly the very same three methods listed by King Saul when he had attempted to obtain Yahweh's guidance. But, exactly as in the case of the Israelite king who received no response, so to the appeals of the Hittite king "the gods did not hearken; the plague did not get better; the Land of the Hittites continued to be cruelly afflicted."

"Matters were becoming too much for me," Mursilis wrote in this annal, and he redoubled his pious appeals to the god Teshub ("The Windblower" or "Storm God," whom the Sumerians called Ishkur and the Semitic peoples Adad, Fig. 80). Finally he managed to receive an oracle; since it was neither an omen nor a prophecy, it must have been a dream-oracle, the third method of divine communication with the king. It was thus that Mursilis learned that his father Shuppiliumas, in whose time the plague began, did transgress in two ways: he discontinued certain offerings to the gods, and he broke his oath in a treaty with the Egyptians to keep the peace, and took Egyptian captives back to Hattiland; and it was with them that the plague came to nest among the Hittites.

If that was so, the king told Teshub in his supplications, he would offer restitution, "acknowledge his father's sins," and accept full responsibility. If more repentance or restitution was required, he asked the god again to "let me see it in a dream, or let it be found by an omen, or let a prophet declare it to me."

He thus listed again the three accepted or expected methods of divine communication. Since the text, when found, ends here, one must assume that with that the wrath of Teshub had ended and so did the plague.

Other Hittite inscriptions recording Divine Encounters through dreams and visions have been found. Some of them concern the goddess Ishtar, the Sumerian Inanna, whose rise to prominence continued well after Sumerian times.

In one such inscription, the Hittite prince who was heir to the throne stated that the goddess appeared to his father in a dream, telling him that the young prince had only a few years to live; but that if he be dedicated as a priest to Ishtar, "then he shall stay alive." When the king followed the oracle dream, the prince lived on and his brother (Muwatallis) inherited the throne in his stead.

The same Muwatallis and Ishtar are the principals in a dream reported by Hattusilis III (1275–1250 B.C.), also a brother of Muwatallis. It tells that Muwatallis, apparently

Figure 80

with some evil motive, ordered that his brother Hattusilis be subjected to a trial "by the sacred wheel" (a procedure or torture whose nature is uncertain). "However," the intended victim's report states, "my Lady Ishtar appeared to me in a dream; in the dream she said to me as follows: 'Shall I abandon you to a hostile deity? Be not afraid!' And with the help of the goddess I was acquitted; because the goddess, my Lady, held me by the hand; she never abandoned me to a hostile deity or an evil judgment."

According to the various Hittite royal annals from that time, the goddess Ishtar announced her support of Hattusilis III in his struggle for the throne with his brother Mutawallis in several oracle dreams. In one report the claim was made that the goddess promised the Hittite throne to Hattusilis in a dream by his wife—a wife, according to another dream-record, espoused by him "upon the command of the goddess Ishtar; the goddess entrusted her to me in a dream." In a third dream report, Ishtar is said to have appeared to Urhi-Teshub, the heir appointed by Mutawallis to succeed him, and told him in a dream that all his efforts to thwart Hattusilis were in vain: "Aimlessly you have tired yourselves out, for I, Ishtar, all the lands of the Hittites to Hattusilis have turned over."

Hittite dream reports, at least to the extent that they have been found, reflect the importance that was attached there to the proper observance of the rites and requirements of worship. In one discovered text "a dream of his majesty the king" is reported thus: In the dream, the Lady Hebat Who Judges (the spouse of Teshub) said again and again to his majesty, 'When the Storm God comes from heaven, he should not find you to be stingy.' While dreaming, the king responded that he had made a golden ritual object for the god. But the goddess said, "It is not enough!" Then another king, the king of Hakmish, entered the dream-conversation, saying to his majesty: "Why have you not given the *Huhupal*-instruments and the lapis-lazuli stones which you have promised to Teshub?"

When the Hittite king awoke from this trialogued dream, he reported it to the priestess Hebatsum. And she said the dream meant that "You must give the *Huhupal*-instruments and the lapis-lazuli stones to the great god."

Uncharacteristically for the record of royal dream reports in the ancient Near East, some of the Hittite ones pertain to dreams by queens, female members of the royalty. One such record, that begins with the introductory statement "A dream of the queen," states that "the queen has made a vow in a dream to the goddess Hebat." In that dream-vow, the queen said to the goddess: "If you, my Lady, Divine Hebat, will make the king well and not give him over to the Evil, I shall make for Divine Hebat a golden statue and a rosette of gold, and for your breast I shall also make a golden pectoral."

In yet another instance, the recorded event was the appearance of an unidentified god to the queen in a dream—perhaps the same queen who sought Hebat's intervention to cure her sick royal spouse. In the dream this god told the queen "regarding the matter which weighs heavily on your heart concerning your husband: He will live; I shall give him 100 years." Hearing that, "the queen made a vow in her dream as follows: 'If you do thus for me and my husband remains alive, I shall give to the gods three *Harshialli*-containers, one with oil, one with honey and one with fruits.'"

The king's illness must have indeed weighed heavily on this queen's heart, for in a third dream record the queen reported that someone whom she could not see said again and again to her in the dream: "Make a vow to the goddess Ningal" (the spouse of Nannar/Sin), promising the goddess ritual objects of gold decorated with lapis lazuli if the king recovers. Here the sickness is described as "fire of the feet."

In another part of Asia Minor, in Lydia where Greek cities prospered, a king named Gyges had—according to his adversary the Assyrian king Ashurbanipal—a dream-vision. In it the sleeping king was shown an inscription that spelled out the name of Ashurbanipal. The divine message said: "Bow before the feet of Ashurbanipal, the King of Assyria; then you will conquer your enemies just by mentioning this name."

According to the Assyrian king's inscription in his annals, King Gyges, "the very same day that he had this dream, sent a horseman to wish me well and report the dream to me; and from the day he bowed before my royal feet, he conquered

Figure 81

the Cimmerians who had been harassing the inhabitants of his country.''

The Assyrian king's interest in, and recording of, the dream of a foreign king was but a reflection of the extent of Assyrian beliefs in the power of dreams as a form of Divine Encounter. The epiphanies and oracles conveyed by royal dreams were a phenomenon eagerly sought after, and reported, by the kings of Assyria; the same held true for the kings of their neighbor and rival Babylonia.

Ashurbanipal himself (686–626 B.C.), who kept extensive annals on baked clay prisms (as this one now in the Louvre Museum—Fig. 81), recorded several dream experiences; often they were by others rather than himself, just as was the case with King Gyges.

In one instance it was a record of a priest who went to sleep and in the middle of the night ''had a dream as follows: There was writing upon the pedestal of the god Sin; the god Nabu, scribe of the world, was reading the inscription again and again: 'Upon those who plot evil against Ashurbanipal, king of Assyria, and resort to hostilities, I shall bring miserable death, I shall put an end to their lives with a quick iron dagger, conflagration, hunger and disease.' '' A postscript by Ashurbanipal to this report of a dream stated: "This dream I heard and put my trust in the word of my Lord Sin."

In another instance it was asserted that one and the same dream—vision might be a better term—was experienced by a whole army. In the relevant record Ashurbanipal explains that when his army reached the river Idide it was a raging torrent and the soldiers were afraid to try a crossing. "But the goddess Ishtar who dwells in Arbela let my army have a dream in the middle of the night." In this mass dream or vision Ishtar was heard to say, "I shall go in front of Ashurbanipal, the king whom I have myself made." The army, Ashurbanipal added as a postscript, "relied upon this dream and crossed the river Idide safely." (Historical data confirm a crossing of this river by Ashurbanipal's army circa 648 B.C.)

In the introduction to another dream concerning his reign Ashurbanipal claimed that the dream, by a priest of the goddess Ishtar, resulted from a prior auditory communication from the goddess directly to the king himself. "The goddess Ishtar heard my anxious sighs and said to me, 'Fear not . . . inasmuch as you have lifted your hands in prayer and your eyes are filled with tears, I have mercy upon you.' "

It was during that very same night of the above epiphany that "a seer-priest went to bed and saw a dream; when he awoke with a start, Ishtar made him see a night-vision." As reported by the priest to Ashurbanipal, what he saw in the nocturnal vision was this: "The goddess Ishtar who dwells in Arbela came in; quivers were hanging at her right and her left; she held the bow in her hand; her sharp sword was drawn for battle. You were standing before her and she spoke to you like a real mother." Then, the priest reported, he heard in the night-vision Ishtar say to the king: "Wait with the attack; wherever you go, I shall go ahead of you . . . Stay here, eat, drink wine and make merry and praise my divinity, while I shall go ahead and accomplish the task that you have asked for." Then, the priest continued to describe the vision: The goddess embraced the king and wrapped him in her protective aura; "her countenance shone like fire, and she left the room." The vision, the seer-priest told the king, meant

Figure 82

Figure 83

that Ishtar will be at his side when he marches against his enemy. The vision of Ishtar armed and as a warlike goddess emitting rays has been recorded in various ancient depictions (Fig. 82).

The annals of Ashurbanipal, who claimed that among his great knowledge was the ability to interpret dreams, are replete with references to oracles—probably through dreams, though this is not specified—given him by this or that of the "great gods, my lords" in connection with his military campaigns. His interest in dreams and their interpretation led him also to have state archives examined for records of past oracle dreams. Thus we learn that an archivist by the name of Marduk-shum-usur reported to Ashurbanipal that his grandfather Sennacherib had a dream in which the god Ashur (Fig. 83), Assyria's national god, appeared to him and said, "O wise one, king, king of kings: You are the offspring of wise Adapa; you surpass all men in the knowledge of Apsu (Enki's domain).''

In the same report the archivist, evidently trained as an omen-priest, also reported to Ashurbanipal the circumstances that made his father, Esarhaddon, invade Egypt. It was when ''thy father Esarhaddon was in the region of Harran that he saw there a temple of cedarwood, and he went in, and saw inside the god Sin leaning on a staff, holding two crowns.'' The god Nusku, the Divine Messenger of the gods, ''was standing there before him; when the father of the king entered, the god placed a crown upon his head, saying, 'You will go to countries, therein you will conquer.' Your father departed and conquered Egypt.''

Though the text does not say so explicitly, it is presumed that the incident at the temple in Harran was also a dream, a vision-dream seen by Esarhaddon. Indeed, both historical and religious texts from that time indicate that Nannar/Sin had left Mesopotamia after Sumer had been desolated and Marduk returned to Babylon to claim supremacy ''on Earth and in Heaven'' (in 2024 B.C. by our calculations). Harran, where Esarhaddon received the permissive oracle from the absent god, had been a twin cult center of Nannar/Sin, emulating that of Nannar/Sin's principal center in Sumer— the city of Ur. It was to Harran that Abraham's father, the priest Terah, took his family when they left Ur. And, as we shall see, Harran came again into prominence when dream-omens and real events once again changed the course of history.

As prophesied by the biblical Prophets, mighty Assyria, the scourge of nations, lay prostrate before Achaemenid (Persian) invaders, who overran Nineveh in 612 B.C. In Babylon Nebuchadnezzar, freed of Assyrian constraints, rushed into the void, capturing lands near and far, destroying the Temple in Jerusalem. But the days of Babylon were also numbered, and the end was foretold to the haughty king in a series of dreams. As recorded in the Bible (Daniel chapter 2) Nebuchadnezzar had a troubling dream. He called in ''the magicians, seers, sorcerers and Chaldeans'' (i.e. astrologers) and asked them to interpret the dream—however, without telling them what the dream was. Unable to do so, he ordered their execution. But then Daniel was brought before the king, and invoked the powers of the "God in heaven who reveals mysteries." As the executioner of the others was told to halt, Daniel first guessed the dream and then solved its meaning. "In your vision," he told the king, "you saw a very large statue, exceedingly bright, terrifying in appearance, standing before thee." The statue's head was made of gold, its chest and arms of silver, its belly and thighs of bronze, the legs of iron, the feet part iron and part clay. Then a stone that no hand held appeared and smote the statue to pieces; the pieces turned to chaff that was carried by a wind into oblivion; and the stone turned into a great mountain.

"This is the dream," Daniel said, and here is its meaning: The statue represents the great Babylon; the golden head is Nebuchadnezzar; after him there shall be three lesser kings; and in the end it will all be swept away like chaff, and a new king from elsewhere shall rise to greatness.

Nebuchadnezzar then had a second dream. He called in the seers, including Daniel. In "visions as he lay in bed," the king said, he saw a tall tree that kept growing until it reached the heavens; it was a fruitful and shade-giving tree. Suddenly,

> In the vision, at the head of my bed,
> a Watcher, a Holy One, came down from heaven.
> He cried out aloud, saying:
> "Cut down the tree and lop off its branches,
> strip off its leaves and scatter its fruit,
> let the beasts flee its shade and the birds its branches;
> but leave in the ground its stump and roots."

And Daniel told the king that the tree was he, Nebuchadnezzar; and the vision was an oracle of things to come—the end of Nebuchadnezzar, doomed to lose his mind and roam the fields like windblown leaves and eat like the beasts. Tradition holds that Nebuchadnezzar indeed went mad, dying seven years after that oracle dream (in 562 B.C.).

As predicted, his three successors were short-lived kings, demised and killed in a series of rebellions. Into the breach stepped the High Priestess of the temple of Sin in Harran;

and in a series of appeals and prayers to Sin, she prevailed on this god to return to Harran and bless the assumption of kingship by her son Nabuna'id (although he was only remotely related to the Assyrian royal line). It was as a result that the last effective king of Babylon and his dreams linked the end of Mesopotamian civilizations to Harran. The time was 555 B.C.

In order for a non-Babylonian and a follower of Sin to rule in Babylon, the approval of Marduk, and a rapprochement between this son of Enki and the son (Sin) of Enlil were required. The double blessing and the rapprochement were confirmed—perhaps achieved—by means of several dreams by Nabuna'id. They were so important that he recorded them on stelas, for all to know.

The omen-dreams of Nabuna'id had some unusual features. In at least two of them planets representing deities made an appearance. In another, the apparition of a dead king took part in the goings-on, and it was divided into two parts as a way to relate a dream within a dream.

In the first of those recorded dreams, Nabuna'id saw "the planet Venus, the planet Saturn, the planet Ab-Hal, the Shining Planet, and the Great Star, the great witnesses who dwell in heaven." He (in the dream) set up altars to them and prayed for lasting life, enduring rule, and a favorable response to his prayers by Marduk. He then—in the same dream or in a sequel thereto—"lay down and beheld in a nightly vision the Great Goddess who restores health and bestows life on the dead." He prayed to her, too, for lasting life "and asked that she might turn her face toward me"; and

> She actually did turn,
> and looked steadily upon me
> with her shining face,
> thus indicating her mercy.

In the preamble to the report of another dream Nabuna'id states that he "became apprehensive in regard to the conjunction of the Great Star and the Moon," the celestial counterparts of Marduk and Nannar/Sin. Then he went on to tell the dream:

In the dream, a man's apparition suddenly stood beside me.

He said to me: "There are no evil portents in the conjunction."

In the same dream Nubuchadnezzar, my royal predecessor, appeared to me. He was standing on a chariot with one attendant. The attendant said to Nebuchadnezzar: "Do speak to Nabunaid so that he would report to you the dream he just had!"

Nebuchadnezzar listened to him and said to me: "Tell me what good omens you have seen."

I answered him, saying, "In my dream I saw with joy the Great Star and the Moon. And the planet of Marduk, high up in the sky, called me by my name."

The conjunction of the celestial counterparts of Marduk and Sin signified, thus, the agreement of both to the ascent of Nabuna'id to the throne; the inquiring departed Nebuchadnezzar and the satisfactory answer given him signified that he, too, in a kind of retrospect, approved this succession.

The third dream carried the rapprochement between Marduk and Sin even farther. In it "the great gods" Marduk and Sin were seen standing together, and Marduk reprimanded the king for not yet beginning the rebuilding of Sin's temple in Harran. In the two-way conversation, Nabuna'id explained that he could not do that because the Medians were laying siege to the city. Whereupon Marduk predicted the enemy's demise by the hand of Cyrus, the Achaemenid king. This indeed has later taken place, Nabuna'id wrote in a postscript to the record of this dream.

Struggling to hold together the disintegrating empire, Nabuna'id appointed his son Belshazzar as regent in Babylon. But there, amid the banqueting intended to forget the surrounding turmoil, there appeared the Handwriting-on-the-Wall. *Mene, mene, tekel u Pharsin* it said—the days of Babylon are numbered, the kingdom shall be divided and given over to the Medians and Persians. In 539 B.C. the city fell to the Achaemenid (Persian) king Cyrus. One of his first acts was to permit the return of exiles to their lands and their freedom to worship in their temples of choice—an edict re-

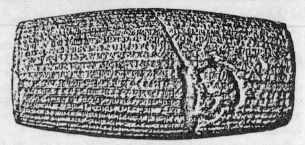

Figure 84

corded on the Cylinder of Cyrus (Fig. 84), now in the British Museum in London. To the Jewish exiles he issued a special proclamation permitting their return to Judaea and the rebuilding of the Temple in Jerusalem; he was doing so, the Bible states, because he was "charged to do so" by "Yahweh, the God of Heaven."

Do Gods Too Dream?

Do all animals who sleep also dream? Or just mammals, or only primates—or is dreaming unique to Humankind?

If, as seems to be the case, dreaming is indeed one of the unique talents and abilities that Man has not acquired by Evolution alone, then it has to be part of the genetic legacy bequeathed to us by the Anunnaki. But to do so, they themselves had to be able to dream. Did they?

The answer is Yes; the Anunnaki "gods" also had oracle dreams.

One instance is the oracle dream in which Dumuzi, the son of Enki who was betrothed to Ishtar, the granddaughter of Enlil, foresaw in a dream his own death, bringing to a tragic end that Anunnaki tale of "Romeo and Juliet." The text titled "His Heart Was Filled With Tears" relates how Dumuzi, having raped his own sister Geshtinanna, goes to sleep and has nightmares. He dreams that all his attributes of status and possessions are taken away from him one by one by a "princely bird" and a falcon. In the end he sees himself lying dead amidst his shattered sheepfolds.

Waking up, he asked his sister for the meaning of the dream. "My brother," she said, "your dream is not favorable." It foretold, she said, his arrest by "bandits" who will handcuff his hands and bind his arms. Soon, indeed, "evil sheriffs" arrive to seize Dumuzi on orders of his elder brother Marduk. A saga of escapes and chases ensues; in the end Dumuzi finds himself among his sheepfolds, as he had seen in the dream. As the evil *Gallu* seize him, Dumuzi is accidentally killed in the struggle; and, as he had seen in the dream, his lifeless body lies among the shattered furnishings.

In the Canaanite texts regarding Ba'al and Anat, it is the goddess Anat who sees, in an omen-dream, the lifeless body of Ba'al and is told where it is, so that she might try to retrieve and revive the dead god.

11

ANGELS
AND OTHER EMISSARIES

A nighttime vision, a UFO sighting, and the appearance of angels come together in one of the most intriguing dream reports in the Bible, known as *Jacob's Dream*. It was a most significant Divine Encounter, for in it Yahweh himself vowed to protect Jacob, the son of Isaac and grandson of Abraham, to bless him and his seed, and to give the Promised Land to him and his descendants forever.

The circumstances leading to this Divine Encounter, in which Jacob—in a vision—saw the Angels of the Lord in action, were the journey of Jacob from Canaan, where the family had settled, to Harran, where other members of the family of Abraham had stayed on when Abraham continued southward toward the Sinai and Egypt. Concerned lest his son Jacob, with whom the divinely ordained succession rested, marry a pagan Canaanite, "Isaac called Jacob and blessed him and ordered him thus: Thou shalt not take a wife from the daughters of Canaan; arise, go to Padan-Aram, to the house of Bethuel thy mother's father, and take thyself from there a wife from among the daughters of Laban, thy mother's brother."

Harran, it will be recalled, was a way station (which is what its name meant) on the northern route from Mesopotamia to the Mediterranean lands and thence to Egypt. It was there that Abraham stayed with his father Terah before he was ordered to proceed southward; and it was there that Esarhaddon (some fifteen hundred years later) received the oracle

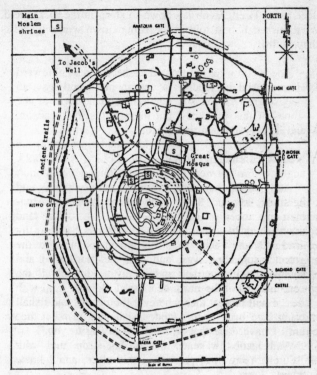

Figure 85

to invade Egypt and Nabunaid was chosen to Kingship over Babylon. (Harran, still called by its ancient name, is still a major city in southern Turkey; but since Moslem shrines have been built upon the ancient mound, with the main mosque where the ancient sacred precinct had been (Fig. 85), archaeologists are prevented from excavating there. But numerous structural remains are still associated with Abraham, and a well northwest of the city is called Jacob's Well—see ensuing tale).

Starting his northward trek from Beersheba, Jacob reached at the end of one day a place where his grandfather Abraham had once encamped on the opposite journey, from Harran to

Beersheba. Tired, Jacob lay down to sleep in the rocky field. What ensued is best told in the Bible's own words (Genesis chapter 28):

> And Jacob went out from Beersheba and went toward Harran. And he reached a certain place and went to sleep there, for the sun had set. And he took of the stones of that place and put them to rest his head on, and he lay down in that place.
>
> And he dreamed, and beheld a ladder set up on the ground with its top reaching up to the sky. And behold, angels of *Elohim* were going up and coming down on it.
>
> And behold, there was Yahweh standing upon it, and he spoke, saying: "I am Yahweh, the *Elohim* of Abraham thy ancestor and the *Elohim* of Isaac. The land upon which thou liest, to thee I will give it and to thy seed. And thy seed shall be spread as dust on the ground, spreading west and east and northward and southward; and in thee and in thy seed shall all the communities of the Earth be blessed. Behold, I am with thee; I will protect thee wherever thou goest, and I shall bring thee back to this land. I shall not abandon thee until I have done that which I am saying to you."
>
> And Jacob awakened out of his sleep, and said, "Surely Yahweh is present in this place, and I knew it not."
>
> And he was afraid, saying: "How awesome is this place! This is none other than an abode of *Elohim,* and this is the gateway to heaven!"
>
> And Jacob got up early in the morning and took the stone that he had used as a pillow, and set it up as a pillar, and poured oil on its top, and called the name of the place *Beth-El.*

In this Divine Encounter, in a nighttime vision, Jacob saw what, without doubt, we would nowadays call a UFO; except that to him it was not an UNidentified Flying Object: he well realized that its occupants or operators were divine beings, "angels of *Elohim,*" and their Lord or commander none other than Yahweh himself, "standing upon it." What he had witnessed left no doubt in his mind that the place was a "Gateway to Heaven"—a place from which the *Elohim* could rise skyward. The wording is akin to that applied to Babylon (*Bab-Ili*, "Gateway of the *Elohim*") where the incident of the launch tower "whose head shall reach to heaven" had taken place.

The commander identified himself to Jacob as "Yahweh, the *Elohim*"—the DIN.GIR—"of Abraham thy forefather and the *Elohim* of Isaac." The operators of the "ladder" are identified as "Angels of *Elohim*," not simply as angels; and Jacob, realizing that he had unknowingly stumbled upon a site used by these divine aeronauts, named the place *Beth-El* ("The House of El"), *El* being the singular of *Elohim*.

A few words on etymology and thus on the identity of these "angels" are required.

The Bible is careful to identify the subordinates of the deity as "Angels of *Elohim*" and not simply as "angels," because the Hebrew term *Mal'akhim* does not mean "angels" at all; it literally means "emissaries"; and the term is employed in the Bible for regular, flesh-and-blood human emissaries who carried royal rather than divine messages. King Saul sent *Mal'akhim* (commonly translated "messengers") to summon David (I Samuel 16:19); David sent *Mal'akhim* (also translated "messengers") to the people of Jabesh Gilead to inform them that he had been anointed king (II Samuel 2:5); King Ahaz of Judaea sent *Mal'akhim* ("emissaries") to the Assyrian king Tiglat-Pileser for help to ward off enemy attacks (II Kings 16:7), and so on. Etymologically, the term stems from the same root as *Mela'kha* which has been variably translated as "work," "craft," "workmanship." The Bible employs the term in this derivation in connection with the "Wisdom and Understanding" that Yahweh gave Bezalel to be able to carry out the *Melakha* required for building the Tabernacle and the Ark of the Covenant in the Sinai wilderness, so a *Mal'akh* (the singular of *Mal'akhim*) signified not a mere messenger but a special emissary, trained and qualified for the task and with some powers of discretion (as an ambassador would have). It is to "Angels of *Elohim*," the *Divine Emissaries*, that the reference will be in the following pages.

The story of Jacob is dotted with oracle dreams and angelic

encounters—continuing, as we shall see, the experiences of the Patriarchs, his grandfather Abraham, and his father Isaac.

Meeting Rachel at the water well in the grazing fields of Harran and discovering that she was the daughter of his uncle Laban, Jacob asked Laban's permission to marry her. The uncle agreed if Jacob would in exchange serve Laban seven years; but when he did, Laban made him marry first his older daughter Leah, demanding that he serve another seven years to have Rachel as a second wife. Upon the insistence of Laban, Jacob, his wives, the children they bore him, and the flocks that he managed to amass, stayed on and on—for twenty years. Then one night Jacob had a dream. In the dream he saw "rams leaping upon the flocks, and they were streaked, and speckled, and grizzled." Puzzled by what he was seeing, Jacob then received a divine oracle in the second part of the dream in which an "Angel of the *Elohim*" appeared and called out his name. "And Jacob said, Here I am. And the angel said, Lift up thy eyes and see thou all of the rams that leap upon the flocks; they are streaked and speckled and grizzled because I have seen all that Laban had done to thee. I am the *El* of Beth-El, the place where thou didst anoint a pillar ... Now arise, and get thee from out of this land, and return to the land of thy birth."

So, acting on this dream-oracle, Jacob picked up his family and belongings, and seizing the opportunity when Laban was away for the shearing of the sheep, left Harran in a hurry. When the news reached Laban, he was furious. "But *Elohim* came unto Laban the Aramean in a nighttime dream, saying to him: Take thou heed! Speak neither threats nor sweettalk Jacob." Thus admonished, Laban in the end consented to Jacob's departure, and the two set up a stone to serve as a boundary between them, not to be crossed by either one of them in anger. In witness of the treaty's vows the *Elohim* were invoked as guarantors.

The placing of such a boundary stone conformed to the customs of the day. Called *Kudurru,* they were rounded at the top; the terms of the boundary agreement were inscribed on them, ending with the oaths and the invoking of the gods of each side as guarantors of the treaty vows; sometimes, the symbols of the celestial counterparts of the invoked deities

Figure 86

were engraved near or on the rounded stone's top (Fig. 86).
It is thus indicative of the Bible's accuracy in describing the
event when the biblical narrative (Genesis 31:53) states that
"the *Elohim* of Abraham and the *Elohim* of Nahor shall judge
between us, the *Elohim* of their father." While the name of
Abraham's God, Yahweh, is not mentioned, a distinction is
made between Him and the gods of his brother Nahor (who
had stayed behind in Harran); all of whom, according to
Laban, were *Elohim* of their father Terah.

The biblical data suggests that the favored route of the
Patriarchs between the Negev (the southern part of Canaan
bordering on the Sinai peninsula), of which Beersheba was
(and still is) the principal city, involved a crossing of the
Jordan River; this indicates that The King's Highway east of
the river was used (rather than the coastal Way of the Sea—
see Map). It was when Jacob, journeying south with his family, retinue, and flocks, reached a place where the Yabbok
tributary created an easier passage to the Jordan through the

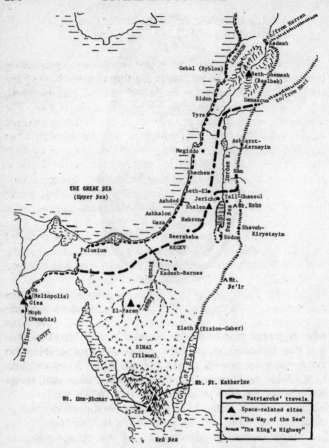

mountains, that his next encounter with *Mal'akhim* took place. This time, however, it was neither in a dream nor in a vision: it was a face-to-face encounter!

The event is reported in chapter 32 of Genesis:

> *As Jacob went on his way,*
> *Angels of* Elohim *encountered him.*
> *And when Jacob saw them, he said:*
> *"An encampment of* Elohim *it is!"*

And he called the place Mahana'im
(the Place of Two Encampments).

The event is recorded here in just two verses, significantly constituting a separate section in the formal enscribing of the Bible. In the following verses the subsequent, but unrelated, tale of Jacob's meeting with his brother Esau is told. The manner in which the ancient editors of the Scriptures treated these two verses brings to mind the manner in which the segment on the Nefilim has been told in chapter 6 of Genesis (preceding the tale of Noah and the ark), where the segment is clearly a retained remnant of a longer text. So must have been this reference to the encounter with an actual group or troup of Divine Emissaries—two verses remaining out of a much longer and detailed record.

The ancient editors of Genesis must have retained the brief mention because of the subsequent episode, that had to be included because it explains why Jacob's name was changed to "Israel."

Reaching the Crossing of Yabbok, and uncertain what his brother Esau's attitude would be to see his rival for the succession return, Jacob adopted a strategy of sending forth his retinue a little at a time. Finally only he and his two wives and two handmaidens and his eleven children remained in his encampment for the night; so, under the cover of darkness, Jacob "took them and had them cross the stream, bringing over all that had remained."

Then the unexpected Divine Encounter happened:

> *And Jacob was left alone;*
> *And there wrestled with him a man*
> *until daybreak at dawn.*
> *And seeing that he could not prevail*
> *against him, he struck against the hollow*
> *of his (Jacob's) thigh; and the hollow of*
> *Jacob's thigh was put out of joint*
> *as he was wrestling with him.*
>
> *And he said: "Let go, for it is daybreak."*
> *But Jacob said: "I will not let thee*

> *leave unless thou bless me.''*
> *And he said to him: ''What is thy name?''*
> *And he said: ''Jacob.''*
> *So he said: ''Thy name shall no longer be*
> *called Jacob; but rather* 'Israel',
> *for thou hast striven with both* Elohim
> *and men, and prevailed.''*

(*Isra-El* is a play on the words meaning "strive, contest" with *El*, a deity).

> *And Jacob asked him, saying:*
> *''Do tell me your name!''*
> *And he said: ''Wherefor dost thou ask for*
> *my name?'' And he blessed him there.*

> *And Jacob named the place* Peni-El
> *(the Face of* El)
> *For I have seen* Elohim *face to face*
> *and my life was preserved.*
> *And it was sunrise when he crossed at*
> *Peniel, limping on his thigh.*

The first reference in the Bible to an Angel of the Lord, in chapter 16 of Genesis, relates an event in the time of Jacob's grandfather Abraham. Abraham and his wife Sarah were getting old—he in his mid eighties, she ten years younger; and still they had no offspring. Abraham had just fulfilled the mission for which he had been ordered to Canaan—to ward off attacks on the Spaceport in the Sinai: the War of the Kings (described in chapter 14 of Genesis). The grateful Lord Yahweh

> *Appeared to Abram in a vision, saying:*
> *''Fear not Abram; I am thy shield;*
> *thy reward shall be exceedingly great.''*

But the childless Abraham (still called by his Sumerian name Abram) responded bitterly: "My Lord Yahweh, what wouldst thou give me? But I am childless!" Without an heir, Abram said, what use is any reward?

> *Then the word of Yahweh came to him, thus:*
> *"None shall inherit thee except he who*
> *shall come out of thy own innards."*
> *And he brought him out, and said:*
> *"Look now up to the heavens, and count the*
> *stars, if thou be able to number them;*
> *that many shall be thy seed."*

"It was on that day that Yahweh had made a Covenant with Abram, saying: Unto thy seed have I given this land, from the Brook of Egypt until the great river, the River Euphrates."

But, the biblical tale continues, in spite of that promise of countless descendants, Sarah still did not bear a child to Abraham. So Sarah said to Abraham that perhaps it was the Lord's intention that Abraham's offspring should not depend on her ability to bear children, and suggested that he "come unto" Hagar, her Egyptian handmaiden. And "Hagar became pregnant," and began to belittle her mistress.

Although it was her own suggestion, Sarah was now furious, "and dealt harshly with Hagar," and Hagar ran away.

> *And an angel of Yahweh found her*
> *by a spring in the desert, the spring*
> *which is on the Way of Shur.*
> *And he said to Hagar, Sarah's handmaiden,*
> *"Whence comest thou and whither goest thou?"*

Explaining that she was running away from her mistress Sarah, the angel told her to go back, for she would have a son and by him numerous offspring. "And thou shalt call his name *Ishma-El*"—'God Has Heard'—for Yahweh hath heard thy plight." So Hagar went back and gave birth to Ishmael; "and Abram was eighty-six years old when Hagar bore Ishmael to Abram." It was not before another thirteen years had passed that Yahweh once again "appeared unto Abram" and, reaffirming the Covenant with Abraham and his offspring, took steps to provide Abraham with legitimate succession through a son by his half sister (Sarah). As part of the legitimization, Abraham and all his male household had to be circumcised; and as part of inheriting Canaan and severing the remaining ties to the Old Country, Sumer, the Hebrew Patriarch and his wife had to shed their Sumerian names (Abram and Sarai) and adopt Semitic versions thereof, Abraham and Sarah. (Our references to "Abraham" and "Sarah" prior to this occurrence were for convenience only; in the Bible, up to that point, they were called Abram and Sarai). And Abraham was ninety-nine years old at the time.

The details of these divine instructions, coupled with the foretelling of the birth of Isaac by Sarah, are given in chapter 17 of Genesis. The circumstances—*the Theophany leading to the upheavaling of Sodom and Gomorrah*—are described in the following chapter, "when Yahweh showed himself" to Abraham. The aging Patriarch was sitting at the entrance to his tent; it was midday, the hottest time of the day. Suddenly, three strangers appeared to Abraham as if from nowhere:

> And he lifted up his eyes and lo,
> he beheld three persons standing above him.
> And when he saw them, he ran toward them
> from the entrance of the tent, and bowed down.
> And he said:
> "My lord, if I find favor in thy eyes,
> please do not pass over above thy servant."

The scene is replete with mystery. Three strangers appear to Abraham suddenly, seen by him as he lifts his eyes skyward. He sees them standing "above him." Though unidentified at this point, he quickly recognizes their extraordinary—divine?—nature. Somehow one of them is distinguished, and Abraham addresses him, calling him "My Lord." His words begin with the most important request: "Please do not *pass over above* thy servant." He recognized, in other words, their ability to roam the skies . . . Yet they were so humanlike that he offers them water, to wash their feet, to rest in the tree's shade, and to sustain their hearts with food, before they "pass over" onward. "And they said, Do as thou hast spoken."

"So Abraham hastened into the tent unto Sarah," and asked her to quickly prepare bread rolls while he oversaw the preparation of a meat dish, and had the meal served to them. And one of them, inquiring about Sarah, said: "In a year's time, when I return to thee, Sarah thy wife shall have a son." Overhearing that in the tent, Sarah laughed, for how could she and Abraham, too old by now, have a son?

> Then Yahweh said unto Abraham:
> "Wherefore did Sarah laugh,
> thinking: Would I really bear a child
> when I have waxed old?
> Is anything too wondrous for Yahweh?
> At the appointed time I will return unto
> thee, at the same time next year,
> and Sarah will then have a son."

And it would be through Isaac and his seed that the Covenant with Abraham shall be everlasting, Yahweh said.

As the tale continues, we read that "the persons rose up from there to survey over upon Sodom; and Abraham went with them to see them off." But while the narrative continues to describe the three sudden visitors as *Anashim*—"persons"—the oracle regarding the coming birth of Isaac (whose Hebrew name, *Itz'hak*, was a play on words on the "laughing" by Sarah) has let us know that one of the three was none other than Yahweh himself. It was a most remarkable Theophany in which the Hebrew Patriarch was privileged to have the Lord Yahweh as his guest!

Arriving at a promontory from which Sodom could be seen down in the valley of the Sea of Salt, Yahweh decided to tell Abraham what was the reason for the visit.

> Because the outcry regarding Sodom and
> Gomorrah has been great, and the accusations
> against them being grievous, [I said:]
> Let me come down and verify:
> If it is as the outcry reaching me,
> they will destroy completely;
> and if not, I wish to know.

This then was the mission of the other two "persons" who were with Yahweh—to verify the truth about, or extent of, the "sinning" of the two cities in the Jordan valley near what is now the Dead Sea, so that the Lord could determine their fate. "And the persons turned from there and went to Sodom, but Abraham remained standing before Yahweh," we read in Genesis 18:22; but when the arrival of the two "persons" at Sodom is reported next (Genesis 19:1), it becomes clear who the two were: "And the two *angels* came to Sodom in the evening." The three visitors who had appeared to Abraham were, thus, Yahweh and two of his emissaries.

Before the Bible focuses on the angels' visit to Sodom and Gomorrah and the ensuing destruction of the "evil cities," the Bible reports a most unusual discourse between Abraham and Yahweh. Approaching the Lord, Abraham took on the role of an intercessor, a defense lawyer, for Sodom (where his nephew Lot and his family have been residing). "Perhaps there be fifty Righteous Ones inside the city," he said to Yahweh, "wilt thou destroy and not spare the place for the sake of the fifty? Surely, far be it from thee, to slay the Righteous with the wicked?"

Reminding Yahweh that he was "Judge of all the Earth," one who would always do justice, Abraham placed the Lord in a dilemma. So the Lord Yahweh answered that if there be fifty Righteous Ones in Sodom, he would spare the whole city. But no sooner had the Lord consented thus, than Abraham—asking forgiveness for his audacity in "taking leave to speak to my Lord"—posed another question: What if the number, fifty, shall fall short by five? "And He said, I will not destroy if I find there forty-five." Seizing the offensive, Abraham then bargained on, reducing the number of Righteous Ones on account of whom the whole city would be spared all the way down to ten. And with that, "*Elohim* went up from over Abraham," rising skyward from whence He had appeared earlier in the day. "And Abraham returned to his place."

"And the two angels came to Sodom in the evening, and Lot was sitting at the gate of Sodom. And Lot, seeing them, rose up toward them and bowed himself with the face to the ground. And he said, If it please my lords, do turn unto thy servant's house for the night, and wash your feet; and in the morning, arising early, continue on your way." As the two stayed in Lot's house, "the people of the city, the people of Sodom, young and old, closed in on the house; and they called out unto Lot: 'Where are the men who had come to thee tonight? Bring them out to us so that we may know them.' " And when the people persisted, even attempting to break down the door to Lot's house, the angels "smote the people at the door, young and old, with a blindness, and they gave up finding the door."

Did the angels use some magical wand, a beam emitter, with whose powerful ray the people who were trying to break down the door were smitten with blindness? In the answer to this question lies the answer to a greater puzzle. In describing the arrival of the visitors to Abraham and then to Lot, the visitors are called *Anashim*—"people" (not necessarily "men" as the term is often translated). Yet in both instances the hosts at once recognize something that made them look different, something "divine" about them. The hosts call them right away "lords," bow to them. If, as it is described, the visitors were fully anthropomorphic, what was nevertheless so different and distinguishing about them?

The answer that comes instantly to mind will no doubt be, Why—of course—their wings! But that, as we shall show, is not necessarily so.

The popular notion of angels, an image sustained and bolstered by centuries of religious art, is that of fully anthropomorphic, humanlike beings who, unlike people, are equipped with wings. Indeed, were they to be stripped of their wings, they would be indistinguishable from humans. Brought over to Western iconography by early Christianity, the undoubted origin of such a representation of angels was the ancient Near East. We found them in Sumerian art—the winged emissary who led Enkidu away, the guardians with the deadly beams. We find them in the religious art of Assyria and Egypt, Canaan and Phoenicia (Fig. 87). Similar Hittite representations (Fig. 88a) were even duplicated in South America, on the

Gate of the Sun in Tiahuanacu (Fig. 88b)—evidence of Hittite contacts with that distant place.

Though modern scholars, perhaps wishing to avoid religious connotations, refer to the depicted beings as "protective geniuses," the ancient peoples considered them to be a class of lesser gods, a kind of rank-and-file divine being that only carries out the orders of the "Great Lords" who were "Gods of Heaven and Earth."

Their representation as winged beings was clearly intended to indicate their ability to fly in Earth's skies; and in that they emulated the gods themselves, and specifically so those who had been depicted as winged deities—Utu/Shamash (Fig. 89) and his twin sister Inanna/Ishtar (Fig. 90). The affinity to the Eaglemen (see Fig. 16) whose commander Utu/Shamash was, is also obvious. In this regard the Lord's statement (Exodus 19:4) that he would carry the Children of Israel "on

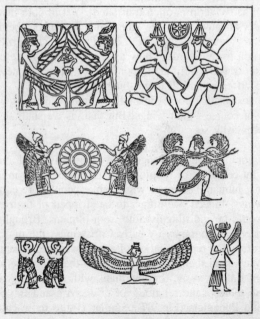

Figure 87

the wings of eagles'' might have been more than allegorical; it also brings to mind the tale of Etana (see Fig. 30) whom an eagle or Eagleman had carried aloft on the orders of Shamash.

But, as the biblical textual descriptions and a glance at Fig.

Figures 88a and 88b

Figure 89

71 will attest, such winged divine assistants were called in the Bible *Cherubim* rather than *Mal'akhim*. *Cherub* (the singular of *Cherubim*) derives from the Akkadian *Karabu*—to "bless, consecrate." A *Karibu* (male) was "a blessed/consecrated one" and a female *Kuribi* meant a Protective Goddess. As such the biblical Cherubim were assigned (Genesis 3:24) to guard "the way to the Tree of Life" lest the expelled Adam and Eve return to the Garden of Eden; to protect with their wings the Ark of the Covenant; and to serve as bearers of the Lord, be it as supporters of the Divine Throne in the Ezekiel vision or by simply carrying Yahweh aloft: "He rode upon a Cherub and flew away," we read in II Samuel 22:11 and Psalms 18:11 (another parallel to the tale of Etana). According to the Bible, then, the winged Cherubim had specific and limited functions; not so the *Mal'akhim,* the Emissaries who had come and gone on assigned missions and, as plenipotentiary ambassadors, had considerable discretionary powers.

This is made clear from the events at Sodom. Having seen for themselves the viciousness of the people of Sodom, the two *Mal'akhim* instructed Lot and his family to leave at once,

Figure 90

"for Yahweh will destroy this city." But Lot tarried, and kept asking the "angels" to delay the upheavaling of the city until he, his wife, and two daughters could reach the safety of the mountains that were not so near. And the emissaries granted him the request, promising that they will postpone the city's upheavaling to give him and his family time to escape.

In both instances (the sudden appearance to Abraham, the arrival at Sodom's gate) the "angels" are called "people," manlike in appearance; if not winged, what then made them recognizable as Divine Emissaries?

We find a clue in the representation of the Hittite pantheon, carved in a rock sanctuary at a site called Yazilikaya in Turkey, not far from the imposing ruins of the Hittite capital. The deities are arranged in two processions, male ones marching in from the left and female ones marching from the right. Each procession is led by the great gods (Teshub leading the males, Hebat leading the females), followed by their offspring, aides, and companies of lesser gods. In the male procession the last to march are twelve "emissaries" whose divinity or role and status are recognized by their headgear and the curved weapon they are holding (Fig. 91a); ahead of them marches a somewhat more important group of twelve, again identified by the headgear and the instrument— a rod with a loop or disc on top—they are holding (Fig. 91b). This wand is also held by the two principal male deities (Fig. 91c).

The twelve-man companies of these lesser gods in the Hittite depiction bring unavoidably to mind the troop of *Mal'akhim* that Jacob encountered on his way back from Harran— in today's Turkey—to Canaan. What comes to mind, then, is that the possession of a handheld device was what made the angels recognizable for what they were (along with, at least sometimes, their unique headgear).

Miraculous deeds performed by *Mal'akhim* abound in the Bible, the blinding of the unruly crowd at Sodom being just one of them; a similar incident of magical blinding is reported in connection with the activities and prophecies of Elisha, the disciple and successor of the Prophet Elijah. In another instance Elijah himself, escaping for his life after having hundreds of the priests of Ba'al killed, was saved by an "Angel of Yahweh'' as he became exhausted without food and water in the Negev desert—in the very same area where the Angel saved the wandering, thirsty, and hungry Hagar. As the weary Elijah lay to sleep under a tree, a *Mal'akh* all of sudden touched him, saying: ''Get up and eat.'' To his utter surprise, Elijah saw placed at his head a roll of baked bread and a water jug. He ate and drank a little and fell asleep—only to be touched again by the Angel, telling him to consume all the food and the water because there is a long way ahead (the destination was ''the Mount of the *Elohim*,'' Mount Sinai, in the Wilderness). Though the narrative (I Kings 19:5–7) does not state how the Angel touched Elijah, one can safely assume that it was not with his hand but with the divine wand or staff.

The use of such an implement is clearly reported in the

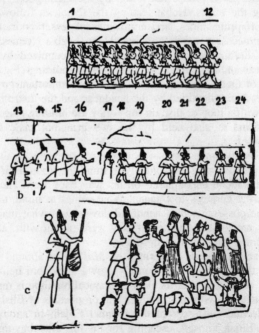

Figures 91a, 91b, and 91c

tale of Gideon (Judges chapter 6). To convince Gideon that his selection to lead the Israelites against their enemies was ordained by Yahweh, the "Angel of Yahweh" instructed Gideon to take the meat and bread that he had prepared as an offering to the Lord, and place them on a rock; and when Gideon had done so,

> *The angel of Yahweh put forth the*
> *end of the wand that was in his hand,*
> *and touched the meat and the breadrolls.*
> *And there flamed up a fire out of the rock*
> *and consumed the meat and the breadrolls.*
>
> *Then the angel of Yahweh disappeared from sight;*
> *and Gideon realized that he was [indeed]*
> *an angel of Yahweh.*

In such instances the magical wand might have looked like the rod held by the more important group of twelve in the Yazilikaya procession. The curved instrument held by the last-to-march group could very well have been the "sword" that was seen held by the *Mal'akhim* when they were sent on destructive missions. One such sighting is reported in Joshua chapter 5. As the Israelite leader of the conquest of Canaan faced his most challenging target—the exceedingly fortified city of Jericho—a Divine Emissary appeared to him to give him instructions:

> *As Joshua was by Jericho,*
> *he lifted up his eyes and lo,*
> *he beheld a man standing opposite him,*
> *a drawn sword in his hand.*
>
> *And Joshua went toward him,*
> *and said to him:*
> *"Art thou one of us or one of our adversaries?"*
> *And he answered:*
> *"Neither; the captain of the host of Yahweh I am."*

Another occurrence in which a warlike *Mal'akh* appeared

with a swordlike object in his hand took place in the time of King David. Not heeding the prohibition against taking a census of his able-bodied men, he received word from the Lord through Gad the Visionary that it was up to David which of three punishments would be meted out by the Lord. When David hesitated,

> *He raised his eyes,*
> *and saw the Angel of Yahweh*
> *hovering between the Earth and the heavens,*
> *and his drawn sword stretched out*
> *over Jerusalem.*
> *And David and the Elders, clothed in sackcloths,*
> *fell face down.*

> > (*I Chronicles* 21:16)

Equally illustrative are the instances when the Angels appeared without such a distinctive object in their hands, for then they had to resort to other magical acts to convince the recipients of the Divine Word that the embassy was authentic. Whereas in the case of the encounter by Gideon the magical wand was specifically mentioned, such a wand was apparently not within sight when the Angel of Yahweh appeared to the barren wife of Mano'ah and foretold the birth of Samson, providing he would be a Nazirite and the woman, like her son once born, abstain from drinking wine or beer or the eating of unclean foods (additionally, the boy's hair was never to be cut). When the Angel appeared a second time to make sure the instructions for conceiving and for raising the boy were being followed, Mano'ah sought to verify the speaker's identity, for he looked like ''a man.'' So he asked the emissary, ''What is thy name?''

Instead of revealing his identity, the ''angel did a wonder'':

> *And the angel of Yahweh said to him:*
> *''Why askest thou for my name,*
> *which is a secret?''*

> *So Manoah took the kid of sacrifice*
> *and placed it on the rock*

as an offering to Yahweh.

And the angel did a wonder,
as Manoah and his wife looked on:
As the flame rose up from the altar,
the angel of Yahweh ascended skyward
within the flame.
And Manoah and his wife were witnessing this;
and they fell on their faces to the ground.

After that the angel of Yahweh did not appear
anymore to Manoah and his wife.
But Manoah then knew that an angel of Yahweh
it was.

A more renowned instance of using fire magically in order
to convince the observer that he is indeed being given a
divine message is the incident of the Burning Bush. It was
when Yahweh had chosen Moses, a Hebrew raised as an
Egyptian prince, to lead the Israelites out of bondage in
Egypt. Having escaped the wrath of the Pharaoh to the Wilderness of Sinai, Moses was shepherding the flock of his
father-in-law, the priest of Midian, "and he came to the
mountain of the *Elohim* in Horeb," where a miraculous sight
drew his attention:

And an angel of Yahweh appeared unto him
in a flame of fire, out of the midst of
a thorn-bush.
And he looked and, behold—
the thorn-bush was burning with fire,
but the thorn-bush was not consumed.

And Moses said [to himself]:
"Let me get closer and observe
this great sight, for why is the
thorn-bush not burning down?"

And when Yahweh saw that Moses had turned
to take a closer look,

Figures 92a, 92b, and 92c

Elohim *called out to him from the thorn-bush*
saying: "Moses, Moses!"
And he said: "Here I am."

Such miracles were not needed for identifying the speaker
as a divine being, as we have recounted, when the speaker
was holding the bent weapon or magical wand.

Ancient depictions suggest that there was probably, at least
in some instances, another distinctive feature by which the
"persons" or "men" were recognized as Divine Emissaries:
the special "goggles" that they wore, usually as part of their
headgear. In this regard the Hittite pictograph that expressed
the term "divine" (Fig. 92a) is instructive, for it represents
the "Eye" symbols that proliferated in the upper Euphrates
region as idols (Fig. 92b) placed atop altars or pedestals.
The latter were clearly emulating depictions of deities whose
outstanding feature (beside their divine helmet) were the goggled eyes (Fig. 92c).

In one instance the statuette, depicting a helmeted and goggled godlike "man" holding a bent instrument (Fig. 93), may
well have represented the way in which the biblical angels
had appeared to Abraham and to Lot.

(If, in those instances, the wand-weapon was used to blind with its beam, the goggles might have been required to protect the "angel" from the blinding effects—a possibility suggested by recent developments (by the United States and several other countries) of blinding weapons as one kind of "nonlethal" weapons. Called Cobra Laser Rifles, these weapons employ a technique derived from both the surgical laser and the lasers that guide missiles. The soldiers using them must wear protective goggles, lest they be blinded by their own weapons).

As a comparison of the above depictions with the helmeted and goggled Ishtar as a pilot (Fig. 33) suggests, the attire and weaponry of the *Mal'akhim* only emulated those of the Great Gods themselves. The great Enlil could "raise the beams that search the heart of all the lands" from his ziggurat in Nippur, and had there "eyes that could scan all the lands," as well as a "net" that could ensnare unauthorized encroachers. Ninurta was armed with "the weapon which tears apart and robs the senses" and with a Brilliance that could pulverize mountains, as well as with a unique IB—a "weapon with fifty killing heads." Teshub/Adad was armed with a "thunder-stormer which scatters the rocks" and with the "lightning which flashes frightfully."

Mesopotamian kings asserted from time to time that their patron deity provided them with divine weapons to assure a victory; it was thus even more plausible that the gods would provide weapons or magical wands to their own emissaries, the Angels.

Indeed, the very notion of Divine Emissaries can be traced

Figure 93

back to the gods of Sumer, the Anunnaki, when they employed emissaries in their dealings with one another rather than with Earthlings.

The one whom scholars refer to as "the vizier of the great gods" was Papsukkal; his epithet-name meant "Father/Ancestor of the Emissaries." He carried out missions on behalf of Anu, conveying Anu's decisions or advice to the Anunnaki leaders on Earth; as often as not, he displayed considerable diplomatic skills. The texts suggest that at times, perhaps when Anu was away from Earth, Papsukkal served as an emissary of Ninurta (although, during the battle with Zu, Ninurta employed his main weapon-bearer Sharur as a Divine Emissary).

Enlil's principal *Sukkal* or emissary was called Nusku; he is mentioned in a variety of roles in most of the "myths" concerning Enlil. When the Anunnaki toiling in the mines of the Abzu (southeastern Africa) mutinied and surrounded the house where Enlil stayed, it was Nusku who blocked their way with his weapons; it was also he who acted as a go-between to diffuse the confrontation. In Sumerian times he was the emissary who brought the "word of Ekur" (Enlil's ziggurat in Nippur) to those—both gods and people—whose fate Enlil had decreed. A *Hymn to Enlil, the All-Beneficent* stated that "only to his exalted vizier, the chamberlain (*Sukkal*) Nusku, does he (Enlil) the command, the word that is in his heart, make known." We have mentioned earlier an instance in which Nusku, standing in the Harran temple with Sin, informed the Assyrian king Esarhaddon of the divine permission to invade Egypt.

Ashurbanipal, in his annals, asserted that it was "Nusku, the faithful emissary," who conveyed the divine decision to make him king of Assyria; then, on the gods' command, Nusku accompanied Ashurbanipal on a military campaign to assure victory. Nusku, Ashurbanipal wrote, "took the lead of my army and threw down my foes with the divine weapon." The assertion brings to mind the reverse incident reported in the Bible, when the Angel of Yahweh smote the army of Assyria besieging Jerusalem:

> *And it came to pass that night*
> *that the Angel of Yahweh*

went out and smote the camp of the Assyrians,
an hundred and fourscore and five thousand.
And when they (the people of Jerusalem)
arose early in the morning, lo and behold:
they (the Assyrians) were all dead corpses.

(II Kings 19:35)

Enki's chief emissary, named Isimud in the Sumerian texts and Usmu in the Akkadian versions, inevitably played a role in the sexual shenanigans of his master. In the "myth" of *Enki and Ninharsag,* in which Enki's efforts to obtain a male successor by his half sister were related, Isimud/Usmu first acted as a confidant and later as the provider of a variety of fruits with which Enki attempted to cure himself of the paralysis with which Ninharsag had afflicted him. When Inanna/Ishtar came to Eridu to obtain the ME's, it was Isimud/Usmu who made the arrangements for the visit. Later on, when the sobered-up Enki realized that he was tricked out of important ME's, it was his faithful *Sukkal* who was ordered to pursue Inanna (who had fled in her "Boat of Heaven") to retrieve the ME's.

Isimud/Usmu was sometimes referred to in the texts as "two faced." This curious description, it turns out, was a factual one; for in both statues and on cylinder seals he was indeed shown with two faces (Fig. 94). Was he deformed at birth, a genetic aberration, or was there some profound reason for depicting him so? While no one seems to know, it occurs to us that this two-facedness might have reflected this emissary's celestial association (see box at the end of this chapter).

There was something unusual also about the *Sukkal* of Inanna /Ishtar, whose name was Ninshubur. The enigma was that Ninshubur sometimes appeared to be masculine, at which times the scholars translate his title as "chamberlain, vizier"; and at other times Ninshubur appears to be feminine, at which times she is called "chambermaid." The question is, was Ninshubur bisexual or asexual? An androgynous, a eunuch, or what?

Ninshubur acts as the confidante of Inanna/Ishtar during her courtship with Dumuzi, in which role she is treated (or assumed to be) female; Thorkild Jacobsen, in *The Treasures of Darkness,* translates her title as "Handmaiden." But in the tale of Inanna/Ishtar's escape with the ME's that she had tricked out of Enki, Ninshubur is a match for the male Isimud/Usmu and is called by the goddess "my warrior who fights by my side"—patently a male role. The diplomatic talents of this emissary were employed to the full when Inanna/Ishtar decided to visit her sister Ereshkigal in the Lower World, in defiance of a prohibition; in this instance the great Sumerologist Samuel N. Kramer (*Inanna's Descent to the Nether World*) referred to Ninshubur as a "he"; so did A. Leo Oppenheim (*Mesopotamian Mythology*).

The enigmatic bisexuality or asexuality of Ninshubur is reflected by her/his contesting with *other beings—mostly but not only the creations of Enki—that seem to be neither male nor female as well as neither divine nor human, a kind of android—automatons in human form.*

The existence of such enigmatic emissaries, and their baffling characteristics, come to light in the above-mentioned text that deals with Inanna's unauthorized visit to the domain of her older sister Ereshkigal in the Lower World (southern

Figure 94

Figures 95a and 95b

Africa). For the trip Inanna put on her attire of an aeronaut; the seven items listed in the texts match her depiction on a life-size statue that was unearthed in Mari (Fig. 95a, b). As an admission fee to the restricted zone Inanna had to give up her possessions, one at a time, as she passed through the domain's seven gates; then, ''naked and bowed low, Inanna entered the throne room.'' No sooner had the two sisters set eyes on each other than both flew into a rage; and Ereshkigal ordered her *Sukkal* Namtar to seize Inanna and afflict her from head to toe. ''Inanna was turned into a corpse, hung from a stake.''

Foreseeing trouble, Inanna had instructed her emissary Ninshubur, before she had left on the risky journey, to raise an outcry for her if she does not return within three days. Realizing that Inanna was in trouble, Ninshubur rushed from god to god to seek help; but none except Enki could counteract the death-dealing Namtar. His name meant ''Terminator;'' the Assyrians and Babylonians nicknamed him *Memittu*— ''The Killer,'' an Angel of Death. Unlike the deities or humans, ''he has no hands, he has no feet; he drinks no water, eats no food." So, to save Inanna, Enki contrived to fashion similar androids who could go to the "Land of No Return" and perform their mission safely.

In the Sumerian version of the "myth" we read that Enki fashioned *two clay androids,* and activated them by giving one the Food of Life and the other the Water of Life. The text calls one *Kurgarru* and the other *Kalaturru,* terms that scholars leave untranslated because of their complexity; referring to the beings' "private parts," the terms suggest peculiar sexual organs: literally translated, one whose "opening" is "locked," and the other whose "penetrator" is "sick."

Seeing them appear in her throne room, Ereshkigal wondered who they were: "Are you gods? Are you mortals?" she asked. "What is it that you wish?" They asked for the lifeless body of Inanna, and getting it, "upon the corpse they directed the Pulser and the Emitter,"; then sprinkled her body with the Water of Life and gave her the Plant of Life, "and Inanna arose."

Commenting on the description of the two emissaries, A. Leo Oppenheim (*Mesopotamian Mythology*) saw the main attributes that qualified them to penetrate the domain of Ereshkigal and save Inanna as having been (a) that they were neither male nor female, and (b) that they were not created in a womb. Moreover, he found a reference to the ability of the gods to create "robots" in the *Enuma elish,* the Babylonian version of the Creation Epic, in which the celestial battle with Tiamat and the wondrous creations that ensued were all attributed to Marduk—including the idea of creating Man.

In this reading of the Babylonian text, it was Marduk, "while listening to the words of the gods, conceived the idea of creating a clever device to help them." Revealing his idea to his father Ea/Enki, Marduk said: "I shall bring into existence a *robot;* his name shall be 'Man' . . . He shall be charged with the service of the gods and thus they will be relieved." But "Ea answered him by making him another proposition, in order to change his mind regarding the [idea] of relieving the gods;" it was, as we have earlier related, to "put the mark" of the gods—their genetic imprint—on "a being that already exists" (and thus bringing about *Homo sapiens*).

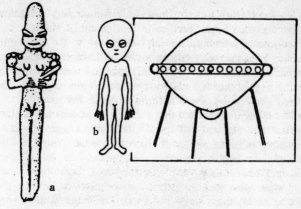

Figures 96a and 96b

In an updated translation of the Sumerian version Diane Wolkstein (*Inanna, Queen of Heaven and Earth*) explains the nature of the two emissaries as "creatures neither male nor female." A more precise explanation is provided, however, by the Akkadian version, in which Enki/Ea created only one being to save Ishtar. As rendered by E.A. Speiser (*Descent of Ishtar to the Nether World*) the relevant verses read:

> *Ea in his wise heart conceived an image*
> *and created Ashushunamir, a eunuch.*

The Akkadian term that is loosely translated "eunuch" is *assinnu*, literally meaning "penis-vagina"—a *bisexual* being rather than a castrated male (which is what "eunuch" means). That this was the true nature of the creature or creatures that baffled Ereshkigal is evident from actual depictions of them in the form of statuettes that have been discovered by archaeologists (Fig. 96a); they appear to possess both male and female organs and thus, by implication, are of no real sex.

Holding a wand or a weapon, these androids belonged to a class of emissaries called *Gallu*—usually translated "demons"—whom we have already encountered in the story of the death of Dumuzi, when Marduk had sent the "sheriffs''—the *Gallu*—to seize him. In a tale dealing with how a son of Enki, Nergal, had come to espouse Ereshkigal, it is related that to safeguard his son on his visit to the dangerous domain, Enki created fourteen *Gallu* to accompany and protect Nergal. In the tale of Inanna/Ishtar's descent to that domain, it is told that Namtar tried to prevent the escape of the revived goddess by sending *Gallu* to block her ascent.

All these texts point out that although the *Gallu* had neither the face nor the body of the divine *Sukkals* that served as emissaries between the gods themselves, they did "hold a staff in their hands, carried a weapon on their loins." Not flesh and blood, they were described as beings "who have no mother, who have no father, neither sister or brother, nor wife or child; they know not food, know not water. They flutter in the skies over Earth like wardens."

Have these Androids of ancient lore come back in recent times?

The question is pertinent because of the way in which the occupants of UFOs have been described by people who claim to have encountered them (or even abducted by them): of undetermined sex, a plastic skin, conical heads, oval eyes—humanlike in shape but definitely nonhuman, behaving like androids. That their depictions (Fig. 96b) by those who claim to have seen them seem so similar to the ancient depictions of the *Gallu* is probably no accident.

There was yet another class of Divine Emissaries—demonic beings. Some were in the service of Enki, some in the service of Enlil. Some were considered the descendants of the evildoer Zu, "evil spirits" that bode no good, bearers of disease and pestilences; demons who as often as not had birdlike features.

In the "myth" of *Inanna and Enki* it is told that when Enki ordered Isimud to retrieve the ME's taken by Inanna, he sent along with him a succession of freakish emissaries capable of seizing the Boat of Heaven: *Uru* giants, *Lahama* monsters, "sound-piercing *Kugalgal,*" and the *Enunun* "sky giants." They were all, apparently, the class of creatures called *Enkum*—"part human, part animal" according to an interpretation by Margaret Whitney Green (*Eridu in Sumerian*

Figure 97

Literature)—looking, perhaps, like the fearsome "griffins" (Fig. 97) that were created to guard temple treasures.

An encounter with a whole troop of such beings is reported in a text known as *The Legend of Naram-Sin;* he was the grandson of Sargon I (the founder of the Akkadian dynasty) and engaged in several military campaigns—on orders of the Enlilite gods, according to his annals. But at least in one instance, when the divine oracles discouraged further warfare, he took matters into his own hands. It was then that a host of "spirits" were sent against him, apparently upon a decision or order of Shamash. They were

> *Warriors with bodies of cave birds,*
> *a race with raven's faces.*
> *The great gods created them;*
> *in the plain the gods built them a city.*

Bewildered by their appearance and nature, Naram-Sin instructed one of his officers to sneak up on these beings and prick one of them with his lance. "If blood comes out, they are men like us," the king said; "If blood does not come

Figure 98

out, they are demons, devils created by Enlil.'' (The officer's report was that he did see blood, whereupon Naram-Sin ordered an attack; none of his soldiers returned alive.)

Of particular prominence among the part-anthropomorphic, part-birdlike demons was the female *Lilith* (Fig. 98). Her name meant both ''She of the night'' and ''The Howler,'' and she specialized, according to beliefs (or, as some prefer, superstitions) that endured for millennia, in enticing men to their deaths and snatching newborn babies from their mothers. Although in some post-biblical Jewish legends she was considered to have been the intended bride of Adam (hating men because she had been rejected in favor of Eve), it is more plausible that she was the erstwhile consort of the evil Zu (or AN.ZU, ''The celestial Zu''); in the Sumerian tale known as *Inanna and the Huluppu Tree,* the unusual tree was home to both the evil, birdlike Anzu and to ''the dark maid'' Lilith. When the tree was cut down to make furnishings for Inanna and Shamash, Anzu flew away and Lilith ''fled to wild, uninhabited places.''

With the passage of time, and as the gods themselves became more distant and less visible, the ''demons'' were held

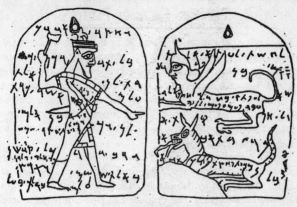

Figure 99

responsible for every malady, mishap, or misfortune. Incantations were composed, prescribed appeals to the gods to call off the evildoers; amulets were made (to be worn or affixed to doorposts) whose "sacred words" could defy the demon depicted on the amulet—a practice that continued well into the latest pre-Christian times (Fig. 99) and has persisted thereafter.

On the other hand, in post-biblical times and the Hellenistic Age that followed the conquests of Alexander, Angels as we think of them nowadays came to dominate popular and religious beliefs. In the Hebrew Bible, only Gabriel and Michael are mentioned, in the Book of Daniel, out of the seven archangels that were listed in post-biblical times. The angelic tales in the *Book of Enoch* and other books of the Apocrypha were just the foundation of a whole array of Angels inhabiting the various heavens and carrying out divine commandments—components of a wide-ranging Angelology that has captivated human imagination and yearnings ever since. And to this day, who does not wish for his or her Guardian Angel?

THE TWO FACES OF PLUTO

The earliest mention of *Usmu* is in the Epic of Creation, in the segment dealing with the rearranging of the Solar System by Nibiru/Marduk after the celestial collision. Having cleaved Tiamat, shunting the intact half of her to become Earth (with its companion, the Moon) and creating out of the shattered half the Asteroid Belt between Mars and Jupiter (and comets), the Invader now turned his attention to the outer planets.

There, *Gaga,* a satellite of Anshar (Saturn), had been pulled off its orbit to "visit" the other planets. Now Nibiru/Marduk, beholden to the planet that "begot" him in the first place—*Nudimmud*/Ea (the one we call Neptune)—presented the roving small planet as a "gift" to Ea's spouse Damkina: "To Damkina, his mother, he offered him as a joyous gift; as *Usmu* he brought him to her in an unknown place, entrusting to him the chancellorship of the Deep."

The Sumerian name of this planetary god, *Isimud,* meant "at the tip, at the very end." The Akkadian name *Usmu* meant "Two Faced." This, indeed, is a perfect description of the odd orbit of the outermost planet (excluding Nibiru). Not only is the orbit unusual in that it is inclined to the common orbital plane of the planets in our Solar System—it is also such that it takes Pluto outward, beyond Neptune, for the better part of its 248–249 year (Earth-years, that is) orbit—but brings it inside the orbit of Neptune for the rest of the time (see following illustration). Pluto, thus, shows two faces to its "master" Enki/Neptune: one when it is beyond it, the other when it is in front of it.

Astronomers have speculated, ever since the discovery of Pluto in 1930, that it was once a satellite—presumably of Neptune; but according to the Epic of Creation, of Saturn. The astronomers, however, cannot account for the odd and inclined orbit of Pluto. The Sumerian cosmogony, revealed to them by the Anunnaki, has the answer; Nibiru did it . . .

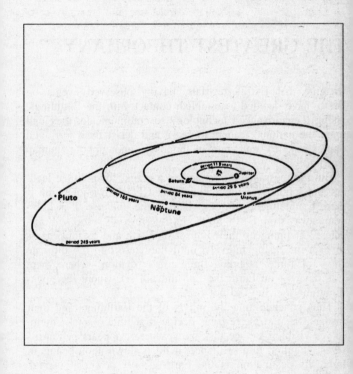

period 11.8 years

period 29.5 years

period 84 years

period 165 years

period 249 years

Jupiter

Saturn

Uranus

Neptune

•Pluto

12

THE GREATEST THEOPHANY

Imagine that Extraterrestrials, having observed events on Earth, have decided to establish contact with the Earthlings. Using their advanced technology to communicate, they call upon the nations' leaders to cease and desist from wars and oppression, to end human bondage and uphold human freedom.

But the messages are treated as a prank, for political leaders and scholarly savants know that UFOs are a joke, and if there be intelligent life elsewhere in the universe, it is light-years away from Earth. So the Extraterrestrials resort to "miracles," stepping up their impact on Earth and its inhabitants in ever-increasing marvels, until they resort to the ultimate show of force: stopping the Earth's rotation—where there was daylight on Earth the Sun did not set, where there was nighttime the Sun did not rise.

Thus concentrating the minds of the Earthlings and their leaders, the Extraterrestrials decide it is time to make themselves visible. A huge disklike spacecraft appears in Earth's skies; engulfed in a brilliance, it floats down upon beams of light. Its destination is the Earth's most powerful capital. There it lands in sight of stunned multitudes. An opening silently unrolls, letting out a shining light. A huge, giant robot steps out, moves forward and freezes. As the people fall to their knees with fear of the unknown, a humanlike figure appears—the actual Extraterrestrial. "I bring you peace," he says.

In truth, the above scenario need not be imagined, for it is the gist of the 1952 movie *The Day The Earth Stood Still,* in which the memorable Michael Rennie was the Extraterrestrial who stepped out in Washington, D.C., and spoke his reassuring words in English . . .

In truth, the above scenario need not be the summary of a science fiction movie; for what we have described—in essence if not in detail—*has really happened*. Not in modern times but in antiquity; not in the United States but in the ancient Near East; and in the actual sequence, the Earth stood still some time after rather than before the spacecraft appeared.

It was, indeed, the greatest Divine Encounter in human memory—the greatest Theophany on record, witnessed by no less than a multitude of 600,000 people.

The site of the Theophany was Mount Sinai, the "Mountain of the Elohim" in the Sinai peninsula; the occasion was the granting of the Laws of the Covenant to the Children of Israel, the high point of an eventful and miracle-filled Exodus from Egypt.

A brief review of the chain of events that culminated in the Exodus would be helpful; it was a path whose milestones were Divine Encounters.

Abraham—still called by his Sumerian name Abram in the Bible—moved with his father Terah (an oracle priest to judge by the meaning of his name) from Ur in Sumer to Harran on the Upper Euphrates. By our calculations this took place in 2096 B.C., when the great Sumerian king Ur-Nammu died unexpectedly and the people complained that the death occurred because "Enlil changed his word" to Ur-Nammu. Against a background of a growing preoccupation in Sumer with "sinning" cities in the west, along the Mediterranean coast, Abram/Abraham was ordered by Yahweh to move southward with his family, retainers, and flocks and take a position in the Negev, the dry area bordering on the Sinai. The move took place upon the death in Sumer of Ur-Nammu's successor (Shulgi) in 2048 B.C., when the Hebrew Patriarch was seventy-five years old. It was the very same year when Marduk, in preparation for his seizing of the supremacy among the gods, arrived in the Land of the Hittites, north of Mesopotamia.

Encountering a famine caused by a drought, Abram continued moving on, all the way to Egypt. There he was received by the Pharaoh—the last Pharaoh of the tenth northern dynasty, who a few years later (in 2040 B.C.) was overthrown by the princes and priests of Thebes in the south.

Two years before, in 2042 B.C. by our calculations, Abram returned to his outpost in the Negev; he was now in command of a retinue of cavalrymen (probably fast camel riders). He returned in time to deflect an attempt, by a coalition of "Kings of the East," to invade the Mediterranean lands and reach the Spaceport in the Sinai. Abram's mission was to guard the Spaceport's approaches, not to take sides in the war of the Easterns with the kings of Canaan. But when the deflected invaders overran Sodom and took Abram's nephew Lot captive, he pursued them with his cavalry all the way to Damascus, rescued his nephew, and retrieved the booty. Upon his return he was greeted as a victor in the environs of *Shalem* (the future Jerusalem); and the exchanged salutations carried a lasting significance:

> *And Melchizedek, the king of Shalem,*
> *brought forth bread and wine,*
> *for he was a priest unto the God Most High.*
> *And he blessed him, saying:*
> *"Blessed be Abram unto the God Most High,*
> *Possessor of Heaven and Earth; and*
> *Blessed be the God Most High*
> *who hath delivered thy foes unto thy hands."*

And the Canaanite kings, who were present at the ceremony, offered Abram to keep all the booty for himself, and hand over just the captives. But Abram, refusing to take anything, said thus under oath:

> *"I hereby lift my hand unto Yahweh,*
> *God Supreme, Posessor of Heaven and Earth:*
> *Neither a thread nor a shoelace*
> *shall I take—nothing that is thine."*

"And it was after these things"—after Abram had carried out his mission to Canaan to protect the Spaceport—"that

the word of Yahweh came unto Abram in an envisioning"
(Genesis 15:1). "Fear not, Abram," the Lord said, "I am
thy shield, [and] thy reward shall be exceedingly great." But
Abram answered that in the absence of an heir, what value
would any reward be? So "the word of Yahweh came to
him," assuring him that he would have his own natural son,
and offspring as many as the stars of heaven, who shall inherit the land on which he stands.

To leave no doubt in the mind of Abram that no matter
what this Promise would come to pass, the deity speaking to
Abram revealed his identity to the childless Abram. Until this
point we had to take the word of the biblical narrative that
it was Yahweh who had spoken or appeared to Abram. Now,
for the first time, the Lord identified himself by name:

> *"I am Yahweh*
> *who had brought thee out of Ur of the Chaldees,*
> *to give thee this land, to inherit it."*
>
> *And Abram said:*
> *"My Lord Yahweh,*
> *By what shall I know that I shall inherit it?"*

Thereupon, to convince the doubting Abram, Yahweh "cut
a covenant with Abram that day, to wit: To thy seed have I
given this land, from the Brook of Egypt to the River Euphrates, the great river."

The "cutting of the covenant" between Yahweh—"God
Supreme, Possessor of Heaven and Earth"—and the blessed
Patriarch involved a magical ritual whose likes are not mentioned anywhere else in the Bible, either before or afterward.
The Patriarch was instructed to take a heifer, a she-goat, a
ram, a turtledove, and a pigeon and cut them apart and place
the pieces opposite each other. "And when the sun went
down, a deep sleep fell upon Abram, and a horror, dark and
great, fell upon him." The prophecy—a destiny by which
Yahweh declared himself bound—was then proclaimed: After
a sojourn of four hundred years in bondage in a foreign land,
the descendants of Abram shall inherit the Promised Land.
No sooner did the Lord pronounce this oracle than "a burning

smoke and a fiery torch passed between the pieces." It was on that day, the Bible states, "that Yahweh cut a covenant with Abram."

(Some fifteen centuries later the Assyrian king Esarhaddon, "seeking the decision of the gods Shamash and Adad, prostrated himself reverently." To obtain a "vision concerning Ashur, Babylon and Nineveh," the king wrote, "I laid down the portions of the sacrificial animals at both sides; the signs of the oracle were in perfect agreement, and they gave me a favorable answer." But in that case, no divine fire came down to pass between the pieces of the sacrificed animals).

At age eighty-six Abram did obtain a son, by the handmaiden Hagar but not by his wife Sarai (as she was still called, by her Sumerian name). It was thirteen years later, on the eve of momentous events concerning the affairs of gods and men, that Yahweh "appeared unto Abram" and prepared him for the new era: the change of names from the Sumerian Abram and Sarai to the Semitic Abraham and Sarah, and the circumcising of all the males as a sign of the everlasting Covenant.

It was in 2024 B.C., by our calculations (based on synchronizations with Sumerian and Egyptian chronologies), that Abraham had witnessed the upheavaling of Sodom and Gomorrah following the visit by Yahweh and the two Angels. The destruction, we have shown in *The Wars of Gods and Men,* was just a sideshow to the main "event"—the vaporizing with nuclear weapons of the Spaceport in the center of the Sinai peninsula by Ninurta and Nergal in order to deprive Marduk of the space facility. The unintentional result of the nuclear holocaust was the blowing of a deathly nuclear cloud eastward; it caused death (but no destruction) in Sumer, bringing to a bitter end that great civilization.

Now it was only Abram/Abraham and his seed—his descendants—that remained to carry on the ancient traditions, to "call on the name of Yahweh," to retain a sacred link to the beginning of time.

To be safe from the nuclear poison, Abraham was ordered out of the Negev (the arid district bordering on the Sinai) and to find haven near the Mediterranean coast, in the district of the Philistines. A year after the event Isaac was born to

Abraham by his wife and half sister Sarah, as Yahweh had foretold.

Thirty-seven years later Sarah died, and the old Patriarch Abraham was concerned about the succession. Fearing that he would die before seeing his son Isaac married, he made his head-servant swear "by Yahweh, the God of Heaven and the God of Earth," that on no account would he arrange for Isaac to marry a local Canaanite.

To be sure, he sent him to get for Isaac a bride from among the daughters of the relatives who had stayed behind in Harran on the Upper Euphrates. At age forty, Isaac married his imported bride Rebecca; and she bore him two sons, the twins Esau and Jacob, twenty years later. The year, by our calculations, was 1963 B.C.

Some time later, when the boys grew up, "there was a famine in the land, other than the first famine that occurred in the time of Abraham." Isaac thought of emulating his father by going to Egypt, whose agriculture did not depend on rains (but on the annual rise of the Nile's waters). But to do that he had to cross the Sinai, and that apparently was still dangerous even decades after the nuclear blast. So "Yahweh was seen to him" and instructed him not to go to Egypt; instead he was to move in Canaan to a district where wells could be dug for water. There Isaac and his family remained for many years, long enough for Esau to marry locally and for Jacob to go to Harran, where he married Leah and Rachel.

In time Jacob had twelve sons: six by Leah, four by concubines, and two by Rachel: Joseph, and the youngest, Benjamin (at whose birth Rachel died). Of them all Joseph was his favorite; and it was therefore that the older brothers, envious of Joseph, sold him to caravaners going to Egypt. And thus the Divine Prophecy, of a sojourn of Abraham's descendants in a foreign land, began to be fulfilled.

Through a series of successful dream-solving, Joseph became Overseer of Egypt, charged with the task of preparing the land during seven plentiful years for a predicted seven-year famine thereafter. (It is our belief that in his ingenuity Joseph used a natural depression to create an artificial lake, and fill it up with water when the Nile was still rising high annually; then use the stored water to irrigate the parched

Figure 100

land. The shrunken lake still waters Egypt's most fertile area, called Elfayum; the canal linking the lake to the Nile is still called The Waterway of Joseph).

When the famine became too harsh to bear, Jacob sent his other sons (except Benjamin) to Egypt to obtain food—only to discover, after several dramatic encounters with the Overseer, that he was none other than their younger brother Joseph. Telling them that the famine would last another five years, Joseph told them to go back and bring over to Egypt their father and remaining brother and all the rest of Jacob's household. The year, by our calculations, was 1833 B.C. and the reigning Pharaoh was Amenemhet III of the twelfth dynasty.

(A depiction found in a royal tomb from that time shows a group of men, women, and children with some of their livestock arriving in Egypt. The immigrants are depicted as, and identified in the accompanying inscription, as ''Asiatics'' (Fig. 100); their colorful robes, vividly painted in the tomb mural, are exactly of the kind of multicolored striped robe that Joseph had worn while in Canaan. While the Asiatics here depicted are not necessarily the caravan of Jacob and his family, the painting does show how they had certainly looked.)

The presence of Jacob in Egypt is directly attested, according to A. Mallon in *Les Hébreux en Egypte*, also by various inscriptions on scarabs that spell out the name *Ya'a-qob* (the Hebrew name that in English is rendered ''Jacob''). Written sometimes within a royal cartouche (Fig. 101), it is spelled hieroglyphically Yy-A-Q-B with the suffix H-R, giv-

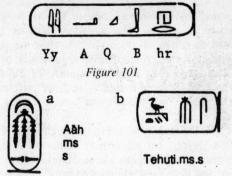

Yy   A   Q   B   hr

Figure 101

a   b

Aäh
ms
s

Tehuti.ms.s

Figures 102a and 102b

ing the inscription the meaning "Jacob is satisfied" or "Jacob is at peace."

Jacob was 130 years old when the Children of Israel began their sojourn in Egypt; as prophesied, it ended in bondage four hundred years later. It is with the death and burial of Jacob, and the subsequent death and mummification of Joseph, that the Book of Genesis ends.

The Book of Exodus picks up the story centuries later, "when there arose a new king over Egypt who knew not Joseph." In the intervening centuries much had happened in Egypt. There were civil wars, the capital shifted back and forth, the era of the Middle Kingdom passed, the so-called Second Intermediary Period of chaos took place. In 1650 B.C. the New Kingdom began with the seventeenth dynasty, and in 1570 B.C. the renowned eighteenth dynasty ascended the Pharaonic throne in Thebes, in Upper (southern) Egypt, leaving behind its magnificent monuments, temples, and statues in Karnak and Luxor and its splendid tombs hidden inside the mountains, in the Valley of the Kings.

Many of the throne names chosen by the Pharaohs of those new dynasties were epithets by which they asserted their status as demigods; such was the name *Ra-Ms-S* (Ramesses or Ramses in English) which meant "From the god Ra emanated." The founder of the seventeenth dynasty called himself *Ah-Ms-S* (Ah-Mose) (Fig. 102a) meaning "From the god

Ah emanated'' (*Ah* being a name of the Moon god). This new dynasty started the New Kingdom that, we have suggested, had forgotten all about Joseph after the passage of some three centuries. Accordingly, a successor of Ahmose called *Tehuti-Ms-S* (Fig 102b) (Thothmose or Tutmosis I)— ''From the god Thoth emanated''—was, we have concluded, the ruler in whose time the story of Moses and the events of the Exodus began.

It was this Pharaoh who, using the might of a unified and invigorated Egypt, sent his armies northward as far as the Upper Euphrates—the region where the relatives of Abraham had stayed and flourished. He reigned from 1525 to 1512 B.C. and it was he, we have suggested in *The Wars of Gods and Men,* who feared that the Children of Israel would join the warfare in support of their Euphratean relatives. So he imposed harsh work on the Israelites, and ordered that any new born Israelite male should be killed at birth.

It was in 1513 B.C. that a Levite Hebrew and his Levite wife had a son born to them. And fearing that he would be killed, the mother put him in a waterproofed box of bulrushes of the Nile and placed the box in the river. And it so happened that the stream carried the box to where the Pharaoh's Daughter was bathing; she ended up adopting the boy as a son, ''and she called him Moses''—*Moshe* in Hebrew. The Bible explains that she called him so for he was ''from the waters extracted.'' But, we have no doubt, what the Pharaoh's Daughter did was to give the boy the epithet common in her dynasty with the component *Mss* (Mose, Mosis), prefixed, we believe, by a deity's name that the Bible preferred to omit.

The chronology suggested by us, placing the birth of Moses in 1513 B.C., meshes the biblical tale with Egyptian chronology and a web of intrigues and power struggles in the Egyptian court.

Having been born to Thothmes I by his half sister wife, their only daughter, called Hatshepsut, indeed bore the exclusive title The Pharaoh's Daughter. When Thothmes I died in 1512, the only male heir was a son born by a harem girl. Ascending the throne as Thothmes II, he married his half sister Hatshepsut to gain legitimacy for himself and for his children. But this couple had only daughters, and the only son this king had was by a concubine. Thothmes II had a short reign, just nine years. So when he died, the son—the future Thothmes III—was just a boy, too young to be a Pharaoh. Hatshepsut was appointed Regent, and after a number of years crowned herself Queen—a female Pharaoh (who even ordered that her carved images show her with a false beard). As can be imagined, it was in such circumstances that the envy and enmity between the king's son and the queen's adopted son grew and intensified.

Finally, in 1482 B.C., Hatshepsut died (or was murdered), and the concubine's son assumed the throne as Thothmes III. He lost no time in renewing the foreign conquests (some scholars refer to him as the "Napoleon of ancient Egypt") and the oppression of the Israelites. "And it came to pass in those days, when Moses was grown up, that he went out unto his brethren and saw their sufferings." Killing an Egyptian slavemaster, he gave the king the excuse to order his death. "So Moses fled from the Pharaoh, and tarried in the land of the Midianites," in the Sinai peninsula. He ended up marrying the daughter of the Midianite priest.

"And it came to pass, after a long time, that the king of Egypt died; and the Children of Israel, bemoaning their bondage, cried out unto the *Elohim*. And *Elohim* heard their laments, and *Elohim* recalled his covenant with Abraham and with Isaac and with Jacob; and *Elohim* beheld the Children of Israel, and *Elohim* found out."

Almost four hundred years had passed since the Lord had last spoken to Jacob "in a nighttime vision," until he has now come to take a look at the Children of Jacob/Israel crying out of their bondage. That the *Elohim* intended here was Yahweh becomes clear in the subsequent narrative. Where was He during those long four centuries? The Bible does not say; but it is a question to be pondered.

Be that as it may, the time was propitious for drastic action. As the biblical narrative makes clear, this chain of new developments was triggered by the death of the Pharaoh "after a long time" of reign. Egyptian records show that Thothmes III, who had ordered that Moses be put to death, died in 1450 B.C. His successor on the throne, Amenhotep II, was a weak ruler who had trouble keeping Egypt united; and with his ascension, the death sentence against Moses expired.

It was then that Yahweh called out to Moses from inside the Burning Bush, telling him that He had decided to "come down and save" the Israelites from their bondage in Egypt and lead them back to the Promised Land, and telling Moses that he was selected to be the God's ambassador to gain this freedom from the Pharaoh and to lead the Israelites on their Exodus from Egypt.

It happened, we are told in Exodus chapter 3, when Moses was shepherding the flock of his father in law, "leading the flock beyond the desert, and he came to the Mount of the *Elohim,* in Horeb," and saw there the thornbush burning without being consumed; so he went closer to take a look at the incredible sight.

The biblical narrative refers to the "Mount of the *Elohim*" as though it was a well-known landmark; the unusual character of the event was not that Moses had led his flock there, nor that there were bushes there. The exceptional aspect was that the bush was burning without being consumed!

It was only the first of a series of amazing magical acts and miracles that the Lord had to employ in order to convince Moses, the Israelites, and the Pharaoh of the authenticity of the mission and the divine determination motivating it. To that purpose Yahweh empowered Moses with three magical acts: his staff could turn into a snake, and back into a staff; his hand could be made leprous and again healthy; and he could pour some Nile water on the ground and the ground would stay dry. "The people who had sought thy death are all dead," Yahweh told Moses; fear no more; face the new Pharaoh and perform the magics that I granted thee, and tell him that the Israelites must be let go to be free to worship their God in the desert. As an assistant, Yahweh appointed Aaron, the brother of Moses, to accompany him.

In the first encounter with the Pharaoh, the king was not responsive. "Who is this Yahweh whom I should heed to let the Israelites go?" he said, "I know not Yahweh and the Israelites I will not let go." Instead of releasing the Israelites, the Pharaoh doubled and trebled their quotas of brickmaking. When the magical tricks with the staff failed to impress the

Pharaoh, Moses was instructed by the Lord to begin the series of plagues—"hits," if one is to translate the Hebrew term literally—that kept escalating in severity as the Egyptian king first refused to release the Israelites, then wavered, then agreed and changed his mind. Ten in all, they ranged from the turning of the Nile's water red as blood for a week, through the swarming of the river and lakes with frogs; the afflicting of the people with lice and the cattle with pestilences; devastation by hailstones and brimstones and locusts; and a darkness that lasted three days. And when all that did not attain the Israelites' freedom, when all the "wonders of Yahweh" failed, the last and decisive blow came: All the firstborn of Egypt, be it men or cattle, were stricken to death 'as Yahweh passed through the land of Egypt.'' But the Israelite homes, marked with blood on their doorposts, were 'passed over'' and spared. That very same night, the Pharaoh let them go out of Egypt; and therefore is the event celebrated to this very day by the Jewish people as the holiday of the Passover. It happened on the night of the fourteenth day of the month Nissan, when Moses was eighty years old—in 1433 B.C. by our calculations.

The Exodus from Egypt was on—but it was not yet the end of the troubles with the Pharaoh. As the Israelites reached the edge of the desert, where the chain of lakes formed a watery barrier beyond the Egyptian forts, the Pharaoh concluded that the escapees were trapped and sent his fast chariots to recapture them. It was then that Yahweh sent an Angel, 'the angel of the *Elohim* who had gone in front of the Israelite host,'' to station himself and a pillar of dark clouds between the Israelites and the pursuing Egyptians, to separate the camps. And during that night ''Yahweh drove back the sea with a strong east wind, and dried up the sea, and the waters were divided, and the Children of Israel went into the sea upon the dried ground.''

By early morning the dazed Egyptians tried to follow the Israelites through the parted waters; but no sooner had they tried that, than the wall of water engulfed them and they perished.

It was only after that miraculous event—so vividly and artfully recreated for all to see by Cecil B. DeMille in the epic movie *The Ten Commandments*—that the Children of Israel were free at last, free to proceed through the desert and its hardships to the edge of the Sinai peninsula—all the while led by the Divine Pillar that was a dark cloud during the day and a fiery beacon at night. Water and food shortages, miraculously averted, and a war with an unexpected Amalekite enemy, still were in store for them. Finally, "in the third month," they arrived in the Wilderness of Sinai "and encamped opposite the Mount."

They had arrived at their predetermined destination: the "Mountain of the *Elohim*." The greatest Theophany ever was about to begin.

There were preparations and stages in that memorable and unique Divine Encounter, and a price to pay by its chosen witnesses. It began with "Moses going up toward the *Elohim*," upon the Mount, as "Yahweh called out to him from the Mount," to hear the precondition for the Theophany and its consequences. Moses was told to repeat to the Children of Israel the Lord's exact words:

> *If you will listen to me*
> *and keep my covenant, then—*
> *out of all the nations—*
> *a treasured possession to me you shall be,*
> *for the whole Earth is mine;*
> *You shall be my kingdom of priests*
> *and a holy nation.*

Earlier, when Moses was given his embassy at this very same mount, Yahweh stated his intention to "adopt the children of Israel as his people," and in turn "to be an *Elohim* unto them." Now the Lord spelled out the "deal" involved in the Theophany. With the Covenant came commandments and laws and restrictions; they were the price to be paid for qualifying for the Theophany—a unique event by which the Israelites will become a Treasured People, consecrated unto God.

"And Moses came and summoned the elders of the people and laid before them all these words as Yahweh had commanded. And all the people answered, all together, saying:

'All that Yahweh hath spoken we will do.' And Moses brought the people's words unto Yahweh."

Having received this acceptance, "Yahweh said unto Moses: Behold, I shall be coming unto thee in a thick cloud, enabling the people to hear when I speak with thee, so that in thee too they shall have faith." And the Lord ordered Moses to have the people consecrate themselves and be ready for three days hence, informing them that "on the third day shall Yahweh come down upon Mount Sinai, in full sight of all the people."

The landing, Yahweh indicated to Moses, would create a danger for anyone coming too near. "Thou shalt set bounds round about" the Mount, Moses was told, to keep the people at a distance, telling them to dare not try to go up or even touch the Mount's edge, "for whosoever toucheth it shall surely be put to death."

As these instructions were followed, "it was on the third day, when it was morning," that the promised *Landing of Yahweh* upon the Mount of *Elohim* began. It was a fiery descent and a noisy one: "There were thundering sounds and flashes of lightning, and a dense cloud [was] upon the Mount, and a *Shofar* sound, exceedingly strong; and all the people in the encampment were terrified."

As the descent of the Lord Yahweh began, "Moses brought forth the people from the encampment toward the *Elohim*, and they stationed themselves at the foot of the Mount," at the boundary that Moses had marked out all around the Mount.

And Mount Sinai was completely engulfed by smoke,
for Yahweh had descended upon it in a fire.
And the smoke thereof rose up like that of a furnace,
and the whole mount quaked greatly.
And the sound of the Shofar *continued to wax louder;*
As Moses spoke, the Elohim *answered him in a loud*
voice.

(The term *Shofar* associated in this text with the sounds emanating from the Mount is usually translated "horn." Literally, however, it means "Amplifier"—a device, we believe, that was used to enable all the Israelite multitude, standing at the foot of the mountain, to hear Yahweh's voice and his talk with Moses).

Thus did Yahweh, in full view of all the people—all 600,000 of them—"descend upon Mount Sinai, on the top of it; and Yahweh called Moses up to the top of the Mount, and Moses went up."

It was then, from atop the mount, from within the thick cloud, that *"Elohim* spoke the following words," pronouncing the Ten Commandments—the essentials of the Hebrew Faith, the guidelines for social justice and human morality; a summary of the Covenant between Man and God, all of the Divine Teachings succinctly expressed.

The first three Commandments established monotheism, proclaimed Yahweh as the *Elohim* of Israel, the sole God, and prohibited the making of idols and their worship:

I I am Yahweh thy Elohim
who hath brought thee out of the land of Egypt,
out of the house of bondage.

II Thou shalt have no other Elohim *beside me;*
thou shalt not make for thyself any sculptured image
of likeness of anything that is in heaven above,
or that is on the earth beneath, or that is in the
waters under the earth. Thou shalt not bow to them
nor worship them . . .

III Thou shalt not utter the name of Yahweh thy Elohim
in vain.

Next came a Commandment intended to express the sanctity of the People of Israel and their subjection to a higher standard of daily life, by setting aside one day a week to be the *Sabbath*—a day devoted to contemplation and rest, applying equally to all people, to humans as well as to their livestock:

IV Remember to keep the day of the Sabbath and sanctify
it.

Six days shalt thou labor and do all thy work;
but the seventh day is the Sabbath of Yahweh, thy
Elohim:
On it thou shalt not do any work—
neither thou, nor thy son, nor thy daughter; neither thy
servant nor thy maidservant, nor thy cattle;
As also the stranger who is within thy gates.

The fifth affirmative Commandment established the family
as the human unit, headed by the patriarch and the matriarch:

V *Honor thy father and thy mother,*
 that thy days may be prolonged upon the land
 which Yahweh thy Elohim *giveth thee.*

And then came the five No's that established the moral
and social code between Man and Man rather than, as at the
beginning, between Man and God:

 VI *Thou shalt not murder.*
 VII *Thou shalt not commit adultery.*
VIII *Thou shalt not steal*
 IX *Thou shalt not bear false witness against thy neighbor.*
 X *Thou shalt not covet thy neighbor's house;*
 Thou shalt not covet thy neighbor's wife,
 neither his servant or maidservant, his ox, his ass,
 nor anything that is his.

Much has been made in countless textbooks of the *Laws
of Hammurabi,* the Babylonian king from the eighteenth century B.C., that he engraved on a stela (now in the Louvre
Museum) upon which he is shown receiving the laws from
the god Shamash. But that was only a listing of crimes and
their punishments. A thousand years before Hammurabi Sumerian kings established laws of social justice—you shall not
take away the donkey of a widow, they decreed, or delay the
wages of a day laborer (to give two examples). But never
before (and perhaps not even thereafter) did just ten commandments state, so clearly, *all* of the essentials that a whole
people and any human being had to be guided by!

To hear the booming divine voice coming from atop the mount had to be an awesome experience. Indeed, we read that as "all the people perceived the thundering and flashes and the *Shofar*'s sound and the mountain engulfed in smoke, they were seized with fear and moved away and stood at a distance. And they said unto Moses: 'Speak thou with us and we will listen, but let not the *Elohim* himself speak to us, lest we die'." And having asked Moses to be the conveyor of the divine words rather than hearing them directly, "the people stood farther away; and Moses went toward the thick fog where the *Elohim* was," for the Lord had summoned him:

> *And Yahweh said unto Moses:*
> *Come up to me, on the Mount, and remain there;*
> *And I will give thee the stone tablets*
> *with the law and the commandment*
> *which I have written, to be taught to them.*

This (in Genesis chapter 24) is the first mention of the Tablets of the Law and the assertion that they were *inscribed by Yahweh himself.* This is restated in chapter 31, where the number of Tablets is stated to be two, "made of stone, inscribed by the finger of *Elohim*"; and again in chapter 32: "Tablets inscribed on both of their sides—on the one side and on the other side were they inscribed; and the Tablets were the craftwork of *Elohim* and the writing was the script of *Elohim,* engraved upon the Tablets." (This is reasserted in Deuteronomy).

Written on the Tablets were the Ten Commandments as well as more detailed ordinances to govern daily conduct by the people, some rules of worship of Yahweh, and strict prohibitions against the worship or even uttering the names of the gods of Israel's neighbors. All that the Lord intended to give Moses as *Tablets of the Covenant,* to be kept forever in the Ark of the Covenant that was to be built according to detailed specifications.

The granting of the Tablets was an event of lasting significance, embedded in the memory of the Children of Israel and therefore requiring witnesses of the highest standing. Therefore Yahweh instructed Moses to come up to receive the

Tablets accompanied by his brother Aaron and Aaron's two priestly sons and seventy of the tribal elders. They were not allowed to come up all the way (only Moses could do that), but close enough "to see the *Elohim* of Israel." Even then all they could see was the space under the Lord's feet, "made as of pure sapphire, like the color of skies in clearness." Coming that close they would have normally lost their lives; but this time, having invited them, "Yahweh against the nobles of Israel did not put forth his hand." They were not struck down, and lived to celebrate the Divine Encounter and witness Moses going up to receive the Tablets:

> *And Moses went up on the Mount,*
> *and the cloud enveloped the Mount.*
> *And the glory of Yahweh rested upon Mount Sinai,*
> *covered by the cloud, for six days;*
> *and on the seventh day He called unto Moses*
> *from inside the cloud ...*
>
> *And Moses went into the cloud*
> *and ascended up the Mount;*
> *And Moses was on the mount forty days*
> *and forty nights.*

Since the two tablets had already been inscribed, the long time Moses stayed atop the Mount was used to instruct him in the construction of the Tabernacle, the *Mishkan* ("Residence") in which Yahweh would make his presence known to the Children of Israel. It was then that, in addition to the architectural details that were given orally, Yahweh also showed Moses the "structural model of the Residence and the model of all of the instruments thereof." These included the Ark of the Covenant, the wooden chest inlaid with gold, in which the two Tablets were to be kept, and on top of which the two golden Cherubim were to be emplaced; that, the Lord explained, would be the *Dvir*—literally, the Speaker—"where I will keep the appointments with thee, speaking to thee from between the two Cherubim."

It was also during that Divine Encounter atop the Mount that Moses was instructed about the priesthood, naming as the only ones who could approach the Lord (besides Moses) and officiate in the Tabernacle Aaron, the brother of Moses, and the four sons of Aaron. Their vestments were elaborately prescribed, to the smallest detail, including the Breastplate of Judgment containing twelve precious stones inscribed with the names of the twelve tribes of Israel. The Breastplate was also to hold in place—precisely against the priest's heart— the *Urim* and *Tumim*. Though the exact meaning of the terms has eluded scholars, it is clear from other biblical references (e.g. Numbers 27:21) that they served as an oracular panel for obtaining a Yes or No answer from the Lord in response to a question. The inquiring person's question was put before the Lord by the priest, "to ask for the Decision of the Urim before Yahweh, and in accordance thereof to act." When King Saul (I Samuel 28:6) sought Yahweh's guidance whether to engage in war with the Philistines, he "inquired of Yahweh in dreams, by the Urim, and through prophets."

While Moses was in the presence of the Lord, back in the encampment his long absence was interpreted as bad news, and his failure to show up after several weeks as an indication that he might have perished by seeing God; "for is there any any flesh"—any mortal human—"who hath heard the voice of a living *Elohim* speaking from inside the fire, and stayed alive?" It was thus that "the people, seeing that Moses was not coming down from the Mount, gathered by Aaron and said to him: 'Come, make for us an *Elohim* who could lead us, for this man Moses, who hath brought us out of Egypt— we know not what is become of him." So Aaron, seeking to invoke Yahweh, built an altar to Yahweh and placed before it the sculpture of a calf inlaid with gold.

Alerted by Yahweh, "Moses turned and went down from the Mount, with the two Tablets of the Testimony in his hand." And when he neared the camp and saw the golden calf, Moses was furious "and he threw the tablets out of his hand, and broke them at the foot of the Mount; and he took the calf which they had made and burnt it by fire, and [its gold] he ground into a powder, and strewed the dust upon the waters." Seeking out the instigators of the abomination and having them put to the sword, Moses beseeched the Lord not to abandon the Children of Israel. If the sin cannot be forgiven, let me alone bear the punishment, he said; let it be me who is "blotted out of the book" of life. But the Lord was not fully appeased, keeping the option of further retribution; "Whosoever hath sinned against me, indeed from my book shall be blotted out."

"And when the people heard these evil tidings, they mourned." Moses himself, discouraged and despairing, picked up his tent and pitched it outside the encampment, far off from the camp. "And when Moses left for the tent, all the people rose up and stood every one at the door of his tent, and watched Moses go, until he would enter the tent." A sense of a failed mission pervaded him and them all.

But then a miracle happened; Yahweh's compassion became manifest:

> *And it came to pass,*
> *when Moses was entering the tent,*
> *that the pillared cloud descended,*
> *and stood at the entrance of the tent,*
> *and a voice spoke to Moses.*
>
> *And when the people, all of them,*
> *saw the pillar of cloud standing*
> *at the entrance to the tent,*
> *the whole people rose up and prostrated*
> *themselves, each at his tent's entrance.*
>
> *And Yahweh spoke unto Moses face to face,*
> *as a man would speak unto his friend.*

When the Lord spoke to Moses from inside the Burning Bush, "Moses covered his face, for he was afraid to look at the *Elohim*." The Elders and nobles who had accompanied Moses up the Mount, went up only halfway and were enabled to see only the Lord's footrest—and even then it was a wonder that they were not smitten. At the end of the forty years of wandering, as the Israelites were ready to enter Canaan, Moses in his testamental review of the Exodus and the great Theophany made a point of stressing that "on the day Yah-

weh hath spoken unto you in Horeb, out of the midst of the
fire, ye saw no visage of any kind:''

> *Ye came near and stood at the foot of the Mount,*
> *and the Mount was engulfed with fire*
> *reaching unto the midst of heaven,*
> *and [there was] a dark cloud and thick fog.*
> *And Yahweh spoke unto you from inside the fire;*
> *ye heard the sound of the words,*
> *but the likeness of a visage ye saw not—*
> *only a voice was heard.*

(Deuteronomy 4:11–15)

This, obviously, was an essential element in the do's and
don'ts of close encounters with Yahweh. But now that the
relenting God was talking to Moses "face to face"—but still
from within the cloud-pillar—Moses seized the moment to
seek a reaffirmation of his role as the leader chosen by the
Lord. "Show me thy face!" he begged of the Lord.

Answering enigmatically, Yahweh said: "Thou canst not
see my face, for no Man can see Me and live."

So Moses pleaded again: "Please, show me thy *glory!*"

And Yahweh said: "Behold, there is a place by me; go
and stand there upon the rock. And when my *glory* shall pass
by there, I will put thee in the cleft of the rock, and will
cover thee with my hand until I have passed by; and I will
then remove my hand, and you shall see my back; but my
face shall not be seen."

The Hebrew word that has been rendered "glory" in English translations, in all the above quoted instances, is *Kabod;*
it stems from the root KBD whose seminal meaning is
"weighty, heavy." Literally then, *Kabod* would mean "the
heaviness, the weighty thing." That a "thing," a physical
object and not an abstract "glory" is meant when applied to
Yahweh is clear from its first mention in the Bible, when the
Israelites "beheld the *Kabod* of Yahweh," enveloped by the
ubiquitous cloud, after the Lord supplied them miraculously
with Manna as their daily food. In Exodus 24:16 we read that

"the *Kabod* of Yahweh rested upon Mount Sinai, covered by the cloud, for six days" until He called Moses up on the seventh day; and verse 17 adds, for the benefit of those who were not present, that "the appearance of the *Kabod* of Yahweh, on top of the Mount in full view of the Children of Israel, was like a devouring fire."

Indicating a manifestation of Yahweh, the term *Kabod* is so used in all five books of the Pentateuch—Genesis, Exodus, Leviticus, Numbers, Deuteronomy. In all instances, called the *"Kabod* of Yahweh," it was something concrete that the people could see—but always engulfed by a cloud, as though within a dark fog.

The term is repeatedly employed by the Prophet Ezekiel in his descriptions of the Divine Chariot (where the footstool is described almost identically as in the verses regarding what the Elders of Israel had seen halfway up Mount Sinai). The Chariot, Ezekiel reported, was engulfed with a bright radiance; this, he said, was "the appearance of the *Kabod* of Yahweh." On his first prophetic mission to the exiles dwelling at the River Khabur, he was addressed by the Lord in a valley where "the *Kabod* of Yahweh was stationed, a *Kabod* like the one seen before." When he was carried aloft and taken to see Jerusalem "in divine visions," he again "saw the *Kabod* of the God of Israel, as the one I had seen in the valley." And when the envisioned visit was completed, the *"Kabod* of Yahweh" stationed itself upon the Cherubim, and the Cherubim raised their wings and "lifted off the earth," carrying the *Kabod* aloft.

The *Kabod,* Ezekiel wrote (10:4) had a luminosity that shone through the cloud that shrouded it, a kind of a radiance. This detail provides an insight into a facet of a Close Encounter by Moses with the Lord Yahweh and his *Kabod.* It was after Yahweh had relented of his anger, and told Moses to fashion two new stone tablets, similar to the first two tablets that Moses had broken, and come up again to the top of Mount Sinai to receive again the Ten Commandments and other ordinances. This time, however, the words were dictated to Moses by the Lord. Again he spent forty days and forty nights atop the Mount; and all that time "Yahweh stood

with him there''—not speaking from a distance, through an
Amplifier, "but staying with him."

And it came to pass,
when Moses was coming down from Mount Sinai
and the two Tablets of the Testimony in his hand
—as Moses was coming down from the Mount—
he knew not that the skin of his face radiated
when He was speaking to him.

And Aaron and all of the Children of Israel,
seeing Moses, saw that the skin of his face radiated;
and they were afraid to come nigh unto him.

So "Moses put a covering-mask upon his face. But when
Moses was coming before Yahweh to speak with him, he
would take off the covering mask until he left and came out
to speak to the Children of Israel whatever he was instructed;
but when the Children of Israel would see the face of Moses,
that the skin of his face was radiating, Moses would put back
the covering-mask, until the next time that he would go to
speak" to the Lord.

It is evident from this that Moses, when he had been in
the proximity of the *Kabod,* was subjected to some kind of
radiation that affected his skin. What exactly the source material of that radiation was we do not know, but we do know
that the Anunnaki could (and did) employ radiation for a
variety of purposes. We read of that in the tale of *Inanna's
Descent to the Nether World,* when she was revived with a
pulsating radiance (perhaps not unlike that depicted on a clay
plaque from Mesopotamia, in which the patient, protected by
a mask, is treated with radiation—Fig. 103). We read of it,
used as a killing beam, when Gilgamesh tried to enter the
Restricted Zone in the Sinai peninsula and its guardians directed the radiation at him (see Fig. 46). And we have read
in the *Tale of Zu* what had happened when he removed the
Tablet of Destinies from the Mission Control Center in Nippur: "Stillness spread all over, silence prevailed; the sanctuary's brilliance was taken away."

A physical object, one that can move about, station it-

Figure 103

**self upon a mountain, rise and take off, shrouded in a
cloud of dark fog, radiating a brilliance—this is how the
Bible describes the *Kabod*—literally, "The Heavy Object"—in which Yahweh moved about. It all describes
what we nowadays call, out of ignorance or disbelief, a
UFO—an Unidentified Flying Object.**

In this regard it will be helpful to trace the Akkadian and
Sumerian roots from which the Hebrew term had derived.
While the Akkadian *Kabbuttu* meant "heavy, weighty," the
similar-sounding *Kabdu* (paralleling the Hebrew *Kabod*)
meant "Wing-holder"—something to which wings are
attached, or perhaps into which wings can retract. And the
Sumerian term KI.BAD.DU meant "to soar to a faraway
place." In one instance, in which a deity's throne is described, the adjective HUSH—"red glowing"—is used to
describe the "Far Soaring" object.

We can only speculate whether the *Kabod* looked like the
winged "Divine Black Bird" of Ninurta, the wingless (or
with wings retracted) bulbous vehicles depicted in the murals
of Tell Ghassul (see Fig. 72)—or as the rocketlike object that
Gilgamesh had seen rise from the Landing Place in Lebanon
(an ascent which, reversed for a descent, reads almost like
the description provided in Exodus chapter 19).

Might it have resembled an American shuttlecraft (Fig.
104a)? We wonder, because of the similarity to it of a small
figurine, discovered a few years ago at a site in Turkey (the
ancient Tuspa). Made of clay, it shows a flying machine that

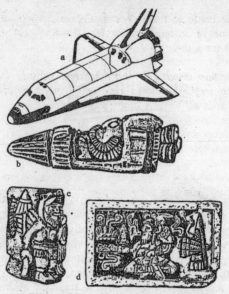

Figures 104a, 104b, 104c, and 104d

combines features of a modern shuttlecraft (including the engine exhausts) with the cockpit of a single-seater plane (Fig. 104b). The partly damaged image of the "pilot" seated in the cockpit, as well as the totality of the artform, bring to our mind Mesoamerican depictions of bearded gods accompanied by rocketlike objects (Figs. 104c, 104d). The Archeological Museum in Istanbul, which has been keeping this figurine, has not put it on display; the official excuse is that its "authenticity" has not been established. If it is authentic, it will serve not only to illustrate ancient "UFOs" but also to add light on the links between the ancient Near East and the Americas.

After Moses had died and Joshua was chosen by the Lord to lead the Israelites, they advanced up the eastern side of the Jordan River and crossed it near Jericho; almost at every turn, they were assisted by divine miracles. Of them all, the one scholars and scientists find the hardest to accept is the tale of the battle in the valley of Gibeon, when—according to the Book of Joshua chapter 10—the Sun and the Moon stood still for a day:

> *And the Sun stood still, and the Moon stayed,*
> *until the people had avenged themselves of the enemies.*
> *Indeed it is all written in the Book of Jashar:*
> *The Sun stood still in the midst of the skies*
> *and it hastened not to go down,*
> *about a whole day.*

What could have caused the Earth's rotation to stop, so that the Sun rising in the east and the Moon setting in the west seemed to stand still, for the better part ("about a whole") of a day (of twenty-four hours)? To those who take the Bible on faith, it is just one more divine intervention in behalf of God's Chosen People. At the other extreme there are those who discount the whole tale as mere fiction, a myth. In between are those who, as for the ten plagues that befell Egypt and the parting of the waters of the Sea of Reeds (associating the events with the volcanic explosion on the Mediterranean island of Thera/Santorini), seek a natural phenomenon or calamity as the cause. Some have suggested an extraordinarily long eclipse; but the Bible states that the Sun was seen, and there was daylight for a prolonged daytime, not that the Sun was obscured. Because the long day began with "great stones" falling from the skies, some have suggested as an explanation the close passage of a large comet (Immanuel Velikovsky, in *Worlds of Collision,* postulated that such a comet was caught into a solar orbit and became the planet Venus).

Both Sumerian and Old Babylonian texts speak of celestial upheavals that were observed in the skies and that called for incantations against the celestial "demons." Treated as "magical texts" (e.g. Charles Fossey, *Textes Magique;* Morris Jastrow, *Die Religion Babyloniens und Assyriens;* and Eric Ebeling, *Tod und Leben*) such texts described an "evil seven, born in the vast skies, unknown in heaven, unknown on Earth" who "attacked Sin and Shamash"—the Moon and the Sun, upsetting at the same time Ishtar (Venus) and Adad

(Mercury). Prior to 1994 the possibility that seven comets would "attack" our celestial region all at once was so remote that the text seemed more a fantasy than a reality witnessed by Mesopotamian astronomers. But when, in July 1994, comet Shoemaker-Levy 9 broke up into twenty-one pieces that impacted Jupiter in quick succession—in full view of observers from Earth—the Mesopotamian texts assume an impressive reality.

Had a comet broken up into seven pieces and caused havoc in our celestial vicinity, impacting Earth and breaking its rotation? Or, as Alfred Jeremias *(The Old Testament in the Light of the Ancient Near East),* reproducing what he called "an important astral-mythological text," treated it as possibly an unusual alignment of seven planets that, with the resulting immense gravitational pull, affected the Sun and Moon from the perspective of Earth—making the Sun and Moon appear to stand still because in reality it was the Earth whose rotation was temporarily halted.

Whatever the explanation, there is corroboration for the occurrence itself from the other side of the world. In both Mesoamerica and South America, "legends"—collective memories—have persisted of a long night of about twenty hours during which the Sun failed to rise. Our investigations (fully reported in *The Lost Realms)* concluded that this long night occurred in the Americas circa 1400 B.C.—the same time when the Sun did not set in Canaan for a similar period. Since one phenomenon is the opposite of the other, the same occurrence—whatever its cause—that made the Sun appear to stand still in Canaan, would have made the Sun fail to rise on the opposite side of the Earth, in the Americas.

The Mesoamerican and South American recollections thus validate the tale of the Day the Earth Stood Still—not the movie script, but the olden biblical tale. And with that, we need neither science fiction nor fantasies to accept the tale of the greatest Theophany ever as the memorable fact that it has been.

CIRCUMCISION: SIGN OF THE STARS?

When Yahweh "cut a covenant" with Abraham, the Patriarch and all the males in his household were required to be circumcised: "Every male among you shall be circumcised in the flesh of your foreskin, and it shall be a token of the covenant betwixt Me and you. He that is eight days old shall be circumcised among you, every male throughout your generations ... This shall be a covenant in your flesh, an everlasting covenant" (Genesis 17:11–14). Failure to do so would have excluded the offender from the people of Israel.

Circumcision was thus intended to serve as a unique "sign in the flesh" distinguishing the descendants of Abraham from their neighbors. Some researchers believe that circumcision was practiced among royalty in Egypt, as evidenced by an ancient illustration (see p. 312)—though the depiction might be that of a puberty rite rather than a religious circumcision.

With or without a precedent, what was the symbolism implied by the requirement to *Mul* (translated "circumcise") the Hebrew males? No one really knows. Unexplained, too, has been the origin of the term; linguists seeking parallels in Akkadian or later Semitic languages have come up empty-handed.

We suggest that the answer to the puzzle lies in Abraham's Sumerian origin. Searching for the meaning there, the term assumes a striking significance, for MUL was the Sumerian term for "celestial body," a star or a planet!

So when Yahweh instructed Abraham to *Mul* himself and the other males, he may have been telling him to put the "sign of the stars" in his flesh—an everlasting symbol of a *celestial connection*.

13

PROPHETS OF AN UNSEEN GOD

The greatest Theophany ever to take place was unique not only in its scope—viewed by 600,000 people, not only in its duration—several months, and not only in its attainments—the Covenant between God and a Chosen People and the proclamation of Commandments and laws of lasting impact. It also revealed a key aspect of the Deity—that of an Unseen God. "No one can see my face and live," He stated; and even approaching too closely to where the *Kabod* rested was a peril.

Yet if He were to be followed and worshiped, how could He be sought, found, and heard? How would Divine Encounters with Yahweh take place?

The immediate answer, in the Wilderness of Sinai, was the Tabernacle, the portable *Mishkan* (literally: Residence) with its Tent of Appointment.

On the first day of the first month of the second year of the Exodus the Tabernacle was completed in accordance with the most detailed and exact specification dictated by the Lord to Moses, including the Tent of Appointment with its Holy of Holies; therein, separated from the other areas by a heavy screen, was placed the Ark of the Covenant that contained the two Tablets and above which the two golden Cherubim touched their wings. There, where the wings touched, was the *Dvir*—literally, the Speaker—by which Yahweh conversed with Moses.

And when Moses had completed "all this work, as Yahweh had commanded," on the prescribed day, a thick cloud landed and engulfed the Tent of Appointment. "The Cloud of Yahweh,'' the last verse of the Book of Exodus states, ''was upon the Residence by day and a fire was in it by night, before the very eyes of the whole house of Israel, throughout their journeys.'' It was only when the divine cloud lifted that they moved on; but when the cloud did not rise off the Residence, they stayed put where encamped until the cloud would rise.

It was during those resting periods (as the first verse in the next book of the Pentateuch, *Leviticus,* states) that ''Yahweh called Moses, and spoke to him from inside the Tent of Appointment.'' The instructions covered the appointment of the House of Aaron as the priestly line, and the precise details of the priestly clothing, consecration, and the rituals of the sacred service of Yahweh.

Even then, in the immediate aftermath of the landing on the Mount and within the consecrated confines of the Tabernacle, it was from inside the thick cloud of a foglike darkness, from behind the screened-off portion, from between the Cherubim, that Yahweh's voice could be heard—the words of the Unseen God. With all those precautions and obscuring veilings, even the High Priest had to raise an additional opaque haze by burning a specific combination of incenses before he could approach the screen that veiled the Ark of the Covenant; and when two sons of Aaron burned the wrong incense, creating a ''strange fire,'' a beam of fire ''emanating from Yahweh'' struck them dead.

It was during those resting periods that Moses was instructed regarding a long list of other rules and regulations—for all manner of sacrifices and the paying of homage to the Lord by the common people, who were all to be considered ''a nation of priests''; for the proper relations between members of the family and between one person and another, prescribing equal treatment of the citizen, the serf, and the strangers. There were instructions for what foods were proper or improper, and in the diagnosing and treatment of various ailments. Throughout and repeatedly, there were strict prohibitions of the customs of ''other nations'' that were associated with the worship of ''other gods''—such as the shaving of the head or beards, the incising of tattoos, or the sacrificing of children as burnt offerings. Forbidden was the ''turning to conjurers and seers,'' and emphatically prohibited was the "making of idols and graven images, and the erection of statues, or of a carved stone to bow upon it.''

"By these shall the Children of Israel be distinguished from the others—a holy nation, consecrated unto Yahweh,'' Moses was told.

As the ensuing biblical books of Judges, Samuel, Kings, and Prophets reveal, it was the last prohibition that was the most difficult to maintain. For all around them the people could *see* the gods they were worshiping—sometimes in fact, otherwise (and most of the time) through their graven images. But Yahweh had asserted that no one could see his face and live, and now the Israelites were required to observe strictly a myriad of commandments and keep faith with a sole deity that could not even be represented by its statue—to worship an Unseen God!

That it was a total departure from the practices everywhere else was readily admitted by Yahweh himself. "After the customs of the Land of Egypt, wherein ye have dwelt, and after the customs of the Land of Canaan whither I am bringing you, ye shalt not do, and their precepts ye shall not follow,'' Yahweh decreed; and He knew well what he was talking about.

Egypt, whence the Children of Israel had come out—as ancient depictions and archaeological finds amply attest—was awash with images and statues of the gods of Egypt. Ptah, the patriarch of the pantheon (whom we have identified with Enki), Ra his son, head of the pantheon (whom we have identified with Marduk), and their offspring who had reigned over Egypt before the Pharaohs and who were worshiped thereafter, sometimes appeared to the kings in person in various Divine Encounters, some other times (and more frequently so) were represented by their images (Fig. 105). The more distant the gods became over time, the more did king and people turn to priests and magicians, seers and diviners to obtain and interpret the divine will. No wonder that Moses, endeavoring to impress the doubting Pharaoh with the powers of the Hebrews' God, had first to engage in magic to outperform the Pharaoh's royal magicians.

In the realms of the Enlilites, the notion of an Unseen

THE CELESTIAL DISC AND THE GODS OF EGYPT

Ptah Ra-Amen Thoth Seker / Osiris Isis with Horus Nephtys Hathor

The gods with their attributes:

Ra/Falcon   Horus/Falcon   Seth/Sinai Ass   Thoth/Ibis   Hathor/Cow

Figure 105

ENLIL   NINURTA   NANNAR/Sin   ISHKUR/Adad

NERGAL   GIBIL   MARDUK

INANNA/Ishtar as Great Lady, Enchantress, Warrior, Pilot

Figure 106

God was surely an oddity. Reclusive, perhaps; selectively accessible, yes; but *unseen*—certainly not. Virtually all the "great gods" of Sumer—with the apparent exception of Anu—were depicted one way or another, in sculptures or engravings or upon cylinder seals (Fig. 106). That they were actually seen by mortals is evident from countless cylinder seals found throughout Mesopotamia, Anatolia, and the Mediterranean lands that depict what scholars call "presentation scenes" in which a king, as often as not wearing priestly

Figure 107

robes, is shown ushered by a lesser god (or goddess) into the presence of a "great god." A similar scene is depicted on a large stone stela found at a site called Abu Habba in Mesopotamia, in which the king-priest is being presented to the god Shamash (Fig. 107)—a scene that recalls those of the granting of codes of law that we have reproduced in earlier chapters. And, one must assume, in instances when a god had a human spouse or during divine encounters of the Sacred Marriage kind, the god or goddess was not unseen.

(That, too, increased the Israelites' consternation, for nowhere throughout the Hebrew Bible is there mention of Yahweh as having a spouse, be it divine or human. This, biblical scholars believe, was why in spite of all admonitions the Israelites digressed toward veneration of Asherah, the principal goddess of the Canaanite pantheon).

Even in Sumer, where the presence of the Anunnaki gods in their ziggurats was an accepted fact, the Divine Word was conveyed to the people through the intermediary of oracle priests. Indeed, the name *Terah* of Abraham's father suggests that he was a *Tirhu,* an oracle priest; and the family's clan designation, *Ibri* ("Hebrew"), we believe, indicates that the family stemmed from Nippur (Enlil's cult center), whose Sumerian name was NI.IBRU—"Beautiful dwelling place of crossing." After the demise of Sumer and the rise of Babylon (with Marduk as head of the pantheon) and later of Assyria (with Ashur as head of the pantheon), a complex plethora of oracle and omen priests, astrologers, dream interpreters, diviners, seers, conjurers, voayers and fortune-tellers filled temples, palaces, and humbler abodes—all claiming to be expert in conveying the Divine Word or being able to guess the Divine Will—"fortune"—from the examination of animal livers, or how oil spreads on water, or celestial conjunctions.

In this respect, too, the Israelites were required to act differently. "Ye shall not practice divination or soothsaying," was the commandment in Leviticus 19:26. "Seek neither seers of spirits nor fortune tellers," admonished Leviticus 19:31. In direct contrast to the inclusion of such "professionals" within the ranks of the priests of other nations in antiquity, the Israelite priests and the Levites selected to serve in the temple were qualified to "stand before Yahweh" by (among other restrictions) never becoming "a magician, a diviner, a wizard or an enchanter, nor one who is a charmer or a seer of spirits, a fortune teller, or one who conjures up the dead; for all of them are an abomination to Yahweh—it is because of those abominations that Yahweh thy *Elohim* doth drive them out before thee." (Deuteronomy 18:10–12).

Practices that were—certainly by the time of the Exodus, in the fifteenth century B.C.—part and parcel of the religious practices throughout the ancient world and the worship of "other gods," were thus strictly forbidden by Yahweh in the religion and worship of Israel. How then could the Children of Israel, once in their Promised Land, receive the Divine Word and know the Divine Will?

The answers were given by Yahweh himself.

First, there will be the Angels, the Divine Emissaries, who would convey the Lord's will and guidance and act in His behalf. "I am sending a *Mal'akh* to be in front of thee, to guard thee on the way to bring thee unto the place which I have prepared," the Lord said to the Children of Israel through Moses; "beware of him and obey him, be not rebellious against him, for he will not forgive your transgressions; my *Shem* is in him" (Exodus 23:20–21). If so hearkened

to, the Lord said, his Angel will bring them safely to the
Promised Land.

There will also be other channels of communication, Yahweh said. They were made explicit as a result of an incident
in which Aaron, the brother of Moses, and Miriam, their
sister, became envious of Moses being the only one summoned to the Tent of Appointment to speak with Yahweh.
As reported in Numbers chapter 12,

> And Miriam and Aaron said:
> "Hath Yahweh spoken only through Moses?
> Hath he not also spoken through us?".
> And Yahweh heard it.
>
> Then, suddenly, Yahweh spoke unto
> Moses and Aaron and Miriam, saying:
> "Come out ye three unto the Tent of Appointment."
> And the three of them came forth.
>
> And Yahweh descended in a pillar of cloud,
> coming to rest at the door of the Tent.
> And He called Aaron and Miriam,
> and the two of them stepped forward.

Thus getting their attention, and bringing them as close as
possible to the "column of cloud" that had descended and
positioned itself in front of the Tent, Yahweh said to them:

> "Hear now my words:
> If there be a prophet of Yahweh among you,
> in a vision will I make myself known to him,
> in a dream will I speak to him.
> Not so is it with my servant Moses,
> faithful in all mine house.
> With him I speak mouth to mouth,
> in appearances and not in puzzles;
> the similitude of Yahweh does he behold;
> How then dared you speak ill of my servant Moses?"
>
> And Yahweh's anger was kindled against them,
> and He departed.

And the cloud lifted off the Tent;
and lo and behold,
Miriam became leprous, her skin white as snow.

So there it was, clearly stated: It will be through the *Prophets of Yahweh,* appearing to them in a vision or in a dream, that the Lord will communicate with the people.

The usual concept of a "prophet" is that of one who engages in *prophecies*—predictions of the future (in this instance under divine guidance or inspiration). But the dictionary correctly defines "prophet" as "a person who speaks for God" in divine matters, or just "a spokesman for some cause, group or government." The prediction aspect is present or assumed; but the key function is that of a spokesman. And indeed, that is what the Hebrew term, *Nabih,* means: a spokesman. A *"Nabih of Yahweh,"* commonly translated (and so quoted above) "a prophet of Yahweh," literally meant "a spokesman of Yahweh," someone (as explained in Numbers chapter 11) "upon whom the spirit of God was bestowed," qualifying him (or her!) to be a *Nabih,* a spokesperson for the Lord.

The term appears for the first time in the Bible in chapter 20 of Genesis, which deals with the transgression of Abimelech, the Philistine king of Gerar, who was about to take Sarah into his harem not knowing that she was married to Abraham. "And *Elohim* came unto Abimelech in a nighttime dream" to warn him off. When Abimelech pleaded innocence, the Lord told him to return Sarah unmolested to her husband, and ask him to pray for forgiveness. "A *Nabih* he is," the Lord said of Abraham, "and pray he will for thee."

Next the term is used (in Exodus chapter 6) in its rudimentary sense. When the mission to the Pharaoh was imposed on Moses, he complained that his was a "halting speaking," which would not be heeded by the Pharaoh. So Yahweh said to him: "Behold, as an *Elohim* I will make thee before Pharaoh, and Aaron thy brother shall be thy *Nabih*"—your spokesman. And once again, after the Children of Israel had crossed the Sea of Reeds when it had parted miraculously, Miriam, the sister of Moses and Aaron, led the daughters of

Israel in a song and dance honoring Yahweh; and the Bible calls her "Miriam the *Nebiah*," "Miriam the prophetess." In yet another instance, when it was necessary to enlist the tribal leaders in administrating a multitude of 600,000,

> *Moses assembled seventy men*
> *from among the elders of the people*
> *and he stationed them around the Tent.*
> *And Yahweh came down in the cloud,*
> *and spoke to him;*
> *And bestowed from the spirit that was upon him*
> *on the seventy elders;*
> *And when the spirit rested upon them,*
> *they became Nabih's (spokesmen)—*
> *then, but not thereafter.*

But two of the elders, the narrative reports, continued to be under the spell of the Divine Spirit, and were acting as *Nabih's* in the encampment. It was expected that they would be punished; but Moses saw it differently: "I wish the whole people would be *Nabihs,* that Yahweh would bestow His spirit upon them," he said to his faithful servant Joshua.

The matter of the *Nabih* as a true spokesman for Yahweh must have needed further elucidation—witness the additional statements in Deuteronomy. Unlike other peoples who "listen to diviners and magicians," the Lord said, to the people of Israel He will provide a *Nabih,* one from their own brethren who "My words shall be in his mouth, who shall speak to them as I will command." Recognizing that some might lay claim to be speaking for God without it being so, Yahweh warned that such a false prophet shall surely die. But how would the people know the difference? "If there arise in the midst of thee a prophet, or a dreamer of dreams, and he giveth thee a sign or a wonder," but it was only to induce you to "follow other *Elohim,* unknown to thee, and worship them—do not hearken to the words of such a *Nabih,*" Yahweh explained through Moses. There could be another test of the prophet's authenticity, it was explained (Deuteronomy chapter 18): "If that which the prophet was saying in behalf of Yahweh will not happen and shall not come to pass, maliciously hath the prophet spoken it—not the words of Yahweh.''

That it was not an easy matter to distinguish between true and false prophets was thus anticipated right from the beginning; the ensuing events offered bitter confirmation of the problem.

''And there arose not a *Nabih* in Israel like Moses, whom Yahweh hath known face to face,'' it is stated at the conclusion of the Book of Deuteronomy (and thus the conclusion of the Pentateuch, the so-called Five Books of Moses); for Moses, as decreed for all those who had known the servitude in Egypt, was doomed not to enter the Promised Land. Before dying, the Lord made him go up Mount Nebo that was on the eastern side of the Jordan facing Jericho, to see from there the Promised Land.

Significantly or ironically, the mount chosen for that final act, Mount *Nebo,* was named after *Nabu,* the son of Marduk. *Il Nabium,* the ''God who is a spokesman,'' Babylonian inscriptions called him; for as historical records show, it was he who, while his father Marduk was in exile, roamed the lands bordering on the Mediterranean, converting the people to the worship of Marduk in preparation for the seizing of the supremacy by Marduk at the time of Abraham.

The function, the mission of the Prophets of Yahweh winds its way through the era of the Judges, finds expression in the biblical books of Samuel and Kings, and reaches its high ground, moral and religious message and its prophetic visions for humanity in the books of the Prophets. Guidance, rage, and solace; teaching, reprimanding, and reassuring, the words and symbolic deeds of these ''spokesmen'' of Yahweh gradually fashion, as the years and the events march by, an *image of Yahweh* and His role in the past and in the future of Earth and its inhabitants.

''It was after the death of Moses the servant of Yahweh, that Yahweh spoke unto Joshua the son of Nun, the minister of Moses, saying: Moses my servant died; now therefore arise and cross the Jordan, thou and all this people, unto the land which I do give to them, the Children of Israel ... as I was with Moses so will I be with thee; I will not fail thee nor forsake thee . . . Only be thou strong and steadfast in observing to act according to all the teachings which Moses my servant commanded thee—turn not to the right or to the left.'' Thus begins the Book of Joshua, with a reiteration of the Divine Promise on the one hand and of the required absolute adherence to Yahweh's commandments on the other hand. And right away Joshua, recognizing that the former depended on the latter, realized that it would be the latter that would be the problem.

As in the time of Moses, divine assistance in the form of miracles was provided the new leader to make the double point: Though unseen, Yahweh was omnipresent as well as omnipotent. The very first obstacle facing the Israelites who had journeyed up the east side of the Jordan was how to cross the river westward; the time was soon after the rainy season and the river's waters were high and overflowing. Reassuring the people that ''Yahweh will show you wonders,'' he told them to sanctify themselves and be ready for the crossing, for Yahweh had directed him to have the priests carrying the Ark of the Covenant step into the river; and lo and behold, the moment the priests' feet touched the waters, the Jordan's waters flowing down from the north froze and were held back as a wall, and the Israelites crossed over on the river's dried bed. And when the priests carrying the Ark crossed over as well, the piled-up waters collapsed and the river was filled again with water.

''By this shall ye know that a living God is among you,'' Joshua announced—proof that though unseen, He is present, He is powerful, He can perform miracles. The miracles indeed did not cease; the one of the Jordan's crossing was soon followed by the appearance of the Angel of Yahweh with the instructions for the toppling of the walls of Jericho, and the use of Joshua's lance the way the staff of Moses was held— this time for the miraculous defeat of the mountain fortress of Ai. Next came the miraculous defeat of an alliance of Canaanite kings in the Valley of Ajalon, when the sun stood still and did not set for some twenty hours.

''And it came to pass after a long time, after Yahweh had given rest unto Israel from all their surrounding enemies, that Joshua waxed old and aged''; thus begins the end of the

Book of Joshua and the record of the events of the conquest and settlement of Canaan under his leadership. It ends, however, as it began: with the need to reaffirm the existence and presence of Yahweh; for, as the Bible explains, not only Joshua but all the elders who could recall the Exodus and the Lord's miracles were passing from the scene.

So Joshua assembled the tribal leaders at Shechem, to review before them the history of the Hebrews from their ancestral beginnings until the present. On the other side of the Euphrates River did your ancestors live, he said—Terah and his sons Abraham and Nahor—"and they worshipped other *Elohim.*" The migration of Abraham, the story of his descendants, the enslavement in Egypt and the events of the Exodus under the leadership of Moses were then briefly reviewed, as well as the crossing of the Jordan and the settlement under Joshua's leadership. Now, as I and my generation are passing on, Joshua said, you are free to make a choice: you can remain committed to Yahweh—or you can worship other gods:

> *Would'st ye hold Yahweh in awe,*
> *and worship Him in sincerity and in truth—*
> *then remove the* Elohim *whom your forefathers*
> *had worshipped across the river [Euphrates]*
> *and in Egypt, and worship [only] Yahweh.*
> *But if it does not please you to serve Yahweh—*
> *choose here and now whom ye shall worship:*
> *whether the* Elohim *which your forefathers had*
> *served on the other side of the River,*
> *or the gods of the Westerners in whose land ye dwell;*
> *and I and my family shall worship Yahweh.*

Faced with this momentous yet clear-cut choice, "the people answered and said: It is unthinkable that we should forsake Yahweh to worship other *Elohim* . . . It is Yahweh our God whom we shall worship, it is Him whom we shall obey!"

So "Joshua said unto the people: Ye all are witnesses against yourselves that ye have chosen Yahweh to worship. And they said: We are witnesses." Thereupon "Joshua made a covenant with the people that day," writing it all down "in the Book of the Teachings of Yahweh." And he erected a stone stela under the oak tree that was beside the Tabernacle in witness of the covenant.

But no admonitions and witnessed covenants could preserve the reality of an Israelite monotheistic enclave within an overwhelming multitude of polytheistic peoples. As pointed out in the writings of the Jewish theologian and biblical scholar Yehezkel Kaufmann *(The Religion of Israel)*, the "Basic Problem" facing the Israelites was that the Bible was "dedicated to fighting idolatry"—the worship of idols, of statues made of wood and stone, or gold and silver—but recognized that other peoples worshiped "other gods." "Israelite religion and paganism are historically related," he wrote; "both are stages in the religious evolution of Man. Israelite religion arose at a certain period in history, and it goes without saying that its rise did not take place in a vacuum."

Among the difficulties inherent in the Religion of Yahweh were the absence of a genealogy and of a primordial realm whence the gods had come. The gods who had been worshiped by the parents and forefathers of Abraham "across the river"—the first set of "other gods" listed by Joshua—included Enlil and Enki, the sons of the Anu, the brothers of Ninharsag. Anu himself had named parents. All of them had spouses, offspring—Ninurta, Nannar, Adad, Marduk, and so on. There was even a third generation—Shamash, Ishtar, Nabu. There had been an original homeland—a place called Nibiru, another world (i.e. planet) whence they had come to Earth.

Then there were the "other gods" of Egypt; Yahweh had shown His might against them when Egypt was afflicted to let the Children of Israel go, but they continued to be venerated and worshiped not only in Egypt but also wherever Egypt's might had reached. They were headed by Ptah, and the great Ra was his son—traveling in Celestial Boats between Earth and the "Planet of Millions of Years," the primordial abode. Thoth, Seth, Osiris, Horus, Isis, Nepthys were related by simple genealogies in which brothers married half sisters. When the Israelites, fearing that Moses had perished

on Mount Sinai, asked Aaron to reinvoke the deity, he fashioned a golden calf—the image of the Apis Bull—to represent
the Bull of Heaven. And when a plague afflicted the Israelites, Moses made a copper serpent—the symbol of Enki/
Ptah—to stop the plague. No wonder that the gods of Egypt,
too, were fresh in the Israelites' mind.

And then there were the "other gods of the Westerners in
whose lands you dwell''—the gods of the Canaanites (Western Asiatics) whose pantheon was headed by the retired olden
god *El* (a proper name or epithet being the singular of the
plural *Elohim)* and his spouse *Asherah;* the active *Ba'al* (simply meaning "Lord"), their son; his favorite female companions *Anat* and *Shepesh* and *Ashtoret,* and his adversaries *Mot*
and *Yam.* Their playgrounds and battlegrounds were the lands
that stretched from the border of Egypt to the borders of
Mesopotamia; every nation in that area worshiped them,
sometimes under locally adjusted names; and the Children of
Israel were now dwelling in their midst . . .

To compound the "Basic Problem" of the missing ingredi-
ents of a genealogy and a primordial abode, was added the
greater difficulty for the Israelites: an Unseen God who could
not even be represented by a graven image.

And so it was that, on and off, "the Children of Israel did
wrong in the eyes of Yahweh, and worshiped the Ba'al gods;
they forsook Yahweh, the *Elohim* of their forefathers who
hath brought them out of Egypt, and followed other *Elohim*
from among the gods of the nations that surrounded them . . .
and paid homage to Ba'al and to Ashtoreth gods" (Judges
2:11–13). And again and again leaders—designated Judges—
arose to return the Israelites to their true faith and thereby
remove Yahweh's wrath.

One of those Judges, the female Deborah, is fondly recalled
by the Bible as *Nebi'ah*—a Prophetess. Inspired by Yahweh,
she chose the right commander and tactics for the defeat of
Israel's northern enemies; the Bible records her victory
song—a poem considered by scholars a unique ancient literary masterpiece. David Ben-Gurion (the first prime minister
of the modern State of Israel), in *The Jews in Their Land,*
wrote that "that religio-national awakening was movingly expressed in the *Song of Deborah* with its reference to the great

and invisible God." In fact the victory hymnal song did more than that: It referred to the celestial nature of Yahweh, asserting that the victory was made possible because Yahweh, whose appearance "makes the Earth tremble, the heavens quake and the mountains melt," caused the "planets, in their orbits," to fight the enemy.

Such a celestial aspect of Yahweh, as we shall see, was to become highly significant in the prophetic utterances of the great Prophets of the Bible.

Chronologically the term *Nabih* and its holder come into play again in the Books of Samuel, the boy who grew to be a combination prophet-priest-judge of his people. We have already described the series of dream-encounters by which he had been called to Yahweh's embassy; "and the boy Samuel grew up and Yahweh was with him, and none of his words went unfulfilled; from Dan to Beersheba did the whole of Israel know that Samuel was confirmed as a *Nabih* of Yahweh. And Yahweh continued to appear in Shiloh, for it was in Shiloh that Yahweh revealed himself there to Samuel, when Yahweh hath spoken."

Samuel's ministry coincided with the rise of a new and powerful enemy of Israel, the Philistines, who commanded the coastal plain of Canaan from five strongholds. The conflict, or when-push-comes-to-shove relationship, had flared up earlier in the time of Samson, and in another incident when the Philistines even captured the Ark of the Covenant and brought it into the temple of their god Dagon (whose statue, the Bible relates, kept falling down before the Ark). It was thereafter that leaders of the twelve tribes assembled before Samuel and asked that he choose a king for them—a system of government "akin to that of all the nations." It was thus that Saul the son of Kish was anointed the first king of the Children of Israel. After a troubled reign, the monarchy passed to David, the son of Jesse, who had come into prominence after he slew the giant Goliath. And after he was anointed by Samuel, "the spirit of Yahweh was upon him, from that time on."

Both Saul and David, the Bible states, "inquired of Yahweh," seeking oracles to guide their actions by. After Samuel had died, Saul sought an oracle from Yahweh but received none "neither in dreams or visions nor through prophets" (he ended up speaking to the ghost of Samuel through a medium). David, we read in I Samuel 30:7, "inquired of Yahweh" by putting on the priestly garment of the High Priest with its oracular breastplate. But thereafter he was given the "word of Yahweh" through prophets—first one named Gad and then another named Nathan. The Bible (II Samuel 24:11) calls the former "Gad the *Nabih,* the Seer of David," through whom the "word of Yahweh" was made known to the king. Nathan was the prophet through whom Yahweh had told David that not he, but his son, would build the Temple in Jerusalem (II Samuel 7:2–17)—"all the words in accordance with the vision did Nathan say unto David."

The function of the *Nabih* as teacher and upholder of moral laws and social justice, and not only as a conduit for divine messages, emerges from the deeds of even such an early Prophet as the enigmatic "Nathan" ("He who was granted"). It happened when David, having seen Bathsheba naked as she washed herself on her home's roof, ordered his general to expose Bathsheba's husband to the most dangerous battlefield spot, so that the king could take Bathsheba as a wife once she was widowed. It was then that Nathan the prophet came to the king and told him a fable of a rich man who had many sheep but nevertheless coveted the only sheep that a poor man had. And when David exclaimed, "such a man must be punished by death!" the prophet told him: "Thou art the man!"

Recognizing his sin and going out of his way to atone for it, David spent ever more time in pious meditation and solitary prayer; many of the king's reflections on God and Man found expression in the *Psalms of David;* in them the celestial aspects of Yahweh echo, and expand upon, the words in the *Song of Deborah.* "These are the words of the song David sang to Yahweh" (II Samuel 22 and Psalm 18):

Yahweh is my rock and my fortress;
He is my deliverer . . .

In my distress I call Yahweh,
to my God I call out;

And he hears my voice in his Great House,
my cry reached his ears.
Then the Earth heaved and quaked,
the Heaven's foundations were disturbed and shook . . .

In the heavens he turned and came down,
thick fog lay under his feet.
Upon a Cherub he rode and flew,
on the windy wings he appeared . . .

From the heavens Yahweh thunders,
the Most High utters his voice . . .
From the heights he reached out
to pick me up . . . to save me from my foe.

"Forty years did David rule over the whole of Israel—seven years he reigned in Hebron and thirty-three in Jerusalem," it is stated at the conclusion of *I Chronicles,* "dying at a ripe old age." "And all that concerns David, from the first to the last words, are recorded in the books of Samuel the Seer, and the book of Nathan the Prophet, and the book of Gad the Man of Visions." The books of Nathan and Gad have vanished, as did other books—the *Book of the Wars of Yahweh,* the *Book of Jashar,* to mention two others—that the Bible speaks of. But Psalms attributed to (or sung by) David make up almost half (seventy-three to be exact) of the 150 Psalms retained in the Bible. They all provide a wealth of insights into the nature and identity of Yahweh.

The significance of the statement that David ruled "over the whole of Israel" becomes evident as the wheels of history turn from the second millennium B.C. to the beginning of the first millennium B.C., when Solomon ascended the throne in Jerusalem; for soon after his death the kingdom split into separate states, that of Judaea in the south and that of Israel in the north. Cut off from Jerusalem and the Temple, the northern kingdom was more exposed to foreign customs and religious influences. The establishment of a new capital by the sixth king of Israel circa 880 B.C. signified both a final break from Judaea as well as from the worship of Yahweh in Jerusalem's temple; he called the new city *Shomron* (Samaria), meaning "Little Sumer," leaning toward gods whose images could be seen.

Throughout those turbulent years, the word of Yahweh was brought to the competing kings by a succession of "Men of God"—sometimes called a *Nabih* (Prophet), other times called *Hozeh* (One who sees visions) or *Ro'eh* (Seer). Some of them relayed the direct Word of God, others were guided by an Angel of Yahweh; some had to prove that they were "true prophets" by performing miracles which the "false prophets"—those whose utterances were meant to always please the king—could not duplicate; all were involved in the struggle against paganism and in efforts to see that the throne was occupied by a king who did "that which was righteous in the eyes of Yahweh."

One whose ministry and record stood out in his time and left an indelible messianic expectation for generations thereafter was the Prophet Elijah *(Eli-yahu* in Hebrew, meaning "Yahweh is my God"). He was called to prophecy in the reign of Ahab (circa 870 B.C.), the king of Israel who succumbed completely to the religious influences of his Sidonite wife, the infamous Jezebel. He "proceeded to worship Ba'al and bow to him;" he built a temple to Ba'al in Samaria and set up an altar to Asherah. Of him the Bible (I Kings 16:31–33) states that "he angered Yahweh the God of Israel more than any other kings of Israel who had reigned before him."

It was then that the Lord called upon Elijah to become a Spokesman, taking care to assure his authority and authenticity through a series of miracles.

The first recorded miracle was when Elijah came to stay with a poor widow; when she told him she was running out of food, he assured her that the little flour and oil she had would last and last for days. And indeed, as they ate of it, the food miraculously never diminished.

While staying with the woman, her son became grievously ill "until at last his breathing ceased." Asking Yahweh to spare the boy, Elijah took the child upstairs and laid his body on the bed, and stretched himself upon the boy three times, crying out to the Lord each time; "and the soul of the child came back into him, and he revived." "And the woman said unto Elijah: Now by this I know that thou art a Man of God, and that the word of Yahweh in thy mouth is truth."

As time went on, Jezebel had no less than 450 "prophets of Ba'al" assembled in her palace, with Elijah alone remaining a "prophet of Yahweh." Told by Elijah to arrange a final showdown, the king assembled the people and the prophets of Ba'al on Mount Carmel. Two bullocks were brought and prepared for sacrifice on two altars, but no fire was lit on the altars: Each side was to cry out and pray to their god for a fire to strike the altar from the heavens. The whole day went by without anything happening on the altar to Ba'al; but when it was the turn of Elijah to seek divine intervention, "a fire from Yahweh fell down and consumed the sacrifice" and the altar itself. "And when all the people saw it, they fell on their faces and said: Yahweh is the *Elohim!*" And Elijah told them to kill all the prophets of Ba'al, letting not one escape.

When the news reached Jezebel, she ordered Elijah killed; but he escaped southward, toward the wilderness of Sinai. Hungry and thirsty he lay exhausted, ready to die; it was then that the Angel of Yahweh miraculously provided him with food and water and showed him the way to a cave on Mount Sinai, the "Mount of the *Elohim.*" There the Lord, speaking to him out of the stillness, instructed him to go back north and anoint a new king in Damascus, the Aramean capital, and a new king over Israel; and to "anoint Elisha son of Shaphat to be a prophet after thee."

This was more than a hint of things to come—the involvement of the Prophets of Yahweh in affairs of state—predicting the downfall of kings and anointing their successors; and not only in Israel or Judaea, but also in foreign capitals!

Several more times the prophetic activity of Elijah is stated to have taken place after the "Angel of Yahweh" had given him instructions, and it appears that this was the manner in which Yahweh's word was communicated to him. Untold by the Bible, though, is the manner by which Elijah was given his most memorable (and final) instructions for *his ascent to heaven in a fiery chariot.* The event, the likes of which harken back to the times of Enmeduranki, Adapa, and Enoch, is described in detail in II Kings chapter 2. It is clear from the tale that the ascent was not a sudden or unexpected occurrence, but rather a planned and prearranged operation whose place and time were communicated to Elijah in advance.

"And it came to pass when Yahweh was to take up Elijah into heaven in a whirlwind, that Elijah went with Elisha from Gilgal"—the place where Joshua had set up a stone circle to commemorate the miraculous crossing of the Jordan River. Elijah sought to leave there his principal disciple and proceed by himself, but Elisha would not hear of it. Reaching Bethel, their students (called "sons of Prophets") assembled there too and said to Elisha: "Knowest thou that Yahweh will, this day, take thy master from above thee?" and Elisha answered, "Yes, I know it too, but keep silent."

Still trying to free himself of companions, Elijah then stated his destination to be Jericho, and asked Elisha to stay behind; but Elisha insisted on coming along. Elijah then made it clear that he alone must proceed to the river; but Elisha insisted on coming along. As their students stood at a distance and watched, "Elijah took his mantle and rolled it together and struck the waters, and the waters parted hither and thither, and the two of them crossed over on dry ground."

Once they were across—about where the Israelites had come across in the opposite direction when they entered Canaan—as the two were walking and talking to each other,

> *There appeared a chariot of fire,*
> *and horses of fire,*
> *and the two were separated.*
> *And Elijah went up into heaven*
> *in a Whirlwind.*
>
> *And Elisha, seeing this, cried out:*
> *"My father! My father!*
> *The Chariot of Israel and its Horsemen!"*
> *And he could see him no more.*

As the biblical detailing of the route shows, Elijah's ascent in a fiery Whirlwind took place near (or at?) the site of

Tell Ghassul, where the UFO-like bulbous vehicles with three extended legs had been depicted (see Fig. 72).

For three days the leaderless disciples searched for the disappeared Master, although Elisha had told them the search would be in vain. Possessing the mantle of Elijah, which the prophet had dropped during the ascent, now Elisha could also perform miracles, including the revival of the dead and the expansion of a little food to satisfy multitudes. His fame and miracles were not limited to the Israelite domain, and foreign dignitaries sought his healing powers; after one such magical treatment, the Aramean leader acknowledged that "indeed there is no *Elohim* on Earth except the one in Israel."

As Elijah before him, Elisha was also involved in royal successions that were divinely ordered; by the time he died, the King of Israel (Joash, circa 800 B.C.) was the fifth successor to Ahab; and as Prophets after him, Elisha was the Divine Spokesman in matters of war and peace. II Kings chapter 3 relates the rebellion by Mesha, the king of the Moabites, against Israelite dominance after the death of Ahab, when Elisha was consulted for Yahweh's ruling whether to fight the Moabites. The veracity of that border war is confirmed by an amazing archaeological find—a stela of that very same King Mesha in which he recorded his version of that border war. The stela (Fig. 108a), now in the Louvre Museum in Paris, is inscribed in the same Old Semitic script which was used at the time by the Hebrews; and in it, the name of the Hebrew God YHWH—exactly as it was written in Israelite and Judean inscriptions—appears in line 18 (Fig. 108b).

It was perhaps no coincidence that the centuries that encompassed the Israelite settlement and conquest of Canaan, through the times of the Judges and early kings, were an intermediate period in what was then World Affairs. The mighty empires of Egypt, Babylon, Assyria, and the Hittites, which arose after the demise of Sumer circa 2000 B.C. and that made the lands of the eastern Mediterranean their battlegrounds, retreated and declined. Their own capitals were overrun or abandoned; age-old religious rites were discontinued, temples fell into disrepair.

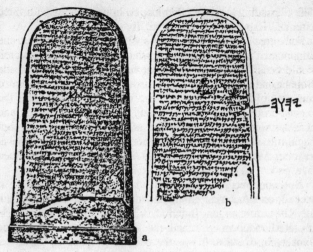

Figures 108a and 108b

Commenting on those times in Babylon and Assyria, H.W.F. Saggs *(The Greatness That Was Babylon)* states that "the dislocation was so bad that a chronicle dating to about 990 B.C. records that 'for nine years successively Marduk did not go forth, Nabu did not come,' that is to say, the New Year Feast, at which Marduk of Babylon went out of the city to a shrine called the *Akitu*-house and Nabu of Borsippa visited him on his return to the city, was not carried out."

In those circumstances not only could the Hebrew kingdoms rise, but also those of their immediate neighbors—the Edomites, Moabites, Arameans, Phoenicians, Philistines. Their border wars and encroachments were small local affairs compared to the titanic battles of the erstwhile empires in past centuries—and to the major onslaughts that were in the offing.

In 879 B.C. a new capital, Kalhu (the biblical Calah) was ceremoniously inaugurated in Assyria; and the event can be historically considered as the start of the Neo-Assyrian period. Its hallmarks were expansion, domination, warfare, carnage, and unparalleled brutality—all in the name of "the great god Ashur" and other deities of the Assyrian pantheon.

The expanding Assyrian domination in time encompassed the city of Babylon—a ghost of its erstwhile glory. As a gesture to the subjugated followers of Marduk the Assyrians appointed "kings" in Babylon, who were no more than viceroy-vassals. But in 721 B.C. a native leader named Merodach-Baladan reinstated the New Year Festival in Babylon, "took the hand of Marduk" and claimed independent Kingship. The action evolved into a full rebellion that saw intermittent warfare for some three decades. In 689 B.C. the Assyrians took back full control of Babylon, and went to the extreme of moving Marduk himself to the Assyrian capital, as a captive god.

But continued resistance in what used to be Sumer and Akkad, and Assyrian entanglements in distant lands, eventually led to a resurgent Babylon. A leader named Nabopolassar declared independence and the start of a new Babylonian dynasty in 626 B.C. It was the beginning of the Neo-Babylonian era; and now it was Babylon that emulated Assyria in conquests near and far—all in the name of "the lords Nabu and Marduk" and, according to the inscriptions, with the active help of "Marduk, the king of the gods, the ruler of Heaven and Earth," who after twenty one years in Assyrian captivity engineered the demise of Assyria and the renewed ascendancy of Babylon.

As border wars grew into world wars (in ancient terms and scope) and as one national god was pitted against another, the Biblical Prophets also expanded their mission to global dimensions. As one reads their prophecies, one is amazed and impressed by their knowledge of geography and politics in distant lands, their grasp of the motives for national intrigues and international conflicts, and their foresight in predicting the outcome of correct or incorrect moves by the kings of Israel and Judaea in the dangerous chesslike game of making and breaking alliances.

To those great Prophets, deemed so important that the Bible included as separate books their words and exhortations, the international turmoil that engulfed Mankind and even involved the nations' *Elohim* was not a series of unrelated struggles but aspects of one great Divine Scheme—all the doing and planning of Yahweh to put an end to individual

nd national inequities and transgressions. As though hark-
ning back to the days before the Deluge, when the Lord
xpressed his dissatisfaction with the way Mankind had
urned out and sought to wipe it off the face of the Earth on
he occasion of the Deluge, so was the Divine Dissatisfaction
reat once again, the remedy being the demise of all king-
oms—of Israel and Judaea included, the destruction of all
emples—that in Jerusalem included, the end of all false wor-
hip that is expressed in sacrifices to cover up constant injus-
ces, and the rise, after such a global catharsis, of a "New
erusalem" that shall be a "Light unto all the nations."

It was, as J.A. Heschel designated it in *The Prophets,* "the
Age of Wrath." Its fifteen Literary Prophets (as scholars des-
gnate them because their words were retained as separate
iblical books) span almost three centuries, from circa 750
.c. when Amos (in Judaea) and Hosea (in Samaria) began
o prophesy through Malachi circa 430 B.C.; they include the
wo great Prophets Isaiah and Jeremiah who, in the eighth
nd seventh centuries B.C., foresaw and saw the demise of
he two Hebrew kingdoms, and the great Prophet Ezekiel,
vho was among the exiles in Babylonia, saw the destruction
f Jerusalem by Nebuchadnezzar in 587, and prophesied
bout the New Jerusalem.

On the individual level, the great Prophets spoke out
arshly against empty piety—rituals that papered over injus-
ices. "I hate, I despise your feasts, I take no delight in your
olemn assemblies," the Lord said through Amos; instead,
"let justice well up as waters, and righteousness as a mighty
tream" (5:21–24). "To what purpose is the multitude of
our sacrifices?" Isaiah said in behalf of Yahweh; "bring no
nore vain oblations ... When ye spread forth your hands, I
vill hide my eyes from you; when ye make many prayers, I
vill not hear"; rather than all that, "seek justice, undo op-
ression, defend the fatherless, plead for the widow" (Isaiah
:17, Jeremiah 22:3). It was a call to return to the essence
f the Ten Commandments, to the righteousness and justice
f ancient Sumer.

On the national level, the Prophets saw futility and foresaw
loom in the making and unmaking of alliances with neigh-
oring kings in efforts to withstand the attacks and domina-

tion of the Great Powers of that time, for those surrounding
nations, too, were themselves doomed in the coming upheavals: "A storm of Yahweh, a wrath shall come forth, a
whirling tempest will burst upon the heads of the wicked,"
Jeremiah (23:19) predicted, asserting that his prophetic words
applied equally to Israel and Judaea, and to all of the "uncir-
cumcised nations" in their region—the Sidonites and Tyrians
the Amonites and Moabites and Edomites, the Philistines, the
desert nations of Arabia.

The two Books of Kings distinguish the various reigns of
the kings of Israel and Judaea according to whether they "did
right" by, or "deviated from," the teachings of Yahweh; and
the Prophets considered the shifting alliances as a major cause
of the deviations. Moreover, whereas in earlier times it was
tolerable that "other nations" would worship "other gods,"
the Prophets deemed that, too, as an abomination, for by their
time the "other gods" of the region were only man-made
idols, crafted by humans of wood and metal and stone—
unlike Yahweh, who was a "Living God." The peoples who
worshiped Ba'al and Ashtoreth, Dagon and Ba'al-zebub,
Chemosh and Molech, were also sinners gone astray.

So were the "false prophets" against whom the True
Prophets of Yahweh had waged a constant struggle. They
were accused not only of speaking in the name of false gods,
but also of pretending to convey the true words of Yahweh
Instead of telling the people of their wrongdoings and the
kings of dangers ahead, they just spoke whatever pleased
kings and people. "They proclaim, Peace! Peace! but there
is no peace," Jeremiah said of them, whereas the True Prophets spared not the kings or the people when reprimand and
warnings were needed.

On the international level, the global arena, the Prophets
displayed an uncanny grasp of geopolitics, and their remarkable insights and foresights ranged far and wide. They knew
of the reemergence of ancient kingdoms, as that of Elam, and
the emergence of a new power farther east, that of the Medes
(later known as Persians); even distant China, the Land of
Sinim, was accounted for. The early city-states of the Greeks
in Asia Minor, their occupation of the Mediterranean islands
of Crete and Cyprus, were recognized. The status of old and

new powers bordering on Egypt in Africa was known. Indeed, "all the inhabitants of the world and the dwellers on Earth" shall be judged by Yahweh, for they have all gone astray.

At center stage were the three longtime powers: Egypt, Assyria, Babylon; of them, Egypt—and its gods—were treated with the least respect. In spite of close and sometimes friendly relationships between the Hebrew kingdoms and Egypt (Solomon married a Pharaoh's daughter and was provided by the Egyptians with horses and chariots), Egypt was considered to be treacherous and unreliable. Its king Sheshonq—the biblical Shishak (I Kings 11 and 14)—ransacked the Temple in Jerusalem, and Necho II, on his way to ward off Mesopotamian armies, killed the Judaean king Josiah who came out to greet him (II Kings 23). Both Isaiah and Jeremiah spoke out at length against Egypt and its gods, prophesying the demise of both.

Isaiah (chapter 19), in an "Oracle on Egypt," envisioned Yahweh arriving in Egypt airborne on the day when He would judge and punish Egypt and the Egyptians:

> *Behold Yahweh,*
> *riding upon a swift cloud,*
> *coming unto Egypt.*
> *The idols of Egypt shall tremble before Him,*
> *the heart of Egypt shall melt as He comes near.*

Predicting—correctly—the coming of internal strife and civil war in Egypt, the Prophet envisioned the Pharaoh futilely seeking the counsel of his seers and wizards to find out Yahweh's intentions. The divine plan, Isaiah announced, was this: "On that day there shall be an altar to Yahweh in the midst of the land of Egypt, and a pillar to Yahweh at its border shall be a sign and a witness to Yahweh, Lord of Hosts, in the land of Egypt ... and Yahweh shall make himself known in Egypt." Jeremiah focused more on the gods of Egypt, relating (in chapter 43) Yahweh's vow to "kindle a fire in the temples of the gods of Egypt and burn them down ... to break the statues of Heliopolis, to destroy by fire the temples of the gods of Egypt." The Prophet Joel (3:19) explained why "Egypt shall be a desolation: Because

Figure 109

of their violence against the sons of Judah and the spilling of innocent blood in their own land.''

The rise of the Neo-Assyrian empire and its onslaught against its neighbors with unparalleled brutality was well-known to the biblical Prophets, sometimes in astounding detail that even included Assyrian court intrigues. The Assyrian imperial expansion, at first directed to the north and northeast, targeted the lands of western Asia by the time of Shalmaneser III (858–824 B.C.). On one of his commemorative obelisks he recorded the sacking of Damascus, the execution of its king Hazael, and the receipt of tribute from Hazael's neighbor Jehu, the king of Israel (Samaria). Accompanying the inscription was a depiction showing Jehu bowing to Shalmaneser under the emblem of the Winged Disc of the god Ashur (Fig. 109).

A century later, when Menahem the son of Gadi was the king in Israel, ''Pul the king of Assyria came against the land, and Menahem gave Pul a thousand talents of silver that his hand might be with him to retain the kingship.'' This biblical record in II Kings 15:19 reveals the impressive familiarity with politics and royal affairs in distant Mesopotamia. The name of the Assyrian king who again invaded the Mediterranean lands was Tiglat-Pileser (745–727 B.C.); yet the Bible was right to call him Pul because this king also assumed the Babylonian throne and renamed himself there *Pulu*—a fact confirmed by the discovery of a tablet (''Baby-

Ionian King List B'') that is now in the British Museum. A few years later Ahaz, the king of Judaea, resorted to the same tactic, "taking the silver and the gold that were in the Temple of Yahweh and in the king's treasury and sending them to the king of Assyria as a bribe."

These subservient gestures, it appears in retrospect, only whetted the appetite of the Assyrian kings. The same Tiglat-Pileser returned and seized parts of the Israelite kingdom and exiled their inhabitants. In 722 B.C. his successor, Shalmaneser V, overran the rest of the Israelite kingdom and dispersed its people throughout the Assyrian empire; the whereabouts of those Ten Lost Tribes of Israel and their descendants are a lingering enigma.

The exile, according to the Prophets, was willed by Yahweh himself because of Israel's transgressions, "they heeded not the words of Yahweh their *Elohim* and transgressed His Covenant and all that Moses the servant of Yahweh commanded." The Prophet Hosea, in words and symbolic deeds, foresaw those events as punishment for Israel's "whoring" after other gods, but made it known that "a quarrel hath Yahweh with the inhabitants of Earth, for there is neither truth nor justice, nor understanding of *Elohim* upon the Earth." Isaiah's prophecies specified that Assyria would be the Lord's instrument for punishment: "I the Lord shall bring upon you the king of Assyria and all his hosts," he said as Yahweh's spokesman.

But that, Isaiah said, was only the beginning. In the "Oracle on Assyria," in which that power was called "the rod of God's wrath" (10:5), Yahweh also expressed his anger at Assyria's excesses, taking it into its haughty heart to annihilate whole nations with unparalleled brutality, whereas Yahweh's intent was only to chastise through punishment, to always leave a remnant that would be redeemed. Assyria's kings can have no more free will than an axe has when in the hands of its wielder, He announced; and when Assyria shall have carried out its initial mission, its own day of reckoning shall come.

Assyria not only failed to realize it was just a tool in the hands of its divine wielder, it also failed to recognize that Yahweh was *the* Lord, a "Living *Elohim*" unlike the pagan gods. The Assyrians exhibited this failure when, having exiled the people of Israel, they resettled the land with foreigners exiled from their lands, letting each group continue to worship their gods. The list, one may note, counts among the idols that were thus set up that of Marduk by the Babylonians, of Nergal by the Cutheans, and of Adad by the Palmyrians. The newcomers to Samaria were devastated, however, by wild lions and saw this as a sign of anger by the "local god," Yahweh. The Assyrian solution was to send back to Samaria one of the exiled priests of Yahweh, to teach the newcomers "the customs of the local god." So, while an Israelite priest was teaching them "how to worship Yahweh," it was only an addition of one more god to the polytheistic worship . . .

That Yahweh was different and that Assyria was subject to His will was demonstrated when Sennacherib (704–681 B.C.) invaded Judaea and, ignoring its tribute, sent his general Rabshakeh and a large army to capture Jerusalem. Surrounding the city, Rabshakeh sought its surrender by suggesting that the Assyrian king was only carrying out Yahweh's wish: "Is it without the will of Yahweh that I have come hither to destroy this place? It is Yahweh who hath said to me, 'Go forth and destroy this land.'"

Since this was not much different from what the Prophet Isaiah had been saying, the people of Jerusalem might have surrendered were it not for the Assyrians' growing haughtiness. If you think that your god Yahweh might change His mind and protect you after all, forget it, he said. Listing the many nations that Assyria conquered, "hath any of the gods of those nations, each one in his country, saved it from the king of Assyria?" he asked rhetorically; "so who is Yahweh that he would save Jerusalem from me?"

The comparison of Yahweh to the pagan gods was such blasphemy that the king, Hezekiah, tore his clothes and put on sackcloth in mourning. Joining the priests in the Temple, he sent word to Isaiah, asking him to seek the help of Yahweh "in this day of distress, of reviling and disgrace," a day on which an emissary of the king of Assyria reviled "a Living God," comparing Him to the gods of other nations "who are not *Elohim* but man-made of wood and stone."

And Isaiah the Prophet sent back to Hezekiah the "word of Yahweh" against the haughtiness of Sennacherib, who dared "raise his voice to revile the God of Israel, He who is enthroned upon the Cherubim." Therefore, the Prophet declared, Jerusalem shall be spared and Sennacherib shall be punished.

"And it came to pass that night that the Angel of the Lord came and smote the camp of the Assyrians, all one hundred and eighty five thousand of them ... And Sennacherib turned and went back to Nineveh; and while he was prostrating himself in the temple of his god Nisroch, his sons Adarmelech and Sharezer slew him with a sword, escaping to the land of Ararat; and his son Esarhaddon became king after him." (The manner of Sennacherib's death and the succession by Esarhaddon are corroborated by Assyrian chronicles).

This reprieve of Jerusalem was only temporary. The divine plan for a global catharsis still was in effect; except that now the chastising had to continue with Assyria itself. The process, as we have mentioned, began in 626 B.C.; and the divine rod to achieve that, Babylon, attained its own imperial reach under the king Nebuchadnezzar II (605–562 B.C.).

Their wayward ways—the social injustices, the insincere sacrifices, the worship of idols—would bring upon them due punishment, the Prophets forewarned the kings and people of Judaea. It would bring upon them Yahweh's wrath in the form of a "great and ferocious nation, coming from the north." It was in the very first year of Nebuchadnezzar, king of Babylon, that Jeremiah made explicit the oracle of punishment against the nation of Judah, the dwellers of Jerusalem, and all the neighboring nations:

So sayeth Yahweh, Lord of Hosts:
Because ye have not hearkened to my words,
I will send for and fetch all the tribes
of the north;
The word of Yahweh [shall be] to Nebuchadnezzar,
the king of Babylon, my servant.
And I shall bring them to this land
against its people
and against all the neighboring nations.

Not only was Babylon a tool in the hands of Yahweh—
the specific king, Nebuchadnezzar, was called by Yahweh
"my servant"!

The prophecy of the end of the Judean kingdom and the
fall of Jerusalem, as we historically know, came true in the
year 587 B.C. But even when that Oracle of Punishment was
pronounced, the ensuing events were also foretold:

> *This whole land shall be desolate and in ruins,*
> *and these nations shall serve the king of*
> *Babylon for seventy years.*

> *And it shall come to pass,*
> *when seventy years shall be completed*
> *—this is the word of Yahweh—*
> *I will call to account the king of Babylon*
> *and the land and the people of Chaldea,*
> *and will put them to everlasting desolation.*

Foreseeing Babylon's bitter end when that nation was just
beginning its ascendancy, the Prophet Isaiah put it thus:
"Babylon, the jewel of kingdoms, the glory and pride of the
Chaldeans, shall be overthrown as the upheavaling by *Elohim*
of Sodom and Gomorrah."

Babylon, as predicted, fell before the onslaught of a new
power from the east, that of the Achaemenid Persians, under
the leadership of their king Cyrus, in 539 B.C. Babylonian
records suggest that the city's fall was made possible by the
falling out between the last Babylonian king, Nabuna'id, and
the god Marduk; according to the annals of Cyrus, as he
captured the city and its sacred precinct and entered the inner
sanctum, Marduk extended his hands to him and he, Cyrus,
"grabbed the extended hands of the god."

But if Cyrus thought that by that he had obtained the blessing of the God Most High, he was wrong, the Prophets said,
for in fact he was only carrying out the grand design of
"Yahweh, the one and only God." Calling Cyrus "My chosen shepherd" and "My anointed," Yahweh thus pronounced
to Cyrus through His spokesman Isaiah (chapter 45):

Though thou knowest Me not,
I am the one who hath called thee by name ...
I am Yahweh, thy Caller,
the God of Israel.

I will enable you to unseat kings and rule nations, I shall thrust open for you brass doors and shall break down for you iron bars, grant to you hidden treasures; all that because you are My chosen to restore the Children of Israel to their homeland—"for the sake of my servant Jacob and my Chosen, Israel, have I summoned thee by thy name; I selected thee, though thou knowest me not," said Yahweh!

It was in his very first year as ruler over Babylon that Cyrus issued an edict calling for the return of the exiles of Judaea to their land and permitting the rebuilding of the Temple in Jerusalem. The cycle of prophecies was completed; Yahweh's words came true.

But, in the eyes of the people, He remained an Unseen God.

IDOLATRY AND STAR WORSHIP

The biblical admonitions against idolatry included the worship of the *Kokhabim*, the visible "stars" that were represented by their symbols on monuments and as emblems erected upon stands in shrines and temples. They included the twelve members of the Solar System and the twelve constellations of the zodiac.

Among the general admonitions there were some that specifically prohibited the worship of the "Queen of Heaven"—Ishtar as the planet Venus, the Sun and the Moon, and the zodiacal constellations that were called *Mazaloth* ("Fortune omens"), a term stemming from the Akkadian word for these celestial bodies.

A passage in II Kings chapter 23, dealing with the destruction of these idollic emblems, specifically names a planet called "The Lord" (The *Ba'al*) in addition to the Sun and the Moon and the rest of the "host of heaven." The Book of Ecclesiastes (12:2) also names a celestial body called "The Light" as appearing between the Sun and the Moon. We believe that these are references to Nibiru, the twelfth member of our Solar System.

These twelve celestial bodies were represented together by the various symbols by which they were worshiped in Mesopotamia, on a stela of King Esarhaddon that is now in the British Museum. On this stela (see Fig. 73) the Sun is represented by a rayed star, the Moon by its crescent, Nibiru by its Winged Disc symbol, and the Earth—the seventh planet as one would count from the outside inward—by the symbol of the Seven Dots.

ENDPAPER
God, the Extraterrestrial

So, who was Yahweh?

Was He one of *them?* Was He an extraterrestrial?

The question, with its implied answer, is not so outrageous. Unless we deem Yahweh—"God" to all whose religious beliefs are founded on the Bible—to have been one of us Earthlings, then He could only be not of this Earth—which "extraterrestrial" ("outside of, not from *Terra*") means. And the story of Man's Divine Encounters, the subject of this book, is so filled with parallels between the biblical experiences and those of encounters with the Anunnaki by other ancient peoples, that the possibility that Yahweh was one of "them" must be seriously considered.

The question and its implied answer, indeed, arise inevitably. That the biblical creation narrative with which the Book of Genesis begins draws upon the Mesopotamian *Enuma elish* is beyond dispute. That the biblical *Eden* is a rendering of the Sumerian E. DIN is almost self-evident. That the tale of the Deluge and Noah and the ark is based on the Akkadian *Atra-Hasis* texts and the earlier Sumerian Deluge tale in the *Epic of Gilgamesh,* is certain. That the plural "us" in the creation of *The Adam* segments reflects the Sumerian and Akkadian record of the discussions by the leaders of the Anunnaki that led to the genetic engineering that brought *Homo sapiens* about, should be obvious.

In the Mesopotamian versions it is Enki, the Chief Scientist, who suggests the genetic engineering to create the Earth-

347

ling to serve as a Primitive Worker, and it had to be Enki whom the Bible quotes as saying "Let us make the Adam in our likeness and after our image." An Epithet of Enki was NU. DIM.MUD, "He who fashions;" the Egyptians likewise called Enki *Ptah*—"The Developer," "He who fashions things," and depicted him as fashioning Man out of clay, as a potter. "The Fashioner of the Adam," the Prophets repeatedly called Yahweh ("fashioner," not "creator"!); and comparing Yahweh to a potter fashioning Man of clay was a frequent biblical simile.

As the master biologist, Enki's emblem was that of the Entwined Serpents, representing the double-helixed DNA— the genetic code that enabled Enki to perform the genetic mixing that brought about The Adam; and then (which is the story of Adam and Eve in the Garden of Eden) to again genetically manipulate the new hybrids and enable them to procreate. One of Enki's Sumerian epithets was BUZUR; it meant both "He who solves secrets" and "He of the mines," for the knowledge of mineralogy was considered knowledge of Earth's secrets, the secrets of its dark depths.

The biblical tale of Adam and Eve in the Garden of Eden— the tale of the second genetic manipulation—assigns to the serpent the role of triggering their acquisition of "knowing" (the biblical term for sexual procreation). The Hebrew term for serpent is *Nahash;* and interestingly, the same word also means soothsayer, "He who solves secrets"—the very same second meaning of Enki's epithet. Moreover, the term stems from the same root as the Hebrew word for the mineral copper, *Nehoshet.* It was a *Nahash Nehoshet,* a copper serpent, that Moses fashioned and held up to stop an epidemic that was afflicting the Israelites during the Exodus; and our analysis leaves no alternative but to conclude that what he had made to summon divine intervention was an emblem of Enki. A passage in II Kings 18:4 reveals that this copper serpent, whom the people nicknamed *Nehushtan* (a play on the triple meaning serpent-copper–solver of secrets) had been kept in the Temple of Yahweh in Jerusalem for almost seven centuries, until the time of King Hezekiah.

Pertinent to this aspect might have been the fact that when Yahweh turned the shepherd's crook that Moses held into a magical staff, the first miracle performed with it was to turn it into a serpent. *Was Yahweh, then, one and the same as Enki?*

The combination of biology with mineralogy and with the ability to solve secrets reflected Enki's status as the god of knowledge and sciences, of the Earth's hidden metals; he was the one who set up the mining operations in southeastern Africa. All these aspects were attributes of Yahweh. "It is Yahweh who giveth wisdom, out of His mouth cometh knowledge and understanding," Proverbs asserted (2:6), and it was He who granted wisdom beyond comparison to Solomon, as Enki had given the Wise Adapa. "The gold is mine and the silver is mine," Yahweh announced (Haggai 2:8); "I shall give thee the treasures of the darkness and the hidden riches of the secret places," Yahweh promised Cyrus (Isaiah 45:3).

The clearest congruence between the Mesopotamian and biblical narratives is found in the story of the Deluge. In the Mesopotamian versions it is Enki who goes out of his way to warn his faithful follower Ziusudra/Utnapishtim of the coming catastrophe, instructs him to build the watertight ark, gives him its specifications and dimensions, and directs him to save the seed of animal life. In the Bible, all that is done by Yahweh.

The case for identifying Yahweh with Enki can be bolstered by examining the references to Enki's domains. After Earth was divided between the Enlilites and the Enki'ites (according to the Mesopotamian texts), Enki was granted dominion over Africa. Its regions included the *Apsu* (stemming from AB.ZU in Sumerian), the gold-mining region, where Enki had his principal abode (in addition to his "cult center" Eridu in Sumer). The term *Apsu,* we believe, explains the biblical term *Apsei-eretz,* usually translated "the ends of earth," the land at the continent's edge—southern Africa, as we understand it. In the Bible, this distant place, *Apsei-eretz,* is where "Yahweh shall judge" (I Samuel 2:10), where He shall rule when Israel is restored (Micah 5:3). Yahweh has thus been equated with Enki in his role as ruler of the Apsu.

This aspect of the similarities between Enki and Yahweh becomes more emphatic—and in one respect perhaps even embarrassingly so for the monotheistic Bible—when we reach

a passage in the Book of Proverbs in which the unsurpassed
greatness of Yahweh is brought out by rhetorical questions:

> *Who hath ascended up to Heaven,*
> *and descended too?*
> *Who hath cupped the wind in his hands,*
> *and bound the waters as in a cloak?*
> *Who hath established the* Apsei-eretz—
> *What is his name,*
> *and what is his son's name—*
> *if thou can tell?*

According to the Mesopotamian sources, when Enki divided the African continent among his sons, he granted the
Apsu to his son Nergal. The polytheistic gloss (of asking the
name of the Apsu's ruler and that of *his son*) can be explained
only by an editorial inadvertent retention of a passage from
the Sumerian original texts—the same gloss as had occurred
in the use of "us" in "let us make the Adam" and in "let
us come down" in the story of the Tower of Babel. The gloss
in Proverbs (30:4) obviously substitutes "Yahweh" for Enki.

Was Yahweh, then, Enki in a biblical-Hebrew garb?

Were it so simple ... If we examine closely the tale of
Adam and Eve in the Garden of Eden, we will find that while
it is the *Nahash*—Enki's serpent guise as knower of biological secrets—who triggers the acquisition by Adam and Eve
of the sexual "knowing" that enables them to have offspring,
he is not Yahweh but an antagonist of Yahweh (as Enki was
of Enlil). In the Sumerian texts it was Enlil who forced Enki
to transfer some of the newly fashioned Primitive Workers
(created to work in the gold mines of the *Apsu*) to the E.DIN
in Mesopotamia, to engage in farming and shepherding. In
the Bible, it is Yahweh who "took the Adam and placed him
in the garden of Eden to tend it and to maintain it." It is
Yahweh, not the serpent, who is depicted as the master of
Eden who talks to Adam and Eve, discovers what they had
done, and expels them. In all this, the Bible equates Yahweh
not with Enki but with Enlil.

Indeed, in the very tale—the tale of the Deluge—where
the identification of Yahweh with Enki appears the clearest,

confusion in fact shows up. The roles are switched, and all of a sudden Yahweh plays the role not of Enki but of his rival Enlil. In the Mesopotamian original texts, it is Enlil who is unhappy with the way Mankind has turned out, who seeks its destruction by the approaching calamity, and who makes the other Anunnaki leaders swear to keep all that a secret from Mankind. In the biblical version (chapter 6 of Genesis), it is Yahweh who voices his unhappiness with Mankind and makes the decision to wipe Mankind off the face of the Earth. In the tale's conclusion, as Ziusudra/Utnapishtim offers sacrifices on Mount Ararat, it is Enlil who is attracted by the pleasant smell of roasting meat and (with some persuasion) accepts the survival of Mankind, forgives Enki, and blesses Ziusudra and his wife. In Genesis, it is to Yahweh that Noah builds an altar and sacrifices animals on it, and it was Yahweh "who smelled the pleasant aroma."

So was Yahweh Enlil, after all?

A strong case can be made for such an identification. If there had been a "first among equals" as far as the two half brothers, sons of Anu, were concerned, the first was Enlil. Though it was Enki who was first to come to Earth, it was EN.LIL ("Lord of the Command") who took over as chief of the Anunnaki on Earth. It was a situation that corresponds to the statement in Psalms 97:9: "For thou, O Yahweh, art supreme over the whole Earth; most supreme art Thou over all the *Elohim.*" The elevation of Enlil to this status is described in the *Atra-Hasis Epic* in the introductory verses, prior to the mutiny of the gold-mining Anunnaki:

> *Anu, their father, was the ruler;*
> *Their commander was the hero Enlil.*
> *Their warrior was Ninurta;*
> *Their provider was Marduk.*
>
> *They all clasped hands together,*
> *cast lots and divided:*
> *Anu ascended to heaven;*
> *The Earth to Enlil was made subject.*
> *The bounded realm of the sea*
> *to princely Enki they had given.*

> *After Anu had gone up to heaven,*
> *Enki went down to the Apsu.*

(Enki, interchangeably called in the Mesopotamian texts E.A.—"Whose home is water"—was thus the prototype of the sea god Poseidon of Greek mythology, the brother of Zeus who was head of the pantheon).

After Anu, the ruler on Nibiru, returned to Nibiru after visiting Earth, it was Enlil who summoned and presided over the council of the Great Anunnaki whenever major decisions had to be made. At various times of crucial decisions—such as to create The Adam, to divide the Earth into four regions, to institute Kingship as both buffer and liaison between the Anunnaki gods and Mankind, as well as in times of crisis between the Anunnaki themselves, when their rivalries erupted into wars and even use of nuclear weapons—"The Anunnaki who decree the fates sat exchanging their counsels." Typical was the manner in which one discussion is described in part: "Enki addressed to Enlil words of lauding: 'O one who is foremost among the brothers, Bull of Heaven, who the fate of Mankind holds.' " Except for the times when the debate got too heated and became a shouting match, the procedure was orderly, with Enlil turning to each member of the Council to let him or her have a say.

The monotheistic Bible lapses several times into describing Yahweh in like manner, chairing an assembly of lesser deities, usually called *Bnei-elim*—"sons of gods." The Book of Job begins its tale of the suffering of a righteous man by describing how the test of his faith in God was the result of a suggestion made by Satan "one day, when the sons of the *Elohim* came to present themselves before Yahweh." "The Lord stands in the assembly of the gods, among the *Elohim* He judges," we read in Psalms 82:1. "Give unto Yahweh, o sons of gods, give unto Yahweh glory and might," Psalms 29:1 stated, "bow to Yahweh, majestic in holiness." The requirement that even the "sons of the gods" bow to the Lord paralleled the Sumerian description of the status of Enlil as the Commander in Chief: "The Anunnaki humble themselves before him, the Igigi bow down willingly before him; they stand by faithfully for the instructions."

It is an image of Enlil that matches the exaltation in the Song of Miriam after the miraculous crossing of the Sea of Reeds: "Who is like thee among the gods, Yahweh? Who is like thee mighty in holiness, awesome in praises, the maker of miracles?" (Exodus 15:11).

As far as personal characters were concerned, Enki, the fashioner of Mankind, was more forebearing, less stringent with both gods and mortals. Enlil was stricter, a "law and order" type, uncompromising, unhesitant to mete out punishments when punishment was due. Perhaps it was because while Enki managed to get away with sexual promiscuities, Enlil, transgressing just once (when he date-raped a young nurse, in what turned out to be his seduction by her), was sentenced to exile (his banishment was lifted when he married her as his consort Ninlil). He viewed adversely the intermarriage between *Nefilim* and the "daughters of Man." When the evils of Mankind became overbearing, he was willing to see it perish by the Deluge. His strictness with other Anunnaki, even his own offspring, was illustrated when his son Nannar (the Moon god Sin) lamented the imminent desolation of his city Ur by the deathly nuclear cloud wafting from the Sinai. Harshly Enlil told him: "Ur was indeed granted Kingship; but an everlasting reign it was not granted."

Enlil's character had at the same time another side, a rewarding one. When the people carried out their tasks, when they were forthright and god-fearing, Enlil on his part saw to the needs of all, assured the land's and the people's wellbeing and prosperity. The Sumerians lovingly called him "Father Enlil" and "Shepherd of the teeming multitudes." A *Hymn to Enlil, the All-Beneficent* stated that without him "no cities would be built, no settlements founded; no stalls would be built, no sheepfolds erected; no king would be raised, no high priest born." The last statement recalled the fact that it was Enlil who had to approve the choice of kings, and by whom the line of Priesthood extended from the sacred precinct of the "cult center" Nippur.

These two characteristics of Enlil—strictness and punishment for transgressions, benevolence and protection when merited—are similar to how Yahweh has been pictured in the Bible. Yahweh can bless and Yahweh can accurse, the

Book of Deuteronomy explicitly states (11:26). If the divine commandments shall be followed, the people and their off-spring shall be blessed, their crops shall be plentiful, their livestock shall multiply, their enemies shall be defeated, they shall be successful in whatever trade they choose; but if they forsake Yahweh and his commandments, they, their homes and their fields shall be accursed and shall suffer afflictions, losses, deprivations, and famines (Deuteronomy 28). "Yah-weh thy *Elohim* is a merciful God," Deuteronomy 4:31 stated; He is a vengeful God, the same Deuteronomy stated a chapter later (5:9) . . .

It was Yahweh who determined who shall be the priests; it was He who stated the rules for Kingship (Deuteronomy 17:16) and made clear that it will be He who chooses the king—as indeed was the case centuries after the Exodus, be-ginning with the selection of Saul and David. In all that, Yahweh and Enlil emulated each other.

Significant, too, for such a comparison was the importance of the numbers seven and fifty. They are not physiologically obvious numbers (we do not have seven fingers on a hand), nor does their combination fit natural phenomena (7×50 is 350, not the 365.25 days of a solar year). The "week" of seven days approximates the length of a lunar month (about 28.5 days) when multiplied by four, but where does the four come from? Yet the Bible introduced the count of seven, and the sanctity of the seventh day as the sacred Sabbath, from the very beginning of divine activity. The accursation of Cain was to last through seven times seven generations; Jericho was to be circled seven times so that its walls would fall down; many of the priestly rites were required to be repeated seven times, or to last seven days. Of a more lasting com-mandment, the New Year Festival was deliberately shifted from the first month Nisan to the seventh month Tishrei and the principal holidays were to last seven days. The number fifty was the principal numerical feature in the construction and equipping of the Ark of the Covenant and the Tabernacle and an important element in the future Temple envisioned by Ezekiel. It was a calendrical count of days in priestly rites; Abraham persuaded the Lord to spare Sodom if fifty just men would be found there. More important, a major social and economic concept of a Jubilee Year in which slaves would be set free, real property would revert to its sellers and so on, was instituted. It was to be the fiftieth year: "Ye shall hallow the fiftieth year and proclaim freedom throughout the land," was the commandment in Leviticus chapter 25.

Both numbers, seven and fifty, were associated in Mesopotamia with Enlil. He was "the god who is seven" because, as the highest-ranking Anunnaki leader on Earth, he was in command of the planet which was the seventh planet. And in the numerical hierarchy of the Anunnaki, in which Anu held the highest numeral 60, Enlil (as his intended successor on Nibiru) held the numerical rank of fifty (Enki's numerical rank was forty). Significantly, when Marduk took over the supremacy on Earth circa 2000 B.C., one of the measures taken to signify his ascendancy was to grant him fifty names, signifying his assumption of the Rank of Fifty.

The similarities between Yahweh and Enlil extend to other aspects. Though he might have been depicted on cylinder seals (which is not certain, since the representation might have been of his son Ninurta), he was by and large an unseen god, ensconced in the innermost chambers of his ziggurat or altogether away from Sumer. In a telltale passage in the *Hymn to Enlil, the All-Beneficent* it is thus said of him:

> *When in his awesomeness he decrees the fates,*
> *no god dares look at him;*
> *Only to his exalted emissary, Nusku,*
> *the command, the word that is in his heart,*
> *does he make known.*

No man can see me and live, Yahweh told Moses in a similar vein; and His words and commandments were known through Emissaries and Prophets.

While all these reasons for equating Yahweh with Enlil are fresh in the reader's mind, let us hasten to offer the contrary evidence that points to other, different identifications.

One of the most powerful biblical epithets for Yahweh is *El Shaddai*. Of an uncertain etymology, it assumed an aura of mystery and by medieval times became a code word for kabbalistic mysticism. Early Greek and Latin translators of the Hebrew Bible rendered *Shaddai* as "omnipotent," leading to the rendering of *El Shaddai* in the King James translation as "God Almighty" when the epithet appears in the tales of the Patriarchs (e.g. "And Yahweh appeared unto Abram and said to him: 'I am *El Shaddai;* walk before me and be thou perfect'," in Genesis 17:1), or in Ezekiel, in Psalms, or several times in other books of the Bible.

Advances in the study of Akkadian in recent years suggest that the Hebrew word is related to *shaddu,* which means "mountain" in Akkadian; so that *El Shaddai* simply means "God of mountains." That this is a correct understanding of the biblical term is indicated by an incident reported in I Kings chapter 20. The Arameans, who were defeated in an attempt to invade Israel (Samaria), recouped their losses and a year later planned a second attack. To win this time, the Aramaean king's generals suggested that a ruse be used to lure the Israelites out of their mountain strongholds to a battlefield in the coastal plains. "Their god is a god of mountains," the generals told the king, "and that is why they prevailed over us; but if we shall fight them in a plain, we shall be the stronger ones."

Now, there is no way that Enlil could have been called, or reputed to be, a "god of mountains," for there are no mountains in the great plain that was (and still is) Mesopotamia. In the Enlilite domains the land that was called "Mountainland" was Asia Minor to the north, beginning with the Taurus ("Bull") mountains; and that was the region of Adad, Enlil's youngest son. His Sumerian name was ISH.KUR (and his "cult animal" was the bull), which meant "He of the mountainland." The Sumerian ISH was rendered *shaddu* in Akkadian; so that *Il Shaddu* became the biblical *El Shaddai.*

Scholars speak of Adad, whom the Hittites called Teshub (see Fig. 80) as a "storm god," always depicted with a lightning, thundering, and windblowing, and thus the god of rains. The Bible credited Yahweh with similar attributes. "When Yahweh uttereth His voice," Jeremiah said (10:13), "there is a rumbling of waters in the skies and storms come from the ends of the earth; He maketh lightnings with the rain, and blows a wind from its sources." The Psalms (135:7), the Book of Job, and other Prophets reaffirmed Yahweh's role as giver or withholder of rains, a role initially expounded to the Children of Israel during the Exodus.

While these attributes tarnish the similarities between Yahweh and Enlil, they should not carry us away to assume that, if so, Yahweh was the mirror image of Adad. The Bible recognized the existence of Hadad (as his name was spelled in Hebrew) as one of the "other gods" of other nations, not of Israel, and mentions various kings and princes (in the Aramean Damascus and other neighboring capitals) who were called Ben-Hadad ("Son of Adad"). In Palmyra (the biblical Tadmor), capital of eastern Syria, Adad's epithet was *Ba'al Shamin,* "Lord of Heaven," causing the Prophets to count him as just one of the Ba'al gods of neighboring nations who were an abomination in the eyes of Yahweh. There is no way, therefore, that Yahweh could have been one and the same as Adad.

The comparability between Yahweh and Enlil is further diminished by another important attribute of Yahweh, that of a warrior. "Yahweh goes forth like a warrior, like a hero He whips up His rage; He shall roar and cry out and over His enemies He shall prevail," Isaiah (42:13) stated, echoing the verse in the Song of Miriam that stated, "A Warrior is Yahweh" (Numbers chapter 15). Continuously, the Bible refers to and describes Yahweh as the "Lord of hosts," "Yahweh, the Lord of hosts, a warring army commands," Isaiah (13:4) declared. And Numbers 21:14 refers to a *Book of the Wars of Yahweh* in which the divine wars were recorded.

There is nothing in the Mesopotamian records that would suggest such an image for Enlil. The warrior *par excellence* was his son, Ninurta, who fought and defeated Zu, engaged in the Pyramid Wars with the Enki'ites, and fought and imprisoned Marduk in the Great Pyramid. His frequent epithets were "the warrior" and "the hero" and hymns to him hailed him as "Ninurta, Foremost Son, possessor of divine powers . . . Hero who in his hand the divine brilliant weapon carries." His feats as a warrior were described in an epic text whose Sumerian title was *Lugal-e Ud Melam-bi* that scholars have called *The Book of The Feats and Exploits of Ninurta.* Was it, one wonders, the enigmatic *Book of the Wars of Yahweh* of which the Bible spoke?

In other words, *could Yahweh have been Ninurta?*

As Foremost Son and heir apparent of Enlil, Ninurta too bore the numerical rank of fifty, and could thus qualify no less than Enlil to have been the Lord who decreed the fifty-year Jubilee and other fifty-related aspects mentioned in the Bible. He possessed a notorious Divine Black Bird that he used both for combat and on humanitarian missions; it could have been the *Kabod* flying vehicle that Yahweh possessed. He was active in the Zagros Mountains to the east of Mesopotamia, the lands of Elam, and was revered there as Ninshushinak, ''Lord of Shushan city'' (the Elamite capital). At one time he performed great dyking works in the Zagros mountains; at another, he diked and diverted mountain rain channels in the Sinai peninsula to make its mountainous part cultivable for his mother Ninharsag; in a way he, too, was ''god of mountains.'' His association with the Sinai peninsula and the channeling of its rainwaters, that come in winter bursts only, into an irrigation system is still recalled to this day: the largest *Wadi* (a river that fills up in winter and dries up in summer) in the peninsula is still called *Wadi El-Arish,* the wadi of the *Urash*—the Ploughman—a nickname of Ninurta from way back. An association with the Sinai peninsula, through his waterworks and his mother's residence there, also offers links to a Yahweh identification.

Another interesting aspect of Ninurta that invokes a similarity to the Biblical Lord comes to light in an inscription by the Assyrian king Ashurbanipal, who at one time invaded Elam. In it the king called him, ''The mysterious god who lingers in a secret place where no one can see what his divine being is about.'' An unseen god!

But Ninurta, as far as the earlier Sumerians were concerned, was not a god in hiding, and graphic depictions of him, as we have shown, were not even rare. Then, in conflict with a Yahweh-Ninurta identification, we come across a major ancient text, dealing with a major and unforgettable event, whose specifics seem to tell us that Ninurta was not Yahweh.

One of the most decisive actions attributed in the Bible to

Yahweh, with lasting effects and indelible memories, was the upheavaling of Sodom and Gomorrah. The event, as we have shown in great detail in *The Wars of Gods and Men,* was described and recalled in Mesopotamian texts, making possible a comparison of the deities involved.

In the biblical version Sodom (where Abram's nephew and his family lived) and Gomorrah, cities in the verdant plain south of the Sea of Salt, were sinful. Yahweh "comes down" and, accompanied by two Angels, visits Abram and his wife Sarai in their encampment near Hebron. After Yahweh predicts that the aged couple would have a son, the two Angels depart for Sodom to verify the extent of the cities' "sinning." Yahweh then reveals to Abram that if the sins would be confirmed, the cities and their residents would be destroyed. Abram pleads with Yahweh to spare Sodom if fifty just men be found there, and Yahweh agrees (the number was bargained by Abram down to ten) and departs. The Angels, having verified the cities' evil, warn Lot to take his family and escape. He asks for time to reach the mountains, and they agree to delay the destruction. Finally, the cities' doom begins as "Yahweh rained upon Sodom and Gomorrah sulfurous fire, coming from Yahweh from the skies; and He upheavaled those cities and the whole plain and all the inhabitants thereof, and all that which grew upon the ground ... And Abraham went early in the morning to the place where he had stood before Yahweh, and gazed in the direction of Sodom and Gomorrah, toward the land of the Plain, and he beheld vapor arising from the earth as the smoke of a furnace" (Genesis chapter 19).

The same event is well documented in Mesopotamian annals as the culmination of Marduk's struggle to attain supremacy on Earth. Living in exile, Marduk gave his son Nabu the assignment of converting people in western Asia to become followers of Marduk. After a series of skirmishes, Nabu's forces were strong enough to invade Mesopotamia and enable Marduk to return to Babylon, where he declared his intention to make it the Gateway of the Gods (what its name, *Bab-ili,* implied). Alarmed, the Council of the Anunnaki met in emergency sessions chaired by Enlil. Ninurta, and an alienated son of Enki called Nergal (from the south African domain), recommended drastic action to stop Marduk. Enki vehemently objected. Ishtar pointed out that while they were debating, Marduk was seizing city after city. "Sheriffs" were sent to seize Nabu, but he escaped and was hiding among his followers in one of the "sinning cities." Finally, Ninurta and Nergal were authorized to retrieve from a hiding place awesome nuclear weapons, and to use them to destroy the Spaceport in the Sinai (lest it fall into Mardukian hands) as well as the area where Nabu was hiding.

The unfolding drama, the heated discussions, the accusations, and the final drastic action—the use of nuclear weapons in 2024 B.C.—are described in great detail in a text that scholars call the *Erra Epic*.

In this document Nergal is referred to as Erra ("Howler") and Ninurta is called Ishum ("Scorcher"). Once they were given the go-ahead they retrieved "the awesome seven weapons, without parallel" and went to the Spaceport near the "Mount Most Supreme." The destruction of the Spaceport was carried out by Ninurta/Ishum: "He raised his hand; the Mount was smashed; the plain by the Mount Most Supreme he then obliterated; in its forests not a tree-stem was left standing."

Now it was the turn of the sinning cities to be upheavaled and the task was carried out by Nergal/Erra. He went there by following the King's Highway that connected the Sinai and the Red Sea with Mesopotamia:

> *Then, emulating Ishum,*
> *Erra the King's Highway followed.*
> *The cities he finished off,*
> *to desolation he overturned them.*

The use of nuclear weapons there broke open the sand barrier that still partly exists in the shape of a tongue (called *El Lissan),* and the waters of the Salt Sea poured south inundating the low-lying plain. The ancient text records that Erra/Nergal "dug through the sea, its wholeness he divided." And the nuclear weapons turned the Salt Sea to the body of water now called the Dead Sea: "That which lives in it he made wither," and what used to be a thriving and verdant plain, "as with fire he scorched the animals, burned its grains to become as dust."

As was the clear-cut case of the divine actors in the Deluge tale, so we find in this one concerning the upheavaling of Sodom, Gomorrah, and the other cities of that plain astride the Sinai peninsula, whom does and whom does not Yahweh match when the biblical and Sumerian texts are compared. The Mesopotamian text clearly associates Nergal and not Ninurta as the one who had upheavaled the sinning cities. Since the Bible asserts that it was not the two Angels who had gone to verify the situation, but Yahweh himself who had rained destruction on the cities, *Yahweh could not have been Ninurta.*

(The reference in Genesis chapter 10 to *Nimrod* as the one credited with starting Kingship in Mesopotamia, which we have discussed earlier, is interpreted by some as a reference not to a human king but to a god, and thus to Ninurta to whom the task of setting up the first Kingships was assigned. If so, the biblical statement that Nimrod "was a mighty hunter before Yahweh" also nullifies the possibility that Ninurta/Nimrod could have been Yahweh).

But Nergal too was not Yahweh. He is mentioned by name as the deity of the Cutheans who were among the foreigners brought over by the Assyrians to replace the Israelites who were exiled. He is listed among the "other gods" that the newcomers worshiped and for whom they set up idols. He could not have been "Yahweh" and Yahweh's abomination at one and the same time.

If Enlil and two of his sons, Adad and Ninurta, are not finalists in the lineup to identify Yahweh, what about Enlil's third son, Nannar/Sin (the "Moon god")?

His "cult center" (as scholars call it) in Sumer was Ur, the very city from which the migration of Terah and his family began. From Ur, where Terah performed priestly services, they went to Harran on the Upper Euphrates—a city that was a duplicate (even if on a smaller scale) of Ur as a cult center of Nannar. The migration at that particular time was connected, we believe, with religious and royal changes that might have affected the worship of Nannar. Was he then

the deity who had instructed Abram the Sumerian to pick up
and leave?

Having brought peace and prosperity to Sumer when Ur
was its capital, he was venerated in Ur's great ziggurat
(whose remains rise awesomely to this day) with his beloved
wife NIN.GAL ("Great Lady"). At the time of the new
moon, the hymns sung to this divine couple expressed the
people's gratitude to them; and the dark of the moon was
considered a time of "the mystery of the great gods, a time
of Nannar's oracle," when he would send "Zaqar, the god
of dreams during the night" to give commands as well as to
forgive sins. He was described in the hymns as "decider of
destinies in Heaven and on Earth, leader of living creatures
. . . who causes truth and justice to be."

It all sounds not unlike some of the praises of Yahweh
sung by the Psalmist . . .

The Akkadian/Semitic name for Nannar was Sin, and there
can be no doubt that it was in honor of Nannar as Sin that
the part of the Sinai peninsula called in the Bible the "Wilderness of Sin" and, for that matter, the whole peninsula
were so named. It was in that part of the world that Yahweh
appeared to Moses for the first time, where the "Mount of
the gods" was located, where the greatest Theophany ever
had taken place. Furthermore, the principal habitat in the
Sinai's central plain, in the vicinity of what we believe is the
true Mount Sinai, is still called *Nakhl* in Arabic after the
goddess Ningal whose Semitic name was pronounced *Nikal*

Was it all indicative of a Yahweh = Nannar/Sin identification?

The discovery several decades ago of extensive Canaanite
literature ("myths" to scholars) dealing with their pantheon
revealed that while a god they called *Ba'al* (the generic word
for "Lord" used as a personal name) was running things, he
was in fact not entirely independent of his father *El* (a generic
term meaning "god" used as a personal name). In these texts
El is depicted as a retired god, living with his spouse Ashera
away from the populated areas, at a quiet place where "the
two waters meet"—a place that we have identified in *The
Stairway To Heaven* as the southern tip of the Sinai peninsula, where the two gulfs extending from the Red Sea meet

This fact and other considerations have led us to the conclusion that the Canaanite El was the retired Nannar/Sin; included in the reasons upon which we had expounded is the fact that a "cult center" to Nannar/Sin has existed at a vital crossroads in the ancient Near East and even nowadays, the city known to us as Jericho but whose biblical/Semitic name is *Yeriho,* meaning "City of the Moon God"; and the adoption by tribes to the south thereof of *Allah*—"El" in Arabic—as the God of Islam represented by the Moon's crescent.

Described in the Canaanite texts as a retired deity, El as Nannar/Sin would indeed have been forced into retirement: Sumerian texts dealing with the effects of the nuclear cloud as it wafted eastward and reached Sumer and its capital Ur, reveal that Nannar/Sin—refusing to leave his beloved city—was afflicted by the deathly cloud and was partly paralyzed.

The image of Yahweh, especially in the period of the Exodus and the settlement of Canaan, i.e. after—not prior to—the demise of Ur, does not sound right for a retired, afflicted, and tired deity as Nannar/Sin had become by then. The Bible paints a picture of an active deity, insistent and persistent, fully in command, defying the gods of Egypt, inflicting plagues, dispatching Angels, roaming the skies; omnipresent, performing wonders, a magical healer, a Divine Architect. We find none of that in the descriptions of Nannar/Sin.

Both his veneration and fear of him stemmed from his association with his celestial counterpart, the Moon; and this celestial aspect serves as a decisive argument against identifying him with Yahweh: In the biblical divine order, it was Yahweh who ordered the Sun and the Moon to serve as luminaries; "the Sun and the Moon praise Yahweh," the Psalmist (148:3) declared. And on Earth, the crumbling of the walls of Jericho before the trumpeters of Yahweh symbolized the supremacy of Yahweh over the Moon god Sin.

There was also the matter of Ba'al, the Canaanite deity whose worship was a constant thorn in the side of Yahweh's faithful. The discovered texts reveal that Ba'al was a son of El. His abode in the mountains of Lebanon is still known as *Baalbek,* "The valley of Ba'al"—the place that was the first destination of Gilgamesh in his search for immortality. The biblical name for it was *Beit-Shemesh*—the "House/abode of

Shamash;'' and Shamash, we may recall, was a son of Nan-
nar/Sin. The Canaanite ''myths'' devote much clay tablet
space to the shenanigans between Ba'al and his sister *Anat;*
the Bible lists in the area of Beit-Shemesh a place called *Beit
Anat;* and we are as good as certain that the Semitic name
Anat was a rendering of *Anunitu* (''Anu's beloved'')—a nickname of Inanna/Ishtar, the twin sister of Utu/Shamash.

All that suggests that in the Canaanite trio El-Ba'al-Anat
we see the Mesopotamian triad of Nannar/Sin-Utu/Shamash-
Inanna/Ishtar—the gods associated with the Moon, the Sun,
and Venus. *And none of them could have been Yahweh,* for
the Bible is replete with admonitions against the worship of
these celestial bodies and their emblems.

If neither Enlil nor any one of his sons (or even grandchil-
dren) fully qualify as Yahweh, the search must turn elsewhere, to the sons of Enki, where some of the qualifications
also point.

The instructions given to Moses during the sojourn at
Mount Sinai were, to a great extent, of a medical nature. Five
whole chapters in Leviticus and many passages in Numbers
are devoted to medical procedures, diagnosis and treatment.
''Heal me, O Yahweh, and I shall be healed,'' Jeremiah
(17:14) cried out: ''My soul blesses Yahweh ... who heals
all my ailments,'' the Psalmist sang (103:1–3). Because of
his piety, King Hezekiah was not only cured on Yahweh's
say-so of a fatal disease, but was also granted by Yahweh
fifteen more years to live (II Kings chapter 19). Yahweh
could not only heal and extend life, he could also (through
his Angels and Prophets) revive the dead; an extreme example was provided by Ezekiel's vision of the scattered dry
bones that came back alive, their dead resurrected by Yahweh's will.

The biological-medical knowledge underlying such capabilities was possessed by Enki, and he passed such knowledge
to two of his sons: Marduk (known as Ra in Egypt), and
Thoth (whom the Egyptians called Tehuti and the Sumerians
NIN.GISH.ZIDDA—''Lord of the Tree of Life''). As for
Marduk, many Babylonian texts refer to his healing abilities;
but—as his own complaint to his father reveals—he was

given knowledge of healing but not that of reviving the dead. On the other hand, Thoth did possess such knowledge, employing it on one occasion to revive Horus, the son of the god Osiris and his sister-wife Isis. According to the hieroglyphic text dealing with this incident, Horus was bitten by a poisonous scorpion and died. As his mother appealed to the "god of magical things," Thoth, for help, he came down to Earth from the heavens in a sky boat, and restored the boy back to life.

When it came to the construction and equipping of the Tabernacle in the Sinai wilderness and later on of the Temple in Jerusalem, Yahweh displayed an impressive knowledge of architecture, sacred alignments, decorative details, use of materials, and construction procedures—even to the point of showing the Earthlings involved scale models of what He had designed or wanted. Marduk has not been credited with such an all-embracing knowledge; but Thoth/Ningishzidda was. In Egypt he was deemed the keeper of the secrets of pyramid building, and as Ningishzidda he was invited to Lagash to help orientate, design, and choose materials for the temple that was built for Ninurta.

Another point of major congruence between Yahweh and Thoth was the matter of the calendar. It is to Thoth that the first Egyptian calendar was attributed, and when he was expelled from Egypt by Ra/Marduk and went (according to our findings) to Mesoamerica, where he was called "The Winged Serpent" (Quetzalcoatl), he devised the Aztec and Mayan calendars there. As the biblical books of Exodus, Leviticus, and Numbers make clear, Yahweh not only shifted the New Year to the "seventh month," but also instituted the week, the Sabbath, and a series of holidays.

Healer; reviver of the dead who came down in a sky boat; a Divine Architect; a great astronomer and designer of calendars. The attributes common to Thoth and Yahweh seem overwhelming.

So was Thoth Yahweh?

Though known in Sumer, he was not considered there one of the Great Gods, and thus not fitting at all the epithet "the God Most High" that both Abraham and Melchizedek, priest of Jerusalem, used at their encounter. Above all, he was a *god of Egypt,* and (unless excluded by the argument that he was Yahweh), he was one of those upon whom Yahweh set out to make judgments. Renowned in ancient Egypt, there could be no Pharaoh ignorant of this deity. Yet, when Moses and Aaron came before Pharaoh and told him, "So sayeth Yahweh, the God of Israel: Let My people go that they may worship Me in the desert," Pharaoh said: "Who is this Yahweh that I should obey his words? I know not Yahweh, and the Israelites I shall not let go."

If Yahweh where Thoth, not only would the Pharaoh not answer thus, but the task of Moses and Aaron would have been made easy and attainable were they just to say, Why— "Yahweh" is just another name for Thoth . . . And Moses having been raised in the Egyptian court, would have had no difficulty knowing that—if that were so.

If Thoth was not Yahweh, the process of elimination alone appears to leave one more candidate: Marduk.

That he was a "god most high" is well established; the Firstborn of Enki who believed that his father was unjustly deprived of the supremacy on Earth—a supremacy to which he, Marduk, rather than Enlil's son Ninurta, was the rightful successor. His attributes included a great many—almost all— the attributes of Yahweh. He possessed a *Shem,* a sky-chamber, as Yahweh did; when the Babylonian king Nebuchadnezzar II rebuilt the sacred precinct of Babylon, he built there an especially strengthened enclosure for the "chariot of Marduk, the Supreme Traveler between Heaven and Earth."

When Marduk finally attained the supremacy on Earth, he did not discredit the other gods. On the contrary, he invited them all to reside in individual pavilions within the sacred precinct of Babylon. There was only one catch: their specific powers and attributes were to pass to him—just as the "Fifty Names" (i.e. rank) of Enlil had to. A Babylonian text, in its legible portion, listed thus the functions of other great gods that were transferred to Marduk:

Ninurta	=	Marduk of the hoe
Nergal	=	Marduk of the attack
Zababa	=	Marduk of the combat
Enlil	=	Marduk of lordship and counsel

Nabu	=	Marduk of numbers and counting
Sin	=	Marduk the illuminator of the night
Shamash	=	Marduk of justice
Adad	=	Marduk of rains

This was not the monotheism of the Prophets and the Psalms; it was what scholars term henotheism—a religion wherein the supreme power passes from one of several deities to another in succession. Even so, Marduk did not reign supreme for long; soon after the institution of Marduk as national god by the Babylonians, it was matched by their Assyrian rivals by the institution of *Ashur* as "lord of all the gods."

Apart from the arguments that we have mentioned in the cases of Thoth that negate an identification with any major Egyptian deity (and Marduk was the great Egyptian god Ra after all), the Bible itself specifically rules out any equating of Yahweh with Marduk. Not only is Yahweh, in sections dealing with Babylon, portrayed as greater, mightier, and supreme over the gods of the Babylonians—it explicitly foretells their demise by naming them. Both Isaiah (46:1) and Jeremiah (50:2) foresaw Marduk (also known as *Bel* by his Babylonian epitheht) and his son Nabu fallen and collapsed before Yahweh on the Day of Judgment.

Those prophetic words depict the two Babylonian gods as antagonists and enemies of Yahweh; *Marduk (and for that matter, Nabu) could not have been Yahweh.*

(As far as Ashur is concerned, the God Lists and other evidence suggest that he was a resurgent Enlil renamed by the Assyrians "The All Seeing;" and as such, he could not have been Yahweh).

As we find so many similarities, and on the other hand crucial differences and contradicting aspects, in our search for a matching "Yahweh" in the ancient Near Eastern pantheons, we can continue only by doing what Yahweh had told Abraham: Lift thine eyes toward the heavens . . .

The Babylonian king Hammurabi recorded thus the legitimization of Marduk's supremacy on Earth:

> *Lofty Anu,*
> *Lord of the Anunnaki,*
> *and Enlil,*
> *Lord of Heaven and Earth*
> *who determines the destinies of the land,*
> *Determined for Marduk, the firstborn of Enki,*
> *the Enlil-functions over all mankind*
> *and made him great among the Igigi.*

As this makes clear, even Marduk as he assumed supremacy on Earth recognized that it was Anu, and not he, who was "Lord of the Anunnaki." Was he the "God Most High" by whom Abraham and Melchizedek greeted each other?

The cuneiform sign for Anu (AN in Sumerian) was a star; it had the multiple meanings of "god, divine," "heaven," and this god's personal name. Anu, as we know from the Mesopotamian texts, stayed in "heaven"; and numerous biblical verses also described Yahweh as the One Who Is in Heaven. It was "Yahweh, the God of Heaven," who commanded him to go to Canaan, Abraham stated (Genesis 24:7). "I am a Hebrew and it is Yahweh, the God of Heaven that I venerate," the Prophet Jonah said (1:9). "Yahweh, the God of Heaven commanded me to build for Him a House in Jerusalem, in Judaea," Cyrus stated in his edict regarding the rebuilding of the Temple in Jerusalem (Ezra 1:2). When Solomon completed the construction of the (first) Temple in Jerusalem, he prayed to Yahweh to hear him from the heavens to bless the Temple as His House, although, Solomon admitted, it was hardly possible that "Yahweh *Elohim*" would come to dwell on Earth, in this House, "when the heaven and the heaven-of-heavens cannot contain Thee" (I Kings 8:27); and the Psalms repeatedly stated, "From the heaven did Yahweh look down upon the Children of Adam" (14:2); "From Heaven did Yahweh behold the Earth" (102:20); and "In Heaven did Yahweh establish His throne" (103:19).

Though Anu did visit Earth several times, he was residing on Nibiru; and as the god whose abode was in Heaven, he was truly an unseen god: among the countless depictions of deities on cylinder seals, statues and statuettes, carvings, wall paintings, amulets—his image does not appear even once!

Since Yahweh, too, was unseen and unrepresented pictorially, residing in "Heaven," the inevitable question that arises is, *Where was the abode of Yahweh?* With so many parallels between Yahweh and Anu, did Yahweh, too, have a "Nibru" to dwell on?

The question, and its relevance to Yahweh's invisibility, does not originate with us. It was sarcastically posed by a heretic to a Jewish savant, Rabbi Gamliel, almost two thousand years ago; and the answer that was given is truly amazing!

The report of the conversation, as rendered into English by S.M. Lehrman in *The World of the Midrash*, goes thus:

When Rabbi Gamliel was asked by a heretic to cite the exact location of God, seeing that the world is so vast and there are seven oceans, his reply was simply, "This I cannot tell you."

Whereupon the other tauntingly retorted: "And this you call Wisdom, praying to a God, daily, whose whereabouts you do not know?"

The Rabbi smiled: "You ask me to put my finger on the exact spot of His Presence, albeit that *tradition avers that the distance between heaven and earth would take a journey of 3,500 years to cover.* So, may I ask you the exact whereabouts of something which is always with you, and without which you cannot live a moment?"

The pagan was intrigued. "What is this?" he eagerly queried.

The Rabbi replied: "The soul which God had planted within you; pray tell me where exactly is it?"

It was a chastened man that shook his head negatively.

It was now the Rabbi's turn to be amazed and amused. "If you do not know where your own soul is located, how can you expect to know the precise habitation of One who fills the whole world with His glory?"

Let us note carefully what Rabbi Gamliel's answer was: according to Jewish tradition, he said, the exact spot in the heavens where God has a dwelling is so distant that it would require a journey of 3,500 years ...

How much closer can one get to the 3,600 years that it takes Nibiru to complete one orbit around the Sun?

Although there are no specific texts dealing with or describing Anu's abode on Nibiru, some idea thereof can be gained indirectly from such texts as the tale of Adapa, occasional references in various texts, and even from Assyrian depictions. It was a place—let us think of it as a royal palace—that was entered through imposing gates, flanked by towers. A pair of gods (Ningishzidda and Dumuzi are mentioned in one instance) stood guard at the gates. Inside, Anu was seated on a throne; when Enlil and Enki were on Nibiru, or when Anu had visited Earth, they flanked the throne, holding up celestial emblems.

(The *Pyramid Texts* of ancient Egypt, describing the Afterlife ascent of the Pharaoh to the celestial abode, carried aloft by an "Ascender," announced for the departing king: "The double gates of heaven are opened for thee, the double gates of the sky are opened for thee" and envisioned four scepter-holding gods announcing his arrival on the "Imperishable Star").

In the Bible, too, Yahweh was described as seated on a throne, flanked by Angels. While Ezekiel described seeing the Lord's image, shimmering like electrum, seated on a throne inside a Flying Vehicle, "the throne of Yahweh is in Heaven," the Psalms (11:4) asserted; and the Prophets described seeing Yahweh seated on a throne in the Heavens. The Prophet Michaiah ("Who is like Yahweh?"), a contemporary of Elijah, told the king of Judaea who had sought a divine oracle (I Kings chapter 22):

> *I saw Yahweh sitting on his throne,*
> *and the host of heaven were standing by Him,*
> *on His right and on His left.*

The Prophet Isaiah recorded (chapter 6) a vision seen by him "in the year in which king Uzziah died" in which he saw God seated on His throne, attended by fiery Angels:

I beheld my Lord seated on a high and lofty throne,
and the train of His robe filled the great hall.
Seraphs *stood in attendance on Him,*
each one of them having six wings:
with twain each covered his face,
with twain each covered his legs,
and with twain each one would fly.
And one would call out to the other:
Holy, holy, holy is the Lord of Hosts!

Biblical references to Yahweh's throne went farther: they actually stated its location, in a place called *Olam.* "Thy throne is established forever, from *Olam* art Thou," the Psalms (93:2) declared; "Thou, Yahweh, are enthroned in *Olam,* enduring through the ages," states the Book of Lamentations (5:19).

Now, this is not the way these verses, and others like them, have been usually translated. In the King James Version, for example, the quoted verse from Psalms is translated "Thy throne is established of old, thou art from *everlasting,*" and the verse in Lamentations is rendered "Thou, O Lord, remainest *for ever;* thy throne from generation to generation." Modern translations likewise render *Olam* as "everlasting" and "forever" (*The New American Bible*) or as "eternity" and "for ever" (*The New English Bible*), revealing an indecision whether to treat the term as an adjective or as a noun. Recognizing, however, that *Olam* is clearly a noun, the most recent translation by the Jewish Publication Society adopted "eternity," an abstract noun, as a solution.

The Hebrew Bible, strict in the precision of its terminology, has other terms for stating the state of "lasting forever." One is *Netzah,* as in Psalm 89:47 that asked, "How long, Yahweh, wilt Thou hide Thyself—*forever?*" Another term that means more precisely "perpetuity" is *Ad,* which is also usually translated "for ever," as in "his seed I will make endure for ever" in Psalm 89:30. There was no need for a third term to express the same thing. *Olam,* often accompanied by the adjective *Ad* to denote its everlasting nature, was itself not an adjective but a noun derived from the root that means "disappearing, mysteriously hidden." The numerous biblical verses in which *Olam* appears indicate that it was deemed a physical place, not an abstraction. "Thou art *from* Olam," the Psalmist declared—God is from a place which is a hidden place (and therefore God has been unseen).

It was a place that was conceived as physically existing: Deuteronomy (33:15) and the Prophet Habakkuk (3:6) spoke of the "hills of Olam." Isaiah (33:14) referred to the "heat sources of *Olam*." Jeremiah (6:16) mentioned the "pathways of *Olam*" and (18:5) "the lanes of *Olam*," and called Yahweh "king of *Olam*" (10:10) as did Psalms 10:16. The Psalms, in statements reminiscent of the references to the gates of Anu's abode (in Sumerian texts) and to the Gates of Heaven (in ancient Egyptian texts), also spoke of the "Gates of *Olam*" that should open and welcome the Lord Yahweh as He arrives there upon His *Kabod*, His Celestial Boat (24:7–10):

> *Lift up your heads, O gates of* Olam
> *so that the King of* Kabod *may come in!*
> *Who is the King of* Kabod?
> *Yahweh, strong and valiant, a mighty warrior!*

> *Lift up your heads, O gates of Olam,*
> *and the King of* Kabod *shall come in!*
> *Who is the King of* Kabod?
> *Yahweh lord of hosts is the King of* Kabod.

"Yahweh is the God of *Olam*," declared Isaiah (40:28), echoing the biblical record in Genesis (21:33) of Abraham's "calling in the name of Yahweh, the God of *Olam*." No wonder, then, that the Covenant symbolized by circumcision, "the celestial sign," was called by the Lord when he had imposed it on Abraham and his descendants "the Covenant of *Olam*:"

> *And my Covenant shall be in your flesh,*
> *the Covenant of* Olam.
> (Genesis 17:13)

In post-biblical rabbinic discussions, and so in modern Hebrew, *Olam* is the term that stands for "world." Indeed, the answer that Rabbi Gamliel gave to the question regarding the Divine Abode was based on rabbinic assertions that it is separated from Earth by seven heavens, in each of which there is a different world; and that the journey from one to the other requires five hundred years, so that the complete journey through seven heavens from the world called Earth to the world that is the Divine Abode lasts 3,500 years. This, as we have pointed out, comes as close to the 3,600 (Earth) years' orbit of Nibiru as one could expect; and while Earth to someone arriving from space would have been the seventh planet, Nibiru to someone on Earth would indeed be seven celestial spaces away when it disappears to its apogee.

Such a disappearing—the root meaning of *Olam*—creates of course the "year" of Nibiru—an awesomely long time in human terms. The Prophets similarly, in numerous passages, spoke of the "Years of Olam" as a measure of a very long time. A clear sense of periodicity, as would result from the periodic appearance and disappearance of a planet, was conveyed by the frequent use of "from Olam to Olam" as a definite (though extremely long) measure of time: "I had given you this land from Olam to Olam," the Lord was quoted as saying by Jeremiah (7:7 and 25:5). And a possible clincher for identifying *Olam* with Nibiru was the statement in Genesis 6:4 that the Nefilim, the young Anunnaki who had come to Earth from Nibiru, were the "people of the *Shem*" (the people of the rocketships), "those who were from Olam."

With the obvious familiarity of the Bible's editors, Prophets, and Psalmists with Mesopotamian "myths" and astronomy, it would have been peculiar not to find knowledge of the important planet Nibiru in the Bible. *It is our suggestion that yes, the Bible was keenly aware of Nibiru—and called it* Olam, *the "disappearing planet."*

Does all that mean that therefore Anu was Yahweh? Not necessarily . . .

Though the Bible depicted Yahweh as reigning in His celestial abode, as Anu did, it also considered Him "king" over the Earth and all upon it—whereas Anu clearly gave the command on Earth to Enlil. Anu did visit Earth, but extant texts describe the occasions mostly as ceremonial state and inspection visits; there is nothing in them comparable to the active involvement of Yahweh in the affairs of nations and individuals. Moreover, the Bible recognized a god, other than Yahweh, a "god of other nations" called *An;* his worship is noted in the listing (II Kings 17:31) of gods of the foreigners whom the Assyrians had resettled in Samaria, where he is referred to as *An-melekh* ("Anu the king"). A personal name Anani, honoring Anu, and a place called Anatot, are also listed in the Bible. And the Bible had nothing for Yahweh that paralleled the genealogy of Anu (parents, spouse, children), his lifestyle (scores of concubines) or his fondness for his granddaughter Inanna (whose worship as the "Queen of Heaven"–Venus was deemed an abomination in the eyes of Yahweh).

And so, in spite of the similarities, there are also too many essential differences between Anu and Yahweh for the two to have been one and the same.

Moreover, in the biblical view Yahweh was more than "king, lord" of *Olam,* as Anu was king on Nibiru. He was more than once hailed as *El Olam,* the God of *Olam* (Genesis 21:33) and *El Elohim,* the God of the *Elohim* (Joshua 22:22, Psalms 50:1 and Psalms 136:2).

The biblical suggestion that the *Elohim*—the "gods," the Anunnaki—had a God, seems totally incredible at first, but quite logical on reflection.

At the very conclusion of our first book in *The Earth Chronicles* series *(The 12th Planet),* having told the story of the planet Nibiru and how the Anunnaki (the biblical Nefilim) who had come to Earth from it "created" Mankind, we posed the following question:

> *And if the Nefilim were the "gods" who "created" Man on Earth, did evolution alone, on the Twelfth Planet, create the Nefilim?*

Technologically advanced, capable hundreds of thousands of years before us to travel in space, arriving at a cosmological explanation for the creation of the Solar System and, as we begin to do, to contemplate and understand the universe—

the Anunnaki must have pondered *their* origins, and arrived at what we call Religion—their religion, *their concept of God.*

Who created the Nefilim, the Anunnaki, on their planet? The Bible itself provides the answer. Yahweh, it states, was not just "a great God, a great king over all of the *Elohim*" (Psalms 95:3); He was there, on Nibiru, before they had come to be on it: "Before the *Elohim* upon *Olam* He sat," Psalm 61:8 explained. Just as the Anunnaki had been on Earth before The Adam, so was Yahweh on Nibiru/Olam before the Anunnaki. The creator preceded the created.

We have already explained that the seeming immortality of the Anunnaki "gods" was merely their extreme longevity, resulting from the fact that one Nibiru-year equaled 3,600 Earth-years; and that in fact they were born, grew old, and could (and did) die. A time measure applicable to *Olam* ("days of *Olam*" and "years of *Olam*") was recognized by the Prophets and Psalmist; what is more impressive is their realization that the various *Elohim* (the Sumerian DIN.GIR, the Akkadian *Ilu*) were in fact not immortal—but Yahweh, God, was. Thus, Psalm 82 envisions God passing judgment on the *Elohim* and reminding them that they—the *Elohim!*— are also mortal: "God stands in the divine assembly, among the *Elohim* He judges," and tells them thus:

> *I have said, ye are* Elohim,
> *all of you sons of the Most High;*
> *But ye shall die as men do,*
> *like any prince ye shall fall.*

We believe that such statements, suggesting that the Lord Yahweh created not only the Heaven and the Earth but also the *Elohim*, the Anunnaki "gods," have a bearing on a puzzle that has baffled generations of biblical scholars. It is the question why the Bible's very first verse that deals with the very Beginning, does not begin with the first letter of the alphabet, but rather with the second one. The significance and symbolism of beginning the Beginning with the proper beginning must have been obvious to the Bible's compilers; yet, this is what they chose to transmit to us:

> Breshit bara Elohim
> et Ha'Shamaim v'et Ha'Aretz

which is commonly translated, "In the beginning God created the Heaven and the Earth."

Since the Hebrew letters have numerical values, the first letter, *Aleph* (from which the Greek *alpha* comes) has the numerical value "one, the first"—the beginning. Why then, scholars and theologians have wondered, does the Creation start with the second letter, *Beth,* whose value is "two, second"?

While the reason remains unknown, the result of starting the first verse in the first book of the Bible with an *Aleph* would be astounding, for it would make the sentence read thus:

> Ab-reshit bara Elohim,
> et Ha'Shamaim v'et Ha'Aretz
>
> The Father-of-Beginning created the *Elohim,*
> the Heavens, and the Earth.

By this slight change, by just starting the beginning with the letter that begins it all, an omnipotent, omnipresent Creator of All emerges from the primeval chaos: *Ab-Reshit,* "the Father of Beginning." The best modern scientific minds have come up with the Big Bang theory of the beginning of the universe—but have yet to explain who caused the Big Bang to happen. Were Genesis to begin as it should have, the Bible—which offers a precise tale of Evolution and adheres to the most sensible cosmogony—would have also given us the answer: the Creator who was there to create it all.

And all at once Science and Religion, Physics and Metaphysics, converge into one single answer that conforms to the credo of Jewish monotheism: "I am Yahweh, there is none beside me!" It is a credo that carried the Prophets, and us with them, from the arena of gods to the God who embraces the universe.

One can only speculate why the Bible's editors, who scholars believe canonized the *Torah* (the first five books of the

Bible) during the Babylonian exile, omitted the *Aleph*. Was it in order to avoid offending their Babylonian exilers (because a claim that Yahweh had created the Anunnaki-gods would have not excluded Marduk)? But what is, we believe, not to be doubted is that at one time the first word in the first verse in the Bible did begin with the first letter of the alphabet. This certainty is based on the statements in the Book of Revelation ("The Apocalypse of St. John" in the New Testament), in which God announces thus:

> *I am Alpha and Omega,*
> *the Beginning and the End,*
> *the First and the Last.*

The statement, repeated three times (1:8, 21:6, 22:13), applies the first letter of the alphabet (by its Greek name) to the Beginning, to the divine First, and the last letter of the (Greek) alphabet to the End, to God being the Last of all as He has been the First of All.

That this had been the case at the beginning of Genesis is confirmed, we believe, by the certainty that the statements in Revelation harken back to the Hebrew scriptures from which the parallel verses in Isaiah (41:6, 42:8, 44:6) were taken, the verses in which Yahweh proclaims His absoluteness and uniqueness:

> *I, Yahweh, was the First*
> *And the Last I will also be!*

> *I am the First*
> *and I am the Last;*
> *There are no* Elohim *without Me!*

> *I am He,*
> *I am the First,*
> *I am the Last as well.*

It is these statements that help identify the biblical God by the answer that He himself gave when asked: Who, O God, are you? It was when He called Moses out of the Burning

Bush, identifying Himself only as "the God of thy father, the God of Abraham, the God of Isaac and the God of Jacob." Having been given his mission, Moses pointed out that when he would come to the Children of Israel and say, "the God of your forefathers has sent me to you, and they will say to me: What is His name?—what shall I tell them?"

> *And God said to Moses:*
> Ehyeh-Asher-Ehyeh—
> *this is what thou shalt say*
> *unto the Children of Israel:*
> Ehyeh *sent me.*
> *And God said further to Moses:*
> *Thus shalt say unto the Children of Israel:*
> Yahweh, *the God of your fathers,*
> *the God of Abraham, the God of Isaac,*
> *and the God of Jacob,*
> *hath sent me unto you;*
> *This is my name unto* Olam,
> *this is my appellation unto all generations.*
>
> (Exodus 3:13–15)

The statement, *Ehyeh-Asher-Ehyeh,* has been the subject of discussion, analysis, and interpretation by generations of theologians, biblical scholars, and linguists. The King James Version translates it "I am that I am ... *I am* hath sent me to you." Other more modern translations adopt "I am, that is who I am ... *I am* has sent you." The most recent translation by the Jewish Publication Society prefers to leave the Hebrew intact, providing the footnote, "meaning of the Hebrew uncertain."

The key to understanding the answer given during this Divine Encounter are the grammatical tenses employed here. *Ehyeh-Asher-Ehyeh* is not given in the present but in the future tense. In simple parlance it states: "Whoever I shall be, I shall be." And the Divine Name that is revealed to a mortal for the first time (in the conversation Moses is told that the sacred name, the Tetragrammaton YHWH, had not been revealed even to Abraham) combines the three tenses from the root meaning "To Be"—the One who was, who is, and who shall be. It is an answer and a name that befit the biblical concept of Yahweh as eternally existing—One who was, who is, and who shall continue to be.

A frequent form of stating this everlasting nature of the biblical God is the expression "Thou art from *Olam* to *Olam.*" It is usually translated, "Thou art everlasting;" this conveys undoubtedly the sense of the statement, but not its precise meaning. Literally taken it suggests that the existence and reign of Yahweh extended from one *Olam* to another—that He was "king, lord" not only of the one *Olam* that was the equivalent of the Mesopotamian Nibiru—but of other Olams, of other worlds!

No less than eleven times, the Bible refers to Yahweh's abode, domain, and "kingdom" using the term *Olamim,* the plural of Olam—a domain, an abode, a kingdom that encompasses many worlds. It is an expansion of Yahweh's Lordship beyond the notion of a "national god" to that of a Judge of all the nations; beyond the Earth and beyond Nibiru, to the "Heavens of Heaven" (Deuteronomy 10:14, I Kings 8:27, II Chronicles 2:5 and 6:18) that encompass not only the Solar System but even the distant stars (Deuteronomy 4:19, Ecclesiastes 12:2).

THIS IS THE IMAGE OF A COSMIC VOYAGER.

All else—the celestial planetary "gods," Nibiru that remade our Solar System and remakes the Earth on its near passages, the Anunnaki "Elohim," Mankind, nations, kings—all are His manifestations and His instruments, carrying out a divine and universal everlasting plan. In a way we are all His Angels, and when the time comes for Earthlings to travel in space and emulate the Anunnaki, on some other world, we too shall only be carrying out a destined future.

It is an image of a universal Lord that is best summed up in the hymnal prayer *Adon Olam* that is recited as a majestic song in Jewish synagogue services on festivals, on the Sabbath, and on each and every day of the year:

> *Lord of the universe, who has reigned*
> *Ere all that exists had yet been created.*
> *When by His will all things were wrought,*
> *"Sovereign" was His name was then pronounced.*

And when, in time, all things shall cease,
He shall still reign in majesty.
He was, He is, He shall remain,
He shall continue gloriously.

Incomparable, unique He is,
No other can His Oneness share.
Without beginning, without end.
Dominion's might is His to bear.

INDEX

381